# AFGHANISTAN

# INVESTMENT AND BUSINESS GUIDE

## VOLUME 1

## STRATEGIC AND PRACTICAL INFORMATION

International Business Publications, USA
Washington, DC USA - Afghanistan

# AFGHANISTAN

## INVESTMENT AND BUSINESS GUIDE

### VOLUME 1 STRATEGIC AND PRACTICAL INFORMATION

**UPDATED ANNUALLY**

**We express our sincere appreciation to all government agencies and international organizations which provided information and other materials for this guide**

Cover Design: **International Business Publications, USA**



**2018 Edition Updated Reprint International Business Publications, USA**
**ISBN 1-4330-0013-X**

For additional analytical, business and investment opportunities information,
please contact Global Investment & Business Center, USA
at (703) 370-8082. Fax: (703) 370-8083. E-mail: ibpusa3@gmail.com
Global Business and Investment Info Databank - www.ibpus.com

Printed in the USA

For additional analytical, business and investment opportunities information,
please contact Global Investment & Business Center, USA
at (703) 370-8082. Fax: (703) 370-8083. E-mail: ibpusa3@gmail.com
Global Business and Investment Info Databank - www.ibpus.com

# AFGHANISTAN

## INVESTMENT AND BUSINESS GUIDE

### VOLUME 1

### STRATEGIC AND PRACTICAL INFORMATION

### TABLE OF CONTENTS

# STRATEGIC AND DEVELOPMENT PROFILES

## BASIC PROFILE

| | |
|---|---|
| Capital and largest city | Kabul 34°32′N 69°08′E |
| Official languages | • Pashto<br>• Dari |
| Ethnic groups | Pashtun, Tajik, Hazara, Uzbek, and others |
| Religion | Islam |
| Demonym | Afghan |
| Government | Unitary presidential Islamic republic |
| • President | Ashraf Ghani |
| • Chief Executive Officer | Abdullah Abdullah |
| Legislature | National Assembly |
| • Upper house | House of Elders |
| • Lower house | House of the People |
| Formation | |
| • Hotak Empire | April 1709 |
| • Durrani Empire | October 1747 |
| • Emirate | 1823 |
| • Recognized | 19 August 1919 |
| • Kingdom | 9 June 1926 |
| • Republic | 17 July 1973 |
| • Current constitution | 26 January 2004 |
| Area | |
| • Total | 652,864 $km^2$ (252,072 sq mi) (40th) |
| • Water (%) | negligible |
| Population | |
| • 2016 estimate | 34,656,032 (40th) |
| • Density | 49.88/$km^2$ (129.2/sq mi) (150th) |
| GDP (PPP) | 2017 estimate |
| • Total | $70 billion |
| • Per capita | $1,888 |
| GDP (nominal) | 2017 estimate |
| • Total | $21 billion |
| • Per capita | $572 |
| Gini | 29<br>low |
| HDI (2014) | ▲ 0.465<br>low · 171st |
| Currency | Afghani (Afs) (AFN) |
| Time zone | D† (UTC+4:30 Solar Calendar) |
| Drives on the | right |
| Calling code | +93 |
| ISO 3166 code | AF |

| Internet TLD | .af افغانستان. |
|---|---|

**Afghanistan** officially the **Islamic Republic of Afghanistan**, is a landlocked country located in the centre of Asia, forming South Asia, Central Asia and the Middle East. With a population of about 29 million, it has an area of 647,500 $km^2$ (250,001 sq mi), making it the 42nd most populous and 41st largest nation in the world. It is bordered by Pakistan in the southeast, Iran in the west, Turkmenistan, Uzbekistan and Tajikistan in the north, and China in the far northeast. The territory that now forms Afghanistan has been an ancient focal point of the Silk Road and human migration. Archaeologists have found evidence of human habitation from as far back as 50,000 BC. Urban civilization may have begun in the area as early as 3,000 to 2,000 BC.

The country sits at an important geostrategic location that connects the Middle East with Central Asia and the Indian subcontinent, which has been home to various peoples through the ages. The land has witnessed many military conquests since antiquity, notably by Alexander the Great, Chandragupta Maurya, and Genghis Khan. It has also served as a source from which local dynasties such as the Greco-Bactrians, Kushans, Saffarids, Ghaznavids, Ghorids, Timurids, Mughals and many others have established empires of their own.

The political history of modern Afghanistan begins in 1709 with the rise of the Pashtuns, when the Hotaki dynasty was established in Kandahar followed by Ahmad Shah Durrani's rise to power in 1747. The capital of Afghanistan was shifted in 1776 from Kandahar to Kabul and part of the Afghan Empire was ceded to neighboring empires by 1893. In the late 19th century, Afghanistan became a buffer state in the "Great Game" between the British and Russian empires. Following the third Anglo-Afghan war and the signing of the Treaty of Rawalpindi in 1919, the nation regained control over its foreign policy from the British.

After the 1978 Marxist revolution, the Soviet Union began a 10-year war in which over a million Afghans lost lives. The mujahidin insurgency generated by the Marxist government and the Soviet invasion signaled the first sustained entry of Islam into Afghan politics as the religion served as a force to unify the tribally divided multiethnic population.

This was followed by the Afghan civil war (1992–1996), the rise and fall of the extremist Taliban government and the 2001-present war. In December 2001, the United Nations Security Council authorized the creation of the International Security Assistance Force (ISAF) to help maintain security in Afghanistan and assist the Karzai administration. While NATO and other countries are rebuilding war-torn Afghanistan, insurgent groups such as the Taliban and Haqqani network are actively involved in a nationwide Taliban-led insurgency, which includes countless assassinations and suicide attacks against civilians, Afghan authorities and western forces. According to the United Nations, the insurgents were responsible for 75% of civilian casualties in 2010 and 80% in 2011.

## STRATEGIC PROFILE

The name Afghanistan literally translates to *Land of the Afghans*. Its modern usage derives from the word *Afghan*. The Pashtuns appear to have begun using the term Afghan as a name for themselves from the Islamic period onwards. According to W.K. Frazier Tyler, M.C. Gillet and several other scholars, *"The word Afghan first appears in history in the Hudud-al-Alam in 982 AD."* The last part of the name *Afghanistan* originates from the Persian word *stān* (*country* or *land*). The English word *Afghanland* that appeared in various treaties between Qajar-Persia and the United Kingdom dealing with the lands between Persia and British Raj inhabited by Pashtun tribes (modern Southeastern Afghanistan) was adopted by the Afghans and became *Afghanistan*.

However, Afghanistan was pronounced by its current name from the 18th century onwards when Ahmed Shah Abdali formed the new government, and was officially named as Afghanistan during the ruling of Abdur Rahman Khan. Before the 18th century, Afghanistan was always known as Khorasan, as today's Afghan territory forms the major regions of the Great Khorasan.

**Afghanistan** (officially the **Islamic Republic of Afghanistan**; is a landlocked country at the crossroads of Asia. Generally considered a part of Central Asia, it is sometimes ascribed to a regional bloc in either the Middle East or South Asia, as it has cultural, ethno-linguistic, and geographic links with most of its neighbors. It is bordered by Iran in the west, Pakistan and India in the south and east, Turkmenistan, Uzbekistan and Tajikistan in the north, and the People's Republic of China to the east. The name Afghanistan is derived from Persian, meaning "land of the Afghans"

Afghanistan is a mosaic of ethnic groups and cultures, and a crossroads between east and west. An ancient land that has often been plundered, and also a focal point of trade, the region of present-day Afghanistan has seen several invading forces come and go, including Aryan nomads, the Mede and Persian Empires, Greeks, Arabs, Turks, and Mongols. Modern Afghanistan arose as an independent state in 1919, when foreign intervention ceased following the Anglo-Afghan wars. The country's recent history has seen it ravaged by the Soviet Invasion of Afghanistan, the Afghan Civil War, the rise and fall of the Taliban, and the United States invasion of Afghanistan in 2001.

As a result of these traumatic events, Afghanistan is in a rebuilding phase, as it attempts to reconcile the devastation that constant warfare has created, with a new government that seeks to unify and rebuild Afghanistan. Afghanistan faces numerous problems, ranging from its devastated economy, the return of millions of refugees, continued warlordism, drug trafficking, and a new government that is struggling with the political forces trying to define the sort of country Afghanistan will become in the 21st century.

| | |
|---|---|
| Background: | Afghanistan was invaded and occupied by the Soviet Union in 1979. The USSR was forced to withdraw 10 years later by anti-communist mujahidin forces supplied and trained by the US, Saudi Arabia, Pakistan, and others. Fighting subsequently continued among the various mujahidin factions, but the fundamentalist Islamic Taliban movement has been able to seize most of the country. In addition to the continuing civil strife, the country suffers from enormous poverty, a crumbling infrastructure, and widespread land mines. |

## GEOGRAPHY

| | |
|---|---|
| **Location:** | Southern Asia, north and west of Pakistan, east of Iran |
| **Geographic coordinates:** | 33 00 N, 65 00 E |
| **Map references:** | Asia |
| **Area:** | total: 647,500 sq km<br>land: 647,500 sq km water: 0 sq km |
| **Area - comparative:** | slightly smaller than Texas |
| **Land boundaries:** | total: 5,529 km<br>border countries: China 76 km, Iran 936 km, Pakistan 2,430 km, Tajikistan 1,206 km, Turkmenistan 744 km, Uzbekistan 137 km |

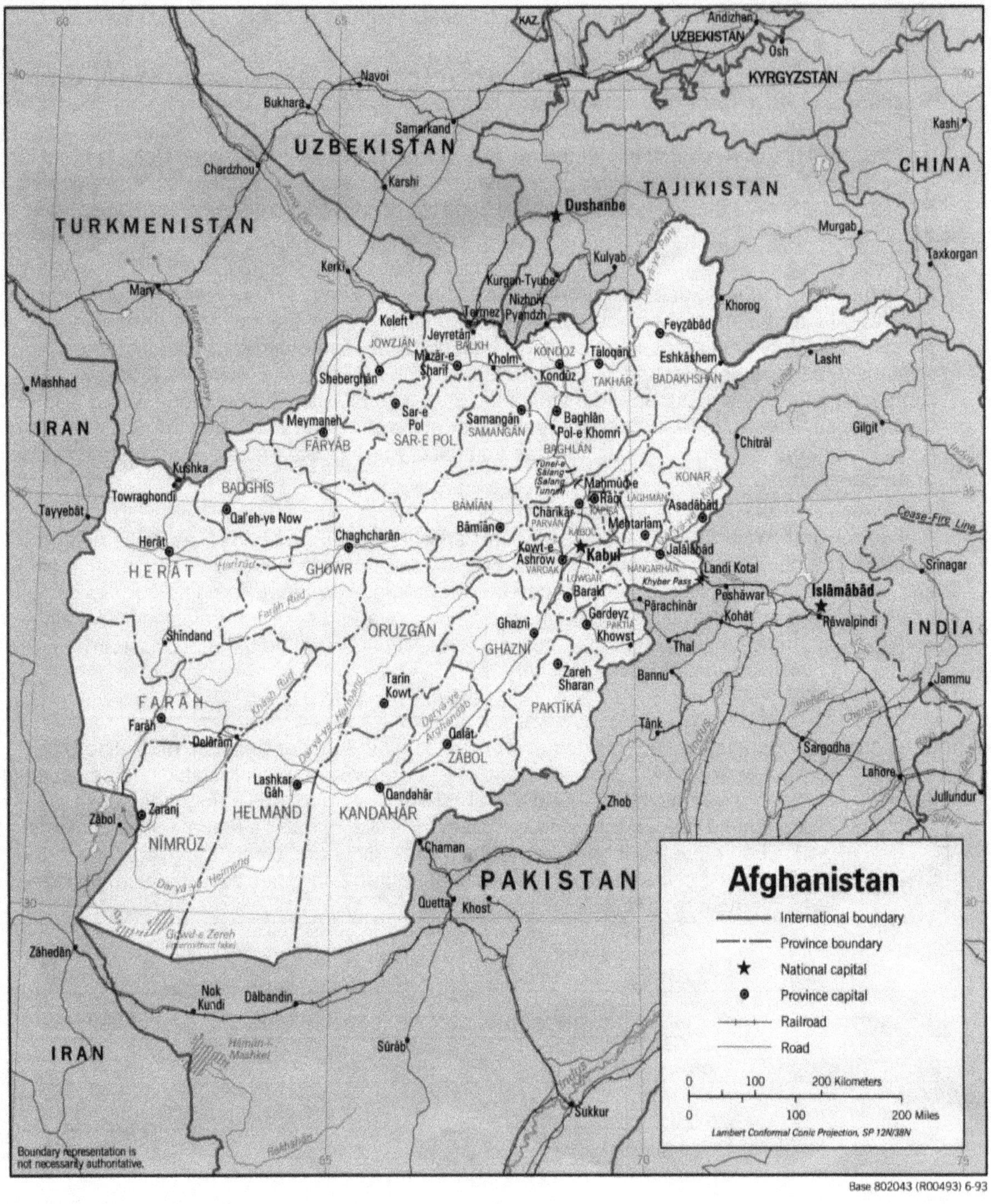


Base 802043 (R00493) 6-93

| | |
|---|---|
| **Coastline:** | 0 km (landlocked) |
| **Maritime claims:** | none (landlocked) |
| **Climate:** | arid to semiarid; cold winters and hot summers |
| **Terrain:** | mostly rugged mountains; plains in north and southwest |
| **Elevation extremes:** | lowest point: Amu Darya 258 m<br>highest point: Nowshak 7,485 m |
| **Natural resources:** | natural gas, petroleum, coal, copper, chromite, talc, barites, sulfur, lead, zinc, iron ore, salt, precious and semiprecious stones |
| **Land use:** | arable land: 12%<br>permanent crops: 0%<br>permanent pastures: 46%<br>forests and woodland: 3%<br>other: 39% |
| **Irrigated land:** | 30,000 sq km |
| **Natural hazards:** | damaging earthquakes occur in Hindu Kush mountains; flooding; droughts |
| **Environment - current issues:** | soil degradation; overgrazing; deforestation (much of the remaining forests are being cut down for fuel and building materials); desertification |
| **Environment - international agreements:** | party to: Desertification, Endangered Species, Environmental Modification, Marine Dumping, Nuclear Test Ban<br>signed, but not ratified: Biodiversity, Climate Change, Hazardous Wastes, Law of the Sea, Marine Life Conservation |

| | |
|---|---|
| **Geography - note:** | landlocked; the Hindu Kush mountains that run northeast to southwest divide the northern provinces from the rest of the country; the highest peaks are in the northern Vakhan (Wakhan Corridor) |
| **Population:** | 26,813,057 |
| **Age structure:** | 0-14 years: 42.2% (male 5,775,921; female 5,538,836)<br>15-64 years: 55.01% (male 7,644,242; female 7,106,568)<br>65 years and over: 2.79% (male 394,444; female 353,046) |
| **Population growth rate:** | 3.48%<br>note: this rate reflects the continued return of refugees from Iran |
| **Birth rate:** | 41.42 births/1,000 population |
| **Death rate:** | 17.72 deaths/1,000 population |
| **Net migration rate:** | 11.11 migrant(s)/1,000 population |
| **Sex ratio:** | at birth: 1.05 male(s)/female<br>under 15 years: 1.04 male(s)/female |

| | |
|---|---|
| | 15-64 years: 1.08 male(s)/female<br>65 years and over: 1.12 male(s)/female<br>total population: 1.06 male(s)/female |
| **Infant mortality rate:** | 147.02 deaths/1,000 live births |

## PEOPLE

| | |
|---|---|
| **Life expectancy at birth:** | total population: 46.24 years<br>male: 46.97 years<br>female: 45.47 years |
| **Total fertility rate:** | 5.79 children born/woman |
| **HIV/AIDS - adult prevalence rate:** | less than 0.01% |
| **HIV/AIDS - people living with HIV/AIDS:** | NA |
| **HIV/AIDS - deaths:** | NA |
| **Nationality:** | noun: Afghan(s)<br>adjective: Afghan |
| **Ethnic groups:** | Pashtun 38%, Tajik 25%, Hazara 19%, minor ethnic groups (Aimaks, Turkmen, Baloch, and others) 12%, Uzbek 6% |
| **Religions:** | Sunni Muslim 84%, Shi'a Muslim 15%, other 1% |
| **Languages:** | Pashtu 35%, Afghan Persian (Dari) 50%, Turkic languages (primarily Uzbek and Turkmen) 11%, 30 minor languages (primarily Balochi and Pashai) 4%, much bilingualism |
| **Literacy:** | definition: age 15 and over can read and write<br>total population: 31.5%<br>male: 47.2%<br>female: 15% |

## GOVERNMENT

| | |
|---|---|
| **Country name:** | conventional long form: Islamic State of Afghanistan; note - the self-proclaimed Taliban government refers to the country as Islamic Emirate of Afghanistan<br>conventional short form: Afghanistan<br>local long form: Dowlat-e Eslami-ye Afghanestan<br>local short form: Afghanestan<br>former: Republic of Afghanistan |
| **Government type:** | no functioning central government, administered by factions |
| **Capital:** | Kabul |
| **Administrative divisions:** | 30 provinces (velayat, singular - velayat); Badakhshan, Badghis, Baghlan, Balkh, Bamian, Farah, Faryab, Ghazni, Ghowr, Helmand, Herat, Jowzjan, Kabol, Kandahar, Kapisa, Konar, Kondoz, |

| | |
|---|---|
| | Laghman, Lowgar, Nangarhar, Nimruz, Oruzgan, Paktia, Paktika, Parvan, Samangan, Sar-e Pol, Takhar, Vardak, Zabol; note - there may be two new provinces of Nurestan (Nuristan) and Khowst |
| **Independence:** | 19 August 1919 (from UK control over Afghan foreign affairs) |
| **National holiday:** | Independence Day, 19 August (1919) |
| **Constitution:** | none |
| **Legal system:** | a new legal system has not been adopted but all factions tacitly agree they will follow Shari'a (Islamic law) |
| **Suffrage:** | NA; previously males 15-50 years of age |
| **Executive branch:** | **chief of state:** President of the Islamic Republic of Afghanistan Ashraf GHANI Ahmadzai (since 29 September 2014 ); CEO Abdullah ABDULLAH (since 29 September 2014); First Vice President Abdul Rashid DOSTAM (since 29 September 2014 ); Second Vice President Sarwar DANESH (since 29 September 2014); note - the president is both chief of state and head of government<br>**head of government:** President of the Islamic Republic of Afghanistan Ashraf GHANI Ahmadzai (since 29 September 2014 ); CEO Abdullah ABDULLAH (since 29 September 2014); First Vice President Abdul Rashid DOSTAM (since 29 September 2014 ); Second Vice President Sarwar DANESH (since 29 September 2014)<br>**cabinet:** Cabinet consists of 25 ministers appointed by the president, approved by the National Assembly<br>**elections/appointments:** president directly elected by absolute majority popular vote in 2 rounds if needed for a 5-year term (eligible for a second term); election last held in 2 rounds on 5 April and 14 June 2014 (next to be held in 2019)<br>**election results:** percent of vote in first round - Abdullah ABDULLAH (National Coalition of Afghanistan) 45%, Ashraf GHANI (independent) 31.6%, Zalmai RASSOUL 11.4%, other 12%; percent of vote in second round - Ashraf GHANI 56.4%, Abdullah ABDULLAH 43.6% |
| **Legislative branch:** | **description:** bicameral National Assembly consists of the Meshrano Jirga or House of Elders (102 seats; 34 members indirectly elected by district councils to serve 3-year terms, 34 indirectly elected by provincial councils to serve 4-year terms, and 34 nominated by the president of which 17 must be women, 2 must represent the disabled, and 2 must be Kuchi nomads; members serve 5-year terms) and the Wolesi Jirga or House of People (249 seats; members directly elected in multi-seat constituencies by proportional representation vote to serve 5-year terms)<br><br>**note:** the constitution allows the government to convene a constitutional Loya Jirga (Grand Council) on issues of independence, national sovereignty, and territorial integrity; it can amend the provisions of the constitution and prosecute |

| | |
|---|---|
| | the president; it consists of members of the National Assembly and chairpersons of the provincial and district councils; no constitutional Loya Jirga has ever been held, and district councils have never been elected; the president appointed 34 members of the Meshrano Jirga that the district councils should have indirectly elected<br>**elections:** the Wolesi Jirga's five-year term expired in 2015, but the president extended its term by decree until elections can be held<br>**election results:** results by party - NA; seats by party - NA |
| **Judicial branch:** | upper courts were non-functioning as of March 1995 (local Shari'a or Islamic law courts are functioning throughout the country) the constitution establishes a nine-member Stera Mahkama or Supreme Court (its nine justices are appointed for 10-year terms by the president with approval of the Wolesi Jirga) and subordinate High Courts and Appeals Courts (note - nine supreme court justices were appointed in the interim in January 2005 pending National Assembly selection of the constitutionally mandated justices); there is also a minister of justice; a separate Afghan Independent Human Rights Commission established by the Bonn Agreement is charged with investigating human rights abuses and war crimes |
| **Political parties and leaders:** | note - includes only political parties approved by the Ministry of Justice: Afghan Millat [Anwarul Haq AHADI]; De Afghanistan De Solay Ghorzang Gond [Shahnawaz TANAI]; De Afghanistan De Solay Mili Islami Gond [Shah Mahmood Polal ZAI]; Harakat-e-Islami Afghanistan [Mohammad Asif MOHSINEE]; Hezb-e-Aarman-e-Mardum-e-Afghanistan [Iihaj Saraj-u-din ZAFAREE]; Hezb-e-Aazadee Afghanistan [Abdul MALIK]; Hezb-e-Adalat-e-Islami Afghanistan [Mohammad Kabeer MARZBAN]; Hezb-e-Afghanistan-e-Wahid [Mohammad Wasil RAHEEMEE]; Hezb-e-Afghan Watan Islami Gond; Hezb-e-Congra-e-Mili Afghanistan [Latif PEDRAM]; Hezb-e-Falah-e-Mardum-e-Afghanistan [Mohammad ZAREEF]; Hezb-e-Hambastagee Mili Jawanan-e-Afghanistan [Mohammad Jamil KARZAI]; Hezb-e-Hamnbatagee-e-Afghanistan [Abdul Khaleq NEMAT]; Hezb-e-Harakat-e-Mili Wahdat-e-Afghanistan [Mohammad Nadir AATASH]; Hezb-e-Harak-e-Islami Mardum-e-Afghanistan [Ilhaj Said Hssain ANWARY]; Hezb-e-Ifazat Az Uqoq-e-Bashar Wa Inkishaf-e-Afghanistan [Baryalai NASRATEE]; Hezb-e-Istiqlal-e-Afghanistan [Dr. Gh. Farooq NIJZRABEE]; Hezb-e-Jamhoree Khwahan [Sibghatullah SANJAR]; Hezb-e-Kar Wa Tawsiha-e-Afghanistan [Zulfiar OMID]; Hezb-e-Libral-e-Aazadee Khwa-e-Mardum-e-Afghanistan [Ajmal SOHAIL]; Hezb-e-Mili Afghanistan [Abdul Rasheed AARYAN]; Hezb-e-Mili Wahdat-e-Aqwam-e-Islami Afghanistan [Mohammad Shah KHOGYANEE]; Hezb-e-Nuhzhat-e-Mili Afghanistan [Ahmad Wali MASOUD]; Hezb-e-Paiwand-e-Mili Afghanistan [Said Mansoor NADIRI]; Hezb-e-Rastakhaiz-e-Islami Mardum-e-Afghanistan [Said ZAHIR]; Hezb-e-Refah-e-Mardum-e-Afghanistan [Mia Gul WASEEQ]; Hezb-e-Risalat-e-Mardum-e-Afghanistan [Noor Aqa ROEEN]; Hezb-e-Sahadat-e-Mardum-e- |

| | |
|---|---|
| | Afghanistan [Mohammad Zubair PAIROZ]; Hezb-e-Sahadat-e-Mili Wa Islami Afghanistan [Mohammad Usman SALIGZADA]; Hezb-e-Sulh-e-Mili Islami Aqwam-e-Afghanistan [Abdul Qahir SHARYATEE]; Hezb-e-Sulh Wa Wahdat-e-Mili Afghanistan [Abdul Qadir IMAMEE]; Hezb-e-Tafahum-e-Wa Democracy Afghanistan [Ahamad SHAHEEN]; Hezb-e-Wahdat-e-Islami Afghanistan [Mohammad Karim KHALILI]; Hezb-e-Wahdat-e-Islami Mardum-e-Afghanistan [Ustad Mohammad MOHAQQEQ]; Hezb-e-Wahdat-e-Mili Afghanistan [Abdul Rasheed JALILI]; Jamahat-ul-Dahwat ilal Qurhan-wa-Sunat-ul-Afghanistan [Mawlawee Samiullah NAJEEBEE]; Jombesh-e Milli [Abdul Rashid DOSTAM]; Mahaz-e-Mili Islami Afghanistan [Said Ahmad GAILANEE]; Majmah-e-Mili Fahaleen-e-Sulh-e-Afghanistan [Shams ul Haq Noor SHAMS]; Nuhzat-e-Aazadee Wa Democracy Afghanistan [Abdul Raqeeb Jawid KUHISTANEE]; Nuhzat-e-Hambastagee Mili Afghanistan [Peer Said Ishaq GAILANEE]; Sazman-e-Islami Afghanistan-e-Jawan [Siad Jawad HUSSAINEE]; Tahreek Wahdat-e-Mili [Sultan Mahmood DHAZI] (30 Sep 2004) |
| **Political pressure groups and leaders:** | Jamiat-e Islami (Society of Islam) [former President Burhanuddin RABBANI]; Ittihad-e Islami (Islamic Union for the Liberation of Afghanistan) [Abdul Rasul SAYYAF]; there are also small monarchist, communist, and democratic groups |
| **International organization participation:** | AsDB, CP, ECO, FAO, G-77, IAEA, IBRD, ICAO, ICCt, ICRM, IDA, IDB, IFAD, IFC, IFRCS, ILO, IMF, Interpol, IOC, IOM, ISO (correspondent), ITU, MIGA, NAM, OIC, OPCW, OSCE (partner), SAARC, SACEP, UN, UNCTAD, UNESCO, UNIDO, UPU, WCO, WFTU, WHO, WIPO, WMO, WToO, WTO (observer) |
| **Diplomatic representation in the US:** | **chief of mission:** Ambassador Kare AAS<br>**chancery:** 2341 Wyoming Avenue NW, Washington, DC 20008<br>**telephone:** [1] (202) 483-6410<br>**FAX:** [1] (202) 483-6488<br>**consulate(s) general:** Los Angeles, New York, Washington, DC |
| **Diplomatic representation from the US:** | **chief of mission:** Ambassador (vacant); Special Charge d'Affaires Hugo LLORENS (since December 2016)<br>**embassy:** Bibi Mahru, Kabul<br>**mailing address:** U.S. Embassy Kabul, APO, AE 09806<br>**telephone:** [00 93] 0700 108 001<br>**FAX:** [00 93] 0700 108 564 |
| **Flag description:** | hree equal vertical bands of black (hoist), red, and green, with a gold emblem centered on the red band; the emblem features a temple-like structure encircled by a wreath on the left and right and by a bold Islamic inscription above |

## ECONOMY

Afghanistan is gradually recovering from decades of conflict. Before 2014, the economy had sustained nearly a decade of strong growth, largely because of international assistance. Since 2014, however, the economy has slowed, in large part because of the withdrawal of nearly 100,000 foreign troops that had artificially inflated the country's economic growth. Despite improvements in life expectancy, incomes, and literacy since 2001, Afghanistan is extremely poor, landlocked, and highly dependent on foreign aid. Much of the population continues to suffer from shortages of housing, clean water, electricity, medical care, and jobs. Corruption, insecurity, weak governance, lack of infrastructure, and the Afghan Government's difficulty in extending rule of law to all parts of the country pose challenges to future economic growth. Afghanistan's living standards are among the lowest in the world.

The international community remains committed to Afghanistan's development, pledging over $83 billion at ten donors' conferences between 2003 and 2016. In October 2016, the donors at the Brussels conference pledged an additional $3.8 billion in development aid annually from 2017 to 2020. Despite this help, the Government of Afghanistan will need to overcome a number of challenges, including low revenue collection, anemic job creation, high levels of corruption, weak government capacity, and poor public infrastructure.

In 2017 Afghanistan's growth rate was only marginally above that of the 2014-2016 average. The drawdown of international security forces that started in 2012 has negatively affected economic growth, as a substantial portion of commerce, especially in the services sector, has catered to the ongoing international troop presence in the country. Afghan President Ashraf GHANI Ahmadzai is dedicated to instituting economic reforms to include improving revenue collection and fighting corruption. However, the reforms will take time to implement and Afghanistan will remain dependent on international donor support over the next several years.

**GDP (purchasing power parity):**

$69.51 billion (2017 est.)
$67.81 billion (2016 est.)
$66.25 billion (2015 est.)
**note:** data are in 2017 dollars
**country comparison to the world:** 100

**GDP (official exchange rate):**
$21.06 billion (2016 est.)

**GDP - real growth rate:**
2.5% (2017 est.)
2.4% (2016 est.)
1.3% (2015 est.)
**country comparison to the world:** 129

**GDP - per capita (PPP):**
$1,900 (2017 est.)
$2,000 (2016 est.)
$2,100 (2015 est.)
**note:** data are in 2017 dollars
**country comparison to the world:** 211

**Gross national saving:**
22.7% of GDP (2017 est.)
25.5% of GDP (2016 est.)
21.4% of GDP (2015 est.)

**country comparison to the world:** 68

**GDP - composition, by end use:**
**household consumption:** 108.6%
**government consumption:** 12.8%
**investment in fixed capital:** 18.2%
**investment in inventories:** 0%
**exports of goods and services:** 6.6%
**imports of goods and services:** -46.2% (2014 est.)

**GDP - composition, by sector of origin:**
**agriculture:** 22%
**industry:** 22%
**services:** 56%
**note:** data exclude opium production (2015 est.)

**Agriculture - products:**
opium, wheat, fruits, nuts; wool, mutton, sheepskins, lambskins, poppies

**Industries:**
small-scale production of bricks, textiles, soap, furniture, shoes, fertilizer, apparel, food products, non-alcoholic beverages, mineral water, cement; handwoven carpets; natural gas, coal, copper

**Industrial production growth rate:**
2.4% (2014 est.)
**country comparison to the world:** 116

**Labor force:**
7.983 million (2013 est.)
**country comparison to the world:** 62

**Labor force - by occupation:**
**agriculture:** 78.6%
**industry:** 5.7%
**services:** 15.7% (FY08/09 est.)

**Unemployment rate:**
35% (2008 est.)
40% (2005 est.)
**country comparison to the world:** 208

**Population below poverty line:**
35.8%

**Household income or consumption by percentage share:**
**lowest 10%:** 3.8%
**highest 10%:** 24% (2008)

**Budget:**
**revenues:** $1.992 billion
**expenditures:** $6.636 billion (2016 est.)

**Taxes and other revenues:**
9.5% of GDP (2016 est.)
**country comparison to the world:** 214

**Budget surplus (+) or deficit (-):**
-22.1% of GDP (2016 est.)
**country comparison to the world:** 218

**Public debt:**
8.3% of GDP (2016 est.)
9.3% of GDP (2015 est.)
**country comparison to the world:** 199

**Fiscal year:**
21 December - 20 December

**Inflation rate (consumer prices):**
6% (2017 est.)
4.4% (2016 est.)
**country comparison to the world:** 183

**Commercial bank prime lending rate:**
15% (31 December 2016 est.)
15% (31 December 2015 est.)
**country comparison to the world:** 45

**Stock of narrow money:**
$6.644 billion (31 December 2014 est.)
$6.192 billion (31 December 2013 est.)
**country comparison to the world:** 93

**Stock of broad money:**
$6.945 billion (31 December 2014 est.)
$6.544 billion (31 December 2013 est.)
**country comparison to the world:** 118

**Stock of domestic credit:**
$-240.6 million (31 December 2016 est.)
$-240.6 million (31 December 2016 est.)
**country comparison to the world:** 191

**Current account balance:**
$999 million (2017 est.)
$1.372 billion (2016 est.)
**country comparison to the world:** 38

**Exports:**
$619.2 million (2016 est.)
$580 million (2015 est.)
**note:** not including illicit exports or reexports
**country comparison to the world:** 171

**Exports - commodities:**

opium, fruits and nuts, handwoven carpets, wool, cotton, hides and pelts, precious and semi-precious gems

**Exports - partners:**
Pakistan 46.3%, India 37.6%

**Imports:**
$6.16 billion (2016 est.)
$7.034 billion (2015 est.)
**country comparison to the world:** 114

**Imports - commodities:**
machinery and other capital goods, food, textiles, petroleum products

**Imports - partners:**
Iran 19.3%, Pakistan 18.3%, China 16.7%, Kazakhstan 9.5%, Uzbekistan 6.1%, Turkmenistan 5.4%, Malaysia 4% (2016)

**Reserves of foreign exchange and gold:**
$6.477 billion (31 December 2016 est.)
$6.232 billion (31 December 2015 est.)
**country comparison to the world:** 87

**Debt - external:**
$1.28 billion (FY10/11)
$2.7 billion (FY08/09)
**country comparison to the world:** 163

**Exchange rates:**
afghanis (AFA) per US dollar -
67.87 (2016 est.)
67.87 (2016 est.)
67.87 (2015)
61.14 (2014 est.)
57.25 (2013 est.)

## ENERRGY

**Electricity access:**
**population without electricity:** 18,999,254
**electrification - total population:** 43%
**electrification - urban areas:** 83%
**electrification - rural areas:** 32%

**Electricity - production:**
1.034 billion kWh (2015 est.)
**country comparison to the world:** 149

**Electricity - consumption:**
4.741 billion kWh (2015 est.)
**country comparison to the world:** 124

**Electricity - exports:**
0 kWh (2016 est.)

**country comparison to the world:** 99

**Electricity - imports:**
3.779 billion kWh (2015 est.)
**country comparison to the world:** 48

**Electricity - installed generating capacity:**
599,100 kW (2015 est.)
**country comparison to the world:** 139

**Electricity - from fossil fuels:**
44.7% of total installed capacity (2015 est.)
**country comparison to the world:** 161

**Electricity - from nuclear fuels:**
0% of total installed capacity (2015 est.)
**country comparison to the world:** 36

**Electricity - from hydroelectric plants:**
55.1% of total installed capacity (2015 est.)
**country comparison to the world:** 33

**Electricity - from other renewable sources:**
0.2% of total installed capacity (2015 est.)
**country comparison to the world:** 160

**Crude oil - production:**
0 bbl/day (2016 est.)
**country comparison to the world:** 102

**Crude oil - exports:**
0 bbl/day (2014 est.)
**country comparison to the world:** 86

**Crude oil - imports:**
0 bbl/day (2014 est.)
**country comparison to the world:** 89

**Crude oil - proved reserves:**
0 bbl (1 January 2017 es)
**country comparison to the world:** 102

**Refined petroleum products - production:**
0 bbl/day (2014 est.)
**country comparison to the world:** 111

**Refined petroleum products - consumption:**
130,000 bbl/day (2015 est.)
**country comparison to the world:** 76

**Refined petroleum products - exports:**
0 bbl/day (2014 est.)
**country comparison to the world:** 129

**Refined petroleum products - imports:**
127,200 bbl/day (2014 est.)
**country comparison to the world:** 52

**Natural gas - production:**
189 million cu m (2015 est.)
**country comparison to the world:** 77
**Natural gas - consumption:**
816 million cu m (2015 est.)
**country comparison to the world:** 104
**Natural gas - exports:**
0 cu m (2013 est.)
**country comparison to the world:** 59
**Natural gas - imports:**
0 cu m (2013 est.)
**country comparison to the world:** 81

**Natural gas - proved reserves:**
49.55 billion cu m (1 January 2017 est.)
**country comparison to the world:** 64

**Carbon dioxide emissions from consumption of energy:**
7.4 million Mt (2013 est.)
**country comparison to the world:** 115

## COMMUNICATIONS

| | |
|---|---|
| **Telephones - main lines in use:** | 50,000 |
| **Telephones - mobile cellular:** | 600,000 |
| **Telephone system:** | *general assessment:* very limited telephone and telegraph service<br>*domestic:* telephone service is improving with the licensing of four wireless telephone service providers by 2005; approximately 3 in 10 Afghans own a wireless telephone; telephone main lines remain limited with only 0.1 line per 10 people<br>*international:* country code - 93; five VSAT's installed in Kabul, Herat, Mazar-e-Sharif, Kandahar, and Jalalabad provide international and domestic voice and data connectivity |
| **Radio broadcast stations:** | AM 21, FM 23, shortwave 1 (broadcasts in Pashtu, Afghan Persian (Dari), Urdu, and English) |
| **Radios:** | 167,000 |
| **Television broadcast stations:** | at least 10 (one government run central television station in Kabul and regional stations in nine of the 30 provinces; the regional stations operate on a reduced schedule; also, in 1997, there was a station in Mazar-e Sharif reaching four northern Afghanistan provinces) |
| **Televisions:** | 100,000 |
| **Internet country code:** | .af |
| **Internet Service Providers (ISPs):** | 76 |
| **Internet users:** | 25,900 |

| | |
|---|---|
| | in March 2003, 'af' was established as Afghanistan's domain name; Internet access is growing through Internet cafes as well as public "telekiosks" in Kabul |

**TRANSPORTATION**

| | |
|---|---|
| **Railways:** | total: 24.6 km<br>broad gauge: 9.6 km 1.524-m gauge from Gushgy (Turkmenistan) to Towraghondi; 15 km 1.524-m gauge from Termiz (Uzbekistan) to Kheyrabad transshipment point on south bank of Amu Darya |
| **Highways:** | total: 21,000 km<br>paved: 2,793 km<br>unpaved: 18,207 km |
| **Waterways:** | 1,200 km<br><br>note: chiefly Amu Darya, which handles vessels with DWT up to about 500 |
| **Pipelines:** | petroleum products - Uzbekistan to Bagram and Turkmenistan to Shindand; natural gas 180 km |
| **Ports and harbors:** | Kheyrabad, Shir Khan |
| **Airports:** | 46 |
| **Airports - with paved runways:** | total: 10<br>over 3,047 m: 3<br>2,438 to 3,047 m: 4<br>1,524 to 2,437 m: 2<br>under 914 m: 1 |
| **Airports - with unpaved runways:** | total: 36<br>Over 3047 m: 1<br>2,438 to 3,047 m: 7<br><br>1,524 to 2,437 m: 13<br>914 to 1,523 m: 4<br>under 914 m: 11 |
| **Heliports:** | 2 |

**MILITARY**

| | |
|---|---|
| **Military branches:** | Afghan National Army (includes Afghan Air Force) |
| **Military manpower - military age:** | 22 years of age |
| **Military manpower - availability:** | males age 15-49: 6,645,023 |
| **Military manpower - fit for military service:** | males age 15-49: 3,561,957 |
| **Military manpower - reaching military age annually:** | males: 252,869 |
| **Military expenditures - dollar figure:** | $NA |
| **Military expenditures - percent of GDP:** | NA% |

## TRANSNATIONAL ISSUES

| | |
|---|---|
| **Disputes - international:** | most Afghan refugees in Pakistan have been repatriated, but thousands still remain in Iran, many at their own choosing; Coalition and Pakistani forces continue to patrol remote tribal areas to control the borders and stem organized terrorist and other illegal cross-border activities; regular meetings between Pakistani and Coalition allies aim to resolve periodic claims of boundary encroachments; regional conflicts over water-sharing arrangements with Amu Darya and Helmand River states |
| **Refugees and internally displaced persons:** | IDPs: 200,000-300,000 (mostly Pashtuns and Kuchis displaced in south and west due to drought and instability) (2005) |
| **Illicit drugs:** | world's largest producer of opium; cultivation dropped 48% to 107,400 hectares in 2005; better weather and lack of widespread disease returned opium yields to normal levels, meaning potential opium production declined by only 10% to 4,475 metric tons; if the entire poppy crop were processed, it is estimated that 526 metric tons of heroin could be processed; source of hashish; many narcotics-processing labs throughout the country; drug trade source of instability and some antigovernment groups profit from the trade; 80-90% of the heroin consumed in Europe comes from Afghan opium; vulnerable to narcotics money laundering through informal financial networks |

# IMPORTANT INFORMATION FOR UNDERSTANDING MODERN AFGHANISTAN

## PROFILE

**OFFICIAL NAME:** Islamic State of Afghanistan

**Geography**
Area: 647,500 sq. km. (249,935 sq. mi.); slightly smaller than Texas.
Cities: *Capital*--Kabul (1,780,000; UN est.). *Other cities* (1988 UN est.; current figures are probably significantly higher)--Kandahar (226,000); Herat (177,000); Mazar-e-Sharif (131,000); Jalalabad (58,000); Konduz (57,000).
Terrain: Landlocked; mostly mountains and desert.
Climate: Dry, with cold winters and hot summers.

**People**
Nationality: *Noun and adjective*--Afghan(s).
Population: 28,513,677. More than 3.5 million Afghans live outside the country, mainly in Pakistan and Iran, although over two and a half million have returned since the removal of the Taliban.
Annual population growth rate: 4.92%. This rate does not take into consideration the recent war and its continuing impact.
Main ethnic groups: Pashtun, Tajik, Hazara, Uzbek, Turkmen, Aimaq, Baluch, Nuristani, Kizilbash.
Religions: Sunni Muslim 80%, Shi'a Muslim 19%, other 1%.
Main languages: Dari (Afghan Persian), Pashto.
Education: Approximately 4 million children, of whom some 30% are girls, enrolled in school during 2003. *Literacy*--36% (male 51%, female 21%), but real figures may be lower given breakdown of education system and flight of educated Afghans.
Health: *Infant mortality rate* --165.96 deaths/1,000 live births. *Life expectancy* --42.27 yrs. (male); 42.66 yrs. (female).

**Government**
Type: Islamic Republic.
Independence: August 19, 1919.
Constitution: January 4, 2004.
Branches: *Executive*—president (chief of state). *Legislative*—bicameral National Assembly (House of the People--249 seats, House of the Elders--102 seats). *Judicial*—Supreme Court, High Courts, and Appeals Courts.
Political subdivisions: 34 provinces.
Suffrage: Universal at 18 years.

**Economy**
Natural resources: Natural gas, oil, coal, copper, chromite, talc, barites, sulfur, lead, zinc, iron, salt, precious and semiprecious stones.
Agriculture (estimated 52% of GDP): *Products*--wheat, corn, barley, rice, cotton, fruit, nuts, karakul pelts, wool, and mutton.
Industry (estimated 26% of GDP): *Types*--small-scale production for domestic use of textiles, soap, furniture, shoes, fertilizer, and cement; hand-woven carpets for export; natural gas, precious and semiprecious gemstones.
Services (estimated 22% of GDP): Transport, retail, and telecommunications.
Trade (2002-03 est.): *Exports*--$100 million (does not include opium): fruits and nuts, hand-woven

carpets, wool, cotton, hides and pelts, precious and semiprecious gems. *Major markets*--Central Asian republics, Pakistan, Iran, EU, India. *Imports*--$2.3 billion: food, petroleum products, machinery, and consumer goods. *Major suppliers*--Central Asian republics, Pakistan, Iran. Currency: The currency is the afghani, which was reintroduced as Afghanistan's new currency in January 2003. At present, $1 U.S. equals approximately 45 afghanis.

# PEOPLE

Afghanistan's ethnically and linguistically mixed population reflects its location astride historic trade and invasion routes leading from Central Asia into South and Southwest Asia. While population data is somewhat unreliable for Afghanistan, Pashtuns make up the largest ethnic group at 38-44% of the population, followed by Tajiks (25%), Hazaras (10%), Uzbek (6-8%), Aimaq, Turkmen, Baluch, and other small groups. Dari (Afghan Farsi) and Pashto are official languages. Dari is spoken by more than one-third of the population as a first language and serves as a lingua franca for most Afghans, though Pashto is spoken throughout the Pashtun areas of eastern and southern Afghanistan. Tajik and Turkic languages are spoken widely in the north. Smaller groups throughout the country also speak more than 70 other languages and numerous dialects.

Afghanistan is an Islamic country. An estimated 80% of the population is Sunni, following the Hanafi school of jurisprudence; the remainder of the population--and primarily the Hazara ethnic group-- predominantly Shi'a. Despite attempts during the years of communist rule to secularize Afghan society, Islamic practices pervade all aspects of life. In fact, Islam served as a principal basis for expressing opposition to communism and the Soviet invasion. Islamic religious tradition and codes, together with traditional tribal and ethnic practices, have an important role in personal conduct and dispute settlement. Afghan society is largely based on kinship groups, which follow traditional customs and religious practices, though somewhat less so in urban areas.

# HISTORY

Afghanistan, often called the crossroads of Central Asia, has had a turbulent history. In 328 BC, Alexander the Great entered the territory of present-day Afghanistan, then part of the Persian Empire, to capture Bactria (present-day Balkh). Invasions by the Scythians, White Huns, and Turks followed in succeeding centuries. In AD 642, Arabs invaded the entire region and introduced Islam.

Arab rule gave way to the Persians, who controlled the area until conquered by the Turkic Ghaznavids in 998. Mahmud of Ghazni (998-1030) consolidated the conquests of his predecessors and turned Ghazni into a great cultural center as well as a base for frequent forays into India. Following Mahmud's short-lived dynasty, various princes attempted to rule sections of the country until the destructive Mongol invasion of 1219 led by Genghis Khan.

Following Genghis Khan's death in 1227, a succession of petty chiefs and princes struggled for supremacy until late in the 14th century, when one of his descendants, Tamerlane, incorporated Afghanistan into his own vast Asian empire. Babur, a descendant of Tamerlane and the founder of India's Moghul dynasty at the beginning of the 16th century, made Kabul the capital of an Afghan principality.

In 1747, Ahmad Shah Durrani, the founder of what is known today as Afghanistan, established his rule. A Pashtun, Durrani was elected king by a tribal council after the assassination of the Persian ruler Nadir Shah at Khabushan in the same year. Throughout his reign, Durrani consolidated chieftainships, petty principalities, and fragmented provinces into one country. His rule extended from Mashad in the west to Kashmir and Delhi in the east, and from the Amu Darya (Oxus) River in the north to the Arabian Sea in the south.

## EUROPEAN INFLUENCE

During the 19th century, collision between the expanding British Empire in the subcontinent and czarist Russia significantly influenced Afghanistan in what was termed "The Great Game." British concern over Russian advances in Central Asia and growing influence in Persia culminated in two Anglo-Afghan wars. The first (1839-42) resulted not only in the destruction of a British army, but is remembered today as an example of the ferocity of Afghan resistance to foreign rule. The second Anglo-Afghan war (1878-80) was sparked by Amir Sher Ali's refusal to accept a British mission in Kabul. This conflict brought Amir Abdur Rahman to the Afghan throne. During his reign (1880-1901), the British and Russians officially established the boundaries of what would become modern Afghanistan through the demarcation of the Durand Line. The British retained effective control over Kabul's foreign affairs.

Afghanistan remained neutral during World War I, despite German encouragement of anti-British feelings and Afghan rebellion along the borders of British India. The Afghan king's policy of neutrality was not universally popular within the country, however.

Habibullah, Abdur Rahman's son and successor, was assassinated in 1919, possibly by family members opposed to British influence. His third son, Amanullah, regained control of Afghanistan's foreign policy after launching the third Anglo-Afghan war with an attack on India in the same year. During the ensuing conflict, the war-weary British relinquished their control over Afghan foreign affairs by signing the Treaty of Rawalpindi in August 1919. In commemoration of this event, Afghans celebrate August 19 as their Independence Day.

## REFORM AND REACTION

King Amanullah (1919-29) moved to end his country's traditional isolation in the years following the third Anglo-Afghan war. He established diplomatic relations with most major countries and, following a 1927 tour of Europe and Turkey--during which he noted the modernization and secularization advanced by Ataturk--introduced several reforms intended to modernize Afghanistan. Some of these, such as the abolition of the traditional Muslim veil for women and the opening of a number of co-educational schools, quickly alienated many tribal and religious leaders. Faced with overwhelming armed opposition, Amanullah was forced to abdicate in January 1929 after Kabul fell to forces led by Bacha-i-Saqao, a Tajik brigand. Prince Nadir Khan, a cousin of Amanullah's, in turn defeated Bacha-i-Saqao in October of the same year and, with considerable Pashtun tribal support, was declared King Nadir Shah. Four years later, however, he was assassinated in a revenge killing by a Kabul student.

Mohammad Zahir Shah, Nadir Khan's 19-year-old son, succeeded to the throne and reigned from 1933 to 1973. In 1964, King Zahir Shah promulgated a liberal constitution providing for a two-chamber legislature to which the king appointed one-third of the deputies. The people elected another third, and the remainder were selected indirectly by provincial assemblies. Although Zahir's "experiment in democracy" produced few lasting reforms, it permitted the growth of unofficial extremist parties on both the left and the right. These included the communist People's Democratic Party of Afghanistan (PDPA), which had close ideological ties to the Soviet Union. In 1967, the PDPA split into two major rival factions: the Khalq (Masses) faction headed by Nur Muhammad Taraki and Hafizullah Amin and supported by elements within the military, and the

Parcham (Banner) faction led by Babrak Karmal. The split reflected ethnic, class, and ideological divisions within Afghan society.

Zahir's cousin, Sardar Mohammad Daoud, served as his Prime Minister from 1953 to 1963. During his tenure as Prime Minister, Daoud solicited military and economic assistance from both Washington and Moscow and introduced controversial social policies of a reformist nature. Daoud's alleged support for the creation of a Pashtun state in the Pakistan-Afghan border area heightened tensions with Pakistan and eventually resulted in Daoud's dismissal in March 1963.

## DAOUD'S REPUBLIC (1973-78) AND THE APRIL 1978 COUP

Amid charges of corruption and malfeasance against the royal family and poor economic conditions created by the severe 1971-72 drought, former Prime Minister Daoud seized power in a military coup on July 17, 1973. Zahir Shah fled the country, eventually finding refuge in Italy. Daoud abolished the monarchy, abrogated the 1964 constitution, and declared Afghanistan a republic with himself as its first President and Prime Minister. His attempts to carry out badly needed economic and social reforms met with little success, and the new constitution promulgated in February 1977 failed to quell chronic political instability.

Seeking to exploit more effectively mounting popular disaffection, the PDPA reunified with Moscow's support. On April 27, 1978, the PDPA initiated a bloody coup, which resulted in the overthrow and murder of Daoud and most of his family. Nur Muhammad Taraki, Secretary General of the PDPA, became President of the Revolutionary Council and Prime Minister of the newly established Democratic Republic of Afghanistan.

Opposition to the Marxist government emerged almost immediately. During its first 18 months of rule, the PDPA brutally imposed a Marxist-style "reform" program, which ran counter to deeply rooted Afghan traditions. Decrees forcing changes in marriage customs and pushing through an ill-conceived land reform were particularly misunderstood by virtually all Afghans. In addition, thousands of members of the traditional elite, the religious establishment, and the intelligentsia were imprisoned, tortured, or murdered. Conflicts within the PDPA also surfaced early and resulted in exiles, purges, imprisonments, and executions.

By the summer of 1978, a revolt began in the Nuristan region of eastern Afghanistan and quickly spread into a countrywide insurgency. In September 1979, Hafizullah Amin, who had earlier been Prime Minister and Minister of Defense, seized power from Taraki after a palace shootout. Over the next 2 months, instability plagued Amin's regime as he moved against perceived enemies in the PDPA. By December, party morale was crumbling, and the insurgency was growing.

## THE SOVIET INVASION

The Soviet Union moved quickly to take advantage of the April 1978 coup. In December 1978, Moscow signed a new bilateral treaty of friendship and cooperation with Afghanistan, and the Soviet military assistance program increased significantly. The regime's survival increasingly was dependent upon Soviet military equipment and advisers as the insurgency spread and the Afghan army began to collapse.

By October 1979, however, relations between Afghanistan and the Soviet Union were tense as Hafizullah Amin refused to take Soviet advice on how to stabilize and consolidate his government. Faced with a deteriorating security situation, on December 24, 1979, large numbers of Soviet airborne forces, joining thousands of Soviet troops already on the ground, began to land in Kabul under the pretext of a field exercise. On December 26, these invasion forces killed Hafizullah Amin and installed Babrak Karmal, exiled leader of the Parcham faction, bringing him back from Czechoslovakia and making him Prime Minister. Massive Soviet ground forces invaded from the north on December 27.

Following the invasion, the Karmal regime, although backed by an expeditionary force that grew as large as 120,000 Soviet troops, was unable to establish authority outside Kabul. As much as 80% of the countryside, including parts of Herat and Kandahar, eluded effective government control. An overwhelming majority of Afghans opposed the communist regime, either actively or passively. Afghan freedom fighters (mujahidin) made it almost impossible for the regime to maintain a system of local government outside major urban centers. Poorly armed at first, in 1984 the mujahidin began receiving substantial assistance in the form of weapons and training from the U.S. and other outside powers.

In May 1985, the seven principal Peshawar-based guerrilla organizations formed an alliance to coordinate their political and military operations against the Soviet occupation. Late in 1985, the mujahidin were active in and around Kabul, launching rocket attacks and conducting operations against the communist government. The failure of the Soviet Union to win over a significant number of Afghan collaborators or to rebuild a viable Afghan army forced it to bear an increasing responsibility for fighting the resistance and for civilian administration.

Soviet and popular displeasure with the Karmal regime led to its demise in May 1986. Karmal was replaced by Muhammad Najibullah, former chief of the Afghan secret police (KHAD). Najibullah had established a reputation for brutal efficiency during his tenure as KHAD chief. As Prime Minister, Najibullah was ineffective and highly dependent on Soviet support. Undercut by deep-seated divisions within the PDPA, regime efforts to broaden its base of support proved futile.

## THE GENEVA ACCORDS AND THEIR AFTERMATH

By the mid-1980s, the tenacious Afghan resistance movement--aided by the United States, Saudi Arabia, Pakistan, and others--was exacting a high price from the Soviets, both militarily within Afghanistan and by souring the U.S.S.R.'s relations with much of the Western and Islamic world. Informal negotiations for a Soviet withdrawal from Afghanistan had been underway since 1982. In 1988, the Governments of Pakistan and Afghanistan, with the United States and Soviet Union serving as guarantors, signed an agreement settling the major differences between them. The agreement, known as the Geneva accords, included five major documents, which, among other things, called for U.S. and Soviet noninterference in the internal affairs of Pakistan and Afghanistan, the right of refugees to return to Afghanistan without fear of persecution or harassment, and, most importantly, a timetable that ensured full Soviet withdrawal from Afghanistan by February 15, 1989. About 14,500 Soviet and an estimated one million Afghan lives were lost between 1979 and the Soviet withdrawal in 1989.

Significantly, the mujahidin were party neither to the negotiations nor to the 1988 agreement and, consequently, refused to accept the terms of the accords. As a result, the civil war continued after the Soviet withdrawal, which was completed in February 1989. Najibullah's regime, though failing to win popular support, territory, or international recognition, was able to remain in power until 1992 but collapsed after the defection of Gen. Abdul Rashid Dostam and his Uzbek militia in March. However, when the victorious mujahidin entered Kabul to assume control over the city and the central government, a new round of internecine fighting began between the various militias, which had coexisted only uneasily during the Soviet occupation. With the demise of their common enemy, the militias' ethnic, clan, religious, and personality differences surfaced, and the civil war continued.

Seeking to resolve these differences, the leaders of the Peshawar-based mujahidin groups established an interim Islamic Jihad Council in mid-April 1992 to assume power in Kabul. Moderate leader Prof. Sibghatullah Mojaddedi was to chair the council for 2 months, after which a 10-member leadership council composed of mujahidin leaders and presided over by the head of the Jamiat-i-Islami, Prof. Burhanuddin Rabbani, was to be set up for 4 months. During this 6-month period, a Loya Jirga, or grand council of Afghan elders and notables, would convene and designate an interim administration which would hold power up to a year, pending elections.

But in May 1992, Rabbani prematurely formed the leadership council, undermining Mojaddedi's fragile authority. In June, Mojaddedi surrendered power to the Leadership Council, which then elected Rabbani as President. Nonetheless, heavy fighting broke out in August 1992 in Kabul between forces loyal to President Rabbani and rival factions, particularly those who supported Gulbuddin Hekmatyar's Hezb-i-Islami. After Rabbani extended his tenure in December 1992, fighting in the capital flared up in January and February 1993. The Islamabad Accord, signed in March 1993, which appointed Hekmatyar as Prime Minister, failed to have a lasting effect. A follow-up agreement, the Jalalabad Accord, called for the militias to be disarmed but was never fully implemented. Through 1993, Hekmatyar's Hezb-i-Islami forces, allied with the Shi'a Hezb-i-Wahdat militia, clashed intermittently with Rabbani and Masood's Jamiat forces. Cooperating with Jamiat were militants of Sayyaf's Ittehad-i-Islami and, periodically, troops loyal to ethnic Uzbek strongman Abdul Rashid Dostam. On January 1, 1994, Dostam switched sides, precipitating large-scale fighting in Kabul and in northern provinces, which caused thousands of civilian casualties in Kabul and elsewhere and created a new wave of displaced persons and refugees. The country sank even further into anarchy, forces loyal to Rabbani and Masood, both ethnic Tajiks, controlled Kabul and much of the northeast, while local warlords exerted power over the rest of the country.

## RISE AND FALL OF THE TALIBAN

The Taliban had risen to power in the mid 90's in reaction to the anarchy and warlordism that arose after the withdrawal of Soviet forces. Many Taliban had been educated in madrassas in Pakistan and were largely from rural southern Pashtun backgrounds. In 1994, the Taliban developed enough strength to capture the city of Kandahar from a local warlord and proceeded to expand its control throughout Afghanistan, occupying Kabul in September 1996. By the end of 1998, the Taliban occupied about 90% of the country, limiting the opposition largely to a small mostly Tajik corner in the northeast and the Panjshir valley.

The Taliban sought to impose an extreme interpretation of Islam--based upon the rural Pashtun tribal code--on the entire country and committed massive human rights violations, particularly directed against women and girls. The Taliban also committed serious atrocities against minority populations, particularly the Shi'a Hazara ethnic group, and killed noncombatants in several well-documented instances. In 2001, as part of a drive against relics of Afghanistan's pre-Islamic past, the Taliban destroyed two Buddha statues carved into cliff faces outside of the city of Bamiyan.

From the mid-1990s the Taliban provided sanctuary to Osama bin Laden, a Saudi national who had fought with the mujahideen resistance against the Soviets, and provide a base for his and other terrorist organizations. Bin Laden provided both financial and political support to the Taliban. Bin Laden and his Al-Qaida group were charged with the bombing of the U.S. Embassies in Nairobi and Dar Es Salaam in 1998, and in August 1998 the United States launched a cruise missile attack against bin Laden's terrorist camp in southeastern Afghanistan. Bin Laden and Al-

Qaida have acknowledged their responsibility for the September 11, 2001 terrorist attacks against the United States.

Following the Taliban's repeated refusal to expel bin Laden and his group and end its support for international terrorism, the U.S. and its partners in the anti-terrorist coalition began a military campaign on October 7, 2001, targeting terrorist facilities and various Taliban military and political assets within Afghanistan. Under pressure from U.S. military and anti-Taliban forces, the Taliban disintegrated rapidly, and Kabul fell on November 13, 2001.

Afghan factions opposed to the Taliban met at a United Nations-sponsored conference in Bonn, Germany in December 2001 and agreed to restore stability and governance to Afghanistan--creating an interim government and establishing a process to move toward a permanent government. Under the "Bonn Agreement," an Afghan Interim Authority was formed and took office in Kabul on December 22, 2001 with Hamid Karzai as Chairman. The Interim Authority held power for approximately 6 months while preparing for a nationwide "Loya Jirga" (Grand Council) in mid-June 2002 that decided on the structure of a Transitional Authority. The Transitional Authority, headed by President Hamid Karzai, renamed the government as the Transitional Islamic State of Afghanistan (TISA). One of the TISA's primary achievements was the drafting of a constitution that was ratified by a Constitutional Loya Jirga on January 4, 2004.

# AFGHANISTAN LEGAL SYSTEM

## GOVERNMENT – THE EXECUTIVE BRANCH

The Executive Branch of the Afghan government consists of a powerful and popularly elected President and two Vice Presidents.

The constitution involves a strong presidential system. The President of Afghanistan is elected directly by the Afghan people to a five-year term, and can be elected no more than twice.

The president must be Muslim, an Afghan citizen born of Afghan parents, and should not be guilty of war crimes. The president is the commander-in-chief of the armed forces.

Presidential responsibilities include:

- Determining policies with the approval of the National Assembly.
- Appointing the nation's ministers, the attorney general, the director of the central bank, and the justices of the Supreme Court with the approval of the main legislative body, the Wolesi Jirga.
- Appointing the nation's first and second vice presidents.

## GOVERNMENT – THE LEGISLATIVE BRANCH

A National Assembly consisting of two Houses, the House of People (Wolesi Jirga) with 249 seats, and the House of Elders (Meshrano Jirga) with 102 seats, forms the Legislative Branch.

There is an independent Judiciary branch consisting of the Supreme Court (Stera Mahkama), High Courts and Appeal Courts. The President appoints the nine members of the Supreme Court with the approval of the Wolesi Jirga.

## Composition of the National Assembly

"The National Assembly of the Islamic Republic of Afghanistan as the highest legislative organ is the manifestation of the will of its people and represents the whole nation. Every member of the National Assembly takes into judgment the general welfare and supreme interests of all people of Afghanistan at the time of casting their vote." *Constitution of the Islamic Republic of Afghanistan (Article Eighty-One)*

The National Assembly, as envisaged in the Constitution, consists of two houses: the Wolesi Jirga (the House of the People) and theMeshrano Jirga (the House of Elders).

Article Ninety of the Afghan Constitution stipulates that the National Assembly shall have the following duties:

- Ratification, modification or abrogation of laws or legislative decrees;
- Approval of social, cultural, economic as well as technological development programs;
- Approval of the state budget as well as permission to obtain or grant loans;
- Creation, modification and or abrogation of administrative units;
- Ratification of international treaties and agreements, or abrogation of membership of Afghanistan in them;
- Other authorities enshrined in this Constitution.

## The Wolesi Jirga (House of People)

The Wolesi Jirga has 249 seats with members directly elected by the people.

Sixty-eight women were elected to the seats reserved under the Constitution, while 17 of them have been elected in their own rights.

Each province was given proportionate representation in the Wolesi Jirga according to its population. Each member of the Wolesi Jirga will enjoy a five year term expiring on the twenty-first of June of the fifth year (June 21, 2010).

An aspiring candidate for the Wolesi Jirga must fulfil the following criteria:

- Be at least 25 years of age
- Be a citizen of Afghanistan
- Be registered as a voter
- Be running as a representative in only one province
- Pay a registration fee of 15,000 Afghanis (approximately US$300) which will be refunded provided the candidate wins at least three percent (3%) of the vote
- Submit a nomination form along with photocopies of 500 voter ID cards supporting the candidacy

In addition, no candidate can have been charged with crimes against humanity.

### THE MESHRANO JIRGA (HOUSE OF ELDERS)

The Meshrano Jirga consists of a mixture of appointed and elected members (total 102 members). Sixty-eight members were selected by 34 directly elected Provincial Councils, and 34 were appointed by the President.

President Karzai's appointments were vetted by an independent UN sponsored election board and included 17 women (50 %), as required by the Constitution.

Each provincial council has elected one council member to serve in the Jirga (34 members), also each district council (34 members). Representatives of provincial councils will serve a term of four years, while representatives of district councils will serve a term of three years. Sebghatulla Mojadeddi was appointed President of Meshrano Jirga.

An aspiring candidate for the Meshrano Jirga must fulfil the following criteria:

- Be at least 35 years of age
- Be a citizen of Afghanistan

In addition, no potential member of the Meshrano Jirga can have been charged with crimes against humanity

### SESSIONS OF THE NATIONAL ASSEMBLY

Both Houses of the National Assembly will convene two regular sessions for the term of nine months annually. The sessions are held concurrently, but separately, unless:

- The legislative term or annual sessions are inaugurated by the President;
- It is deemed necessary by the President.

The speaker of the Lower House shall preside over the joint sessions of the National Assembly. The sessions are open, except when the Speaker of the National Assembly or ten members of the House request its secrecy and it is granted by the National Assembly.

The President can order extraordinary sessions of the National Assembly during recess.

### THE SECRETARIAT OF THE NATIONAL ASSEMBLY

Upon commencement of their work period, each of the two houses of the National Assembly elects one member as the Speaker for the term of the legislature, and two members as, first and second deputies, and two members as secretary and assistant secretary for a period of one year.

These individuals shall form the administrative teams of the Lower House as well as the Upper House.

The Lower House has the authority to establish a special commission on the proposal of one third of its members to review, as well as, investigate the actions of Government.

## THE COURT OF APPEALS

The Court of Appeals is established in all the provinces in accordance with this law. The Court of Appeals is composed of chief of the court, heads of Dewans and other judicial members. Head of the Court of Appeals shall be selected from among the judges who have enough qualification, experience and competency. Head of the General Criminal Dewan is the deputy head of court of appeals.

**Structure of Dewans of Courts of Appeal**

The Courts of Appeal contains the following Dewans:

- General Criminal Dewan
- Public Security Dewan
- Civil and Family Dewan
- Public Rights Dewan
- Commercial Dewan
- Juveniles Dewan

There can not be more than six judicial members within each Dewan of the Court of Appeals.

The Supreme Court may as needed establish other Dewans within the structure of the Court of Appeals with the approval of the President.

**Powers of the Court of Appeals**

- The Court of Appeals oversees the rulings and decisions of the lower courts, in situations according to the provisions of the related laws.
- The Court of Appeals while resolving cases reconsiders the whole legal process. It may correct, overturn, amend, confirm or repeal the rulings and decisions of the lower courts.

**Duties and Powers of head of the Court of Appeals**

The head of the Court of Appeals has the following responsibilities and powers:

- lead and organize activities of the respective Dewans
- preside over the judicial meetings of the Dewans, when necessary
- assign member of one Dewan to another on temporary basis.
- assign one of the judges of the court of appeals to the primary courts when necessary.
- delegate the authority of resolving a certain case from one Dewan to another, when necessary.
- coordinate judicial experiences of respective Dewans.
- preparation of activity reports of Dewans and courts and delivery of the reports to the Supreme Court.

## THE PRIMARY COURTS

In the jurisdictional area of each Court of Appeals, there are these primary courts:

- Central provincial primary court
- Juveniles Court
- Commercial Primary Court

- District Primary Court
- Family Issues primary court

The Supreme Court may establish more courts in the centres of provinces when required after approval of the president.

**Primary Court Structure**

A Central Primary Court comprises of the following Dewans:

- General Criminal Dewan
- Civil Dewan
- Public Rights Dewan
- Public Security Dewan
- Traffic Criminal Dewan

The Dewans of Central Primary Court shall have one head and no more than four members.

**Resolving cases by Dewans of primary courts**

Central provincial primary courts have the relevant Dewans to resolve cases in primary level in accordance with law:

- Resolving general criminal cases by General Criminal Dewan.
- Resolving civil disputes between natural persons by Civil Dewan.
- Resolving civil disputes between natural and legal individuals/entities or among legal entities by Public Rights Dewan.
- Resolving criminal cases of public security and interest, drug trafficking and other crimes by Public Security Dewan in accordance with law.
- Resolving traffic criminal cases by Traffic related Crimes Dewan.

**Leading Court and Dewans**

There is a head for the central provincial primary court to lead and manage the judicial and administrative activities of the Dewans and to attend their meetings when required.

## JUVENILE COURT

There is a juvenile primary court in the centre of every province. The juvenile primary court is made up of a head and four members. In case the head is absent due to any reason, his/her powers and duties shall be transferred to one of the judicially experienced judges. The method to resolve juveniles' offences is to be determined by a special regulation.

## THE COMMERCIAL COURT

A commercial court is to be established in centre of every province. This court shall have a chief and four other members. In provinces where commercial court is not available, dealing with commercial cases is the jurisdiction of the civil Dewan of the provincial central primary court.

### Resolving special cases

Based on the case, the commercial, public rights and public security cases within the judicial jurisdiction of a Court of Appeals shall be initiated in the commercial court and in the relevant Dewans of the provincial central primary court.

## DISTRICT PRIMARY COURT STRUCTURE

The District primary court shall consist of a chief and two members. In the areas where there are no members available, the cases shall be decided by fewer than three. The chief of the district primary court shall lead the court. In his/her absence, the responsibilities and powers shall be transferred to the most judicially experienced judge on the court.

### District Primary Court Jurisdiction

District Primary courts shall deal in primary stage with all ordinary criminal, civil and family cases which are legally presented to them.

### Responsibility

The chief of each Primary Court, heads of Dewans and their judicial members shall be responsible for deciding cases in a timely manner according to the law, correct application of the law, and for explaining the ground for their decision.

### Finality of Decision

The decisions of the primary courts are absolute and final in the following situations:

- When both parties agree upon the issued decision of the court.
- When the time for appealing has expired.
- When the disputed property is worth up to 100,000 Afgs.
- When the order for a cash fine of 50,000 Afgs is issued
- Other situations set forth in law.

## REGISTRATION OF DOCUMENTS AND DEEDS BRANCHES

In the structure of every Court of Appeals, there is a Directorate of Documents and Deeds Registration (DDDR). There shall be a head in charge of a directorate and shall lead and manage the activities of the directorate. In the districts where there is no such directorate for legal documents registration, the district courts shall have the authority to perform these duties. Duties and powers of the DDDR's are regulated through special legislation.

## REGISTRATION OF DOCUMENTS AND TRADEMARKS

Registration of commercial documents and trade marks shall be the jurisdiction of the commercial court.

## CONDITIONS OF BEING A JUDGE

On the recommendation of the Supreme Court and with approval of the president, any qualified person meeting following requirements shall be appointed as a judge:

- Upon appointment as judge, hold the citizenship of Islamic Republic of Afghanistan for at least ten yeas.
- Not be convicted of any crime or intentional misdemeanour by absolute and final decision of an authorized court.
- Hold the BA degree from any faculties of law or Shari a or above it or holds diploma on Religious Studies from an officially recognized centre or equivalent.
- Not have any illness or disability which impedes a judge performance of duties.
- Has completed the age of 25 upon appointment.
- Have passed the practical stage of judicial training course successfully.

### OATH TAKING

Before occupying the position as judge, a person must swear in front of chief and members of Supreme Court as follow:

"I swear by the name of the Almighty Allah that I perform my duty with full trust and dignity and impartiality, respect and implement provision of Islamic shariah, constitution of Afghanistan and other laws of the country , respect confidentiality of my duty ,will not commit any crime , violation of other rights, injustice and bribery directly and in directly."

# STRATEGIC INFORMATION FOR CONDUCTING BUSINSS

## INVESTMENT AND BUSINESS CLIMATE

**Contact for More Information**

Jeffrey L. Otto
Economic Section
Embassy of the United States of America
Kabul, Afghanistan
+93 (0)700-10-7532

The Afghan economy has experienced steady economic growth averaging 10 percent between 2005 and 2013. That growth was driven largely by the international presence, including spending by international security forces and international aid agencies. As international assistance declines, growth is expected to be one to two percent per year in the short term and three to four percent per year in the medium term. This growth is not expected to be sufficient to cover anticipated government budget deficits, and the Afghan government must therefore focus on improving domestic revenue generation. The success of private sector led development will depend on the government's ability to convince reluctant investors of the business opportunities in the country and that security risks are manageable.

With a population growth rate of 2.8 percent, the Afghan government recognizes that the development of a vibrant private sector is crucial to the reconstruction of an economy impaired by decades of conflict and mismanagement. The government has stated a commitment in principle to fostering private-sector-led economic development and increasing domestic and foreign investment, as reflected in the Afghanistan National Development Strategy (ANDS). Its efforts to build an enabling environment for a competitive private sector; to expand the scope of private investment by developing natural resources and infrastructure; and to promote investment have been limited by institutional capacity, rent seeking behavior, and the political will to undertake necessary reforms.

At present, Afghanistan's legal and regulatory frameworks and enforcement mechanisms remain underdeveloped and irregularly implemented. Much of the framework necessary for encouraging and protecting private investment is not yet in place, and the existence of three overlapping legal systems Sharia (Islamic Law), Shura (traditional law and practice), and the formal statutory system instituted under the 2004 Constitution can be confusing to both investors and legal professionals. Moreover, corruption affects the consistency of the application of the laws. The Afghan government continues to modify existing legislation and draft new laws in anticipation of future World Trade Organization (WTO) accession. It has sometimes failed, however, to complement new laws with implementing rules and regulations that translate into revamped administrative practices.

Although most senior Afghan government officials express strong commitment to a market economy and foreign investment, many businesses maintain that this attitude is not always reflected in practice. Some government officials levy unofficial taxes and inflict bureaucratic delays in order to engage in corrupt practices. Commercial regulatory bodies are often understaffed and hampered by limited capacity. Financial data systems are limited.

Security threats limit investors' opportunities to develop businesses in some provinces. Certain sectors, such as mining and hydrocarbons still lack a regulatory environment that fully supports investment. Domestic and foreign investors rank corruption high on the list of impediments.

## 1. OPENNESS TO, AND RESTRICTIONS UPON, FOREIGN INVESTMENT

### Attitude toward Foreign Direct Investment

The government of Afghanistan welcomes foreign direct investment (FDI). Following the 2014 elections and the establishment of the Government of National Unity (GNU), President Ghani and the Afghan government has spoken out publicly about the need to attract inward investment. Article 16 of the Private Investment Law of 2005 (PIL) stipulates that foreign investors are provided national treatment.

### Other Investment Policy Reviews

Afghanistan is not a World Trade Organization member. A working party was established at the General Council meeting in 2004. Afghanistan's Memorandum on the Foreign Trade Regime was circulated in March 2009. The Draft Working Party Report, prepared by the Secretariat, was circulated in 2013. The Working Party met for the fourth time in July 2013 to continue the examination of Afghanistan's foreign trade regime.

Neither the U.N. Commission on Trade and Development (UNCTAD) nor the Organization on Economic Cooperation and Development (OECD), have conducted an Investment Policy Review.

The Afghanistan National Development Strategy (ANDS), which was developed with the assistance of the United Nations Development Program (UNDP) and covered the period 2008-2013, was Afghanistan's last major investment policy review. It continues to guide development investments in three main areas: 1) agriculture and rural rehabilitation, 2) human-capacity development, and 3) economic development and infrastructure through implementation of high priority programs chosen for their ability to contribute to significant job creation, broad geographic impact, and likelihood of attracting additional investment. In 2013 the government released an Investment Incentive Policy (IIP), which sought to channel foreign direct investment into five sectors: 1) industry, 2) construction, 3) exports, 4) agriculture, and 5) mining. The IIP's associated incentives expired in March 2015.

### Laws/Regulations of Foreign Direct Investment

In the Private Investment Law of 2005 (PIL), investment is defined as currency and contributions in kind, including, without limitation, licenses, leases, machinery, equipment, and industrial and intellectual-property rights provided for the purpose of acquiring shares of stock or other ownership interests in a registered enterprise. The PIL permits investments in nearly all sectors of the economy with the exception of nuclear power, gambling establishments, and production of narcotics and intoxicants. There are also limitations in place on the total value of service transactions or assets with respect to motion pictures, road transport (passenger and freight), and on the total number of people that can be employed in security companies.

### Industrial Promotion

The High Commission on Investment (HCI) is responsible for investment policy making. The commission includes participation by the Ministers of Agriculture, Economy, Finance, Foreign

Affairs, Mines and Industries, the Governor of the Central Bank (Da Afghanistan Bank), and the Chief Executive Officer of the quasi-governmental Afghan Investment Support Agency (AISA). The Minister of Commerce and Industries chairs it. The High Economic Council, which is chaired by the President and includes both the HCI ministers and representatives from academia and the private sector, also plays a role in investment policy development.

**Limits on Foreign Control**

Although the HCI has the authority to limit the share of foreign investment in some industries, specific economic sectors, and specific companies, that authority has never been exercised. In practice, investments may be 100 percent foreign owned. The PIL authorizes the HCI, with the agreement of the relevant ministries, to provide, on a case-by-case basis, different terms from those generally applied to investments. Exceptionally large investments may be granted different terms, provided those investments result in significant economic growth and development within a limited timeframe.

While there is no requirement for foreigners to secure Afghan partners, the Afghan Constitution and the PIL prohibit foreign ownership of land. In practice most foreign firms find it necessary to work with an Afghan partner and many businesses cite lack of land ownership as one of the greatest impediments to investment in Afghanistan. Foreigners may lease arable land for periods up to 50 years and non-arable land for longer. Some businesses have negotiated leases with an automatic renewal clause for terms of up to 99 years.

**Privatization Program**

There are no active privatization programs ongoing in Afghanistan.

**Screening of FDI**

Investment in certain sectors, such as production and sales of weapons and explosives, non-banking financial activities, insurance, natural resources, and infrastructure (defined to include power, water, sewage, waste-treatment, airports, telecommunications, and health and education facilities) is subject to special consideration by the HCI, in consultation with relevant government ministries. The HCI may choose to apply specific requirements for investments in restricted sectors. Direct investment exceeding USD 3 million requires HCI approval of the investment application.

Any potential investor is required to obtain a corporate registration from the Afghanistan Central Business Registry (ACBR), to register with AISA, and to obtain a Tax Identification Number (TIN). AISA approval can be denied to investors (whether domestic or foreign) if the investment license application is incomplete or contains inaccurate information, the investment is not made through a registered Afghan enterprise, or if the investment is proposed for a prohibited sector.

**Competition Law**

While not official policy, small groups of businessmen reported to have close familial or tribal ties with provincial leaders and government officials dominate trading markets in many areas. These individuals enjoy excessive advantages that result in a non-competitive environment in several fields, due to their wealth and insider access to land, credit and contacts, and their ability to manipulate prices and forestall competition. In addition, some industries, including money changing and carpet production, have well-organized guilds that protect existing firms and create barriers to entry.

**Investment Trends**

In 2014, Afghanistan maintained its ranking of 24 out of 189 in the Ease of Starting a Business category in the World Bank's Doing Business Report. However, for overall Ease of Doing Business, they remain close to the bottom of the list at 183 out of 189 economies surveyed. It is widely understood within Afghanistan's private sector, especially among international companies operating in Afghanistan, that while starting a business in Afghanistan might be relatively easy, renewing a business license can be a difficult exercise. Most AISA licenses must be renewed annually and applications for renewal are contingent upon certification from the Ministry of Finance (MOF) that all tax obligations have been met. Some companies have seen their AISA license renewals delayed while MOF audits their tax status, despite MOF assurances that an ongoing tax audit should not impede AISA license renewal. According to credible private sector contacts, corruption and bribery related to the license renewal process are commonplace.

*Table 1*

| Measure | Year | Index or Rank | Website Address |
|---|---|---|---|
| TI Corruption Perceptions index | 2014 | 172 of 175 | transparency.org/cpi2014/results |
| World Bank's Doing Business Report "Ease of Doing Business" | 2015 | 183 of 189 | doingbusiness.org/rankings |
| Global Innovation Index | 2014 | Not ranked | globalinnovationindex.org/content.aspx?page=data-analysis |
| World Bank GNI per capita | 2013 | USD 690 | data.worldbank.org/indicator/NY.GNP.PCAP.CD |

*Millennium Challenge Corporation Country Scorecard*

The Millennium Challenge Corporation, a U.S. Government entity charged with delivering development grants to countries that have demonstrated a commitment to reform, produced scorecards for countries with a per capita gross national income (GNI) of USD 4,125 or less. A list of countries/economies with MCC scorecards and links to those scorecards is available here: http://www.mcc.gov/pages/selection/scorecards. Details on each of the MCC's indicators and a guide to reading the scorecards are available here: http://www.mcc.gov/pages/docs/doc/report-guide-to-the-indicators-and-the-selection-process-fy-2015.

## 2. CONVERSION AND TRANSFER POLICIES

**Foreign Exchange**

Private investors have the right to transfer capital and profits out of Afghanistan, including for off-shore loan debt service. There are no restrictions on converting, remitting, or transferring funds associated with investment, such as dividends, return on capital, interest and principal on private foreign debt, lease payments, or royalties and management fees, into a freely usable currency at a legal market clearing rate. The PIL states that an investor may freely transfer investment dividends or proceeds from the sale of an approved enterprise abroad.

Afghanistan does not maintain a dual-exchange-rate policy, currency controls, capital controls, or any other restrictions on the free flow of funds abroad. It is illegal to transport more than AFN 1,000,000 (approximately USD 17,200) or the foreign currency equivalent out of Afghanistan via land or air; amounts over AFN 500,000 (approximately USD 8,600), but beneath AFN 1,000,000, must be declared. Enforcement of this law is haphazard, particularly for passengers traveling through the VIP lounge at Kabul International Airport, where belongings receive little if any inspection from Afghan authorities to ensure that they are in compliance with reporting requirements.

*Remittance Policies*

Access to foreign exchange for investment is not restricted by any law or regulation. In practice, however, particularly in the provinces, many banks might not have the capacity to deal with foreign exchange. There are large, yet informal, foreign exchange markets in major cities and provinces such as Jalalabad, Kabul, Kandahar, Herat and Mazar-e Sharif, where U.S. dollars, British pounds, and Euros are readily available. Entities wishing to buy and sell foreign exchange in Afghanistan must register with the central bank, Da Afghanistan Bank, but thousands of unlicensed money changers ("hawalas") continue to practice their trade. Non-official money service providers often cite the lack of enforcement in the currency exchange sector, and the resulting competitive disadvantage to licensed exchangers, as a disincentive to becoming licensed.

In mid-2014, due in part to Afghanistan's failure to pass Financial Action Task Force (FATF)-compliant Anti-Money Laundering/Combating the Financing of Terrorism (AML/CFT) laws in a timely manner, some international correspondent banks began closing USD accounts held for Afghan banks abroad, which increased costs and processing times for inbound and outbound international funds transfers. Since then, the government has continued to work with FATF on updating their AML/CFT laws.

## 3. EXPROPRIATION AND COMPENSATION

The PIL allows for expropriation of investments or assets by the government on a non-discriminatory basis and only for the purposes of public interest." The law stipulates that the government shall provide prompt, adequate, and effective compensation in conformity with the principles of international law, equivalent to the fair market value. In cases of investment in a foreign currency, the law requires compensation to be made in that currency. The government may also confiscate private property to settle bad commercial debts. According to the PIL, investors with an ownership share of more than 25 percent may challenge the expropriation. There have been no reports of government expropriation of foreign assets, "creeping" or otherwise.

## 4. DISPUTE SETTLEMENT

### Legal System, Specialized Courts, Judicial Independence, Judgments of Foreign Courts

The legal system of Afghanistan consists of Islamic, statutory and customary rules. The supreme law of the land is the Constitution. The judiciary system is composed of the Supreme Court, the Courts of Appeal and the Primary Courts. Since 2002, NGOs have been working to strengthen the rule of law in Afghanistan by identifying peaceful means for dispute resolutions, developing partnerships between state and community actors in the hopes of improving access to justice. Despite these efforts, as much as 80 percent of legal disputes are still resolved outside the formal justice system by community based tribal leaders. Contract law in Afghanistan is set out in the Afghanistan Commercial Code 1955 and the Afghanistan Civil Code 1977. Under these codes, parties are generally free to: a) enter into and perform a contract on any commercial subject matter provided that subject matter or performance is not contrary to law, public policy, or sharia; and b) agree to have the law of a foreign state govern their contract.

**Bankruptcy**

Provisions in the Banking Law provide special procedures for bank insolvency. Afghanistan's general Law of Insolvency and Bankruptcy, however, is outdated and ineffective. The Department of Commerce Commercial Law Development Program (CLDP) is providing technical assistance to the Ministry of Commerce and Industry as it moves towards the drafting of replacement insolvency legislation.

**Investment Disputes**

The Embassy is unaware of any ongoing investment disputes.

**International Arbitration**

Since 2005, Afghan law has expressly recognized alternative dispute resolution provisions. In October 2014 the Afghanistan Centre for Dispute Resolution (ACDR) was established with the support of USAID and CLDP. The ACDR offers mediation and expert witness services in a limited number of cases referred by the commercial courts and in the future plans to expand its services to include arbitration.

*ICSID Convention and New York Convention*

Since 2005, Afghan law has expressly recognized within their domestic law, alternative dispute resolution mechanisms. In 2005, Afghanistan became a signatory to the Convention on the Recognition and Enforcement of Foreign Arbitral Awards (1958 New York Convention). Under the New York Convention, Afghanistan has agreed to: a) recognize and enforce awards made in another contracted state, and b) apply the convention to commercial disputes. Under the PIL and the Commercial Arbitration Law of 2007 (Arbitration Law): a) parties can agree to have foreign law govern their contract and agree to have their disputes resolved through arbitration or other mechanisms inside or outside of Afghanistan, and b) the Afghan courts must enforce any resulting award or agreement.

Since 1966, Afghanistan has been a member state to the International Centre for the Settlement of Investment Disputes (ICSID convention)

**Duration of Dispute Resolution**

According to credible contacts, civil cases in the commercial court system can sometimes take more than 18 months for parties to obtain resolutions. Cases are frequently resolved more quickly through an informal system or, in some cases, pursuant to negotiations facilitated by formal justice system actors or private lawyers. Because there is often limited access to the formal legal system in rural areas, local elders and shuras (consultative gatherings, usually of men selected by the community) are often the primary means of settling both criminal matters and civil disputes, and they are known to levy unsanctioned punishments. Some estimates suggested that 80 percent of all disputes are resolved by shuras/jirgas.

Investors should be aware that the 2014 Human Rights Report notes that arbitrary arrests occur in most provinces and that there have been a number of cases in which the Attorney General's office, with the complicity of some police officials, imposed or threatened to impose criminal penalties on persons who may only be indirectly connected to a contractual dispute between a foreign company and an Afghan person or entity. For example, in September 2012, authorities arrested two Philippine citizens because their foreign employer allegedly failed to pay for goods and services it had received from Afghan subcontractors. When government authorities could not locate any senior managers of the company, they initially detained 20 employees as collateral for the alleged debt, eventually releasing all but two. After being held without charge for more than a year with no opportunity to contest their detention, the remaining two Filipinos were brought before a judge in October 2013. They were released in November 2013, following intensive diplomatic engagement with Afghan officials.

Although incommunicado imprisonment remains a problem and prompt access to a lawyer is rare, the men did eventually have access to a lawyer. The 2014 Human Rights Report also notes that some detainees are subjected to torture and other mistreatment.

## 5. PERFORMANCE REQUIREMENTS AND INVESTMENT INCENTIVES

### WTO/TRIMS

Afghanistan is not currently a member of the World Trade Organization; it therefore does not adhere to the agreement on Trade-Related Investment Measures.

### Investment Incentives

Not applicable.

### Research and Development

Not applicable

### Performance Requirements

Afghanistan has no formal regulations or laws governing performance requirements. There are no existing government-imposed conditions on investment, beyond the procedures required for establishing or acquiring a business.

There are no discriminatory export or import policies affecting foreign investors. In 2013 the Afghan cabinet approved a series of incentives intended to encourage private investment. The package included tax holidays of up to 10 years, subsidized land, public loans with five to ten year maturities, and automatic licenses to artisanal and small-scale mining activities without a bidding process. While the government has provided a limited amount of subsidized land for industrial development, most of the incentive package has yet to be implemented. In July 2014 the Government of Afghanistan adjusted the renewal period for trader's licenses from one year to three years though implementation has been geographically uneven.

The Public Procurement Law of 2005 covers government procurement. That law specifies that procuring entities are obliged to procure goods, works, or services produced/furnished domestically in accordance with bidding documents, provided that the price of domestic procurement was not higher than imported procurement by a percentage set between five and 10 percent. The procuring entity specifies the margin in its bidding documents. Furthermore, in comparing bids of bidders who did not have a resident representative in Afghanistan, or who were not subject to Afghan taxes, with the bids of those that had a resident representative or were subject to Afghan taxes, the bid prices of the former would be increased by a percentage set in the bidding procedures.

Businesses report that they find it very difficult and time consuming to obtain visas for tourist passport holders coming to Afghanistan for business reasons. In 2014 the government passed legislation providing for one-year multiple entry visas for American citizens engaged in business in Afghanistan. Before it will issue a visa, the Afghan government requires proof that the company the applicant represents is licensed in Afghanistan and that non-Afghans working for the company have work permits. In order for employees to obtain a work permit, they must have a valid Afghan visa.

### Data Storage

The Afghan government does not require the use of domestic content in goods or technology related to data storage. There are no requirements for foreign IT providers to turn over source code and/or provide access for surveillance purposes. The Ministry of Communications and Information Technology does not have domestic data storage requirements.

## 6. RIGHT TO PRIVATE OWNERSHIP AND ESTABLISHMENT

Under the PIL, foreign and domestic private entities have equal standing and may establish and own business enterprises, engage in all forms of remunerative activity, and freely acquire and dispose of interests in business enterprises.

## 7. PROTECTION OF PROPERTY RIGHTS

### Real Property

Property rights protection is weak due to a lack of cadasters or a comprehensive land titling system, disputed land titles, incapacity of commercial courts, and widespread corruption. Land laws in Afghanistan are inconsistent, overlapping, incomplete, or silent with regard to details of effective land management. Judges and attorneys are generally without expertise in land matters. An estimated 80 percent of land is held and transferred informally, without legally recognized deeds, titles, or a simple means to prove ownership.

At present, the acquisition of a clear land title to purchase real estate or a registered leasehold interest is complicated and cumbersome. The World Bank estimated in its 2014 "Doing Business Report" that it takes an average of 250 days and entails legal fees of five percent of the property value to register property. Investment disputes are common in the areas of land titling and contracts. Many documents evidencing land ownership are not archived in any official registry. Frequently, multiple "owners" claim the same piece of land, each asserting rights from a different source. These disputes hinder the development of commercial and agricultural enterprises. Real estate agents are not reliable. Instances of parties falsely claiming title to land that they do not own undermines investor confidence. Foreign investors seeking to work with Afghan citizens to purchase property should conduct thorough due diligence to identify reliable partners.

**Intellectual Property Rights**

The Intellectual Property Office at the Ministry of Commerce and Industries is responsible for issuing patents, trademarks, industrial designs, geographical indications, and genetic resources. The Copyright Directorate at the Ministry of Information and Culture deals with copyright and related rights. The Government of Afghanistan is working to bring its legislation on patents, trademarks and copyrights into compliance with World Trade Organization (WTO) standards. In December 2014, President Ghani signed a comprehensive trademarks law which meets WTO standards. If Afghanistan accedes to the WTO, it will become a party to the WTO Trade Related Intellectual Property Rights (TRIPS) Agreement. Afghanistan is not a party to the World Intellectual Property Organization (WIPO).

Theoretically, intellectual property right-holders have recourse to judicial protection through Afghanistan's civil court system. Courts are empowered to take evidence from all parties, make factual findings, render final decisions and order payment of damages and court costs. Yet, there is no serious enforcement of intellectual property rights. Pirated DVDs and software are sold throughout the country. Counterfeit pharmaceuticals and building materials are also widespread. No cases have yet been filed under the recently adopted trademarks law.

Afghanistan is not listed in the United States Trade Representative's (USTR) Special 301 report, or in its notorious market report. The Government of Afghanistan has been a member of the World Intellectual Property Organization (WIPO) since 2005.

*Resources for Rights Holders*

Contact at U.S. Embassy Kabul:
Jeffrey L. Otto
Economic Section
+93 (0)700-10-7532
Contact at American Chamber of Commerce in Afghanistan:
Soraya Ahmadyar
Executive Director
+93 (0)704-702-957
sorayaahmadyar@amcham-af.org
www.amcham-af.org

## 8. TRANSPARENCY OF THE REGULATORY SYSTEM

Parliament must approve all legislation, but when Parliament is in recess, the president may issue decrees that have the force of law. In these cases, Parliament has the right to review and reject the decrees.

Afghanistan's Law on Publication and Enforcement of Legislation requires publication in the Official Gazette of official declarations, laws, decrees, and other legislative documents. In contracts, there is no legal requirement or practice for publication and comment for domestic laws, regulations, or other measures of application that will become legally enforceable. In general, the Afghan government shares draft legislation with interested parties for comment and some ministries publish draft legislation in national newspapers for comment by the general public.

Afghanistan has invested in a business registration website. Foreign and national investors will find a link to the official business registration website and an assessment of the site's user-friendliness at www.ger.co. Click on Afghanistan. Information about other administrative procedures may also be accessible from the official business registration website. Putting business registration and other administrative processes online and simplifying them are significant steps towards a more transparent, welcoming investment climate.

## 9. EFFICIENT CAPITAL MARKETS AND PORTFOLIO INVESTMENT

Most Afghans remain outside the formal banking sector. Only a small minority currently hold bank deposits. Afghans continue to rely on an informal trust-based process referred to as hawaladas to access finance and transfer money, due in part to unfamiliarity with a functioning banking system and limited access to banks in rural areas. Three of the four mobile network operators - Etisalat, AWCC, and Roshan - offer mobile money services, with MTN expected to roll out their mobile money products in 2015.

Still, finance is Afghanistan's second-largest service industry (behind telecommunications) and is potentially an important driver of private investment and economic growth. As of December 2013, 17 commercial banks were operating in Afghanistan, with total assets of approximately USD 4.07 billion. There are three state banks: Bank-e Millie Afghan (Afghan National Bank), Pashtany Bank, and New Kabul Bank (formerly the privately owned Kabul Bank), and there are also branch offices of foreign banks, including Alfalah Bank (Pakistan), National Bank of Pakistan, Habib Bank of Pakistan, Punjab National Bank (India), and Arian Bank (Iran). Punjab National Bank closed in late 2014, but the latest bank asset data available is from fiscal year 2013.

### Money and Banking System, Hostile Takeovers

Banking remains highly centralized, with a considerable majority of total loans made in Kabul Province. Bank lending is undermined by a deficient legal and regulatory infrastructure that impedes the enforcement of property rights and development of collateral. The aggregate loan-to-deposit ratio for the banking sector is 22 percent, and most banks concentrate on short-term credit to well-known customers. The difficulty of accessing credit through banks and other formal financial institutions makes existing firms dependent on family funds and retained earnings, limits opportunities for entrepreneurialism, and reinforces dependence on the informal financial sector.

The 2010 exposure of pervasive fraud at Kabul Bank revealed the underlying weaknesses in banking regulation and supervision. Despite receiving significant technical assistance, Da Afghanistan Bank (DAB -- the Afghan central bank) has been unable to match the pace of banking sector growth with requisite improvements in monitoring and supervision. Following his inauguration in September 2014, President Ghani moved to reopen the Kabul Bank investigation. Subsequently, the Supreme Court upheld an October 2014 appellate court ruling that froze the assets of certain debtors and extended the sentences of previously convicted officials involved in the case. The Afghan Government is developing an asset recovery plan from perpetrators of the large-scale bank fraud.

Formal credit to the private sector stands at less than 10 percent of GDP, significantly lower than other countries in the region. Afghanistan ranks 86 out of 189 economies for ease of obtaining credit in the World Bank's Doing Business 2014. Afghan entrepreneurs complain interest rates for commercial loans from local banks range from 15 to 20 percent. In response to this situation, investment funds, leasing, micro-financing and SME-financing companies have entered the market. Yet, despite strong donor support for many of their activities, these firms have been handicapped by difficulties in securing repayment. USAID is working with the Afghan government and the banking sector to promote improved access to finance and the expansion of financial inclusion. In March 2015, the U.S. Department of Treasury and the Afghan Ministry of Finance signed a memorandum of understanding to reinitiate financial capacity building and technical assistance at both DAB and the MOF.

## 10. COMPETITION FROM STATE-OWNED ENTERPRISES

The Government of Afghanistan operates 35 “active” or “partially active” state-owned enterprises (SOEs), ranging across sectors from public security to construction to meat processing. In total, SOEs make up a very small share of overall economic activity. All SOEs are overseen and regulated by the Ministry of Finance and directly operated by specific ministries depending on the nature of the operations. The Law on State Owned Enterprises includes specific targets for R&D investment, social development measures, and employee profit sharing, but compliance is negligible. Only a small number of the SOEs are profitable. The Afghan government is also a stakeholder in several state-owned corporations (SOCs), entities that have independent boards and are not operated or directly supervised by the government.

## 11. CORPORATE SOCIAL RESPONSIBILITY

The Afghan government encourages large companies and foreign investors to invest in corporate social responsibility (CSR). Large mining contracts include stipulations for environmental protection and community inclusion. Afghanistan law prohibits mining that would result in the destruction of antiquities, unless the mining company has prior approval from the Ministry of Information and Culture. A comprehensive mining law passed in October 2014 requires mining contract holders to consult with communities that will be affected by mining projects and to implement a community development agreement that includes details of the firm’s environmental and social impact assessment. USAID continues to implement its Mining Investment and Development for Afghan Sustainability (MIDAS) project, a portion of which provides guidance to communities living near mines through training and governance support.

### OECD Guidelines for Multinational Enterprises

All four competing mobile network operators in the country have well-developed CSR outreach programs that include health, education, job creation, environmental protection and outreach to refugees. Some Afghan charities are also benefiting from CSR funds from companies outside of the country. The American Chamber of Commerce in Afghanistan has identified CSR as one of its core focus areas. In addition, some Afghan entrepreneurs, such as Ihsanullah Bayat, the Barakat Group, the Ghazanfar Group, Hotak Azizi and the Alokozay Group, have foundations that provide assistance in the fields of health, education, and the eradication of poverty.

## 12. POLITICAL VIOLENCE

The U.S. Department of State continues to warn Americans against travel to Afghanistan. U.S. citizens should review the Consular Information Sheet and Travel Warning for Afghanistan for the most up-to-date information on the security situation and possible threats.

Anti-government and political violence are common and public concerns regarding security constrain economic activity. As the international forces draw down in the coming year, security remains a primary concern for investors. Foreign firms operating in country report spending a significant percentage of their revenues on security infrastructure and operating expenses.

## 13. CORRUPTION

Reports indicate corruption is endemic throughout society. Systemic corruption at border crossings hampers development of the licit market economy. Afghan officials collect bribes in exchange for undervaluing, under-weighing, or not scanning shipments, which facilitates smuggling of illegal goods and the illicit trade of legal goods, while also weakening Afghan revenue collection and regulatory institutions.

The practice of criminalizing commercial complaints is commonly used to settle business disputes or extort money from wealthy international investors. The government does not implement criminal penalties for official corruption effectively, and officials are reported frequently to engage in corrupt practices with impunity. There are reports of low-profile corruption cases successfully tried at the provincial level. President Ghani has made anti-corruption efforts a major focus of his attention. In some instances corrupt officials have been relieved of duty. Despite the recent high-level attention, the problem remains systemic.

Disputes over land and land grabbing have risen over the last decade. Land grabbing has been an ongoing inter-generational conflicts, which remains a serious issue, if left unresolved, disagreements over land ownership can quickly escalate from a civil dispute, to a criminal, up to acute acts of violence. The most common type occurred when businesses illegally obtained property deeds from corrupt officials and sold the deeds to unsuspecting homeowners, who would then get caught in criminal prosecutions. Other reports indicated that government officials grabbed land without compensation to swap the land for contracts or political favors. Occasionally, provincial governments illegally confiscated land without due process or compensation to build public facilities.

*UN Anticorruption Convention, OECD Convention on Combatting Bribery*

Afghanistan has signed and ratified the UN Anticorruption Convention. The country, however, is not party to the OECD Convention on Combating Bribery of Foreign Public Officials in International Business Transactions.

*Resources to Report Corruption*

The Afghan Government body responsible for combating corruption is the High Office of Oversight & Anti-corruption.

Afghan Government Point of Contact:
Aminullah Amini
Head of Information and Communication Technology Department
High Office of Oversight & Anti-corruption
+93 777 628220
aminullaha@anti-corruption.gov.af
Watchdog Organization Contact:
Sayed Ikram Afzali
Executive Director
Integrity Watch Afghanistan
ikram.afzali@iwaweb.org

## 14. BILATERAL INVESTMENT AGREEMENTS

In 2004, Afghanistan signed a Trade and Investment Framework Agreement (TIFA) with the United States. Afghanistan does not have a bilateral investment treaty (BIT) with the United States.

Afghanistan has signed 31 bilateral trade and investment agreements/memoranda of understanding and a further 10 bilateral economic agreement/memoranda of understanding. In 2010, Afghanistan and Pakistan signed the Afghanistan Pakistan Transit Trade Agreement (APTTA), and an investment-related agreement with China and Kazakhstan. In November 2014, the Afghan government signaled its interest in expanding the APTTA agreement to include Tajikistan. Preliminary negotiations are ongoing.

The European Union, the United States, India, Canada, and Japan have granted Afghan exports preferential treatment under their Generalized Systems of Preference. Afghanistan is a member of the Economic Cooperation Organization (ECO), the South Asia Free Trade Area (SAFTA), and the South Asian Association for Regional Cooperation (SAARC), and of Central Asian Regional Economic Cooperation (CAREC). The Afghan government has stated its intent to formally join the Transport Corridor Europe Caucasus Asia organization (TRACECA).

**Bilateral Taxation Treaties**

Afghanistan does not have a bilateral taxation treaty with the United States.

## 15. OPIC AND OTHER INVESTMENT INSURANCE PROGRAMS

The Overseas Private Investment Corporation (OPIC) offers financing (from large structured finance to small business loans), political risk insurance, and support for private-equity investment funds. Since 2003, OPIC has committed more than USD 295 million in financing and political risk insurance to support 38 projects in Afghanistan.

OPIC operates its programs in Afghanistan under the Investment Incentive Agreement ("IIA") signed in 2004 with the Afghan government. Since 2013, however, the Afghan government has attempted to levy a 20 percent withholding tax on interest paid to OPIC by several OPIC clients, in direct contravention of the IIA.

In January 2014, OPIC President and CEO Elizabeth Littlefield sent a formal letter to the Afghan Minister of Finance notifying the Afghan government that its efforts to tax interest payments made by loan recipients to OPIC ignores the terms of the IIA. This practice gave OPIC "no choice but to suspend consideration of and support for any new transactions in Afghanistan."

In February 2014, the Afghan government provided the Embassy with a diplomatic note indicating that loan recipients would not owe any taxes on their payments to OPIC for the 2013 tax year. The Afghan government diplomatic note also stated, however, that the government would undertake a review of the provisions of the IIA and make recommendations on its future. In October 2014, then-Finance Minister Zakhilwal sent a letter to OPIC stating Afghan intentions to comply with the terms of the IIA. In response, the U.S. Embassy in Kabul sent a diplomatic note acknowledging the letter.

In early 2015 the issue remained outstanding. Given high-level attention to the matter, the U.S. Embassy is cautiously optimistic the final outcome will be positive, though the timing of a final resolution remains uncertain.

## 16. LABOR

There is a critical shortage of skilled labor in Afghanistan. Only 32 percent of the population over the age of 15 can read and write. Decades of war, a low level of education and a lack of training facilities have resulted in a serious scarcity of skilled technicians, qualified managers and educated professionals. U.S. companies that establish training programs for their employees should expect significant returns in enhanced productivity, but there is a risk of high turnover as skilled employees seek higher-paying opportunities, especially outside of Afghanistan.

Labor-management relations are undeveloped. While there are major and smaller trade union organizations in the country, there is little knowledge or practice of collective bargaining. A 2005 labor regulation allows for the employment of foreign workers, but requires priority be given to equally qualified Afghan workers. The 2007 Labor Law guarantees basic workers' rights, such as wages, overtime, leave, and other benefits, and bans forced labor and child labor. The law does not contain provisions for criminal penalties for violations, and the Ministry of Labor, Social Affairs, Martyred and Disabled (MoLSAMD) lacks the capacity to conduct widespread inspections or enforce current regulations. There is little awareness of the law's provisions in either the government or the private sector. A 2014 law introduced penalties for labor violations, guaranteed rights to union membership and collective bargaining, and strengthened the authority of labor inspectors. The law is currently in the Ministry of Justice for review.

Under the law on Foreigners Employment in Afghanistan, foreigners can be employed on the basis of a work permit issued by the Ministry of Labor and Social Affairs. Work permits are issued for one year and are renewable. Foreign citizens traveling to Afghanistan for employment are required to obtain resident and business visas.

## 17. FOREIGN DIRECT INVESTMENT AND FOREIGN PORTFOLIO INVESTMENT STATISTICS

The Afghanistan Investment Support Agency (AISA) is responsible for facilitating registration, licensing and promotion of all investments in Afghanistan. It concentrates on proactive measures to attract industrial investment from both within and outside Afghanistan, thus generating employment and economic growth. While the Afghan government data collection methods have improved in recent years, significant data capture and data entry problems and persistent data gaps result in discrepancies between sources, as demonstrated in the chart below.

*Table 2: Key Macroeconomic Data, U.S. FDI in Host Country/Economy*

| | Host Country Statistical source* | | USG or international statistical source | | USG or International Source of Data: BEA; IMF; Eurostat; UNCTAD, Other |
|---|---|---|---|---|---|
| Economic Data | Year | Amount | Year | Amount | |
| Host Country Gross Domestic Product (GDP) ($M USD) | 2014 | 20,310 | 2013 | 20,366 | www.worldbank.org/en/country |
| Foreign | Host Country | | USG or | | USG or international Source of data: BEA; IMF; Eurostat; |

| Direct Investment | Statistical source* | | international statistical source | | UNCTAD, Other |
|---|---|---|---|---|---|
| U.S. FDI in partner country ($M USD, stock positions) | N/A | | 2013 | 3 | http://bea.gov/international/factsheet/factsheet.cfm?Area=600 |
| Host country's FDI in the United States ($M USD, stock positions) | N/A | | 2013 | 1 | http://bea.gov/international/factsheet/factsheet.cfm?Area=600 |
| Total inbound stock of FDI as % host GDP | N/A | | N/A | | |

*Table 3: Sources and Destination of FDI*

Foreign direct investment position data are not available for Afghanistan.

*Table 4: Sources of Portfolio Investment*

Portfolio investment data are not available for Afghanistan.

## IMPORTANT CONTACTS

### Law Firms

**Motley Legal Services**

Lawyers practicing in Afghanistan, the United States, and UAE
Kimberley Cy. Motley, Esq.
Ph: +93 (0) 788 887 887 (Afg), +1(704) 765-4887 (Int'l)
Email: kmotley@motleylegal.com
Website: http://www.motleylegal.com/
English: Native

## LAWYERS AND ACCOUNTANTS LICENSED IN THE U.S. AND AFGHANISTAN

**Afghanistan Financial Services, LLC/Afghan Legal Services**

House 1319, Street 7, Karte 4, District 3, Kabul, Afghanistan
Sanzar Kakar and Asiyah Sharifi, Esq

Phone: +93 796 000 111, +93 797 09 555
Email: info@afs.af
Website: http://www.afs.af/
English: Native

**Massoudi Legal Consultancy**

Khair Khana, 11th District, Kabul
Mohammad Khalid Massoudi
Phone: +93 776 218 204
Email: khalid.massoudi@gmail.com
English: Fluent

**Shajjan and Associates**

Street address: Blossom Hospital St. Kolola Poshta, District 4, Kabul, Afghanistan
Saeeq Shajjan
Office phone number: +93 202 200 709 / +93 799 286 888
Email: saeeqpr@gmail.com; Shajjan@shajjanlaw.com
Web site: www.shajjanlaw.com
English: Fluent

**PRIVATE ATTORNEYS**

**Abdul Rahman Turani**

Mazar-e-Sharif, Afghanistan
Phone: 0778-870-521
E-mail: turani_andkhui@gmail.com
English: Satisfactory

**Mohammad Akbar Sakhi**

4th Zone, Jalalabad, Afghanistan
Phone: 0700-603-838
E-mail: akbarsakhi2527@yahoo.com
English: Satisfactory

**Mohammad Amin Samandar**

Kabul
Phone: 0700-280-947
E-mail: amin.samandar@gmail.com
English: Satisfactory

**Mohammad Azim Farighi**

Kabul
Phone: 0786-885-279
E-mail: azimfarighi@yahoo.com
English: Satisfactory

**Kakar Advocates LLC**

Kawun Kakar
House 397, Lane 4, Street 15, Wazir Akbar Khan
Phone: +93 795 600 800
www.kakarAdvocates.com
Skype: kawun.kakar
English: Fluent

**Rosenstock Legal Services**

U.S. and New Zealand licensed attorneys
Tom Rosenstock
Phone: + 93 (0) 772-164-044
Email: Tom@rosentocklegal.com
Chantal Grut
Phone: + 93 (0) 780340 679
Email: Chantal@rosenstocklegal.com
English: Native

**Najibullah Azizi**

House # 112, Street # 1st left hand, Charahi Haji Yaqoob, Shahr-e-now, Dist # 10, Kabul
Phone: 0799-721-011
E-mail: azizi_najibullah@yahoo.com
English: Limited

**NGO ATTORNEYS**

**Khalid Sekander**

USAID Rule of Law Project
Charayee Debre, 2nd Alley, Fifth House on Left, Kabul, Afghanistan
Phone: 0706-140-167
E-mail: ksekander2003@yahoo.com
English: Satisfactory

**Sharifa Khalili**

Norwegian Refugee Council (NRC)
Ab-Bakhsh-e-Badmorghan Street, opposite ex. Atoon Herawi Secondary School, Herat
Phone: 0708-445313 / 040222970
E-mail: sharifa.khalili@afg.nrc.no
Website: http://www.nrc.no/
English: Satisfactory

**Ward E Scott II, Esq**

Scott Kakar Advocates LLP
Kabul, Afghanistan
AFG: +93 (0)795 338 617 +93 (0)798 383 438

US: +1 202 436 9038
UK: +44 (0)20 8133 9014 | UAE: +971 (0)507 281 819
US Mob: +1 603 738 9028 | Skype: WEScottii
E-Mail: WScott@ScottAdvocates.com
Linked-In: http://af.linkedin.com/in/WardScottEsq
Web: www.ScottAdvocates.com
English: Native

**Domenic Senger-Schenck**

Rosenstock Legal Services
domenic@rosenstocklegal.com
+93 (0) 784-682-188
+1 (646) 583-2379
Web Site: www.rosenstocklegal.com
Shahr-e-Naw, Kabul, Afghanistan
English: Native

**Law Offices of A. Rahman Rahimghiyasa**

Abdul Rahman
Phone: +93 (0) 702515121
PO Box 538 Kabul, Afghanistan
www.afghanlawfirm.com
English: Native

## AFGHANISTAN ENERGY SECTOR - STRATEGIC INFORMATION AND OPPORTUNITIES

Afghanistan's significance from an energy standpoint stems from its geographical position as a potential transit route for oil and natural gas exports from Central Asia to the Arabian Sea. This potential includes the possible construction of oil and natural gas export pipelines through Afghanistan, which was under serious consideration in the mid-1990s. The idea has since been undermined by Afghanistan's instability. Since 1996, most of Afghanistan has been controlled by the Taliban movement, which the United States does not recognize as the government of Afghanistan.

On December 19, 2000, the UN Security Council imposed additional sanctions against Afghanistan's ruling Taliban movement (which controls around 95% of the country), including an arms embargo and a ban on the sale of chemicals used in making heroin. These sanctions (Resolution 1333) are aimed at pressuring Afghanistan to turn over Osama bin Laden, suspected in various terrorist attacks, including the August 1998 US Embassy bombings in Kenya and Tanzania. These latest sanctions are in addition to sanctions (Resolution 1267) imposed on Afghanistan in November 1999, which included a freeze on Taliban assets and a ban on international flights by Afghanistan's national airline, Ariana. The Taliban reacted sharply to the new sanctions, ordering a boycott of US and Russian goods, and pulling out of UN-mediated peace talks aimed at ending the country's civil war.

On November 29, 1999, UN Secretary General Kofi Annan issued a report on Afghanistan which listed the country's major problems as follows: civil war (which has caused many casualties and refugees, and which has devastated the country's economy), record opium production, wide-scale human rights violations, and food shortages caused in part by drought.

According to the 2001 CIA World Factbook, Afghanistan is an extremely poor, landlocked country, highly dependent on farming and livestock raising. Afghanistan has experienced over two decades of war, including the nearly 10-year Soviet military occupation (which ended in 1989). During that conflict one-third of the population fled the country, with Pakistan and Iran sheltering a combined peak of more than 6 million refugees. Large Afghan refugee populations remain in Pakistan and Iran. Gross domestic product has fallen substantially over the past 20 years because of the loss of labor and capital and the disruption of trade and transport. The severe drought of 1998-2000 added to these problems. The majority of the population continues to suffer from insufficient food, clothing, housing, and medical care. Inflation remains a serious problem throughout the country. International aid can deal with only a fraction of the humanitarian problem, let alone promote economic development. The economic situation did not improve in 1999-2000, as internal civil strife has continued, hampering both domestic economic policies and international aid efforts. Numerical data are likely to be either unavailable or unreliable. Afghanistan was by far the largest world producer of opium poppies in 2000, and narcotics trafficking is a major source of revenues.

## ENERGY OVERVIEW

The Soviets had estimated Afghanistan's proven and probable natural gas reserves at up to 5 trillion cubic feet (Tcf) in the 1970s. Afghan natural gas production reached 275 million cubic feet per day (Mmcf/d) in the mid-1970s. However, due to declining reserves from producing fields, output gradually fell to about 220 Mmcf/d by 1980. At that time, the Jorquduq field was brought online and was expected to boost Afghan natural gas output to 385 Mmcf/d by the early 1980s. However, sabotage of infrastructure by the anti-Soviet mujaheddin fighters limited the country's total production to 290 Mmcf/d, an output level that was held fairly steady until the Soviet withdrawal in 1989. After the Soviet pullout and subsequent Afghan civil war, roughly 31 producing wells at Sheberghan area fields were shut in pending the restart of natural gas sales to the former Soviet Union.

At its peak in the late 1970s, Afghanistan supplied 70%-90% of its natural gas output to the Soviet Union's natural gas grid via a link through Uzbekistan. In 1992, Afghan President Najibullah indicated that a new natural gas sales agreement with Russia was in progress. However, several former Soviet republics raised price and distribution issues and negotiations stalled. In the early 1990s, Afghanistan also discussed possible natural gas supply arrangements with Hungary, Czechoslovakia, and several Western European countries, but these talks never progressed further. Afghan natural gas fields include Jorqaduq, Khowaja Gogerdak, and Yatimtaq, all of which are located within 20 miles of the northern town of Sheberghan in Jowzjan province. Natural gas production and distribution is the responsibility of the Taliban-controlled Afghan Gas Enterprise. In 1999, work resumed on the repair of a distribution pipeline to Mazar-i-Sharif. Spur pipelines to a small power plant and fertilizer plant also were repaired and completed. Mazar-i-Sharif is now receiving natural gas from the pipeline, as well as some other surrounding areas. Rehabilitation of damaged natural gas wells has been undertaken at the Khowaja Gogerak field, which has increased natural gas production.

In February 1998, the Taliban announced plans to revive the Afghan National Oil Company, which was abolished by the Soviet Union after it invaded Afghanistan in 1979. Soviet estimates from the late 1970s placed Afghanistan's proven and probable oil and condensate reserves at 95 million barrels. Oil exploration and development work as well as plans to build a 10,000-bbl/d refinery were halted after the 1979 Soviet invasion. A very small amount of crude oil is produced at the Angot field in the northern Sar-i-Pol province. It is processed at a primitive topping plant in Sheberghan, and burned in central heating boilers in Sheberghan, Mazar-i-Sharif, and Kabul. Another small oilfield at Zomrad Sai near Sheberghan was reportedly undergoing repairs in mid-2001.

Petroleum products such as diesel, gasoline, and jet fuel are imported, mainly from Pakistan and Turkmenistan. A small storage and distribution facility exists in Jalalabad on the highway between Kabul and Peshawar, Pakistan. Turkmenistan also has a petroleum product storage and distribution facility at Tagtabazar near the Afghan border, which supplies northwestern Afghanistan.

Besides oil and natural gas, Afghanistan also is estimated to have 73 million tons of coal reserves, most of which is located in the region between Herat and Badashkan in the northern part of the country. Although Afghanistan produced over 100,000 short tons of coal annually as late as the early 1990s, as of 1999, the country was producing only around 1,000 short tons.

Afghanistan's power grid has been severely damaged by years of war. Currently, the ruling Taliban are concentrating on rebuilding damaged hydroelectric plants, power distribution lines, and high-voltage cables. Production of power by Afghanistan's hydroelectric dams was negatively affected by the drought of 1998-2000, resulting in blackouts in Kabul and other cities. Increased rainfall in 2001 has improved power production. The Kajaki Dam in Helmand province near Kandahar is undergoing the addition of another generating turbine with assistance from the Chinese Dongfeng Agricultural Machinery Company. This will add 16.5 megawatts (MW) to its generating capacity when completed. Transmission lines from the Kajaki Dam to Kandahar were repaired in early 2001, along with a substation in the city, restoring supplies of electricity. The Dahla Dam in Kandahar province also has been restored to operation, along with the Breshna-Kot Dam in Nangarhar province, which has a generating capacity of 11.5 MW. The 66-MW Mahipar hydro plant also is now operational.

Turkmenistan supplies electricity to much of northwestern Afghanistan. In October 1999, Afghanistan announced that it had reached agreement with Turkmenistan for electricity imports into northwestern Afghanistan, including power to the city of Herat and the Herat cement plant. Another transmission line has been built from Turkmenistan to the city of Andkhoy, and one was under construction in 2001 to Sheberghan. Electricity has previously been imported from Uzbekistan for Mazar-i-Sharif, but supplies were cut off during the winter of 1999 due to payment arrears.

## REGIONAL PIPELINE PLANS

In January 1998, an agreement was signed between Pakistan, Turkmenistan, and the Taliban to arrange funding on a proposed 890-mile, $2-billion, 1.9-billion-cubic-feet-per-day natural gas pipeline project. The proposed pipeline would have transported natural gas from Turkmenistan's 45-Tcf Dauletabad natural gas field to Pakistan, and most likely would have run from Dauletabad south to the Afghan border and through Herat and Qandahar in Afghanistan, to Quetta, Pakistan. The line would then have linked with Pakistan's natural gas grid at Sui. Natural gas shipments had been projected to start at 700 Mmcf/d in 1999 and to rise to 1.4 Bcf/d or higher by 2002. In March 1998, however, Unocal announced a delay in finalizing project details due to Afghanistan's continuing civil war. In June 1998, Gazprom announced that it was relinquishing its 10% stake in the gas pipeline project consortium (known as the Central Asian Gas Pipeline Ltd., or Centgas), which was formed in August 1996. As of June 1998, Unocal and Saudi Arabia's Delta Oil held a combined 85% stake in Centgas, while Turkmenrusgas owned 5%. Other participants in the proposed project besides Delta Oil included the Crescent Group of Pakistan, Gazprom of Russia, Hyundai Engineering & Construction Company of South Korea, Inpex and Itochu of Japan

On December 8, 1998, Unocal announced that it was withdrawing from the Centgas consortium, citing low oil prices and turmoil in Afghanistan as making the pipeline project uneconomical and too risky. Unocal's announcement followed an earlier statement -- in August 1998 -- that the company was suspending its role in the Afghanistan gas pipeline project in light of U.S. government military action in Afghanistan, and also due to intensified fighting between the Taliban and opposition groups. Unocal had previously stressed that the Centgas pipeline project would not proceed until an internationally recognized government was in place in Afghanistan. To date, however, only three countries -- Saudi Arabia, Pakistan and the United Arab Emirates -- have recognized the Taliban government (note: in late September 2001, Saudi Arabia and the United Arab Emirates both cut ties with the Taliban).

Besides the gas pipeline, Unocal also had considered building a 1,000-mile, 1-million barrel-per-day (bbl/d) capacity oil pipeline that would link Chardzou, Turkmenistan to Pakistan's Arabian Sea Coast via Afghanistan. Since the Chardzou refinery is already linked to Russia's Western Siberian oil fields, this line could provide a possible alternative export route for regional oil production from the Caspian Sea. The $2.5-billion pipeline is known as the Central Asian Oil Pipeline Project. For a variety of reasons (i.e. war and political instability), however, this project remains highly doubtful for the time being.

In April 1999, Pakistan, Turkmenistan and the Taliban authorities in Afghanistan agreed to reactivate the Turkmenistan-Pakistan gas pipeline project, and to ask the Centgas consortium, now led by Saudi Arabia's Delta Oil (following Unocal's withdrawal from the project), to proceed. Periodic meetings to discuss the project have continued. It remains unlikely, however, that this pipeline will be built.

## ENERGY INFRASTRUCTURE

### OIL

| | |
|---|---|
| Angot Oilfield | Produces a small quantity of crude oil; located in Sar-i-Pol province |
| Zomrad Sai Oilfield | Reportedly undergoing rehabilitation; near Sheberghan |
| Sheberghan Topping Plant | Primitive topping plant which processes crude oil for consumption in heating boilers in Kabul, Mazar-i-Sharif, and Sheberghan |
| Jalalabad Storage Facility | Petroleum product storage and distribution facility |

### GAS

| | |
|---|---|
| Sheberghan Area Gas Fields | The Jorqaduk, Khowaja Gogerak, and Yatimtaq gas fields are all located within 20 miles of Sheberghan |
| Pipeline to Mazar-i-Sharif | A pipeline connects these gas fields to Mazar-i-Sharif.Gas is used for a small power plant, a fertilizer plant, and domestic use. |
| Local pipelines | Small local pipelines near the gas fields distribute gas in small quantities to nearby villages and Sheberghan |

### ELECTRICITY

| | |
|---|---|
| Kajaki Dam | Located in Helmand province near Kandahar; undergoing upgrade which will add a third generating turbine and increase its installed capacity by 16.5 MW (from its current 33 MW capacity); transmission lines to Kandahar repaired in early 2001. |
| Mahipar Dam | Installed capacity of 66 MW.Repaired and operational. |
| Breshna-Kot Dam | Installed capacity of 11.5 MW.Repaired and operational.In Nangarhar province near Jalalabad. |
| Breshna-Kot Substation | Reportedly undergoing repairs. |
| Dahla Dam | Kandahar province.Repaired and operational. |
| Mazar-i-Sharif Power Plant | Small gas-fired power plant near Mazar-i-Sharif, with an installed capacity of 35 MW. |
| Transmission Lines from Turkmenistan | Transmission lines from Turkmenistan supply power to several cities in northwestern Afghanistan, including Herat, and Andkhoy.A line was under construction in early 2001 to Sheberghan. |

*Note: This listing of Afghanistan's energy infrastructure was compiled from information available in press and media sources, and should not necessarily be considered comprehensive. Only facilities which have been reported to be functional or under repair have been included.*

# PRACTICAL INFORMATION FOR CONDUCTING BUSINESS AND OPPORTUNITIES

Afghanistan, a country slightly smaller than the size of Texas, is landlocked, being surrounded by Iran, Turkmenistan, Uzbekistan, Tajikistan, China, and Pakistan. While precise data on Afghanistan's population is sketchy, the present in-country population is estimated at 20 to 25 million (if all refugees were to return). Afghanistan's various ethnic groups have a profound impact on its political, social and business fabric. The mix includes Pashtuns (38%, est.), Tajiks (25%, est.); Hazaras (19%, est.), Uzbeks and other minor ethnic groups. Kabul, Afghanistan's capital, has a population of over two million, with other major cities including Kandahar (pop. 235,000), Herat (200,000), Mazar-i-Sharif (150,000) and Jalalabad (70,000) (note: figures are 1988 UN estimates and are likely now much higher). Afghanistan's 20-plus years of conflict generated the largest refugee outflow in the world, with, at its peak, nearly six million refugees living primarily in Pakistan and Iran. Over one million refugees returned to Afghanistan in the first six months of 2002. The primary languages are Dari (Afghan Persian) and Pashtu. Afghanistan has primarily an arid climate with warm summers and cold winters. The Hindu Kush mountain range runs from northeast to southwest through the middle of the country.

Afghanistan is only now emerging from an extended period of war, extended drought, and chaos. A 1978 communist coup and the December 1979 Soviet invasion of Afghanistan began a period marked by dramatic economic decline, social upheaval, and bloodshed. The departure of Soviet forces in February 1989 began a period of civil war through 1996. In September 1996, the Taliban came to power (although civil war continued), beginning a period of deep international isolation, further economic decline, and another exodus of Afghans to neighboring countries. Dramatic political and military changes have taken place in Afghanistan following the terrorist attacks of September 11, 2001. The military intervention of U.S.-led coalition forces resulted in the ouster of the Taliban in late 2001. This led to the formation of a provisional government, the beginning of a massive reconstruction effort, and an extensive U.S. and international presence that will support Afghanistan's economic recovery and generate opportunities for U.S. firms. The TISA is currently working towards establishing the necessary institutions and structures to convene the Constitutional Loya Jirga in December 2003 and hold national elections in June 2004.

## GETTING STARTED

### STEP 1: INITIAL DESKTOP RESEARCH

Initial desktop research on the Afghan market has become easy as more up-to-date and in-depth information - both on **general issues** as well as on **specific market** segments - is being released via the internet. Please kindly refer to the following websites for further references and regular updates AISA with its Research & Policy Department, too, is in the position to supply the investor with updated information regarding the investment climate in Afghanistan and sector specific studies.

Other organizations able to provide insights into the investment opportunities and investment climate in Afghanistan are:

- Multilateral Investment Guarantee Agency (Investment Horizons: Afghanistan, MIGA 2005, available for download at www.miga.org).
- The recent UNDP study on opportunities for small and medium enterprises in different market sectors (Market Sector Assessments – SME Development, UNDP 2005, available

for download at www.undp.org/afghanistan) offers valuable insights into market and supply chain mechanisms as well as SME financing in the Afghan market.

Further to the websites indicated always check the country-specific websites of the World Bank and the Asian Development Bank: www.worldbank.org/afghanistan and www.adb.org/afghanistan. Both organizations are channeling much of donor aid and investments. You should also directly refer to the website and the news services of the Afghan ministries which best cover your area of interest - for opportunities and background information alike. A list of Afghan ministries can be found in paragraph "Useful Addresses" of this website or in the "A-Z Guide" by the Afghanistan Research and Evaluation Unit. Copies can be obtained at their office.**www.areu.org.af**

**Finally, the following website may also be helpful in finding the information you require www.developmentgateway.org**

Select 'Afghanistan' for latest information on reconstruction and development projects, procurement opportunities, and related information.
**www.aims.org.af**

Afghan Information Management Service is a large scale data base run by UNDP and its partners to generate manage and provide extensive information related to the reconstruction efforts in Afghanistan.

**www.afghanistan21.com**
A privately-run information service featuring up to date press releases, tender information and contact data related to business in Afghanistan.

**www.afghanchamberofcommerce.com**
The business directory of the Afghan Chamber of Commerce offers more than 1,500 contacts to companies in different countries involved in Afghan business. Data may be searched by sector, city, state, or country.

**www.a-acc.org**
The Afghan-American Chamber of Commerce is the first international affiliate of the Afghanistan International Chamber of Commerce. AACC publications, reports and articles give valuable insights in ongoing discussions related to trade and private business in Afghanistan.
**www.afghanbusinesscentre.com**

A joint initiative of the Afghan Ministry of Commerce (MoCI), United Nations Development Programme (UNDP) and the Afghan Chambers of Commerce and Industry (ACCI).
**www.export.gov/afghanistan**

Official website of the Afghan Investment and Reconstruction Task Force (AIRTF) of the US Department of Commerce.

For a first overview and regular updates regarding on-going and forthcoming large-scale reconstruction projects as well as related contracting and procurement opportunities, please refer to the following websites:
**www.developmentgateway.org**

Select 'Afghanistan' for latest information on reconstruction and development projects, procurement opportunities, and related information.
**www.aims.org.af**

Afghan Information Management Service is a large scale data base run by UNDP and its partners to generate manage and provide extensive information related to the reconstruction efforts in Afghanistan.
**www.afghanistan21.com**

A privately-run information service featuring up to date press releases, tender information and contact data related to business in Afghanistan.

Please note that the Procurement Unit of the Government of Afghanistan handles procurement for most World Bank-financed projects and for donors which have selected to use the Procurement Unit's services. The Procurement Unit assists ministries with tenders, evaluations, and contracting and provides advice on a range of procurement issues.

All procurement is carried out according to the procedures of the respective donor, e.g. the World Bank, the EU, and the Asian Development Bank. For more details, please check the Procurement Unit's website at:
**www.eafghanistan.gov.af/procurement**.

In some cases procurement may be carried out directly by donors, multilateral organizations or the relevant Afghan ministry. To be aware of all major opportunities and relevant details in time, double-checking of necessary information is recommended.
Further to the websites indicated always check the country-specific websites of the World Bank and the Asian Development Bank:
**www.worldbank.org/afghanistan** and **www.adb.org/afghanistan**. Both organizations are channeling much of donor aid and investments.

You should also directly refer to the website and the news services of the Afghan ministries which best cover your area of interest - for opportunities and background information alike. A list of Afghan ministries can be found in paragraph "Useful Addresses" of this guide. Updated links can be found at the government's website at www.af. Specific information on small-scale procurement and respective procedures can be found at the website of the recently founded Afghanistan International Chamber of Commerce (AICC). The Chamber has also set up a Procurement Technical Assistance Center. Please refer to
**www.en.aicc-online.org**.

For more specific information on trade issues, please additionally check the following websites:
**www.afghanchamberofcommerce.com**

The business directory of the Afghan Chamber of Commerce offers more than 1,500 contacts to companies in different countries involved in Afghan business. Data may be searched by sector, city, state, or country.
**www.a-acc.org**

The Afghan-American Chamber of Commerce is the first international affiliate of the Afghanistan International Chamber of Commerce. AACC publications, reports and articles give valuable insights in ongoing discussions related to trade and private business in Afghanistan.
**www.commerce.gov.af**

This is the official website of the Afghan Ministry of Commerce.
To Explore investment opportunities in Afghanistan, After visiting AISA's website You may also have a look at the recent study on the investment climate in Afghanistan as edited by the

Multilateral Investment Guarantee Agency (Investment Horizons: Afghanistan, MIGA 2005, available for download at www.miga.org).

The recent UNDP study on opportunities for small and medium enterprises in different market sectors (Market Sector Assessments – SME Development, UNDP 2005, available for download at www.undp.org/afghanistan) offers valuable insights into market and supply chain mechanisms as well as SME financing in the Afghan market.

## STEP 2: BUSINESS-TRIP TO AFGHANISTAN

AISA recommend taking at least one trip to Afghanistan to assess the situation on the ground and get a realistic feeling for your investment here. Prior to you coming here AISA can reserve accommodation for you and arrange for airport pick up. We will also bring you anywhere you need to meet with authorities, potential business partners, to the business parks etc. Such look-see visits will put you in touch with Afghanistan and will enable you to make reality-based business decisions – with the assistance of AISA.
Following some recommendations on how to go about planning your trip to Afghanistan:

### 1. Applying for Visa

Applying for a business or tourist visa to Afghanistan is straight forward. Visitors need to approach the Afghan Embassy or Consulate nearest to them for the application procedure. The following website contains a comprehensive list: **http://www.afghangovernment.com/Embassy.htm**

### 2. Buying your Air Tickets

The following airlines fly to Kabul. You may buy the tickets through an agent in your home country or make reservations online and collect the tickets upon your arrival in Delhi or Dubai respectively.

**Ariana Airlines**
Ariana Airlines provides direct international flights into Kabul from Frankfurt, Istanbul, Dubai, Sharjah, Tehran, Delhi and Islamabad.
**www.flyariana.com**

**Kam Air**
Kam Air flies daily between, Delhi, Dubai and Kabul and has also begun a route via Almaty.
**www.flykamair.com**

**Indian Airlines** from and to Delhi

**Pamir Airways** from and to Dubai

**Kabul International Airport**
Kabul Airport (KBL) is 16km from the city center and taxi service is available. Airport facilities now include banking, a restaurant and parking facilities.

### 3. Accommodations

We recommend the following hotels:

- **Kabul Serena Hotel (5 Stars)**
  Froshgah Street, Kabul
  http://www.serenahotels.com/afghanistan/kabul/home.asp

Tel. +(93) 799 654 000
Email: sales@serena.com.af or reservation@serena.com.af
Rates: $120/night and upwards plus Government Tax (AISA Corporate Rate)

- **Safi Landmark Hotel (4 Stars)**
  P.O. Box 430, Shahr-e-Naw
  Char-Rahi-Ansari, Kabul
  Tel. +(93) 20 2203131
  Fax +(93) 20 2203121
  Email: sales@safilandmarkhotelsuites.com
  Rates: $75-125/night plus Government Tax (AISA Corporate Rate)
- **Hotel Intercontinental Kabul (4 Stars)**
  Baghe Balla Road
  Tel. +93 (020) 2201321
  www.intercontinentalkabul.com
  Email: Frontoffice@intercontinentalkabul.com
  Rates: $75-145/night plus Government Tax (AISA Corporate Rate)

There are also a number of quality guesthouses available. One website to inform about them is **www.kabulguide.net**

### 4. GETTING AROUND

When on a look-see business trip to Afghanistan AISA will bring you around in our vehicles wherever possible.

If you have to get around yourself we suggest Afghan Logistics & Tours taxi service. The drivers speak English and know about most localities popular with foreigners. Contact details for car-rentals and taxi service can be found on their website
Afghan Logistics & Tours also offer travel around the country**www.afghanlogisticstours.com**
The second travel company to do the same is The Great Game.**http://www.greatgametravel.co.uk**

## STEP 3: ASSESSING YOUR INVESTMENT OPPORTUNITIES

Make an appointment with our Investor Support Department and discuss all questions you have regarding doing business in Afghanistan: **info@aisa.org.af**

**Consult us on:**

**a.** Our **priority sectors** – into which our consultants will be happy to give you an in-depth insight – offer areas with extensive opportunities. Other areas, however, may offer more of a niche market. Your product/service might be one to fit this niche market.

**b.** Financial analysis – if you are unable to carry out a financial feasibility analysis in-house AISA's Investor Support Department can do one for you. This might assist you in making the right investment decision, particularly if you want to decide between two or more possible projects.

**c.** Land availability – several industrial parks are open for business in Afghanistan these days and our **Industrial Parks Department**which manages most of them will be happy to advise you on plot availability and application procedures.

After considering carefully the opportunities for your business in Afghanistan you have to license your business.

### STEP 4: LICENSING YOUR BUSINESS

Obtaining a government license and registering one's company with the Commercial Courts is very simple in Afghanistan. The Afghanistan Investment Support Agency (AISA) is the responsible government institution for the registration and licensing of an economic entity. AISA also provides the complete necessary support before, during and after the registration. In contrast to many other countries, in Afghanistan a notary public is not necessary.

At AISA it is possible to register a company as a "natural person" and as a "legal person". We issue a license for investment, which clarifies the legal status of the company. AISA is currently offering the following four economic entity options: Sole Proprietorship, Partnership, Corporation and Limited Liability Company. These definitions of economic entities are currently awaiting further detailed legal regulations in a corresponding "law of incorporation", due in the near future. These laws will confirm such details as the minimum capital stock and other details for Corporations and Limited Liability Companies.

The AISA license is compulsory (our investor support department can advise on the application procedure) as it defines the legal status of the business.

Some businesses require an additional license from the respective ministries, we call this operation license. Details about application procedures and fees can be obtained at AISA's Investor Support Department in hard and soft copy.

## AFGHANISTAN BUSINESS REGISTRATION PROCEDURES FOR U.S COMPANIES

### HOW DO I REGISTER MY COMPANY IN AFGHANISTAN AS A FOREIGN BUSINESS?

A company must first be licensed and in good standing in the U.S to be licensed as a U.S/foreign company in Afghanistan. You must also have a physical address, telephone # and contact for your office in Afghanistan. You may begin by having notarized a copy of your U.S Business License, (if not incorporated) Articles of Incorporation (if incorporated) and any powers of Attorney and have each of these documents attested by your state and Federal Government authorities in the U.S.

Have any Powers of Attorney translated into Dari (Farsi) or Pashto and include along with your original U.S attested documents (from Step 1 above) to the Consulate Section of the Embassy of Afghanistan in Washington D.C for attestation of the final set of documents by the Afghan Government in the U.S.

Take the final set of Consulate attested documents along with your company's IRS tax ID # and a copy of U.S passports of key Principals of the company (President, V.P) to the U.S Embassy in Kabul (Economic Section) for issuance of a referral letter to the Ministry of Foreign Affairs of Afghanistan in Kabul.

Bring your U.S Embassy referral letter together with all documents to the Ministry of Foreign Affairs in Kabul (the Trade, Transit and Investment Directorate) who will the issue a final referral letter either to the Afghanistan Investment Support Agency (AISA) or the Ministry of Commerce & Industry (MoCI) depending on the nature of your work.

If your company deals with investment-related sectors including Services, Consulting, Logistics, Transport (see www.aisa.org.af for full list and information), take all documents from above steps together with the license application to AISA to obtain an "Investment License" . In order to obtain a "Trade" Business License (for Import/ Export activities) follow all the above stated procedures except that you should go to the MoCI Business Licensing Department for final processing of your license. In some cases you will need to register in both places, depending on the nature of your company's work.

## KEY CONTACTS FOR BUSINESS LICENSING IN AFGHANISTAN:

### U.S Embassy in Kabul – Economic Section

Website: http://kabul.usembassy.gov/econsection.htlm
Telephone: 0093 (0) 700-10-8001
Email: KabulEcon@state.gov
Address: Embassy of the United States – Kabul, Afghanistan

### Ministry of Foreign Affairs – Trade, Transit and Investment Directorate

Website: www.mfa.gov.af
Telephone: +93(0)20-210-0377
Address: Malik Azghar Road, Kabul, Afghanistan
Email: contact@mfa.gov.af

### Afghanistan Investment Support Agency (AISA)

Website: www.aisa.af.org
Telephone: 0093(0) 20-210-3404
Address: Opposite Ministry of Foreign Affairs, Kabul, Afghanistan
Email: invest@aisa.org.af

### Ministry of Commerce and Industry (MoCI)

Website: www.commerce.gov.af
Telephone: 0093-(0)700-225-718
Address: Darul Aman Road, Karte Se, Kabul, Afghanistan

## AFGHANISTAN'S TAX REQUIREMENTS:

### Rental Tax Withholding

When paying a monthly rent of **0 Afs to 10,000 Afs**, then you should withhold **0%** and file within 15 days after the end of month in which payment was made.
When paying a monthly rent of **10,000 Afs to 100,000 Afs**, then you should withhold **10% flat** and file within 15 days after end of month in which payment was made.
When paying a monthly rent of **over 100,000**, then you should withhold **15% flat** and file within 15 days after end of month in which payment was made.

### Employee Tax Withholding

When paying a monthly salary of **0 Afs to 5,000 Afs**, then you should withhold **0%** and file within 10 days after the end of the month in which the payment was made.
When paying a monthly salary of **5,000 Afs to 12,500 Afs**, then you should withhold **2% of amount over 5,000 afs** and file within 10 days after the end of the month in which the payment was made.
When paying a monthly salary of **12,500 Afs to 100,000 Afs**, then you should withhold **150 Afs + 10% over 12,500 Afs** and file within 10 days after the end of the month in which the payment was made.
When paying a monthly salary of **over 100,000 Afs**, then you should withhold **8,900 Af+ 20% over 100,000 Afs** and file within 10 days after the end of the month in which the payment was made.

### Contractor Tax Withholding

When paying a sub-contractor **under 500,00 Afs per year**, then you should withhold **0 Afs** and file within 10 days after the end of the month in which payment was made.
When paying a sub-contractor **over 500,00 Afs per year to a company with an AISA license**, then you should withhold **2% flat** and file within 10 days after the end of the month in which payment was made.
When paying a sub-contractor **over 500,00 Afs per year to a company without an ASIA license**, then you should withhold **7% flat** and file within 10 days after the end of the month in which payment was made.

### Business Receipts Tax Return

When revenue is from a contract with a valid contract specific tax exemption on file with the Ministry of Finance, then you should pay **0%** and file within 15 days after the end of quarter in which the payment was made.
When revenue is from all other contracts, then you should pay **2% flat** and file within 15 days after the end of quarter in which the payment was made.

### Annual Income Tax Return

When revenue is from a contract with a valid contract specific tax exemption on file with the Ministry of Finance, then you should pay **0 Afs** and file within 3 months after the end of the year.
When revenue is from all other contracts, then you should pay **20% of profit after all allowable expenses** and file within 3 months after the end of the year.

**INQUIRIES PLEASE CONTACT:**

**Consulate Section of Afghanistan** (Office Hours Mon. – Fri, 9:00am – 1:00pm)

Address: (Georgetown Plaza) 2233 Wisconsin Ave. NW Suite # 216 Washington, D.C 20007
Telephone: 202-298-9125 Fax: 202-298-9127
Website: www.embassyofafghanistan.org
Services: Visas, legalization of documents, attesting, powers of attorney, etc.
Note: Other official Afghan Consulates are located in New York and Los Angeles.

**Embassy of Afghanistan, Washington, D.C., Commercial Attaché**

Website : www.afghanistanbusinessgateway.com
Telephone: (202) 483-6410 exts. 8029
Email: Shakib.Noori@embassyofafghanistan.org

## LICENSING PROCEDURES

In order to operate a business legally in Afghanistan it needs to obtain a business license. This license is awarded through AiSA and is to be renewed yearly. Certain industries, e.g. the Health Sector, require an additional license from the respective ministries. Both need to be obtained prior to starting business operations. Below please find detailed information on both the AISA license as well as all other additional licenses. Please check with our Investor Support Department whether or not your type of business requires such an additional license.

## AFGHAN SECTORS FOR BUSINESS AND INVESTMENTS

The expectations placed on the private sector in Afghanistan are high. The private sector to deliver sustained high levels of growth in an extremely difficult investment environment, and, moreover, this growth should be "pro-poor" in nature. There are fears that Afghanistan may not achieve the hoped-for sustained growth rates of 7–9 percent per year of licit GDP as the immediate recovery period passes and the high real exchange rate, and lack of economic diversification take effect. There is a real need for further investigation of these growth expectations, to assess whether they are realistic. High levels of GDP growth in the medium and long term will be vital to Afghan reconstruction and development.

When promoting Afghan exports one has first to remind himself of the age-old export tradition of the country and its specific strengths. However, traditional export markets have changed over the last 20-30 years, foreign competitors have not hesitated to take over market shares once self understandingly belonging to Afghan exporters. Customer and market requirements became much more demanding especially in terms of quality. So, Afghan producers and exporters have to newly understand international market conditions and – at the same time – re-establish market and trade contacts to potential clients. To properly encounter these challenges and substantially increase Afghan exports it is therefore reasonable to build on export potential and capacities in traditional export sectors, while at the same time making all efforts to adjust to international market requirements and demand.

Initially, EPAA focuses on four sectors with traditionally considerable export potential.

- gribusiness
- Carpet
- Handicrafts and Decorative Articles
- Marble, Minerals Gemstones

### AGRIBUSINESS

Afghanistan is an agricultural country. The development of the agricultural sector is therefore pivotal for Afghanistan´s overall development strategy.

The agriculture sector contributes slightly more than half of GDP and employs almost 70 % of the labour force. Given the seize and the strategic importance of agriculture, the development of the agricultural sector has high priority in all government decisions.

Agriculture production is constrained by an almost total dependence on erratic winter snows and spring rains for water.Relatively little use is made of machines, chemical fertilizer, or pesticides. The policies aimed at rebuilding agriculture and the efforts of farmers, local communities and agro-business are already starting to bear fruit.

Agricultural production has been substantially increased over the last two years and the various elements of the production and marketing chain are increasingly functioning. Irrigated areas are rapidly expanding and orchards are being replanted. International support is also strongly geared towards the sector. Further improvements in irrigation systems, fertilizer use, extension services, and improved infrastructure will further translate into increasing production. Support from international donors for the agricultural sector is likely to remain strong over the next years. However, private investment in agriculture and agro-processing has been low. While agriculture represents the biggest sector of the economy, investment in agro-processing only amounts to about 1% of the investment registered in 2004.

The development of an agro-processing industry is closely tied to the development of the agricultural sector. For some agricultural products such as cotton, processing is even crucial, since no alternative demand exists. Thus, increase in demand for processing creates incentives for farmers to increase output and farmers have shown to be very responsive to such price and demand changes. On the other hand, for agro-processing to occur, an increasing and stable supply of agricultural products at attractive prices is a prerequisite for successful investment in agro-processing activities. Improved irrigation, better seeds and extension service have substantial potential to increase production of particular products. For a variety of Afghan agricultural products regional markets posses a large potential. In particular, Pakistan and India with a population of about 1.3 billion people represent a rapidly growing market. India has been growing at an average of 6 % over the last decade with an accordingly strong growth in import demand. Pakistan has been the destination for 69 % of all Afghan exports, India for about 8 % in 2003/2004. A preferential trade agreement with India has already boosted exports but the potential remains immense. Similar negotiations are going on with other neighbouring countries. Equally interested are the United Arab Emirates, as an export destination. They also serve as a major hub for the entire Middle East region, so that this market is a door opener to many other markets. The success of various quite diverse countries such as New Zealand, Chile, Turkey, Kenya and others, who have successfully penetrated particular agricultural markets in far way countries demonstrate that in today´s globalization a well directed specialisation can be extremely rewarding.

Given the long tradition, the entrepreneurial spirit of its farmers and traders, and the particular potential of many of Afghanistan´s agricultural product quality, the country possess the prerequisites to re-enter the international markets. However, to be successful in these markets require supplying high-quality products

## CARPET

The carpet sector is of strategic importance for the future development of the Afghan economy. Clearly, with carpet exports accounting for 47 % of the country´s export earnings in 2002/2003 (IMF 2004), this sector is a key candidate for increased export earnings.

Carpet weaving is also an important source of income for the rural population, particularly for women. The structure of carpet production is dominated by home production. It typically takes place in the form of some profit-sharing arrangements, where the weavers remain independent producers, or, increasingly, in the form of wage-paid weavers. Within the traditional system, high-quality weaving is often concentrated in particular village, where the necessary skills are passed on within the families. While this preserves ancient traditional designs it is not very open to innovations from the outside and does not offer the possibility for widespread dissemination of skills. Over the last years, a number of carpet factories have been established in urban areas. Currently, no machine made carpet are being produced in Afghanistan. An important aspect of the carpet trade is its non-competitive structure. The national and international trade is dominated by few players which have the capital and the information networks necessary for national and international trade. This is reinforced by the structure of trading networks which are often organized along ethnic lines and exclude outsiders. This privileged position gives these traders substantial monopsony power. The fragmented structure and market power of few key actors is reflected in the high mark-ups observed in the trade.

A particular severe problem is the limited direct access to the overseas markets. Currently, most of the production for the overseas market is transported to Pakistan for washing trimming and finishing, and re-exported from there to the overseas markets. Given the particular skills of the Afghan weavers, the existing traditions and the richness and the uniqueness in designs, a promising strategy should focus on the promotion of high quality carpets made in Afghanistan. Establishing a unique image of the Afghan carpet industry is a necessary and promising product differentiation strategy that would allow Afghan carpets to re-enter the overseas markets and command a price premium for the Afghan carpets on these markets.

EPAA is recently developing a nationally recognised branding strategy called: "REVIVING THE TRADITION – SHAPING THE FUTURE". This strategy will focus on the quality of the carpets, the tradition, the uniqueness of the design and also capitalize on the mystery that surrounds Afghanistan as a remote place that few know.

## HANDICRAFTS AND DECORATIVE ARTICLES

Afghanistan has a century old tradition in furniture making, woodcarving, leatherwork, sewing and jewellery and other quality handicrafts. Afghan design is unique and respective knowledge is given from farther to son. Handicraft companies are making currently great efforts to develop new designs, thereby blending age-old Afghan traditions with international fashion and demand. However, this can only be achieved while keeping the unique Afghan taste and work approach - which makes these artefacts finally exceptional!
Key Items include Jewelry (inc. Turkmen Jewelry, Hazara Jewelry, and more), Furniture (inc. Nouristan Furniture, Herat Glass, Istalif Pottery and more), and antique style decorative items (including keepsafes, teapots, marble items, and more

## MARBLE, MINERALS GEMSTONES

There are substantial quantities of marble deposits within Afghanistan. The marble that is mined within the country is typically exported and only a tiny fraction is processed, typically in handicraft activities, or for local construction use, in Afghanistan. The minerals industry in Afghanistan is beginning to show signs of revival after years of conflict and a chronic lack of investment. The booming construction industry has increased demand for raw materials, and high metal prices and increased political stability have increased the interest of mining companies in the country's undoubted mineral potential.

**Marble**

There is a wide variety of marble in Afghanistan currently extracted from quarries in Badakhshan, Balkh, Bamyan, Helmand, Heart, Kabul, Kandahar, Logar, Faryab, Wardak, Nabgarhar, Paktia, Parwan and
Samangan provinces. Marbles developed in rocks of Proterozoic age are considered to be the highest
quality for use as dimension stone. Marble deposits can be found in the provinces of Kabul, Logar,
Wardak, Badakhan, Herat, and Nangarhar amongst others.

**Onyx Marble.**

Onyx is a banded variety of chalcedony, a cryptocrystalline form of quartz. Onyx is highly valued as a high quality marble and the colour of its bands range from white to almost every other colour. Afghan onyx is quarried from several provinces including Bamyan, Helmand and Faryab, with colours including shades of yellow, green or brown. Some of these may in fact be a variety of aragonite (calcium carbonate) called travertine, however the traditional name of onyx has remained in place and is still used to this day.

The Chesht and Khogiani marble are currently worked for dimension stone and have been favourably compared to Carrara marble, an Italian marble recognised to be one of the finest in the world. During the past five years the political situation in the country has stabilised. Democratic Presidential and parliamentary elections were held peacefully in 2004 and 2005 – the first such elections for over 30 years. The government, with the help of the international community, has passed a raft of essential new laws and begun to reform the civil service. One result of this reform process has been a new Minerals Law, which was written with the assistance of the World Bank and passed in July 2005. The new law aims to encourage investment by local and international companies and changes the role of the Ministry of Mines and Industries (MMI) from a state-run minerals producer to a regulatory and promotional organisation. Although security is a problem in the south and east of the country, most of the northern provinces are stable, with few security concerns that would affect mineral exploration.

The country is well endowed with minerals, which include copper, gold, iron ore, chromium, precious and semi-precious stones, industrial minerals, coal, oil and natural gas. Despite decades of turmoil, most of the records of the Russian exploration work carried in the 1970s and 1980s still exist in the Afghanistan Geological Survey, which now occupies a newly refurbished building in Kabul. These records form an essential archive and the basis for more modern exploration techniques that have not been applied in much of the country.
Afghanistan sits astride the collision zone between the Eurasian and Indian tectonic plates and its geology is complex. The northern part of the country contains most of the known hydrocarbon resources and forms part of the Eurasian platform; a succession of small blocks that originally formed part of the Gondwana supercontinent have accreted on to its southern margin before the final docking with the Indian plate in Miocene times. These complex processes have led to a wide variety of mineral-deposit styles ranging from sediment-hosted copper to porphyry Cu-Au, epithermal gold and pegmatite-hosted rare-metal and gem deposits.

### Copper:

The Aynak copper deposit is situated about 35 km south of Kabul and is a very large, stratabound deposit hosted by Vendian-Lower Cambrian carbonate rocks of the Kabul Block. Extensive Russian exploration was carried out on the prospect in the 1970s and 1980s, including 120 km of drilling. Historic inferred resources are 240 Mt of ore at an average grade of 2.3% Cu. The MMI is going out to international tender for the rights to the deposit and Tender Advisors have been appointed to manage the tender process, which should be completed in 2006. Development of this deposit will give a dramatic boost to the mining industry in Afghanistan and encourage further exploration for copper in the Kabul Block.

### Gold:

There are a large number of gold occurrences in the country, including a notable number in a belt extending southwest from Ghazni to Zabul and Kandahar. Although many are described as Cu-Au skarn deposits, the close association with Miocene granites and porphyries shows that they are more closely related to porphyry-style Cu-Au deposits, and form part of the Tethyan Metallogenic Belt extending from the Carpathians, through Eastern Turkey, Iran (Songun, Sar Chesmeh) and Pakistan (Reko Diq).

Other prospective areas include the Herat area, where a small UK junior company is reported to have signed an exploration licence agreement with the MMI. Another gold deposit, in Baghlan Province, is believed to be under negotiation. In a country with poor infrastructure, gold exploration may be the most attractive option for small mining companies.

### Iron ore:

A large iron-ore deposit has been outlined at Hajigak, 100 km west of Kabul in Bamyan Province. The deposit extends for 32 km along strike, is up to 380 m wide and has been traced down dip for 550 m. The surface ore is haematitic but below 100 m the orebody comprises magnetite plus some pyrite and chalcopyrite, and averages 61.3% Fe. Resources are estimated at 1,700 Mt of ore. Export of the iron-ore would be difficult but the presence of good quality coal not far to the north could form the basis for an integrated iron and steel plant supplying the domestic and export markets.

### Chromium:

A number of chromite deposits occur in Afghanistan, the best known being near Logar, some 40 km south of Kabul. This deposit occurs in the Logar ophiolite, which was obducted on to the Kabul Block in the Eocene. A number of small lensoid bodies are known and an estimated, near surface resource of 180,000 t at 42.4% $Cr_2O_3$ has been outlined. In addition, small-scale working of chromite from an Eocene peridotite is reported from Paktia Province, with the ore being exported to Pakistan.

### Uranium:

Afghanistan formerly produced uranium from the mountains of Khawaja Rawash north of Kabul after the discovery of deposits in 1983. Soviet engineers were also said to be mining uranium at Koh Mir Daoud, between Herat and Shindand, and also in the Khakriz area of Kandahar Province. Very little information on this work is available but Afghanistan has a high potential for further discoveries.

### Precious and semi-precious stones

A number of semi-precious stones are currently exploited in Afghanistan, the most famous being lapis lazuli from the Sary-Sang deposit in Badakhshan. Production figures are difficult to determine but are thought to be around 9,000 kg/y, with speculative reserves of 1,300 t. Most of the material is exported to Pakistan where it is cut and polished. A wide variety of gemstones are known, including emerald, ruby, sapphire, aquamarine, kunzite, garnet and tourmaline. Emeralds are worked on a small scale in the Panjsher Valley, and most of the annual production, worth an estimated US$9-12 million, is traded through Peshawar.

### Construction and industrial minerals:

Building and reconstruction work in Kabul has increased demand for aggregate minerals, with hard rock and alluvial sand and gravel being exploited. A major road-building programme linking Kabul to the main cities has also increased the demand for roadstone and rockfill.

The marble industry has a long history in the country and a variety of white, grey, black, pink and green marbles are exploited, but poor extraction methods using explosives have hindered production. Increased investment in new machinery and better training will be needed to increase production of blocks for export or for cutting and polishing locally.

Salt is produced on a small scale in the north of the country near the Tajikistan border. Deposits of barite, fluorite and gypsum have been exploited to a limited extent.

### Coal

Coal is presently exploited at Karar in the Pul-e-Khumri; at Ishputa near Doshi; and Dar-e-Suf to the south of Mazar. Current production is probably below the historical level of 180,000 t/y and is hindered by obsolescent and broken equipment. The coal is used for local power generation and the cement industry but good coking coal at the last named locality could be used for blast furnaces.

### Oil and gas

Afghanistan`s untapped oil and natural gas reserves may be significantly larger than previously thought. The USGS estimates that the upper range of Afghanistan`s unproven oil reserves roughly matches Sudan`s. The USGS survey shows that two northern regions could contain as much as 1.6 billion barrels of oil, and 15.7 trillion cubic feet of natural gas. Much of the petroleum resource potential of Afghanistan and all of the known crude oil and natural gas reserves are in northern Afghanistan, located in parts of two geologic basins – the Amu Darya Basin to the west and the Afghan-Tajik Basin to the east. Most of the undiscovered crude oil is believed to be in the Afghan-Tajik Basin, and most of the undiscovered natural gas in the Amu Darya Basin.

The government passed a hydrocarbons law in 2005 that grants the Afghan State full control over these resources, but allows fully foreign-owned companies to lease, explore, and develop oil and gas fields, subject to negotiable royalties contracts. Afghanistan is drawing up oil and gas exploration blocks and will soon be seeking production-sharing agreements with foreign companies to develop what it hopes are larger-than-expected reserves

## AFGHANISTAN COMMERCIAL MISSIONS ABROAD

Dubai - U.A.E
Name : Sayed Mohammad Muslem Alawi
Email : t_attache_ae@yahoo.com
Telephone: 00971 4 3988229, 00971 50 3298009, 00971 50 3558301
Fax : 00971 4 3988441
Address : Street 38, Jafellia, Behind Bur Dubai Immigration, Dubai, UAE. P.O.Box: 113233- Dubai- United Arab Emirates

Mumbai - India
Name : Abdul Azim Wardak
Email : azim_wardak2004@hotmail.com
Telephone: 0091 22 - 2363 3777, 0091 9987122673
Fax : 0091 22-2363 5437
Address : Not Available

Peshawar - Pakistan
Name : Sayed Zarif (Ahmadzai)
Email : wtafghani@yahoo.com
Telephone: (+92) 3349231089
Fax : None
Address : Qissa Khwani Bazar, Afghani building, Peshawar, PakistanNot Available

Delhi - India
Name : Abdul Munir Yousofzai
Email : comm._dept_afg@yahoo.com

Telephone: Not Available
Fax : Not Available
Address : Not Available

Karachi - Pakistan
Name : Alhaaj Ajer Khan "Zaheer"
Email : com_attache_khi@hotmail.com
Telephone: 0092-21-5821268
Fax : 0092-21-5838380
Address : Office of the Commercial Attaché .Consulate General of Afghanistan. ST-26 Block, Clifton .Karachi. Pakistan

Mashhad - Iran
Name : Said Aqa Zia Alawee
Email : Trade_agencyafg_inmashhad@yahoo.com
Telephone: 0085940941633
Fax : None
Address : Not Available

Tehran,Iran
Name : Khudadad Faqiehi
Email : afghancommerce@yahoo.com
Telephone: (+98) 329133004
Fax : None

Address : Not Available

Beijing, China
Name : Abdul Sallam Munir
Email : shuhmunir@yahoo.com

Telephone: (010) – 65326325, 13671269114
Fax : Not Available
Address : Commercial Attaché of Islamic Republic of Afghanistan to China. No. 8 Dony Zhi Men Wai Da. Jie Beijing. China 100600

South Korea
Name : Khowaja Mohammad Yahya Siddiqi
Email : yahya_farhad@yahoo.com
Telephone: 00822-793-3535, 0082-10-5250-2344
Fax : 00822-795-2662
Address : 101 HYUNG WOO BEST VILL BUILDING 27-2 HANNAM-DONG, YONGSAN-GU SEOUL 140-210 KOREA

Germany
Name : Alishah Ranjbryan
Email : alishah@ranjbaryan.de
Telephone: (0099) 171 261 32 54
Fax : (0099) 4102 21 10 23
Address : Not Available

Uzbekistan
Name : Bashir Ahmad Sayat
Email : bashirsayet@hotmail.com
Telephone: Not Available
Fax : +998909550547
Address : Khwajasrai District Bakhtepa street 74 Tashkant

Chaman, Pakistan
Name : Moh.Hasan Tolwar
Email : dambla_2004@yahoo.com
Telephone: (+92) 2826612509
Fax : None
Address : None

Zabiullah Momin Zada
Name : Bashir Ahmad
Email : mominzade@yahoo.com
Telephone: 00 966 503610528 - 0093 – 799 23 33 33
Fax : None
Address : Not Available

Moscow , Russia

Name : Sayed Ali Ahmad Mansori
Email : moscowcommerce@gmail.com
Telephone: 00 70959215922, 00 70957784849
Fax : 00 70959215922, 00 70957784849
Address : Not Available

Tajikistan
Name : Najibullah Rahimi
Email : rahimi_n33@yahoo.com
Telephone: (+99) 2935221111
Fax : None
Address : Not Available

United State of America
Name : Khaleda Atta
Email : atta@embassyofafghanistan.org
Telephone: (202) 292 – 42 86
Fax : (202) 483 – 6488
Address : Embassy of Afghanistan 2341 Wyoming Ave ., NW Washington D.C.20008
Website : www.embassyofafghanistan.org

Kazakhstan
Name : Sardar Sakhi
Email : Commercial_attache@yahoo.com
Telephone: 00 998711348432, 00 99652597314
Fax : 00 996312543428
Address : Not Available

London, England
Name : Khalid Yousuf Zai
Email : khalid_yousufzai@hotmail.com
Telephone: 020-7584-4801
Fax : 22 North House Grove Street, London SE8 3LY
Address : None

Kuwait City, Kuwait
Name : Shir Hussain Sultani
Email : Sultani_kw@yahoo.com
Telephone: 00 965-25329461 / 66134106
Fax : 00 96525326274
Address : Kuwait – Alsurra – block 6 – house 13.

Ashgabat, Turkmenistan
Name : Abdul Majid Wafiq
Email : emb.attache@gmail.com
Telephone: 00 999 312 480 757 – 0099366 735056
Fax : (0099312) 480 463
Address : Not Available

Istanbul, Turkey
Name : Hedayatullah Watanyar

Email : Afghancattache_ist@yahoo.com
Telephone: +90 212 2965236,
Fax : +90 2122965237
Address : Cumhuriyet Cad. No: 141. Kat. 3 D.9 Elmadag- sisli, Istanbul Turkey

Jeddah, Kingdom of Saudi Arabia

Name : Qadiri
Email : Qadiri_haq786@yahoo.com
Telephone: None
Fax : None
Address : Not Available

## INDUSTRIAL PARKS

The current industrial property development framework in Afghanistan is inadequate. It relies on public sector planning, development, and management of zoned industrial areas, a responsibility for which the public sector does not have adequate resources. There are 21 industrial parks planned in 17 provinces, which 7 are established in the 1960s and 1970s, without necessary infrastructure and proper management.

The Industrial Parks Development Department of AISA endeavors to develop and offer modern, strategically located, well-managed, regulated and attractive Industrial Parks. Its currently concluded projects include the Bagrami Industrial Park, a 24 hectare (52.8 acres) park located 7 km east of central Kabul; Mazar Industrial Park, a 26 hectare (57.2 acres) park located 7 km north of Mazar-e-Sharif; Kandahar Industrial Park, a 15 hectare (33 acres) park located 10 km east of Kandahar. These project were funded by USAID.

A second phase is also underway, which includes Industrial Parks in Kamari, a 120 hectares park located 13 km from central Kabul. Hisar-e-Shahi Industrial Park, a 200 hectare park located 22 Km South East of Jalalabad city. The World Bank has provided $ 25 million to AISA for the development of the latter two parks.
AISA is committed to establish industrial parks in other provinces of Afghanistan in response to growing demand for these parks. Our future plan includes industrial parks in Helmand, Khost, Kunduz, Ghazni and Farah.
Our industrial park projects represent a unique opportunity for investors to establish and expand their business in Afghanistan's increasingly important market and profitable business environment while enjoying the benefits of attractive tax incentives and versatile and low cost workforce.
Afghanistan's industrial parks will help in:
Reducing risk and avoid potentially costly title disputes
Reducing delays related to site acquisition, zoning and permitting
Benefiting from high quality infrastructure, reliable power supply, and a professionally managed modern industrial park facility

# DOING BUSINESS IN AFGHANISTAN - PRACTICAL INFORMATION

## MARKET OVERVIEW

* Afghanistan continues to rebuild after nearly 30 years of conflict and is transitioning from a state-based model to a free market economy.

* The Government of Afghanistan is improving the country's physical infrastructure with significant donor help and is committed to providing more basic services and humanitarian assistance to a growing population with some of the most challenging social indicators in the world. The Kabul Conference in July 2010 recommitted Afghanistan and its international donors to improved development, governance and stability.

* Corruption remains a persistent problem which increases costs.

* A multi-billion dollar international effort to help reconstruct Afghanistan is ongoing, led by the United States and other international donors. Many, if not most, current business opportunities are linked to these reconstruction efforts.

* The Government of Afghanistan has taken steps to create attractive conditions for foreign investment, however, there is still much more to be done, particularly in completing the process of reforming the legal and regulatory framework.

* Doing business in Afghanistan, however, is more difficult than in other countries in the region. In the World Bank's Doing Business Index 2011 , Afghanistan ranks 167 out of 183 economies in the ease of doing business.

* Afghanistan has enjoyed mostly favorable macroeconomic conditions, with a historically high GDP growth (22.5 percent) and declining prices in 2009/10, according to the World Bank. Since 2002/03, Afghanistan has seen average growth rates in the double digits, but with significant volatility due to the heavy reliance on agriculture which is subject to weather fluctuations. Afghanistan's growth outlook for 2010/11 is cautiously optimistic, with anticipated GDP growth of 8.5-9.0 percent, and inflation around 5 percent, according to the World Bank.

* Currency reform was completed in early 2003, resulting in a stable exchange rate. Since then, inflation has been relatively low and the nominal exchange rate stable. The tax code was restructured and clarified in 2005. Customs tariffs have been rationalized, existing trade agreements are being renewed and new agreements entered into force.

* The economy is dominated by small-farm agriculture and approximately 80 percent of all economic activity remains informal. Illicit opium production remains a major activity and accounts for an amount equivalent to nearly a third of total licit GDP.

* Comprehensive foreign direct investment (FDI) statistics for Afghanistan are unavailable. Figures, which are available, are not reliable because of inconsistencies in data collection. The United Nations 2010 World Investment Report estimated 2009 FDI

flow into Afghanistan at USD 185 million and total FDI stocks at USD 1,550 million, representing 10.3% of GDP.

* Significant investment in Afghanistan comes from United Arab Emirates, Canada, the United States, Turkey, Iran, China, Pakistan, India, and the United Kingdom.

* According to the World Bank, trade as a share of GDP declined significantly in 2009/10. Since 2006, exports as a percent of GDP declined from 23 percent to 15 percent, while imports declined from 87 percent to 64 percent. This partly reflects growth in the domestic economy, but the official trade statistics show a 25% and 45% declines respectively in the value of exports to Pakistan and India that does not appear to reflect the actual trade flows.

* Afghanistan's top export markets are India, Pakistan, Iran, Saudi Arabia, Central Asian Republics and the European Union. Imports primarily come from China, Japan, Pakistan, Iran, the Central Asian Republics and the European Union.

* Afghanistan's history and location give it the potential to develop into a vital trade and transit hub for the region.

## MARKET CHALLENGES

* Poor infrastructure, including power, transport and telecommunications.

* A weak legal framework, regulatory enforcement, and dispute resolution mechanisms.

* Corruption is a serious challenge to doing business in Afghanistan.

* Foreign legal persons may not own land, and securing clear title to land is a long, time-consuming, expensive process.

* The commercial banking system provides limited commercial financing.

* Customs regulations and procedures are neither transparent nor consistent.

* A shortage of skilled labor and trained personnel in both the government and the private sector.

* A critical threat security situation.

## MARKET OPPORTUNITIES

* Business opportunities are largely driven by Afghanistan's need to renovate its infrastructure which was weakened by years of war and neglect. Substantial opportunities for U.S. firms are linked to military spending, donor and international finance institutions (IFIs), including the World Bank and Asian Development Bank, that fund reconstruction efforts. Companies are advised to monitor donor and IFI programs for potential opportunities.

* The security economy generates significant demand for goods and services, equipment and operations and maintenance of the national army and police forces.

* Agriculture remains a strong market driver with significant opportunities in agri-business and agriculture distribution and infrastructure. Dried fruits, nuts and seeds have overtaken carpets to account for half of total exports, but the export of fresh produce accounted for just 6 percent of trade due to limited infrastructure (cold and dry storage facilities.)

In the past 5 years, services have contributed about half of GDP output. The most dynamic services subsectors have been Information & Communications Technology, Finance & Insurance, Transport and Construction. Although Extractive Industries growth has been minimal, recent estimates of mineral deposits and natural resources ensure that this sector will play a prominent role in Afghanistan's future economic growth. Afghanistan has set the target of acceding to fully compliant status in the Extractive Industries Transparency Initiative (EITI) by February 2012 and has established a Secretariat in the Ministry of Finance funded by the World Bank to run the process. The Ministry of Mines plans to offer 24 tenders for various mineral deposits for bidding by investors over the next two years.

## MARKET ENTRY STRATEGY

* Strong local knowledge is a vital part of business development in Afghanistan.

* Be familiar with key players both in business and in government.

* Visit the country, get to know your potential partners and their capabilities to do business with U.S. firms, and meet with local Chambers of Commerce, the Afghanistan Investment Support Agency (AISA) and the Export Promotion Agency of Afghanistan (EPAA). Many U.S. firms may find it beneficial to partner with a local firm which knows the region and can advise on security, and other issues of doing business in the region.

* Expect high costs associated with doing business in an insecure and volatile region.

* Before travel, U.S. citizens should review the Consular Information Sheet (Country Specific Information) and Travel Warning for Afghanistan. These documents can be found at: http://travel.state.gov/travel/cis_pa_tw/cis/cis_1056.html and http://travel.state.gov/travel/cis_pa_tw/tw/tw_2121.html

* Personal relationships are especially important in Afghanistan, and with the legal and regulatory framework still in a nascent stage, businesses are built almost entirely on trust.

# EXPORT AND INVESTMENT OPPORTUNITIES BY SECTOR

## AGRICULTURE AND AGRICULTURE-RELATED INDUSTRIES

Afghanistan is predominantly an agricultural country; agriculture represents nearly 50% of licit GDP and supports 85% of its people. At one time, high quality Afghan agricultural product exports such as dried fruits, nuts, almonds and pistachios occupied a prominent share of the world market. Following almost three decades of conflict, farmers in Afghanistan have recently made great strides in reviving agro business in the country. Development of the agricultural sector is a high priority of the government and is the focus of international donor efforts to revive rural economic activity. Improvements in irrigation systems, fertilizer use and extension services have increased production and reduced input prices.

The domestic market potential for agricultural products is huge and demand is increasing with a rise in population and income across the country. Currently, most processed food is being imported. With rapidly improving supply conditions for agricultural products, there is a large potential for import competition and early entrants stand to benefit as the first domestic suppliers of their products. In addition, Afghan agricultural products represent a potentially valuable export product for investors, particularly in regional markets such as India and Pakistan. There are also significant opportunities in cold and dry storage, processing, particularly cleaning and packaging, or in other elements of the value chain such as testing and certification for both international and domestic markets.

### DRIED FRUITS AND NUTS

The world market for raisins, pistachios, dried apricots, almonds and walnuts is over $2.2 billion, of which Afghanistan currently claims less than 3%. Many of these products were formerly produced on a large scale and continue to enjoy international recognition for quality. Raisins, for example, are Afghanistan's primary agricultural export commodity and once accounted for 60% of the world's market. Pakistan, India and Russia offer large, nearby markets in which Afghan products could begin regaining market share. Existing raisin processors are ripe for new investment to increase and improve production. Ideal growing conditions exist for almonds, pistachios and apricots. The world's largest importers of these products - India for almonds and Russia for dried apricots – are natural regional markets. Low productivity of existing orchards and production facilities as well as a lack of machinery for sorting, drying and packaging, are issues facing the industry.

### JUICES, PASTES, JAM

Local demand for fruit juices, jams and tomato paste is high. Industrially processed products available on the local market are almost entirely imported, primarily from Iran and Pakistan. The abundance of local fruits and tomatoes offers substantial business opportunities in import substitution. Afghan pomegranates are among the best in the world, so production of pomegranate concentrate for export has very good prospects.

### DAIRY PRODUCTS

Most industrially processed and packaged dairy products are imported. Many regions in Afghanistan have a well-established dairy production tradition, particularly in yoghurt, but lack the infrastructure to expand beyond local consumption. U.S. investments in collection, processing, packaging, and a cold storage and transportation chain have good prospects.

## SKINS AND LEATHER

Karakul skins were formerly one of Afghanistan's major exports. With the number of livestock increasing, this industry has rebounded. Investment opportunities and potential for U.S. exports of machinery exist in skin processing and leather manufacturing.

## MEAT PROCESSING

Existing meat processing facilities do not meet international standards. Given the increase in livestock, good opportunities exist for U.S. exports and investment in the upgrade of these facilities and equipment.

## COTTON AND SUGAR

Afghanistan formerly produced substantial quantities of cotton and sugar (beet and cane) crops well suited to the climate of some regions of the country. Foreign investment has been involved in the rehabilitation of former state-owned enterprises in these areas as well as in greenfield operations. The Spinzar plant in Kunduz and the Balkh Gin and Press in Mazar-e-Sharif were privatized under a long term leasing agreement with cotton specialist Dagris of France. KWS of Germany has successfully invested in a joint venture sugar factory in Baghlan. Similar opportunities exist for interested investors.

## MILLS AND BAKING

Most baking and wheat processing activities currently are carried out on a very small scale. However, in large cities such as Kabul, Herat, Kunduz, Mazar-e-Sharif and Kandahar, medium-scale commercial wheat mills are operating. There remain, however, substantial opportunities for expansion of the industry.

## NON-TRADITIONAL PRODUCTS

Afghanistan has a number of native plants with unrealized commercial potential. Ideal climatic and ground conditions for many natural ingredients for the flavor, fragrance, and pharmaceutical industries exist. For example, conditions are ideal for the cultivation of roses and the production of rose oil. A number of spices, rare herbs and medicinal plants can also be found. Various market studies have demonstrated substantial possibilities in these areas.

## PROCESSING AND PACKAGING

Most processing and packaging facilities currently in use for agricultural goods are technologically outdated. This sector represents attractive opportunities for investment and U.S. export of technology and equipment to crush, press, pasteurize, filtrate, dry, sort, grade, fill, and package a variety of agricultural products.

## COLD STORAGE AND TRANSPORTATION

There are few cold storage facilities in Afghanistan. As the agro business sector strengthens and power and fuel supplies become more reliable, cold storage and cold transportation represent one area where U.S. investment and technology could achieve strong export growth and returns on investment.

## CONSTRUCTION MATERIALS

Demand for all types of materials is booming and will remain strong over the next several years given the magnitude of the reconstruction process, a growing population and rising income. Projects range from large scale reconstruction of transportation, power and water infrastructure to small scale retail and residential construction. International donor demands for high quality and quantity represent opportunities for both the export market and local investment. This sector offers perhaps the highest potential for both U.S. investment and exports.

Most available construction materials are currently imported and are of poor quality. Cement, for example, is primarily imported from Pakistan and Iran and is reportedly of such poor quality that it is considered not saleable in those countries. Afghanistan has high-quality limestone deposits, but just one active cement plant, and production does not begin to meet domestic demand.

High transportation costs, an abundance of raw materials, and a supply of local workers with adequate skills in this sector combine to offer promising opportunities for investment in local production that could under-price foreign rivals. The national market for materials is well integrated, with competitive wholesaling and retailing and established distribution channels. There is medium-term potential for local production for export as well, particularly in the marble and marble cutting industry, as Afghanistan's wealth of natural resources offers it a comparative advantage over neighboring countries.

Profitable investment opportunities also exist in the manufacture of final construction inputs, such as doors or windows. Often these activities are carried out on a small scale, but many opportunities exist to expand to mass production.

### Cement and Concrete Block

Afghanistan is in an earthquake prone region. Demand for quality cement is high and is forecasted to remain strong, both in Afghanistan and in regional countries where industries are operating at capacity levels. Local conditions for the production of cement (i.e., adequate limestone) exist. Given the high transportation costs for this product, investment in locally produced cement has potential.

Concrete blocks are a popular local construction material. Upgrading and expanding existing production facilities or establishing new facilities offers good investment potential.

### Bricks

Baked and unbaked bricks are used for construction in Afghanistan. Both are produced by small, local enterprises. Given high transportation costs, there are business opportunities in the expansion and upgrade of local production facilities.

### Doors and Windows

Current local production of doors and windows uses obsolete technology and does not meet local demand. Investment opportunities exist in the improvement and expansion of this process.

### Marble and Natural Stone

There are substantial marble deposits within Afghanistan. Only a small fraction of what is mined is processed locally for construction or handicrafts. Most is exported to

Pakistan, where it is cut into blocks and slabs. Investment in the local cutting process has high profit potential. The abundance of natural stone also offers potential in mining and processing. Some of Afghanistan's natural marble deposits are damaged by mining techniques such as blasting, which creates micro-cracks throughout the deposit. Extraction of marble by diamond blade cutting, the best practice, has begun, but it is still extremely limited.

Tiles

The raw materials for the production of ceramic tiles and other ceramic products can be found in Afghanistan. High demand and prohibitive transportation costs represent great potential for investment in local production facilities.

Sand, Gravel and Aggregate

Many production sites for sand, gravel and aggregate are present. However, quality is mixed. Investment and U.S. export opportunities exist in upgrading the quality of production, equipment sales, and exploitation of new mining sites.

Asphalt

Local asphalt production capacity does not meet the booming demand from large scale road construction and reconstruction activities. High profit potential exists in expansion of local production.

## TELECOMMUNICATIONS

Four mobile telecommunications service providers currently supply the Afghan market with increased competition and price pressures. By early 2010, the number of mobile telephone subscriptions was estimated to be about four million, and the mobile telephone networks cover about 80 percent of the population. Forecasts suggest that by the end of 2011 subscriptions will reach 19 million. The reach of mobile telephony – where more than half of Afghan households have at least one mobile telephone – was achieved through private sector participation. The telecommunications revolution in Afghanistan has been one of the success stories of the country's recent past.

While there are still growth opportunities for mobile service providers, significant market opportunities exist in the other supply and service areas of the telecommunication sector, including data processing, basic business-processing operations, information and communication technology, data transfer and process control. Internet users are only about five percent of the population and services are limited to major urban areas, such as Kabul, Herat, and Mazar-e-Sharif.

Investments in the IT sector are particularly attractive as they often do not depend on the overall infrastructure of Afghanistan such as roads and airports, but investors can develop and rely on their own infrastructure such as satellite communication equipment.

## TRANSPORTATION AND LOGISTICS

Afghanistan has long been a trade hub connecting Asia, Europe and the Middle East. A landlocked country bordering Iran, Turkmenistan, Uzbekistan, Tajikistan, China and Pakistan, it is considered a —land bridgell connecting trading partners and offering a point of access to an expanded regional market of more than two billion people. In addition, this sector represents a vital support industry to other sectors which will not be able to achieve growth without an upgraded transportation and logistics industry.

Inadequate transportation infrastructure is a major obstacle to increased commerce. Road construction is a focus of the reconstruction effort. Major highway projects have been ongoing since 2002, including a nearly complete 2,400 km ring road circling the country and 700 km of links with neighboring countries. The reopening of the Salang Tunnel in 2002 was a major step forward in opening road links with northern Afghanistan. Bridges connect Afghanistan to Uzbekistan and Tajikistan, and rail lines are under construction from the Uzbek border to Mazar-i-Sharif and from Iran to the western suburbs of Herat.

Transportation is a high-growth sector and the demand for transport services is expected to remain strong in the medium to long term. Transport of commercial goods is expected to rise as the commercial infrastructure improves and domestic production of products with strong export potential, such as carpets and dried fruits and nuts, increases.

The market for logistics and transportation services offers first mover advantage to prospective investors with little competition and steady demand. Early investors have reported modest start-up costs, relatively low overhead and high profit margins.

Opportunities exist in areas such as:

* Cold cargo and perishables storage

* Overland transportation

* Truck maintenance

* Customs facilitation

* Air freight and cargo services

* Package and document delivery

* Procurement and supply

* Warehousing.

## MINING AND POWER

The mining industry offers considerable growth potential for U.S. investment and export of technology. Afghanistan has a large quantity of known mineral resources as well as vast areas where the potential is unknown. Early exploration work indicates that Afghanistan possesses substantial mineral wealth ($1 – 3 trillion dollars based on exploration of 10% of the country), but much work remains to be done to determine the economic feasibility of extraction. There is no doubt that the sector will play a leading role in the economy in years to come, as the government proceeds with ambitious plans to develop and market tenders. More information on Afghanistan's natural resources can be found at http://afghanistan.cr.usgs.gov/documents

Afghanistan's mineral resources include copper, iron, coal, uranium, chromite, zinc, lithium, gold, lead, silver and marble. The country's known precious and semi-precious minerals include lapis lazuli, emerald, ruby, tourmaline, sapphire, quartz, alabaster, amethyst, and beryl. While some of these materials are used in the handicrafts market, few of the reserves are being commercially exploited and there is room for expansion of this industry. A reconstruction boom is generating significant local demand for mineral-based construction materials, including marble, paving stones, cement and concrete blocks, bricks, gravel, wood, steel, sand, glass and tile. High transportation costs provide an advantage to locally produced products. Domestic energy needs remain unmet, despite coal deposits and natural gas. Afghanistan has producing oil and natural gas fields, but there is potential for much more as studies show significant geological upside potential in these producing areas.

This sector represents medium to long term potential. Privatization of Afghanistan's State-Owned Enterprises (SOE), which control some of the country's mining resources, such as coal, is not complete. The government of Afghanistan is making progress to improve capacity to effectively regulate its mineral and hydrocarbon resources sectors. Afghanistan is an Extractive Industries Transparency Intitiative (EITI) candidate country and an EITI Secretariat has been established in the Ministry of Finance to oversee the EITI compliance process.

The market for U.S. technology, equipment and expertise in this sector will be substantial.

## LABOR-INTENSIVE MANUFACTURING

Afghanistan is eager to establish a low-cost, labor-intensive manufacturing sector which can employ many Afghans. Industries suitable for investment are those which can first supply the local market and later become export products. The following manufactured products are all imported into Afghanistan which indicates that there currently exists a market within the country:

* Bicycles

* Consumer goods

* Industrial and automotive tools and supplies

* Textiles, apparel and footwear.

Carpets

Carpets are still among Afghanistan's most important exports. The industry has a centuries-old tradition that enjoys world renown. Afghan carpets are internationally competitive, even with the challenges of a post-war economy—a reflection of the capabilities of generations of skilled Afghan weavers. The government places a high priority on the development of the carpet sector, particularly because of its importance as a source of income for the rural population, including women and refugees.

Production is concentrated in several regions of the country. While some carpet factories have been established in urban centers over the last two years, production remains primarily home-based and fragmented. A lack of available and appropriate land has inhibited the development of consolidated production sites.

As few local post-weaving facilities exist, most Afghan carpets destined for overseas markets are exported as unfinished products to Pakistan to undergo the final steps of washing, trimming, and drying. The carpets are then exported from Pakistan as Pakistani products to overseas markets. This process amounts to millions of dollars in lost revenue for Afghanistan.

Hand-knotted Afghan carpets enjoy preferential access to important overseas markets. No customs duty is levied on their import into the United States, Canada or the European Union.

The Afghan carpet industry offers high potential for investment, particularly in re-establishing those elements of the production chain which now take place outside the country. It is estimated that the value of sector exports could increase two to five times if goods were sold directly to foreign markets rather than through intermediaries.

Post Weaving Facilities: Washing, Trimming, Finishing

Facilities for washing, trimming, and finishing carpets are scarce in Afghanistan. The absence of such facilities has created a major bottleneck in the development of direct access to overseas markets. As a result, the carpet industry is dominated by Pakistan-based middlemen. The establishment of such facilities in Afghanistan represents the largest investment potential in this sector.

Carpet Factories

While a few carpet factories exist, the industry is still largely dependent on home production. The establishment of additional factories means increased productivity and increased quality control.

Wool Scouring and Spinning

Quality carpets require quality wool and yarn. While most producers of high quality carpets strive to exclusively use local, handspun wool, supply is insufficient to meet demand. Growing numbers of livestock in Afghanistan have created the potential for investment in additional wool scouring facilities. Spinning of high quality yarn, either from local or imported wool, also represents substantial opportunities.

## OPPORTUNITIES AND RESOURCES

This chapter draws largely on research, market evaluations and case studies conducted by the organizations listed below. Complete materials can be found on their websites.

The Afghan Investment Support Agency http://www.aisa.org.af/english/resources.html /

*Investment opportunity brochures and market studies*

The Multilateral Investment Guarantee Agency http://www.miga.org/

*Investment Horizons: Afghanistan study*

The World Bank http://www.worldbank.org/

*Afghanistan Economic Update and World Bank Doing Business 2011 reports*

Afghanistan Research and Evaluation Unit http://www.areu.org.af/

*Market case studies in raisins, carpets and construction materials*

Donors and international financial institution-funded activities in the sectors discussed in this chapter generate business opportunities for interested companies. Please consult the Project Financing section in Chapter 7 for more details on the activities of organizations such as USAID, World Bank and the Asia Development Bank and how firms can receive notification on procurements and contracting.

# TRADE REGULATIONS, CUSTOMS AND STANDARDS

## IMPORT TARIFFS

Afghanistan maintains the lowest import tariffs in the region. A new tariff regime (dated March 21, 2010 and amended in December 2010) reduced tariff rates for 18 tariff lines (covering beverages and textile items) and increased tariff for 177 tariff lines (mostly on fruits and vegetables, timber, ceramic tiles and some steel products.)

The simple average tariff in 2009 was 5.86% and in 2010, 5.61%. In 2009 the average weighted rate was 6.4% and in 2010, 7.5%.

The total number of tariff bands was simplified to the following 11 categories:

* essential food and non-food products, 2.5%;

* raw materials, 1%;

* fats and oils, 3.5%;

* food and textile, metals, 10%;

* kerosene, oil products and articles from leather, 8%;

* gasoline for vehicles and jet fuel, 12%;

* machinery equipment 0%;

* petroleum products, 5%;

* other import goods, 16%;

* marble, 20%;

* luxury and non-priority products, 25%.

Even at these revised tariff rates, Afghan tariffs will remain the lowest in the region, compared with average tariff rates in Pakistan of 15%, India, 13% and Tajikistan, 11%.

## TRADE BARRIERS

Afghanistan has few trade barriers for imported products. However, deficient infrastructure, a still evolving legal and commercial regime, high levels of corruption and a volatile security situation act as de facto trade barriers.

## IMPORT REQUIREMENTS AND DOCUMENTATION

All imported goods and products must have an original bill of lading and inventory documents. Transit permission is required for shipments transiting through Pakistan; the Central Board of Revenue's Customs Division in Islamabad, Pakistan, oversees transit permission. Importers and exporters must consider whether supporting documentation should be sought from ‗interested' Ministries prior to Customs declaration; e.g., armored vehicles require Ministry of Interior certification; communication equipment requires Ministry of Communications approval; medicines require Ministry of Public Health certification, etc.

## U.S. EXPORT CONTROLS

In June 2002, the U.S. lifted most restrictions on exports and re-exports to Afghanistan. Such transactions are now subject to export control policies applicable to most countries who are not members of multilateral export control regimes. The majority of everyday commercial goods does not require specific U.S. Government authorization for export or re-export to Afghanistan. However, certain items on the Commerce Control List do require a license from the U.S. Department of Commerce's Bureau of Industry and Security (BIS). These include items controlled for chemical and biological weapons, nuclear nonproliferation, national security, and missile technology reasons. There are also foreign policy controls in place for regional stability and crime control reasons. These requirements can be found in Part 742 of the Export Administration Regulations (EAR).

The U.S. Government generally reviews license applications to export controlled goods to Afghanistan on a case-by-case basis. Note that a license is required to export an item

subject to the EAR even when one would not otherwise be necessary, if you know, have reason to know, or are otherwise individually informed by BIS with respect to a specific transaction that the item will be used in activities related to nuclear, chemical, or biological weapons or missile delivery systems as defined in part 744 of the EAR. In addition, certain restrictions administered by the U.S. Department of the Treasury's Office of Foreign Assets Control (OFAC) continue in effect with respect to transactions involving members of the Taliban. Detailed information on U.S. export policies can be found at the BIS website at http://www.bis.doc.gov/index.htm . Specific guidance on U.S. export controls with respect to Afghanistan can be found at http://www.bis.doc.gov/policiesandregulations/afghanfacts.html . You may also contact the BIS Export Counseling Division at (202) 482-4811 for specific guidance.

On July 1, 2010, President Obama signed into law a sweeping new Iran sanctions bill - the Comprehensive Iran Sanctions, Accountability and Divestment Act of 2010 (CISAD) which strengthens U.S. sanctions against Iran by restricting that country's access to, among other things, gasoline and other petroleum products, petroleum-related investment, credit and financial services; and by otherwise tightening the U.S. trade embargo against Iran. Significantly, CISAD authorizes sanctions not only on those

entities conducting Iran-related business but also on those that own or control such entities.

OFAC administers and enforces the Iran Transactions Regulations (ITR), 31 C.F.R. Part 560. Under the previous Iran sanctions legislation, the transshipment of Afghan carpets and foodstuffs to the U.S. through Iran has been done pursuant to a general license (31 C.F.R. sec. 560.534(a)), but section 103 of CISAD prohibits imports into the United States of goods and services of Iranian origin. The new Act preserves OFAC's ability to make exceptions using licenses, but revokes the existing general license for Afghan transshipment through Iran to the United States. For more information on Iran sanctions, go to: http://www.treasury.gov/resource-center/sanctions/Programs/pages/iran.aspx

## TEMPORARY ENTRY

Article 114 of the Afghan Customs Code states that temporary entry goods will be taxed at 3% of the monthly total customs duty if the goods were being imported. Personal belongings, luggage and samples are exempt from payment of duty if they have no commercial purposes.

## LABELING AND MARKING REQUIREMENTS

Afghanistan currently has no laws or regulations governing labeling and marketing requirements for products.

## PROHIBITED AND RESTRICTED IMPORTS

The following items are prohibited from entry in Afghanistan:

* firearms, explosives, daggers

* obscene and subversive literature

* alcohol and pork

Although not prohibited from entry into Afghanistan, Pakistan currently maintains an extensive list of items on its Negative List -- that are barred from transiting its territory for import into Afghanistan.

## CUSTOMS REGULATIONS AND CONTACT INFORMATION

Although there is a focused Afghan and donor country effort to improve governance, practices, and facilities at the major border crossing points, the customs regulations and procedures in Afghanistan are neither transparent nor consistent. Coordination between customs and other government authorities is minimal though improving. Customs officials have received basic training on the customs code, and will have increased opportunities for training and development in the coming years through the new Afghanistan National Customs Academy (ANCA) which was inaugurated in January 2010. Basic communications and support for automated processes are hindered by lack of reliable electricity at major crossing points. Several border crossing facilities have been upgraded in recent years, including Torkham Gate (East), Shir Kan Bandar and Hairatan (North), Islam Qalah (West); plans for infrastructure improvements at several

other border crossing points are underway. Traders face unclear procedures at the borders as well as extra-legal duties and bureaucratic obstructions.

Customs reform is a priority of the Afghan Government. Large-scale reform efforts are underway to establish standardized fees and procedures for incoming goods, as well as streamlined procedures for exports, and a trained cadre of professional staff. In December 2003 the Customs Department introduced a Single Administrative Document (SAD) system pilot program, based on the European Union customs regime, for five key provinces and is now implemented nation-wide. In March 2005, implementation of the Automated System for Customs Data (ASYCUDA) system began on a limited scale and its Import/Export Declaration Processing Module has now been implemented in six locations, with expansion to four more expected soon. Simplified exemptions processing documentation is being introduced and amendments to the Customs Code have been drafted and are moving through Afghanistan's legislative process. A system of Licensed Customs Brokers was launched in 2003, requiring an examination, but due to high levels of illiteracy in the provinces, has been difficult to enforce (Licenses are issued without taking the exam). Improved conditions on cross-border trade are expected with ratification of the South Asian Free Trade Area (SAFTA) agreement and the newly ratified Transit Trade Agreement between Afghanistan and Pakistan (APTTA). Adoption of both agreements will require outreach to the business community and Customs Officers responsible for implementation.

The Afghan Customs Department , a division of the Ministry of Finance , can be contacted at:

Telephone: +(93) 752 004 199

Email: http://www.customs.gov.af/contactus.php

## STANDARDS

Afghanistan is currently in the process of developing a national standards regime. The Afghan National Standards Authority (ANSA) is an independent agency under the Ministry of Commerce and Industries and was established in 2005. ANSA is responsible for the establishment, maintenance, dissemination and enforcement of national standards and technical regulations. ANSA can be contacted at:

Telephone: +(93) 799 079 258.

ANSA was originally established based on Presidential Decree 952 in 2004 under the Ministry of Commerce and Industries. At that time, it had only a symbolic role within government. In August 2007, the Council of Ministers approved ANSA as an independent entity and the Parliament of Afghanistan ratified this decision in February 2008. Soon after that, ANSA obtained membership in the Economic Committee of the Council of Ministers.

ANSA's overall goal is to develop essential national standards and to enhance technical infrastructure for testing. The U.S. Trade and Development Agency helped draft a Standard Law, which was enacted by Presidential Decree 77 dated September 16, 2010. A five year strategy was developed by ANSA and will be expected to be launched at the end of February 2011. ANSA's website at www.ansa.gov.af is currently under construction.

## TRADE AGREEMENTS

In October 2010, one of the most important trade agreements in decades was signed by the Governments of Afghanistan and Pakistan. The Afghanistan-Pakistan Transit Trade Agreement (APTTA), which enters into force February 2011, will strengthen commercial ties across the region and promote global trade as well as contribute to greater regional security as Afghanistan and Pakistan dismantle trade barriers and work together to reduce the cost and difficulties of trade in transit.

Under APTTA, Afghan trucks will be allowed to carry Afghan exports up to the borders of India and China as well as to the rest of the world through the seaports of Karachi, Port Qasim and Gwador. The new transit regime increases the number of transport routes available to trucks from both countries lowering the cost of imports and making exports of both countries more competitive. Pakistan will benefit from easier trade into Central Asia and beyond and improved access to important raw materials for its industries. Afghanistan will gain from increased speed and efficiency in exporting its goods.

Under APTTA, there will be no customs charges for trucks in transit, and customs procedures will be simplified and harmonized to reduce costs and delays. It will also have a multiplier effect, creating jobs along transit corridors, including lodging, food services, repair shops, and service stations.

Afghanistan is a member of the Economic Cooperation Organization (ECO) and the Central Asia Regional Economic Cooperation (CAREC). It became a full member of the South Asian Association for Regional Cooperation (SAARC) in the spring of 2007.

In January 2011, Afghanistan's President signed the Agreement for the South Asia Free Trade Area (SAFTA), which will go into effect 90 days after official notification to the SAARC Secretariat. At that time, under SAFTA, Pakistan, India and Sri Lanka will be required to lower tariffs immediately on many Afghan exports, with the other SAFTA countries (Bangladesh, Bhutan, Maldives, and Nepal) to follow suit over a five year period. Afghanistan has also signed bilateral Trade and Economic Cooperation Agreements with Russia and Turkey, a bilateral Reciprocal Promotion and Protection of Investments Agreement with Turkey, a bilateral Preferential Trade Agreement with India and a bilateral Investment Treaty with Germany.

Afghan products enjoy duty free and quota free access under an LDC Market Access Initiative with Canada and a Generalized Preferences Treatment agreement with Japan. Afghan products also enjoy an —Everything But Arms‖ (EBA) agreement with the European Union.

As a least-developed country, Afghanistan is eligible for duty-free access to the U.S. market for approximately 5,700 products under the Generalized System of Preferences (GSP) program. Afghanistan has signed a bilateral Investment Incentive Agreement with the United States to encourage and protect investment activities in Afghanistan through the provision of insurance and investment guarantees under the OPIC program.

In 2004, a Trade and Investment Framework Agreement (TIFA) was signed with the United States which institutionalized economic relations between the U.S. and Afghanistan. Since that time, there have been annual meetings of the U.S. – Afghanistan Council on Trade and Investment, established under the auspices of the

TIFA, to further the bilateral cooperation needed to achieve Afghanistan's goals of creating an environment conducive to economic reform, private sector development and trade expansion.

Afghanistan became an observer to the World Trade Organization (WTO) in December 2004 and established a Working Party (WP) to begin membership negotiations. The WTO Secretariat scheduled the first meeting for Afghanistan's Working Party for January 31, 2011 as the Afghan Government had replied to all questions submitted by WTO members on the Afghan Memorandum on Foreign Trade Regime (MFTR). This Memorandum, which Afghanistan submitted on March 31, 2009, outlines all aspects of a country's trade and legal regime, and is among the first steps in the accession process. The U.S. Government, through USAID's Trade and Accession Facilitation for Afghanistan (TAFA) project, has been providing technical assistance for such trade regime reform. USTR estimates accession negotiations will take a number of years, though should be somewhat less contentious since Afghanistan is a Least Developed Country (LDC), which can limit concession requests during negotiations.

### WEB RESOURCES

U.S. Department of Commerce's Bureau of Industry and Security (BIS) http://www.bis.doc.gov/
U.S. Department of Treasury's Office of Foreign Assets Control (OFAC)
http://www.treasury.gov/about/organizational-structure/offices/Pages/Office-of-Foreign-Assets-Control.aspx
Afghan Customs Department (ACD) http://www.customs.gov.af/
Afghan Ministry of Finance http://www.mof.gov.af/
Afghan National Standards Authority (ANSA) http://www.ansa.gov.af/
World Trade Organization (WTO) http://www.wto.org/
Afghan Ministry of Finance http://www.mof.gov.af/
Economic Cooperation Organization (ECO) http://www.ecosecretariat.org/
Central Asia Regional Economic Cooperation (CAREC) http://www.adb.org/carec/
South Asian Association for Regional Cooperation (SAARC) http://www.saarc-sec.org/
Office of the U.S. Trade Representative http://www.ustr.gov/
Canadian Department of Foreign Affairs and International Trade
http://www.dfait-maeci.gc.ca/
United Nations Conference on Trade and Development (UNCTAD) http://www.unctad.org/
Turkish Ministry of Foreign of Affairs http://www.mfa.gov.tr/
Japanese Ministry of Foreign Affairs http://www.mofa.go.jp/
Gateway to the European Union http://europa.eu/index_en.htm/
Indian Ministry of Commerce http://www.commerce.nic.in/

## TRADE AND PROJECT FINANCING

### METHODS OF PAYMENT)

Most local businesses operate on a cash basis. Import and export letters of credit are available at several banks as well as electronic funds transfer. Due to wide mistrust and general underdevelopment of the banking system, many local businesses depend on the informal *hawala* system to make payments and transfer funds. The *hawala* system is an informal value transfer system whereby money is transferred through a network of brokers, or *hawaladars*. Promissory instruments are not exchanged; the transaction is based on the honor system.

### HOW DOES THE BANKING SYSTEM OPERATE

Finance is Afghanistan's second largest service-based industry (behind telecommunications) and contributes to private investment and economic growth. The sector has grown rapidly since the end of Taliban rule. Today, 17 commercial banks operate in Afghanistan, with total assets of $4.1 billion (compared to assets of less than $300 million in 2004). However, despite the boom in banking, most Afghans remain —unbanked,‖ with only 5 percent of Afghans currently holding bank deposits. Moreover, many Afghans continue to rely on money service providers (or hawalas) to access finance and transfer money, due to the unfamiliarity with a functioning banking system and limited access to banks in rural areas. Banking remains highly centralized, with 75% of total loans made in Kabul Province. Bank lending is also undermined by a deficient legal and regulatory infrastructure that impedes the enforcement of property rights and development of collateral. The difficulty of accessing credit through banks and other formal financial institutions makes existing firms dependent on family funds and retained earnings, limits opportunities for entrepreneurialism, and reinforces dependence on the informal credit market.

Access to credit has been identified as one of the largest obstacles to investment in Afghanistan and credit to the private sector, according to 2008 data, stands at only around 9% of GDP (low relative to other developing countries). Afghanistan ranks 128th out of 183 countries for obtaining credit in the World Bank's 2011 "Doing Business Report.‖ In response to this situation, investment funds, leasing, micro-financing, and SME-financing companies have begun to enter the market.

Afghanistan has a small public debt market. The Central Bank issues Capital Notes (akin to U.S. Treasury Bills) with maturities of one and six months. Interest rates on both

maturities have stabilized at around 6 percent. Licensed commercial banks, money service providers, and foreign exchange dealers are eligible to participate in the primary auction of these securities and the Central Bank is currently working on a plan to encourage development of a secondary market for Capital Notes.

Afghanistan's Central Bank, the Da Afghanistan Bank (DAB), has taken important steps to improve banking regulation and supervision in recent years. However, serious challenges remain, including lack of capacity, limited operational transparency, a weak legal framework, and further need for improvements in supervision. The Central Bank is now conducting both on- and off-site supervision of all 17 commercial banks. Most bank loans have traditionally been structured as lines of credit rather than term loans, which tends to obscure the true level of non-performing loans. Under the guidance of the DAB, banks are converting lines of credit to term loans.

## FOREIGN-EXCHANGE CONTROLS

Exchange rate policy is determined by the Central Bank, and is implemented through a weekly foreign exchange auction of U.S. Dollars. No foreign exchange restrictions or multiple currency practices are currently in place.

## U.S. BANKS AND LOCAL CORRESPONDENT BANKS

There are currently no U.S. banks operating in Afghanistan. However, in October 2010, Citi entered into a banking agreement with the Afghanistan International Bank (AIB) to serve as Citi's correspondent bank in Afghanistan. AIB is also an ING-affiliated enterprise with American equity.

## PROJECT FINANCING

Project financing is available from the following organizations:

The Overseas Private Investment Corporation (OPIC) is an independent agency of the U.S. Government that offers specialty insurance (stand alone terror/sabotage and political risk coverage), loans and guarantees to help U.S. businesses of all sizes invest and compete in more than 140 emerging markets and developing nations worldwide. A $100 million line of credit is available for projects that demonstrate substantial U.S. participation, promise significant benefits to the economic and social development of Afghanistan, and foster private sector competition in Afghanistan. OPIC is active in Afghanistan and gives preferential consideration to projects that significantly involve U.S. small businesses. For a list of current OPIC projects in Afghanistan, go to: http://www.opic.gov/projects/current-opic-projects and select *Afghanistan.*

The International Finance Corporation (IFC) promotes sustainable private sector investment in developing countries and is the largest multilateral source of loan and equity financing for private sector projects in the developing world. IFC provides loans, equity finance and quasi-equity. It also offers financial risk management products and intermediary finance. For information on IFC's Afghanistan portfolio, go to: http://www.ifc.org/ifcext/mena.nsf/Content/Afghanistan .

The U.S. Trade and Development Agency (USTDA) advances economic development and U.S. commercial interests in developing and middle-income countries. The agency funds various forms of technical assistance, feasibility studies, training, orientation visits and business workshops that support the development of a modern infrastructure and a fair and open trading environment. USTDA moved quickly to establish its program and has provided more than $9 million in funds for projects benefiting Afghanistan since 2002. USTDA has financed projects in telecommunications, civil aviation, oil and gas, higher education, private sector development, and power.

The Export-Import Bank of the United States (Ex-Im) provides financing for the sale of U.S. products and services overseas. Although Ex-Im is currently not open for business in Afghanistan, it will continue to survey future opportunities.

Many business opportunities are connected to the reconstruction effort. The following agencies have large programs through which opportunities for interested businesses are available.

U.S. Agency for International Development (USAID)

USAID has taken a leading role in Afghanistan's reconstruction effort, focusing on health clinics and basic health services, school construction and education programs, revitalizing agriculture through irrigation systems, farm-to-market roads, market centers, SME development and infrastructure, including the Kabul-Kandahar-Herat highway. USAID is also funding programs that enhance the central Government's capacity and provide it with the tools and technical assistance to govern effectively. Between 2006 and 2010, USAID received $8 billion for Afghanistan assistance, of which $4.4 has been disbursed as of September 30, 2010. USAID's Afghanistan web site, http://afghanistan.usaid.gov/en/home , has information on procurement opportunities and doing business with USAID. U.S. firms interested in bidding on USAID projects in Afghanistan can review requests for applications, proposals, quotations and invitation for bids on this website. U.S. firms should also review the main portal for U.S. Government procurements at http://www.fedbizopps.gov .

World Bank

World Bank projects primarily focus on improving rural livelihoods by rebuilding infrastructure and providing employment opportunities, education and basic health services. It is the largest international donor to the Government's flagship National Solidarity and National Emergency Employment Programs, which, respectively, channel block grants through elected community councils to around 17,000 villages and offer cash-for-work on infrastructure projects. In addition, the World Bank administers the multi-donor Afghanistan Reconstruction Trust Fund (ARTF), which provides coordinated financing of unfunded priority expenditures in Afghanistan's reconstruction program as well as supporting the recurrent costs of government. The World Bank's website includes an information portal for the business community seeking to participate in opportunities that are generated from World Bank-financed projects at http://www.worldbank.org . Afghanistan-specific projects, programs and results can be found at: http://www.worldbank.org.af/external/default/main?menuPK=306016&pagePK=141155&piPK=141124&theSitePK=305985 . Projects can also be tracked at http://www.dgmarket.com/ .

Asian Development Bank (ADB)

As of December 31, 2009, ADB had provided Afghanistan with $2.1 billion in loans, grants, guarantees, technical assistance, ADB-administered co-financing, and private sector investments. Afghanistan is ADB's 18th largest borrower.

ADB projects focus in the areas of agriculture and natural resources, energy, gender, governance, financial and private sector development, transport and communications. A detailed description of ADB's Afghanistan strategy and programs can be found at http://www.adb.org/Afghanistan/main.asp and http://www.adb.org/Documents/CSPs/AFG/2005/default.asp . Projects can be also be tracked at http://www.dgmarket.com/ .

In addition, there are also opportunities to bid on donor-funded projects administered by Afghanistan. The Afghanistan Reconstruction and Development Service (ARDS) manages the purchase of goods and services on behalf of the Afghan Government. Companies that wish to receive procurement notices can do so by registering through

email at ards.procurement@ards.org.af .

Political risk insurance is available both through OPIC and the Afghanistan Investment Guarantee Facility, a program of the World Bank's Multilateral Investment Guarantee Agency (MIGA).

## WEB RESOURCES

Export-Import Bank of the United States (Ex-Im): http://www.exim.gov /
Country Limitation Schedule: http://www.exim.gov/tools/country/country_limits.html
Overseas Private Investment Corporation (OPIC): http://www.opic.gov /
U.S. Trade and Development Agency (USTDA): http://www.ustda.gov/
U.S. Small Business Administration (SBA) Office of International Trade: http://www.sba.gov/oit/
U.S. Department of Agriculture (USDA) Commodity Credit Corporation: http://www.fsa.usda.gov/ccc/default.htm /
U.S. Agency for International Development: http://www.usaid.gov /
Afghanistan Central Bank, Da Afghanistan Bank http://www.centralbank.gov.af/
International Finance Corporation http://www.ifc.org/
The World Bank http://www.worldbank.org /
Asian Development Bank http://www.adb.org/
Afghanistan Reconstruction and Development Services http://www.ards.gov.af/

Multilateral Investment Guarantee Agency http://www.miga.org/

## SELLING U.S. PRODUCTS AND SERVICES

### USING AN AGENT OR DISTRIBUTOR

Many international companies find it invaluable to hire an Afghan individual or company as a local agent or partner. In many cases, local connections prove essential in navigating the business world. When looking for a partner, a good start is to contact the various trade associations that operate in Afghanistan, including the American Chamber of Commerce in Afghanistan (AmCham Afghanistan), the Afghanistan Chamber of Commerce and Industries (ACCI) and its U.S.–based affiliate, the Afghan-American Chamber of Commerce (AACC), the Afghan-California Business Council (ACBC) and the Afghanistan Builders Association (ABA).

The NGO Peace Dividend Trust (PDT) maintains a business portal with approximately 6,500 licensed, screened and verified Afghan-owned businesses. PDT services also include business matchmaking activities; tender distribution by e-mail, SMS alerts and office visits; training on procurement processes and market information and advocacy in support of the Afghan First initiative.

AACC, in conjunction with ACCI, the trade associations listed above and various Afghan government ministries, holds an annual matchmaking conference in the fall in the Washington, DC area. These organizations all have a wealth of local knowledge and contacts. The Afghanistan Investment Support Agency (AISA), a quasi-government agency focused on investment promotion, can also help make recommendations.

### ESTABLISHING AN OFFICE

Afghanistan ranks an impressive 25 out of 183 countries in ease of starting a business, according to the World Bank's Doing Business Index 2011 . The Afghanistan Investment Support Agency (AISA) is a —one-stop shop for investors‖, foreign and domestic, for

registering and establishing a business in Afghanistan. AISA is mandated to carry out the legal processes (ie. license) all private businesses and investments in Afghanistan as well as provide investors with assistance and the most up-to-date information on Afghanistan business and investment opportunities.

To operate a business legally in Afghanistan requires a business license. This license is awarded through AISA and is to be renewed annually. Certain industries, e.g. the health sector, require an additional license from the responsible ministry. Both need to be obtained prior to starting business operations. AISA's website provides detailed information on both the AISA license as well as all other additional licenses.

AISA's Investor Support Department will assist the investor in determining whether or not a business requires an additional license and with the following procedures, which are necessary to obtain a business license:

1. Completion of the Investment Application Form and Application Form for Tax ID Number

2. Registration of the Investment Application Form

3. Provision of guidance on the requirements for submission of a business plan and review of the project documents to ensure it is within the country's legal framework

4. Registration of investment documents in commercial court and announcement of investors' business/investment details in a reputable Afghan newspaper

5. Payment of License Fee and Issuance of Investment License. (Fees are based on the type of business and are commensurate with the amount invested.)

To register, a company must first proceed to the Ministry of Foreign Affairs (MoFA) with an introductory letter from its embassy. The U.S. Embassy's Economic/Commercial Section can provide this letter upon provision of the following:

--Federal Tax ID Number on IRS Letterhead;

--Articles of Incorporation from the U.S. State the company is registered with;

--Short (one sentence) description of the business;

--Copy of Passport ID Page of President; Vice-President; and/or Country Representative

The MoFA then sends the information to AISA to license the entity. Once the AISA forms are completed, information on the organization is also sent to the Afghanistan Central Business Registry (ACBR) for registration. The ACBR is a —one stop shopǁ to register businesses, combining all of the functions previously performed by the Commercial Court, the Ministry of Justice (MoJ) and the Ministry of Finance (MoF). The ACBR facilities the registration process for all businesses. The ACBR issues the partner a tax identification number (TIN), registers the business and publishes the information in the Official Gazette of the MoJ. The partner receives a registration number from the ACBR which then allows AISA to issue the license.

The entire process takes about one to two weeks. Licensing fees range from USD $100 to $1000, depending on the size of initial investment.

If a business intends to engage in import/export, additional steps are required. In addition to the Investment License, the Ministry of Commerce & Industries (MoCI) will also issue an Export License. To obtain an Export License, the Ministry requests businesses to provide a bank statement and police verification from their country of domicile.

Other types of licenses may require this police verification (sometimes referred to as a —criminal background checkǁ) that verifies that the police have done a criminal records check and there are no records indicating that an individual has been charged or convicted of a crime.

These are common and most police agencies in the U.S. are familiar with these requests. You should contact your local police department where you reside or last resided in the United States, request that the police conduct a criminal records search and provide you with a document reflecting that there is no history of a criminal record.

For more information on criminal records checks, please see:
http://travel.state.gov/travel/tips/emergencies/emergencies_1201.html

Non-profit/non-governmental organizations must also register with the Government of Afghanistan. To register, a non-profit must first proceed to the Ministry of Foreign Affairs (MoFA) with an introductory letter from its embassy. The U.S. Embassy's Economic/Commercial Section can provide this letter upon provision of the following:

--Federal Tax ID Number on IRS Letterhead;

--Articles of Incorporation from the U.S. State the non-profit is registered with;

--Short (one sentence) description of the organization;

--Copy of Passport ID Page of President; Vice-President; and/or Country Representative

That letter is then taken to the Ministry of Economy (MoEC) for registration of the non-profit/non-governmental organization.

There are no separate licensing procedures for joint ventures.

While AISA has the mandate to host business, trade and investment events and conferences, as well as refer companies to potential partners, sources of finance and opportunities in industrial parks, its services in these areas are lacking.

Establishing a physical office in Afghanistan can be challenging. Potential investors face an overheated real estate market with rents comparable to large U.S. or European cities. Renters are also required to pay a 20% renters tax, which they must personally withhold from their monthly rent payment and remit to the Afghan Government. Foreign investors are not permitted to purchase real estate in Afghanistan (see Chapter 6 for more details). Basic infrastructure, such as electricity, heating and telecommunications, remains a constant challenge.

Under the Afghan government-launched Industrial Park Program, established industrial parks offer clear land title, reliable power and water supply, and security. The industrial park in Bagrami (near Kabul) is expanding due to the large demand for land. Parks in Mazar-e-Sharif and Kandahar are in the process of securing occupants and overcoming

infrastructure challenges. The privately-owned industrial park in Herat is host to nearly 200 companies and is growing rapidly. The Industrial Park Program is administered by AISA.

## FRANCHISING

While the establishment of brand-name businesses in Afghanistan could make a significant impact on improving the investment climate, U.S. and international franchises are currently entering Afghanistan only in limited cases. When those large firms do choose to enter this market, they will seeks franchisees possessing high integrity, business experience in the market, a history of success, ability to work well with a franchisor, retail experience, knowledge of the real estate market, and significant capital. This value chain experience is critical to maintaining brand quality.

Small and medium size franchise concepts may be more adaptable to the Afghan market. The U.S. Embassy encourages potential Afghan franchisees to contact the International Franchise Association to learn about franchise opportunities, attend trade shows such as the International Franchise Expo and to take advantage of their training programs.

## SELLING TO THE GOVERNMENT

The Government of the Islamic Republic of Afghanistan (GIRoA) has established a procurement agency to facilitate the purchase of goods and services for the Government. This agency, the Afghanistan Reconstruction and Development Service (ARDS), uses internationally recognized procurement procedures. Companies that wish to receive procurement notices can do so by registering through email at ards.procurement@ards.org.af . Notices on new procurements are sent electronically to all companies registered with ARDS. ARDS also maintains a list of suppliers.

## DISTRIBUTION AND SALES CHANNELS

Formal distribution and sales channels are not well developed in Afghanistan. Most commerce is confined to small store fronts, markets and informal roadside trading although some major distribution centers are Kabul, Herat, Mazar-e-Sharif, Jalalabad, and Kandahar. Many commercial goods destined for Afghanistan are shipped through ports in Karachi or Port Qasim, Pakistan, moved overland by rail or truck and enter the country via the Torkham (Nangarhar province) or Chaman (Kandahar province) border crossings. In addition, a significant amount of Afghanistan's imports pass through Hairatan, the country's third largest port, in northern Afghanistan. In January 2010, construction of a 75 km rail link from Uzbekistan to Marzar-e-Sharif was launched and completion is planned for June 2011. Goods are currently distributed throughout Afghanistan by truck. Another major overland route is through Iran via Bandar-i-Abbas, entering Afghanistan at the border with Herat province. U.S. law prohibits transshipment through Iran by American companies or individuals without written approval by the U.S. Department of Treasury's Office of Foreign Assets Control . There is no internal rail network in Afghanistan. Though a growing number of air cargo companies are offering their services, this sector is still undeveloped and expensive.

## SELLING FACTORS/TECHNIQUES

Due to limited understanding of English among Afghans, sales materials should be in Dari and/or Pashto. Direct marketing is a relatively unused sales technique because the postal system is largely defunct and land-line telephone connections are limited. Due to the low literacy rate, businesses may want to consider using radio or television advertising to reach potential clients. With a growing population of cellular users, currently reaching over four million, direct marketing via cellular phone could likely become more widespread in the near future. Electronic commerce is not common in Afghanistan due to still developing telecommunications infrastructure, however, it is growing rapidly and several telecommunications companies have undergone large-scale expansions. Surveys shows that only 15% of businesses use email to communicate with their clients and 9% have websites.

The United Nations Development Program has conducted a Market Sector Assessment of small and medium size enterprises in Afghanistan that includes information on existing marketing practices in some sectors. The study as well as other useful information can be found at: http://www.undp.org.af/

## TRADE PROMOTION AND ADVERTISING

The Afghanistan Investment Support Agency (AISA), the quasi-government agency responsible for investment promotion, organizes trade promotion events. The Export Promotion Agency of Afghanistan (EPAA), the quasi-government agency responsible for export promotion, organizes export promotion events. The Afghanistan Chamber of Commerce & Industries (ACCI) also has a Trade and Investment Promotion Office.

Businesses in Afghanistan spend limited resources on advertising. Only a handful of Western-style advertising agencies exist. Commercial advertising is available through major television and radio outlets such as Tolo TV , Ayna TV, Shamshad TV , Ariana TV , 1 TV , Radio Television Afghanistan, Radio Arman, Radio Khillid, Radio Salam Wastandar. Advertisements in newspapers reach a limited audience.

## PRICING

Factors to consider in pricing are as follows:

* Corporate income tax of 20%; low by regional standards. Personal income tax ranges from 0 – 20%.

* Business Receipts Tax ranging from 2 – 10%, based on sector, revenue and billing.

* Import tariffs in the range of 0 – 25%.

* High transport costs.

* Competition from cheap, low-quality goods and services from Pakistan, China and Iran.

## SALES SERVICE/CUSTOMER SUPPORT

Customers in Afghanistan are not accustomed to a high degree of sales service and customer support, with the possible exception of those who use mobile and internet service providers. However, appreciation for higher levels of service is increasing as the general population becomes more market savvy.

## PROTECTING YOUR INTELLECTUAL PROPERTY

Afghanistan currently has no laws enforcing intellectual property rights. Investors should have no expectation of protection (see Chapter 6 for more information.)

Several general principles are important for effective management of intellectual property (—IP‖) rights in Afghanistan. It is important to have an overall strategy to protect your IP. Your U.S. trademark and patent registrations will not protect you in Afghanistan. There is no such thing as an —international copyright‖ that will automatically protect an author's writings throughout the entire world. Protection against unauthorized use in a particular country depends, basically, on the national laws of that country. However, most countries do offer copyright protection to foreign works under certain conditions, and these conditions have been greatly simplified by international copyright treaties and conventions.

Registration of patents and trademarks is on a first-in-time, first-in-right basis, so you should consider applying for trademark and patent protection even before selling your products or services in the Afghan market. It is vital that companies understand that intellectual property is primarily a private right and that the U.S. Government generally cannot enforce rights for private individuals in Afghanistan. It is the responsibility of the rights' holders to register, protect, and enforce their rights where relevant, retaining their own counsel and advisors. Companies may wish to seek advice from local attorneys or IP consultants who are experts in Afghan law. The U.S. Embassy provides a list of local lawyers on its website .

While the U.S. Government stands ready to assist, there is little which can be done if the rights holders have not taken these fundamental steps necessary to securing and enforcing their IP in a timely fashion. Moreover, in many countries, rights holders who delay enforcing their rights on a mistaken belief that the USG can provide a political resolution to a legal problem may find that their rights have been eroded or abrogated due to legal doctrines such as statutes of limitations, laches, estoppel, or unreasonable delay in prosecuting a lawsuit. In no instance should U.S. Government advice be seen as a substitute for the obligation of a rights holder to promptly pursue its case.

It is always advisable to conduct due diligence on potential partners. Negotiate from the position of your partner and give your partner clear incentives to honor the contract. A good partner is an important ally in protecting IP rights. Consider carefully, however, whether to permit your partner to register your IP rights on your behalf. Doing so may create a risk that your partner will list itself as the IP owner and fail to transfer the rights should the partnership end. Keep an eye on your cost structure and reduce the margins (and the incentive) of would-be bad actors. Projects and sales in Afghanistan require constant attention. Work with legal counsel familiar with Afghanistan laws to create a solid contract that includes non-compete clauses, and confidentiality/non-disclosure provisions.

It is also recommended that small and medium-size companies understand the importance of working together with trade associations and organizations to support efforts to protect IP and stop counterfeiting. There are a number of these organizations, both Afghan or U.S.-based. These include:

* The U.S. Chamber and local American Chambers of Commerce

* National Association of Manufacturers (NAM)

* International Intellectual Property Alliance (IIPA)

* International Trademark Association (INTA)

* The Coalition Against Counterfeiting and Piracy

* International Anti-Counterfeiting Coalition (IACC)

* Pharmaceutical Research and Manufacturers of America (PhRMA)

* Biotechnology Industry Organization (BIO)

IP Resources

A wealth of information on protecting IP is freely available to U.S. rights holders. Some excellent resources for companies regarding intellectual property include the following:

* For information about patent, trademark, or copyright issues -- including enforcement issues in the US and other countries -- call the STOP! Hotline: 1-866-999-HALT or register at www.StopFakes.gov .

* For more information about registering trademarks and patents (both in the U.S. as well as in foreign countries), contact the US Patent and Trademark Office (USPTO) at: 1-800-786-9199.

* For more information about registering for copyright protection in the US, contact the US Copyright Office at: 1-202-707-5959.

* For more information about how to evaluate, protect, and enforce intellectual property rights and how these rights may be important for businesses, a free online training program is available at www.stopfakes.gov .

* For US small and medium-size companies, the Department of Commerce offers a "SME IP Advisory Program" available through the American Bar Association that provides one hour of free IP legal advice for companies with concerns in numerous countries including Brazil, China, Egypt, India and Russia (but not Afghanistan). For details and to register, visit: http://www.abanet.org/intlaw/intlproj/iprprogram_consultation.html

* For information on obtaining and enforcing intellectual property rights and market-specific IP Toolkits visit: www.StopFakes.gov This site is linked to the USPTO website for registering trademarks and patents (both in the U.S. as well as in foreign countries), the U.S. Customs & Border Protection website to record registered trademarks and copyrighted works (to assist customs in blocking imports of IP-infringing products) and allows you to register for Webinars on protecting IP.

## DUE DILIGENCE

It is essential to conduct adequate due diligence on potential local partners before entering into business in Afghanistan. As the country currently has no contracts law in place and the commercial court system is inadequate, businesses should tread carefully when entering into commercial agreements or partnerships. The Afghan Government

enacted arbitration and mediation laws in January 2007. The Ministries of Commerce, Interior, AISA, The Afghan National Police, and the courts have all played roles in recent disputes involving Americans. If involved in a commercial dispute, hiring an Afghan attorney early can be beneficial. Visiting the country to learn more about the business environment and the potential partner is recommended.

The Afghanistan Chamber of Commerce & Industries (ACCI) and the Afghanistan Investment Support Agency (AISA) can be helpful in providing background on a potential partner. In addition, there are a few local attorneys who specialize in business and commerce that can be contacted for assistance. Please contact the U.S. Embassy Commercial Section for that listing. Additionally, the U.S. Embassy provides a list of local lawyers on its website .

## LOCAL PROFESSIONAL SERVICES

The Embassy of Afghanistan in Washington, DC has developed a resource listing services available to facilitate investment. The guide can be downloaded at: http://www.embassyofafghanistan.org/resourceguide.html

## WORKING AS A CONTRACTOR

The legal foundation for taxation in Afghanistan (Article 42 of the Constitution and Article 2 of the Income Tax Law) stipulates that any individual or company that makes a profit in Afghanistan must pay taxes in accordance with the law. There are a number of bilateral agreements in place that provide tax and other exemptions for U.S. Government (USG) personnel, contractors, and subcontractors. USG contractors are required to follow Afghan official registration procedures for companies operating in Afghanistan (see —Establishing an Officell section earlier in this chapter.)

Although the registration requirements are generally uniform for all entities operating in Afghanistan, tax exemptions differ depending on which USG agency is the contracting entity and whether there is an agreement with the Afghan Government applicable to the activities of that USG department or agency. The general information provided here is only a guide and cannot substitute for specific registration and tax advice pertaining to each firm. The U.S. Embassy is prohibited from giving direct tax advice to private firms. The U.S. Government expects each of its implementing partners, including contractors and subcontractors, to comply fully with the laws of the Government of the Islamic Republic of Afghanistan. It is important to note that no firm is exempt from all tax requirements. Even firms exempt from taxation due to development assistance-related contracts must register for the exemption with the Ministry of Finance .

Non-profit/non-governmental organizations (NGOs) working in Afghanistan may want to consider if Afghanistan‘s NGO Law provides tax or other exemptions for their operations. The NGO Department of the Ministry of Economy has responsibility for all NGOs operating in country. Article 30 of the NGO Law relates to tax exemptions.

Questions related to tax exemptions and problems encountered with registration and the collection or payment of taxes when exemptions apply should be brought to the attention of contracting officers immediately.

Tax Exemptions for U.S. Department of Defense (DoD) Contractors: An exchange of diplomatic notes concluded in 2003 constitutes the Status of Forces Agreement (SOFA) applicable to the U.S. Department of Defense (DOD), including U.S. Forces-Afghanistan (USFOR-A). It establishes exemptions for contractors and subcontractors carrying out work for U.S. Forces-Afghanistan. The SOFA provides that DOD —its military and civilian personnel, contractors and contractor personnel shall not be liable to pay any tax or similar charge assessed within Afghanistan.ll It also provides that DOD —contractors and contractor personnel may import into, export out of, and use in the Republic of Afghanistan any personal property, equipment, supplies, materials, technology, training or services required to implement this agreement. Such importation, exportation and use shall be exempt from any inspection, license, other restrictions, customs duties, taxes or any other charges assessed within Afghanistan.ll Further, the SOFA provides that —acquisition of articles and services in the republic of Afghanistan by or on behalf of the [DOD] in implementing this agreement shall not be subject to any taxes, customs duties or similar charges in Afghanistan.ll DOD contractors, subcontractors and their employees making acquisitions and providing services to or on behalf of DOD are exempt from all Afghan taxes on such articles and services.

International Security Assistance Forces (ISAF) Contractors: NATO‘s ISAF contractors operate under the Military Technical Agreement (MTA), which provides some exemptions. Please note that the MTA is not the same as the bilateral U.S.-Afghanistan SOFA and therefore provides a different exemption framework. A U.S. company contracting with ISAF would receive the benefit of the MTA's exemptions.

Tax Exemptions for USAID Contractors: USAID has four over-arching Strategic Objective Grant Agreements (SOAGs) with the Government of Afghanistan that encompass all of the programs USAID finances in Afghanistan. For detailed information on USAID-related tax policy, please refer to: http://afghanistan.usaid.gov/en/about/legal/taxation/ .

Tax Exemptions for Department of State (DoS) Contractors: The State Department's Bureau of International Narcotics and Law Enforcement (INL) has negotiated agreements on tax exemption. Contractors should consult their contracting officer to determine applicable tax exemptions.

### WEB RESOURCES

American Chamber of Commerce in Afghanistan (AmCham) http://www.amcham-af.org/
Afghanistan Chamber of Commerce and Industry (ACCI) http://www.acci.org.af/
Afghan-American Chamber of Commerce (AACC) http://www.a-acc.org/
Afghan-California Business Council (ACBC) http://www.acbconline.org/
Afghanistan Builders Association (ABA) http://www.aba.af/
Peace Dividend Marketplace Afghanistan http://afghanistan.buildingmarkets.org/
Afghanistan Investment Support Agency (AISA) http://www.aisa.org.af/
World Bank Doing Business 2011 Report
http://doingbusiness.org/data/exploreeconomies/afghanistan
Afghan Ministry of Foreign Affairs (MoFA) http://www.mfa.gov.af/
Afghanistan Central Business Registry (ACBR) http://www.acbr.gov.af/
Afghan Ministry of Justice (MoJ) http://www.moj.gov.af/
Afghan Ministry of Finance (MoF) http://www.mof.gov.af/
Afghan Ministry of Commerce & Industries (MoCI) http://www.commerce.gov.af/
Afghan Ministry of Economy (MoEC) http://www.moec.gov.af/index_eng.aspx
International Franchise Association (IFA) http://www.franchise.org/
Afghanistan Reconstruction and Development Service (ARDS) http://www.ards.gov.af/
Office of Foreign Assets Control (OFAC) http://www.treasury.gov/about/organizational-structure/offices/Pages/Office-of-Foreign-Assets-Control.aspx
United Nations Development Program (UNDP) http://www.undp.org.af/
Export Promotion Agency of Afghanistan (EPAA) http://www.epaa.org.af/
Embassy of Afghanistan in Washington, DC http://www.embassyofafghanistan.org/index.html

## BUSINESS TRAVEL

### BUSINESS CUSTOMS

Business meetings are conducted in Dari, Pashto or English. Green or black tea, nuts and raisins are typically served. The form of greeting is —Asalam Aleikum‖ (Peace be with you), followed by a firm handshake and then, for courtesy and to pay homage to the host (you don't necessarily have to), briefly place your right hand over your heart. It is

best to take a few minutes initially to engage in pleasantries about each other's country, rather than going straight to business. Afghan interlocutors may appear vague and non-committal during meetings. In order to build trust and "get to yes," be patient, share meals and other social events and discuss matters other than business. Capture the essence of your business meetings and agreements in a follow up letter to your Afghan interlocutor. Be clear about what you have committed yourself or your U.S. firm to do, or in many cases, have not committed to do. A promise to "look into" or "research" an issue, quote, or pricing policy may be interpreted as a firm commitment.

Do not rely heavily on email and the internet when doing business in Afghanistan. Most Afghan businesspeople do not have access to the internet outside of work hours, and many are only able to log on once or twice a week. Afghans prefer to meet in person, or to talk over the phone when a face-to-face meeting is impractical.

DOs and DON'Ts in Afghan Culture

Do greet everyone when entering a room. Shake hands with the men, but not with a woman unless she extends her hand first.

Do eat with your right hand as much as possible.

Do dress modestly. At a minimum, women in Afghanistan typically cover their head with a scarf, wear long sleeves and either slacks and a tunic or a floor-length skirt,

Do accept a chair if someone brings you one to sit on, even if you would rather stand. This is a sign of respect.

Do read about the country's history, culture, and people before you come, as this will be treated as a sign of respect for Afghanistan.

Don't show impatience if your interlocutor isn't giving you direct answers. Afghans like to elaborate and want to be clear in communicating.

Don't panic. The Afghan Government can be bureaucratic. It may take you several days to get a simple authorization signed. Keep in mind that the Afghan Government is undergoing a reform process.

Don't call an Afghan "Afghani." Afghani is the currency; Afghans are the people of Afghanistan.

Don't drink alcohol in front of an Afghan.

## TRAVEL ADVISORY

While the U.S. Embassy in Kabul encourages U.S. companies to review business opportunities in Afghanistan, it is important to keep in mind the volatile security situation in the country. Travelers should consult the State Department Travel web site http://travel.state.gov prior to any travel and review both the Consular Information Sheet and Travel Warning for Afghanistan. These documents can be found at http://travel.state.gov/travel/cis_pa_tw/cis/cis_1056.html . U.S. citizens should register with the U.S. Embassy through the State Department's Smart Traveler Enrollment Program (STEP) at https://travelregistration.state.gov/ibrs/ui/ . Enrolling in STEP will allow the U.S. Embassy to more easily communicate with you in the event of an emergency.

## VISA REQUIREMENTS

A passport and valid visa are required to enter and exit Afghanistan. Afghan entry visas are not available at Kabul International Airport. American citizens who arrive without a visa are subject to confiscation of their passport and face heavy fines and difficulties in

retrieving their passport and obtaining a visa, as well as possible deportation from the country.

For the most updated requirements to obtain an Afghan visa, please contact the Embassy of Afghanistan located at 2341 Wyoming Ave. NW, Washington, D.C. 20008, phone 202-483-6410, fax 202-483-6488, http://www.embassyofafghanistan.org .

U.S. companies that require travel of foreign businesspersons to the United States should know that it can take an average of between 60 and 90 days for an Afghan citizen to receive a visa to visit the United States due to a lengthy clearance process. The visa application process, including the appointment request must now be completed on-line. Please see the U.S. Embassy website at: http://kabul.usembassy.gov/visas.html for instructions.

State Department Visa Website: http://travel.state.gov/visa/

U.S. Embassy in Afghanistan: http://kabul.usembassy.gov/

## TELECOMMUNICATIONS

There are approximately 50,000 fix-line telephones, provided by state-owned Afghan Telecom (AfTel). The vast majority of Afghanistan's 12 million telephone users subscribe to mobile service. Cellular service is available in Kabul and all 34 provinces, and subsidized rural access programs have improved coverage in remote areas. Eighty percent of the population lives within a coverage area. There are currently four nationwide GSM wireless service providers: Roshan, owned by an international consortium led by the Aga Khan Fund for Economic Development; Afghan Wireless Communications Company (AWCC), a joint venture between U.S.-based Telephone Systems International and the Afghan Ministry of Communications; MTN (also known as Areeba), a subsidiary of South Africa-based MTN Group and a subsidiary of UAE-based Etisalat, and AfTel, which serves approximately 10,000 CDMA wireless customers. The country has multiple internet service providers, assisted by a new fiber-optic cable that connects to Pakistan, Iran, Uzbekistan and Tajikistan and link Afghanistan's major population centers.

## TRANSPORTATION

Several commercial airlines serve Afghanistan at Kabul International Airport, primarily through Dubai, U.A.E. Afghan carriers KamAir, Pamir Air, and Safi Airways operate daily flights between Dubai and Kabul. Pakistan International Airlines has three weekly flights to and from Islamabad and Peshawar. Azerbaijan Airways has twice weekly flights to and from Baku. Indian Airlines flies four times a week to and from Delhi. The U.S. Embassy does not recommend use of Ariana Afghan Airlines or Pamir Air to any destination because their maintenance and operations do not meet international aviation standards. Please see the State Department's Consular Information Sheet at http://travel.state.gov/travel/cis_pa_tw/cis/cis_1056.html for more information.

Taxis around Kabul should range between AFS 50 to 100 ($1 or $2, depending on where you are going) per trip, but a dedicated car and driver are recommended. For travel within Kabul, a car and driver (no English) will run up to $15 to $50 per day, depending on the model of car. Some international firms employ expat drivers and security personnel which run approximately $400 a day or $12,000 a month, depending on the vehicle and experience of the security personnel. Public buses are not recommended.

## LANGUAGE

Dari and Pashto are the official languages of the country. Few native Afghans speak English, but many returning expatriate Afghans speak English or German. A reliable interpreter fluent in English, Dari and Pashto may earn between $150 - $2,000 per month.

Translation of names and words from Arabic script to the Latin/Roman alphabet can have several variations. Accordingly, a company's name may appear slightly differently on different documents.

## HEALTH

The climate in Afghanistan is dry. Summer temperatures reach into the 100s Fahrenheit and winter lows dip into the 20s Fahrenheit, with snow. Kabul is very dusty, and shoes and clothes are difficult to keep clean

Well-equipped medical facilities are few throughout Afghanistan. European and American medicines are available in limited quantities and may be expensive or difficult to locate. There is a shortage of standard medical supplies. Basic medicines manufactured in Iran, Pakistan, and India are available, but their quality can be questionable. Travelers should bring all necessary medications, both prescription and over-the-counter. A couple of western-style private clinics have opened in Kabul recently: the DK-German Medical Diagnostic Center (http://www.medical-kabul.com) and CURE International Hospital (ph. 0799-883-830) offer a variety of care; Americans seeking treatment should request American or Western health practitioners. American travelers may seek emergency medical services at the International Security Assistance Forces (ISAF) medical facilities in the Kabul area, but routine care is not available. The ISAF Hospital and the combined forces ISAF clinic, adjacent to Kabul International Airport, may provide medical care to American citizens who can show appropriate ID and who request emergency care, but payment must be made at the time of service in USD or Euros (credit card not accepted). Shino Zada Private Hospital located in Microrayon 4, opposite the central heating center, provides general surgery, maternity care, ambulance and pharmacy facilities 24 hours a day. Imran Clinic, across from the Ministry of Interior, has limited laboratory and x-ray facilities. Contact information for medical providers in Kabul can be found on the Embassy's website: http://kabul.usembassy.gov/medical_information2.html/

Afghan public hospitals should be avoided. Individuals without government licenses or even medical degrees often operate private clinics; there is no public agency that monitors their operations. Travelers will not be able to find Western-trained medical personnel in most parts of the country outside of Kabul, although there are some international aid groups temporarily providing basic medical assistance in various cities and villages. For any medical treatment, payment is required in advance. Commercial medical evacuation capability from Afghanistan is limited and safe pick-up and transport of a patient, when available, can take 30-60 hours to accomplish. Information on vaccinations and other health precautions, such as safe food and water

precautions and insect bite protection, may be obtained from the Centers for Disease Control and Prevention's hotline for international travelers at 1-877-FYI-TRIP (1-877-394-8747) or via the CDC's Internet site at http://wwwn.cdc.gov/travel/destinationAfghanistan.aspx . For information on outbreaks of infectious diseases abroad consult the World Health Organization's website at http://www.who.int/en . Further health information for travelers is available at http://www.who.int/ith .

### LOCAL TIME, BUSINESS HOURS, AND HOLIDAYS

Local time is GMT +4.5 hours. Afghanistan government officials observe a five and a half day workweek; Thursday afternoon and Friday are off. Business hours are typically 7:30 AM to 4:30 PM, Saturdays to Thursdays. Commercial shops keep longer but varying hours, usually from 7 AM to 11 PM. Religious Holidays follow the lunar cycle and are determined by the Islamic calendar, based on the lunar cycle and the visibility of the lunar crescent. Variable Holidays include three days for Eid-ul-Qurban, three days for Eid-Al-Fitr, and one day for the Prophet's Birthday; 10th of Maharam, March 21

(Nawrooz - New Year) and August 18 (Independence Day) are fixed in the solar calendar.

### TEMPORARY ENTRY OF MATERIALS AND PERSONAL BELONGINGS

Article 114 of the Afghan Customs Code states that temporary entry goods will be taxed at 3% of the monthly total customs duty. Personal belongings, luggage and samples are exempt from payment of duty if they have no commercial purposes.

### WEB RESOURCES

State Department Travel web site http://travel.state.gov/

Embassy of Afghanistan http://www.embassyofafghanistan.org/

State Department Visa Website: http://travel.state.gov/visa/

U.S. Embassy in Afghanistan: http://kabul.usembassy.gov/

U.S. Embassy's website – medical providers: http://kabul.usembassy.gov/medical_information2.html/

U.S. Embassy's website – lawyers: http://kabul.usembassy.gov/judicial_services.html/

Centers for Dissease Control http://wwwn.cdc.gov/travel/destinationAfghanistan.aspx/

World Health Organization http://www.who.int/ith

## IMPORTANT CONTACTS

### U.S. GOVERNMENT CONTACTS

U.S. Embassy Kabul
Great Massoud Road
Tel: +1 (301) 490-1042; +93 (20) 230-0436; +93 (0) 700-108-001/002
http://kabul.usembassy.gov/

Karl W. Eikenberry, Ambassador

Ambassador William E. Todd, Coordinating Director for Development and Economic Activity
Economic/Commercial Section
Jim Boughner, Economic Counselor
Robyn Kessler, Senior Commercial Officer, robyn.kessler@trade.gov ; KesslerRF@state.gov ; Ext. 8498
Feraidoon Zaki, Commercial Specialist, ZakiFX@state.gov ; Ext. 8536
http://kabul.usembassy.gov/economicsection.html

Consular Section – American Citizen Services
Tel: +93 (0) 700-108-499
Email: usconsulkabul@state.gov
http://kabul.usembassy.gov/information_for_travelers.html

Consular Section – Visa Services
Email: Afghanvisainfo@state.gov
http://kabul.usembassy.gov/visas.html

U.S. Department of Commerce
Afghanistan Investment and Reconstruction Task Force
Susan H. Mann, Director
1401 Constitution Avenue, N.W.
Washington, DC 20230
Tel: +1 (202) 482-1812
Fax: +1 (202) 482-0980
Email: AfghanInfo@ita.doc.gov
http://trade.gov/afghanistan/

The Advocacy Center
1401 Constitution Avenue, N.W., Rm. 3814-A
Washington, DC 20230
Tel: +1 (202) 482-3896
Fax: +1 (202) 482-3508
Bryan Lopp, Country Manager, Afghanistan
Tel: +1 (202) 482-4519
Email: Bryan.Lopp@trade.gov
http://www.export.gov/advocacy

U.S. Agency for International Development (USAID) - Afghanistan
Great Massoud Road
Earl W. Gast, Mission Director
Robert Hellyer, Senior Deputy Mission Director
Tel: +1 (202) 216-6288
Email: kabulusaidinformation@usaid.gov
http://afghanistan.usaid.gov/en/Index.aspx

USAID/Washington Headquarters
Robyn Melzig, Afghanistan Desk Officer
1300 Pennsylvania Avenue, N.W.
Ronald Reagan Building
Washington, DC 20523-1000
Tel: +1 (202) 712-0518; +1 (202) 712-0316
Email: rmelzig@usaid.gov

Overseas Private Investment Corporation (OPIC)
John Aldonas, Managing Director, Small & Medium Enterprise Finance
1100 New York Avenue, N.W.
Washington, DC 20527
Tel: +1 (202) 336-8400
Fax: +1 (202) 408-9859
Email: John.Aldonas@opic.gov
http://www.opic.gov

U.S. Trade & Development Agency (USTDA)
Scott Greenip, Country Manager, Afghanistan
1000 Wilson Boulevard, Suite 1600
Arlington, VA 22209
Tel: +1 (703) 875-4357
Fax: +1 (703) 875-4009
Email: sgreenip@ustda.gov
http://www.ustda.gov/

Export-Import Bank of the U.S. (Ex-Im)
811 Vermont Avenue, N.W.
Washington, DC 20571 Tel: +1 (202) 565-3946 (EXIM); +1 (800) 565-3946 (EXIM)
http://www.exim.gov

### INTERNATIONAL FINANCIAL INSTITUTIONS CONTACTS

World Bank
House 19, Street 15, Wazir Akbar Khan
Kabul, Afghanistan
Contact: Abdul Raouf Zia
Tel: +93 (0) 702-80-800
Email: azia@worldbank.org
http://www.worldbank.org/af

U.S. Commercial Service Liaison to World Bank – Washington, DC
David Fulton, Senior Commercial Officer
Tel: +1 (202) 458-0120
Email: David.Fulton@trade.gov

Asian Development Bank
Afghanistan Resident Mission
Robert Gordon Rinker, Country Director
P. O. Box 3070 Kabul, Afghanistan Tel: +93 (20) 210-3602; +63 (2) 632-5535 Email: afrm@adb.org
http://www.adb.org/Afghanistan/main.asp

U.S. Commercial Service Liaison to Asian Development Bank – Manila, Philippines
Joel Fischl, Senior Commercial Officer
Tel: +63 (2) 887-1345
Email: Joel.Fischl@trade.gov

### AFGHAN GOVERNMENT CONTACTS

Afghanistan Investment Support Agency (AISA)
Tel: +93 (20) 210-3404

Email: info@aisa.org.af , invest@aisa.gov.af
http://www.aisa.org.af

Mr. Noorullah Delawari
President & CEO
Tel: +93 (0) 700-276-741
Email: delawari@aisa.org.af

Mr. Naseem Akbar
Vice President
Tel: +93 (0) 700-288-304
Email: NaseemA@aisa.org.af

Embassy of Afghanistan
Mr. Murtaza Bahrami, Acting Commercial Attaché
Economic, Trade and Investment Department
2341 Wyoming Avenue, N.W.
Washington, DC 20006
Tel: +1 (202) 483-6410
Fax: +1 (202) 483-6487
Email: bahrami@afghanistanembassy.org , commerce@embassyofafghanistan.org
http://www.embassyofafghanistan.org

Afghanistan Reconstruction and Development Services (ARDS)
Email: ards.procurement@ards.org.af
http://www.ards.gov.af
Ministry of Commerce & Industry Dr. Anwar ul-haq Ahady, Minister of Commerce
Abdul Hamid Rahimi , Secretary to the Minister
Tel: +93 (20) 250-0356
Email: info@commerce.gov.af
http://www.commerce.gov.af

Ministry of Finance
Dr. Omar Zakhilwal, Minister of Finance
Abdul Razaq Vahidi, Acting Chief of Staff
Tel: +93 (20) 210-3272
Email: info@mof.gov.af
http://www.mof.gov.af

Export Promotion Agency of Afghanistan (EPAA)
Mr. Ahmad Jawaid, CEO
Tel: +93 (0) 700 211 135
Email: ahmad.jawaid@epaa.org.af
Mr. Fazel Wasit, Deputy CEO
Tel: +93 (0) 787 381 150
fwasit@epaa.org.af
http://www.epaa.org.af

Afghan National Standards Authority (ANSA)
Dr. Mujiburrahman Khateer, Technical Deputy Director General
Tel: +93 (0) 752-045-158; +93 (0) 700-215-246
Email: admin.ansa@gmail.com
http://www.ansa.gov.af

### PRIVATE SECTOR CONTACTS

American Chamber of Commerce in Afghanistan (AmCham Afghanistan)
Mr. Dom LaVigne, Executive Director
Tel: +93 (0) 702-032-323
Email: Dom@amcham-af.org
http://www.amcham-af.org

Afghanistan Chamber of Commerce & Industries (ACCI)
Mr. Mohammed Qurban Haqjo, CEO/President
Tel: +93 (0) 752-025-854; +93 (0) 707 644 482
Email: ceoacci@acci.org.af
Mr. Atiqullah Nusrat, Chief Operating Officer
Tel: +93 (0) 799 462 388; +93 (0) 787 698 952
Email: atiqullah.nusrat@acci.org.af
http://www.acci.org.af

Afghan-American Chamber of Commerce (AACC)
Mr. Sulaiman Lutfi, Chairman
Hon. Don Ritter, President & CEO
8201 Greensboro Drive, Suite 103
McLean, VA 22102
Tel: +1 (703) 442-5005
Fax: +1 (703) 442-5008
Email: info@a-acc.org
http://www.a-acc.org

Afghan California Business Council (ACBC)
Mr. Asad Zafari, President
Tel: +1 (925) 776-1701; +93 (0) 708-770-986 Email: asad@afghancaliforniabusinesscouncil.org ; asad@acbconline.org
http://www.afghancaliforniabusinesscouncil.org ; http://www.acbconline.org

Afghanistan Builders Association (ABA)
Mr. Naeem Yassin, President
Tel: +93 (0) 786-363-650; +93 (0) 700-224-822
Email: aba@aba.af ; Yassin@aba.af
http://www.aba.af

## INFORMATION AND CONTACTS FOR DOING BUSINESS

### INVESTING IN AFGHANISTAN

The Afghan Investment Support Agency (AISA) is responsible for registering all foreign and domestic businesses in Afghanistan and assisting companies with navigating the multitude of profitable investment opportunities in Afghanistan. The World Bank's Doing Business Survey has consistently rated AISA's ability to register a new business among the best in the world, with fewer procedures than any other developing country or even the United States!

Market Information, including reports from world experts in the field, on Afghanistan's many vibrant economic sectors from agriculture to telecommunications.

The Afghanistan Chamber of Commerce and Industry is the leading private sector organization in Afghanistan. They can also assist prospective investors to find partners and navigate the exciting Afghan market. Their global partners include:
Afghan-American Chamber of Commerce (McLean, VA)
Afghan Business Council in Dubai

The American Chamber of Commerce of Afghanistan (AmCham/Af) is affiliated with the U.S. Chamber of Commerce. The AmCham/Af is located in Afghanistan and hosts events, incoming delegations, and international businesses and corporations. The AmCham/Af is endorsed by the US Ambassador to Afghanistan and works closely in-country with the Department of Commerce to attract and support international business. AmCham/Af's mission is to promote US business interests in Afghanistan and members have access to a vast network of business information and contacts in country. Highly respected, long-term American, Afghan and Asian companies belong to the AmCham.

Afghanistan Procurement Directory, a vetted company directory produced by the Canadian NGO Peace Dividend Trust, can help you find a partner for your business venture in Afghanistan.

## IMPORTING AFGHAN PRODUCTS

Afghan craftsmen are world famous for their handmade carpets and jewelry, while Afghan's fertile soil fed by deep snow-fed aquifers produce world-class quality agricultural products. Top exports to the United States include handmade carpets, gemstones, pine nuts, licorice root, and other dried fruits and nuts. Regional exports include raisins, pistachios, pomegranates, onions, and marble/granite materials. For more information on some of these specific sectors, refer to our Market Informationpage, which features reports from world experts in the field, or contact the Afghanistan Investment and Reconstruction Task Force at: 1-202-482-1812 or AfghanInfo@trade.gov.

The Export Promotion Agency of Afghanistan is dedicated to promoting Afghanistan's processing, marketing, and distribution of its many commodities. It is primarily focused on Afghanistan's three most export competitive sectors: agricultural goods (especially dried fruits and nuts), carpets, and mined materials (especially marble and gemstones).

Afghanistan Procurement Directory, a vetted company directory produced by the Canadian NGO Peace Dividend Trust, can help you find a vendor for the Afghan goods or services you seek.

Treasury Clarification on Iran Transshipment
*March 13, 2008*
The Treasury Department's Office of Foreign Assets Control (OFAC) issued some interpretative guidance regarding U.S. imports of Afghan goods, which have transshipped Iran. In summary, U.S. persons (citizens, companies, etc.) are allowed to import, purchase, resell, etc. carpets and foodstuffs (fruits, nuts, spices, etc.) whether or not they transshipped Iran. Indeed, U.S. persons are allowed to even engage in loading such Afghan goods at an Iranian port. For further details, please refer to the OFAC letter or to the OFAC website on U.S. sanctions policy towards Iran.

Gemstones, Jewelry, and Handicraft Products from Afghanistan
A list of various sources for Afghan-origin products!

## CONTRACTING/EXPORTING TO AFGHANISTAN

### *U.S. Government*

Federal Business Opportunities (FedBizOpps.Gov) The primary portal for U.S. government procurement opportunities. TheVendors Guide details the process of searching for procurement opportunities. Vendors may initiate a search for Afghanistan-related procurement opportunities by selecting the Find Business Opportunities link on the FedBizOpps.gov homepage and creating a search for Afghanistan.

The Joint Contingency Contracting System is a database of existing DOD contracts available in Afghanistan.

Central Contractor Registration (CCR) Database is where U.S. companies seeking U.S. Government prime contracts are required to register prior to award of any federal contract, basic agreement, basic ordering agreement, or blanket purchase agreement on or after October 01, 2003. Please also refer to the Central Contractor Registration (CCR) Handbook (900KB PDF only) for more information.

The U.S. Agency for International Development (USAID) in Afghanistan has numerous projects to expand economic opportunity, agricultural productivity, and improve the efficiency and accountability of government. Some procurement opportunities can be found on project specific websites such as:
Afghanistan Infrastructure and Rehabilitation Program

### *Related Information*

Contingency Contracting and Contractor on the Battlefield Policy, Guidance, Doctrine, and Other Relevant Information
Background information on contracting with the U.S. military in a battlefield.

Guide to Determining Business Size (120KB PDF only)
The Pentagon Renovation Program's "Guideline to Small Business Size Determination and Category Definitions" helps U.S. companies understand how to qualify as a small business.

Defense Base Act (DBA) Insurance Coverage
The U.S. Department of Commerce offers a guide to Defense Base Act insurance coverage, a requirement on all U.S. government contractors and subcontractors working outside the United States to cover civilian employees, including U.S. citizens, as well as third-country and local nationals.

Federal Acquisition Regulation (FAR)

## AFGHAN GOVERNMENT

### *Procurement Unit*

The Procurement Unit of the Afghan government is the main facilitator for the awarding of contracts on behalf of Afghan ministries and the municipality of Kabul. The Unit is supervised by the Minister of Planning and Minister of Reconstruction and is part of the Afghanistan Reconstruction and Development Services. The World Bank and the Asian Development Bank

(ADB) fund the majority of projects. Interested firms are advised to register using the "PU registration" link on the home page.

The Unit contacts consultants and firms from this registry. Firms may also register by e-mailing information toprocurement@afghanistangov.org. Companies are also encouraged to refer to industry ministry websites for sector specific opportunities.

## MULTILATERAL DEVELOPMENT BANKS

### *World Bank*

The World Bank is the most active multilateral institution in Afghanistan. Since April 2002, the World Bank has committed $456 million in grants and $436 million in loans for projects in Afghanistan.
The World Bank also manages the Afghanistan Reconstruction Trust Fund (ARTF), which provides a coordinated financing mechanism to the Interim Administration of Afghanistan. Funded by more than $400 million from donor countries, the Trust Fund helps with priority projects and programs to rebuild Afghanistan and facilitate the return of skilled expatriate Afghans to the country. It also provides short-term emergency funding for salaries of civil servants.

The World Bank projects such as those listed below, include infrastructure, transportation, agriculture, and public administration. Read the complete list of World Bank projects in Afghanistan.

Information about procurement opportunities from the World Bank (and other international donors) can be obtained for a fee from the United Nations Development Business.
U.S. firms may obtain assistance and more information about World Bank projects from the U.S. Commercial Liaison to the World Bank.
Contact:

U.S. Commercial Liaison to the World Bank
Mr. Will Center, Senior Commercial Officer
Tel: (202) 458-0120
Fax: (202) 477-2967
E-mail: wcenter@worldbank.org
Website: www.buyusa.gov/worldbank

### *Asian Development Bank (ADB)*

The ADB is a multilateral development finance institution dedicated to reducing poverty in Asia and the Pacific. The ADB plans to extend $600 million in assistance from 2004 through 2006 in the areas of natural resources, transport, energy, financial services, and the public sector. Read the complete list of ADB projects in Afghanistan.

The Asian Development Bank projects include:
Promoting International Trade and Cross-Border Trade Facilitation
Consulting firms and consultants must register on the ADB's DACON (Data on Consulting Firms) and DICON (Data on Individual Consultants) systems in order to be able to submit Expressions of Interest.

Information about procurement opportunities from the Asian Development Bank (and other international donors) can be obtained for a fee from the United Nations Development Business. U.S. firms may obtain assistance and more information about ADB projects from the Office of the Commercial Liaison to the ADB in Manila. This office works closely with the Office of the U.S. Executive Director to the ADB to increase American awareness of, and participation in, the ADB's activities.
Contact:

U.S. Commercial Liaison to the ADB
Mr. Frank Foster, Senior Commercial Officer
Tel: (63-2) 887-1345
Fax: (63-2) 887-1164
E-mail: manila.adb.office.box@mail.doc.gov
Website: www.buyusa.gov/adb

# AFGHANISTAN'S NATURAL RESOURCES

## AFGHANISTAN

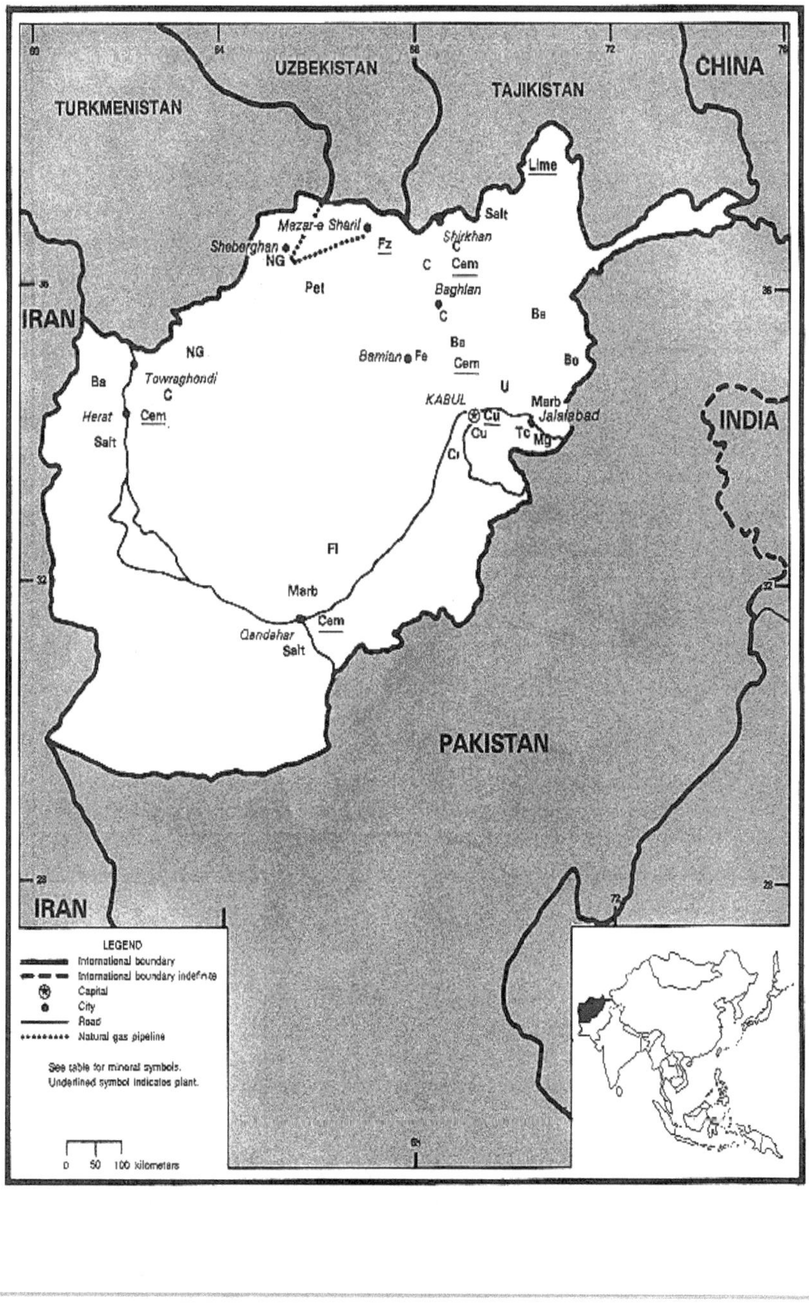


AGRICULTURE

The Afghan economy continues to be overwhelmingly agricultural, despite the fact that only 15% of its total land area is arable and less than 6% currently is cultivated. Agricultural production is constrained by an almost total dependence on erratic winter snows and spring rains for water; irrigation is primitive. Relatively little use is made of machines, chemical fertilizer, or pesticides.

Grain production is Afghanistan's traditional agricultural mainstay. Overall agricultural production declined an average of 3.5% per year between 1978 and 1990. This can be attributed to sustained fighting, instability in rural areas, prolonged drought, and deteriorated infrastructure. Soviet efforts to disrupt production in resistance-dominated areas also contributed to this decline. furthermore, Soviet efforts to centralize the economy through state ownership and control and consolidation of farmland into large collective farms contributed to lower production.

The war against the Soviet Union and the ensuing civil war also led to migration to the cities and refugee flight to Pakistan and Iran, further disrupting normal agricultural production. Recent studies indicate that agricultural production and livestock numbers are less than one-half of what they were in 1978. It is estimated that Afghanistan's food production levels are about 15% lower than what is necessary to feed the population. Shortages are exacerbated by the country's already limited transportation network, which has deteriorated due to damage and neglect resulting from war and the absence of an effective central government.

Opium is increasingly becoming a source of cash for many Afghans, especially since the breakdown in central authority after the Soviet withdrawal. Opium is easy to cultivate and transport and offers a quick source of income for returning refugees and other impoverished Afghans. Afghanistan is the second-largest producer of raw opium in the world, after Burma. In 1993, despite efforts by the U.S. and others to encourage alternative crops, poppy and opium production increased 8% and 7%, respectively, from a year earlier. Much of Afghanistan's opium production is shipped to laboratories in Pakistan and refined into heroin which is either consumed by a growing South Asian addict population or exported, primarily to Europe and North America.

## TRADE AND INDUSTRY

Trade accounts for a small portion of the Afghan economy, and there are no reliable statistics relating to trade flows. Since the Soviet withdrawal and the collapse of the Soviet Union, other limited trade relationships appear to be emerging with Iran, Pakistan, and the West. Afghanistan trades little with the United States; its 1992 trade is estimated at $6 million. Afghanistan does not enjoy U.S. most-favored-nation (MFN) trading status, which was revoked in 1986.

Afghanistan is endowed with a wealth of natural resources, including extensive deposits of coal, salt, chromium, iron ore, gold, fluorite, talc, copper, and lapis lazuli. Unfortunately, the country's remote and rugged terrain, and inadequate transportation network, usually have made mining these resources unprofitable.

The most important resource has been natural gas, first tapped in 1967. At their peak during the 1980s, natural gas sales accounted for $300 million a year in export revenues (56% of the total). Ninety percent of these exports went to the Soviet Union to pay for imports and debts. However, during the withdrawal of Soviet troops in 1989, Afghanistan's natural gas fields were capped to prevent sabotage by the mujahidin. Restoration of gas production has been hampered by internal strife and the disruption of traditional trading relationships following the collapse of the Soviet Union.

## TRANSPORTATION

Landlocked Afghanistan has no rail-ways, but the Amu Darya (Oxus) River, which forms part of Afghanistan's border with Turkmenistan, Uzbekistan, and Tajikistan, has barge traffic. During their occupation of the country, the Soviets completed a bridge across the Amu Darya and built a motor vehicle and railroad bridge between Termez and Jeyretan.

Most roadbuilding occurred in the 1960s, funded by the U.S. and the Soviet Union. The Soviets built a road and tunnel through the Salang Pass in 1964, connecting northern and southern Afghanistan. A highway connecting the principal cities of Herat, Kandahar, Ghazni, and Kabul forms the primary road system.

The highway system requires significant reconstruction, and regional roads are in a state of disrepair. The poor state of the Afghan transportation and communication networks has further fragmented and hobbled the struggling economy.

## ECONOMIC DEVELOPMENT AND RECOVERY

Afghanistan embarked on a modest economic development program in the 1930s. The government founded banks, introduced paper money, established a university, expanded primary, secondary, and technical schools, and sent students abroad for education. In 1956, the Afghan Government promulgated the first in a long series of ambitious development plans. By the late 1970s, these had achieved only mixed results due to flaws in the planning process as well as inadequate funding and a shortage of the skilled managers and technicians needed for implementation.

These constraints on development have been exacerbated by the flight of refugees and the disruption and instability stemming from the Soviet occupation and ensuing civil war. Today, economic recovery and long-term development will depend on establishing an effective and stable political system.

The UN and the international donor community continue to provide considerable humanitarian relief. Since its inception in 1988, the umbrella UN Office for the Coordination of Humanitarian Assistance to Afghanistan (UNOCHA) has channeled $512 million in multilateral cash assistance to Afghan refugees and vulnerable per-sons inside Afghanistan. The U.S. and Japan are the leading contributors to this relief effort. One of its key tasks is to eliminate from priority areas (such as villages, arable fields, and roads) some of the estimated 10 million land-mines which continue to litter the Afghan landscape. Afghanistan is the most heavily mined country in the world; mine-related injuries number up to 100 per month. Without successful mine clearance, refugee repatriation, political stability, and economic reconstruction will be severely constrained.

The UN, through the UN Development Program (UNDP), is expected to play a major role in post-war recovery and reconstruction of Afghanistan. In November 1993, the UNDP Action Plan for the Immediate Rehabilitation of Afghanistan identified more than $600 million in quick-impact development projects which could be implemented within two years where security conditions permit.

## THE CURRENT STATUS OF THE ECONOMY

Despite continued destruction, blockades of some of the supply routes and fighting in various parts of the country, trade and agriculture remained active. The section below provides a more elaborate study of agriculture and trade activities and their role in sustaining the Afghan economy.

## AGRICULTURE

***Increase in cereal production:*** Agriculture forms the largest sector of the economy and the source of livelihood for over 85% of the population. With the return of security to most parts of the country, following the Taliban's control over 75-80 percent of the territory, agricultural production has increased over the past few years. The Crop and Food Supply Assessment carried out by a FAO/WFP mission in 1997 and in May 1998 estimated the last two years' cereal production to be the highest in the past several years.

The total 1998 cereal production was estimated to be 3.85 million tonnes, which is 5 percent higher than 1997, and perhaps the largest since 1978. The farmers' response to high cereal prices of the year before (US$ 300 per tonne), favourable precipitation during winter and spring, and enhanced security are cited as the main factors for the increase. In the north, surplus cereal could not be moved to Kabul, Bamyan or Badakhshan provinces where food scarcity and high prices for grain prevailed due to the blockade of the supply routes. This led to a reduction in the price of wheat and other major cereals in the northern provinces.

***Food imports/dependency***: A large segment of the Afghan population still depends on food imported from abroad or that distributed by the aid community. The total import requirement for the period of June 1998 to July 1999 is estimated by FAO at 740,000 tonnes, of which an estimated 140,000 tonnes of wheat would be food assistance provided by the international community. The bulk of the remaining imported food comes from Pakistan via Torkham in the east and Chaman in the south, as well as through a few small border points in the southeast. Table 1 in Annex 1 shows the yield and production of main crops for 1997/98 and 1998/99.

***Increase in livestock production***: Livestock forms a main source of the household economy in rural areas. Many families in rural areas sell their livestock to purchase wheat during the spring months when they run out of stocks. While this sector has sustained enormous loss due to prolonged hostilities, there are indications that livestock production has improved over the past few years, especially in areas under the control of the Taliban. Table 2 in Annex 1 shows the estimated number and type of major livestock produced in Afghanistan during 1998.

***Decrease in poppy yields***: While cereal production has increased there seems to be a significant decrease in poppy yields during 1998. According to UNDCP Annual Opium Poppy Survey of 1998, although there was a 9 percent increase in poppy cultivation, UNDCP estimated a 25 percent reduction in poppy yields when compared to 1997. The total opium production for 1998 was estimated at 2,102 tonnes against a total of 2,804 tonnes in 1997. This reduction in the level of poppy production was reported to be due to unusual climatic conditions such as heavy and continuous rains and hailstorms in some of the major poppy producing provinces.

## FOOD PRICES/INFLATION

Over the past six months, Afghanistan has experienced growing inflation, which has been influenced largely by cost-push and demand-pull forces. The Afghani to US$ rate changed from 36,000 Afs. to a dollar in October 1998 to 45,000 Afs. to a dollar in mid-April 1999, a devaluation of more than 25 percent in six months.

The prices of essential items have also increased in different parts of the country. Table 3 (in Annex 1) provides a list of prices of wheat flour in six provinces for the months of October 1998 through March 1999. Tables 3 and 4 reflect an interesting picture in the Afghan markets, in particular the relationship between income through casual labour and household expenditure. For instance, in Kabul, a family of seven can earn 1.14 US$ a day if the head of the family is lucky enough to find employment, while they need to spend US$ 0.63 to buy twenty-one loaves of bread for the family.

This implies that over 50 percent of an individual's income is spent only on bread. The isolated food deficit province of Badakhshan is the most expensive place to live. During last winter, WFP distributed over 2,000 tonnes of food in nine districts of Badakhshan and approximately 4,000 tonnes to the most vulnerable populations in Hazarajat.

## LABOR MARKET

A great majority of the Afghan labour force is self-employed, mostly in agriculture and domestic trade but also, to a smaller extent, in cross-border trade. Working as a casual laborer inside Afghanistan as well as in neighboring Pakistan and Iran is another major source of employment for many Afghans. While the income from remittances is not known, Table 4 (Annex 1) provides interesting information on income through casual labor. The table reflects a downward pattern in most cities except for Kandahar, where income through casual labor has increased by 15 percent.

The worst situation prevails in Faizabad (47 percent decrease) and in Mazar-i-Sharif (43 percent decrease). In Herat and Jalalabad, income through casual labor increased between October and December last year and decreased between January and March 1999. One reason, among others, could be the reduction in demand for casual labor during the winter months. Recruitment in military activities has gone up due to the need by warring factions and lack of employment opportunities. Unemployment has increased in services, industries and other formal institutions.

## TRADE

***Domestic trade***: Despite continued conflict and blockades of supply routes in some parts of the country, domestic trade continues throughout the country. The closure of the Salang Tunnel has created many difficulties for domestic merchants, as they are no longer able to bring the agricultural products of the north to Kabul and to other parts of the country via Kabul. Even in blockaded areas, merchandise continues to move, albeit in smaller quantities and with more difficulties.

***Cross-border trade***: Cross-border trade in domestic goods and foreign commodities has increased between Afghanistan, Pakistan and Turkmenistan over the past several years. According to a recent newspaper report, there has been an 11 percent increase in the volume of trade between Afghanistan and Turkmenistan during the last year. In September 1998, the Taliban authorities signed an agreement with the Government of Turkmenistan on the import of petrol, diesel and jet fuel. The first consignment of the fuel reportedly arrived in mid-December via Torghundi.

This has, to some extent, reduced Afghanistan's dependency on fuel imports from Iran. In December, the Taliban Government signed another agreement with Turkmenistan for the import of 600 tones of liquefied natural gas.

With souring relations between the Taliban and Iran, Uzbekistan and Tajikistan, the border points with these countries have been closed and trade activities have come to a halt, which has limited Afghanistan's access to these markets for its exports and imports. However, the Torghundi border in Herat has remained open as the Taliban managed to establish a cordial relation with Turkmenistan. In the past, Afghan traders used to import goods through Bander-Abbas and Islam Qala, while now they have switched to Bander-Abbas-Turkmenistan and Torghundi, which has increased their transportation costs.

Both Pakistan and Afghanistan benefit from cross-border trade, despite their claim to have been affected by the existing trading mechanism--i.e. the Afghan Transit Trade. Under the agreement of the Afghan Transit Trade, Pakistan allows Afghanistan to have access to the sea and to undertake trade and commerce with the international community to the extent required by Afghanistan's economy and commerce requirements. Most of the goods imported under the ATT are reportedly electronics and other consumer items, which cross Pakistan's territory duty free. Some of these are then re-exported illegally through smuggling back into Pakistan.

On several occasions, the Government of Pakistan has tried to limit the amount of goods imported under the ATT by dropping some thirty items from the ATT list. In 1995, for instance, the Government of Pakistan made a unilateral decision and took seventeen items including artificial silk fibre and clothing off the list of the ATT. During an interview on 2 January 1999, Pakistan's Federal Finance Minister Ishaq Dar said that the government had requested the Afghan authorities to review their transit trade and agree either to pay duties equal to those in Pakistan or reduce the quantity of commodities to be imported (*The Frontier Post*, 3 January, 1999). The Taliban authorities have not replied to this request.

Despite these efforts by the Government of Pakistan, there are indications that the volume of re-exports from Afghanistan to Pakistan has increased during the last fiscal year. After the ban on the ATT, most of these items are imported via Gulf countries to the Afghan cities of Kandahar and Jalalabad and then re-exported into Peshawar and Quetta in Pakistan. A recent newspaper report indicates that India-made "Modi" tires are smuggled into Pakistan through Afghanistan via Central Asia and the Russian port of Vladivostok since the import of tires under the ATT was banned 1994 (Inter Press Service 20/4/99).

According to a report published by *The News* (30 December 1998), it was estimated that goods worth Rs. 23 billion (US$ 500 million) have been imported under the ATT during the current fiscal year while the same imports for the previous fiscal year amounted to RS 10 billion (approximately US$ 218 million). According to another report, between July and December 1998, the total trade has increased by around US$ 43 million over the same period in 1997 (Inter Press Service 20/4/99). According to a World Bank report, the total trade between Afghanistan and Pakistan was estimated to be US$ 2.5 billion in 1996/97, of which US$ 1.96 billion was estimated to be the value of re-exported goods from Afghanistan into Pakistan.

These examples indicate that banning the Afghan Transit Trade facility alone does not help reduce smuggling activities in Pakistan and may have negative repercussions for Pakistan in the longer term. Once Afghanistan manages to have access to other neighboring markets, they may retaliate against Pakistan's unilateral decision and strengthen their trade relations with other countries where they may have a comparative advantage.

Realising the benefit from trade, and upon requests from the business community in NWFP, the Government of Pakistan issued Statute Regulatory Order (SRO) No. 138 on 3 March 1999, which allows the export of all commodities produced or manufactured in Pakistan, excluding those produced by manufacturing bond, via land routes to Afghanistan against Pakistani rupees. These exports will not be entitled to any duty drawback or zero rating of sales tax (*The Frontier Post*, 17 March 1999).

# INVESTMENT IN MINING AND INDUSTRIES; RESPONSIBILITIES AND FACILITIES AS ENVISAGED FOR DOMESTIC AND FOREIGN INVESTORS AS PER THE LAW OF MINING AND INVESTMENT

1. Hundred percent private domestic capital.
2. Foreign and private domestic capital: private foreign and government share should not exceed then 49%.
3. Domestic, private and government joint capital: the share of government should not exceed 51%.
4. Domestic, foreign private and government joint capital: the share of government should not exceed 33% of the total capital and the foreign share 49% of the remaining capital.
5. According to the Investment Law, the Investment Promotion Department completes administration procedures of investment.

## EXEMPTIONS AND ASSISTANCE

Approved private enterprises can get benefits from the following exemptions and assistance:

6. Exemption on Income Taxes, consuming items, financial and profitable transactions taxes.
7. The exemption period is not less than two years and not more than six years. In the provinces, this period is based upon location of the enterprise, and in view of identical projects in Kabul city, it (the exemption period) will be determined by the permanent commission of the Executive Committee of the Council of Ministers for the Private Investment, which will not be less than three years.
8. At emergency cases, the extension of the exemption period beyond its approved period, will be permitted by the approval of Coordination Board of the Executive Committee of the Council of Ministers.
9. The exemption period of the private enterprise commences from the beginning of its activity.
10. The investor's income gained from the private enterprise annual profit according to exemption period, is exempted from annual tax. The extension of exemptions period after the approval of the private enterprise can not exceed 30 percent of the specified period.
11. If an approved private enterprise imports capital goods, parts, raw materials, semi-finished and finished items which can not be supplied from inside the country in order to use them for manufacturing, assembling and production as shown in Specification Form, can get benefits from the following exemption and custom assistance.

A. The exemption of the private enterprise capital goods from customs duties.
B. Based upon the total cost price of the parts (as calculated) at the Custom House of destination only 10% custom duty will be levied on the goods.
C. Five percent duty is charged on machinery imported by the private enterprise to supplement or replace private investment machinery.
D. Custom duty is charged according to the custom tariff of raw and semi-finished goods and in case which have not been prescribed in the industrial tariff, at the rate of 10% of the cost price of the materials or as per independent price.

12. The approved private enterprise in order to increase and diversify its production, can get benefits from exemption and assistance mentioned at this law after the approval of the Executive Committee of the Permanent Commission for private Investment Affairs of the Council of Ministers.

13. The approved Investment while completing their legal documentation, will be exempted from stamp taxes, registration fees and other related taxes at courts. But the Court services fee will be charged at the rate of One Afghani per Thousand Afghanis of the total amount.
14. The export of production of private enterprise, while its export is permissible(item) is exported by the private enterprise itself, is exempted from custom tax payment.
15. At those places which are specified for Industrial Parks, the Government will give the required land at the disposal of the private enterprise after the payment of its price. The price of the land is determined according to the price which the government has paid, including some basic expenses paid by the government, but it should not exceed than the triple price of the same land that the government has paid.
16. It is the duty of the Emirate to build up roads, electric system, security posts, communication system, fire extinguishing and water network systems and canalization for the industrial parks.
17. The safety of the private entrepreneurs as well as the industrial parks, is guaranteed by the Emirate and it will encourage and support them for further promotions.
18. It is the duty of the Emirate to provide materials and possibilities under its monopoly to private enterprises with favorable conditions.
19. The private enterprise has the duty to carry out some activities during the exemption period. If, due to some reasons, it is dissolved before the exemption period or it is not able to perform its duty and if these reasons couldn't satisfy the authorities, the entrepreneur is duty - bound to pay his custom duty, taxes and other obligation of the Emirate.
20. The private enterprise's internal and external debt interest is deductable as expenditure at the annual balance.

## REGARDING MINES

1. Entrepreneur can invest for the purpose of study, search and extraction of the following minerals provided the share of government is (51%) together with domestic and foreign enterprise:
Burning items (crude oil, natural gas, coal tar), semi precious stones (lapis- lazuli, serpentine Granite) colored metals (Copper, Lead, Zinc, Aluminium), black metals (iron, manganese (Mg)), scarce metals like Lithium Li, Berelium Be, Tantalum TA, Neubium NB, Sesium CS, Tin Sn, Molbodeum MO, Welfram W, Robedum RU,
Cadmium Cd, Starriest St, and semi metals (Besmote BI, Antemone St, Arsenic As, Mercury Hg).

2. The study and extraction of non-metal items, optical items, the tariff of decorative and mass constructional items, under ground deep water, mineral water, naphta water can be undertaken with domestic and external entrepreneurs with participation or without participation of government.
3. The export of precious stones, precious metals and crude items outside the country in order to sell them is prohibited. Precious metals before their monolect, and precious stones before their engraving, prior to their price being determined and added to the government income, are considered as crude items.
4. Government with the approval of Council of Ministers at some special occasions can export some engraved special stone to foreign country after the sorting out and specifying of their prices for selling purposes.
5. The crude materials of colored metals and their concentrates can be exported to foreign countries by the proposal of the Council of Ministers and the approval of the Emirate Authority.
6. The crude materials of other mineral items could be exported abroad for sale by the proposal of the Ministry of Mines and Industries and the approval of the Council of Ministers.
7. The import of mineral items from abroad is forbidden, if the same items with the same quality to meet the requirements is available in the country.
8. Those mineral items identified as first necessities could be sold with government subsidy.
9. The completion of the mining project phase is the basic prerequisite for utilization.

10. The permission of the activities in the mining activities for physical and incorporate persons is given by the Ministry of Mines and Industries based upon a contract according to the articles of domestic foreign private investment law.
11. Domestic and foreign private entrepreneurs are duty bound to utilize the local experts for running of their activities and to pay keen attention to uplift scientifical and technical knowledge of their employees.
12. According to the mining Law, the basic conditions for the contract are as follows:

A. Specify the boundary of the area of activities on the map.
B. Specify the type of activity and its period.
C. Specify of the mines and estimate of the mineral amounts to be extracted.

13. Those additional mining materials gained during the study and utilization process by domestic and foreign private entrepreneurs which are not specified in the contract signed by both sides, belong to the state.
14. Those domestic and foreign entrepreneurs which according to the Law obtain right to carry out activities in the field of mining, have the following responsibilities:

A. Have to observe the Mining Law and its related instructions during the study and extraction of the minerals.
B. Have to observe safety techniques and environmental norms and principles.
C. Have to submit the result of their activities (1/3) copies to the authorities at the Ministry at the end of their activities.

15. Domestic and foreign private entrepreneurs are not allowed to sell items of first necessity minerals items at more than 10% profit in the domestic market.
16. Domestic and foreign entrepreneurs can export the surplus first necessity materials abroad according to the instructions and articles of the Law.
17. If during the implementation of this Law and its rules and regulations, some conflicts arise between the Ministry of Mines and domestic or foreign entrepreneurs, such conflicts shall be settled through the articles of Domestic and Foreign private Investment Law and those international conventions which have been accepted by Afghanistan.

## FACTORIES FOR INVESTMENT

| Factory | Area | Product | Working |
|---|---|---|---|
| Kabul Textile Mill | Kabul | 1.6 million mtr silk cloth | 100% |
| Kandhar Textile Mill | Kandhar | 6 million mtr silk cloth<br>500 ton wool | 100% |
| Kandhar Cotton Textile | Kandhar | 40 million mtr cloth<br>1000 ton wool | 70% |
| Herat Cotton Textile | Herat | 12.5 million mtr cloth<br>500 ton thread | 100% |
| Afghan Roll Industry | Kabul | 420,000 mtr cotton cloth | 100% |

| | | | |
|---|---|---|---|
| | | and blankets | |
| Gulbahar Cotton Textile | Kapisa | 52 million mtr cloth and dying | 100% |
| Jabul-us-Siraj Textile | Parwan | 6 million mtr double cloth | 100% |
| Kabul Thread Textile | Kabul | 1,200 cotton thread | 50% |
| Kabul Textile | Kabul | 2.8 million mtr woollen cloth | 50% |
| Herat Cement Factory | Herat | 210,000 tonne | 80% |
| Jabal-us-Siraj Cement Fac. | Parwan | 20,000 tonne | 100% |
| Marble Factory | Helmund | | 90% |
| Herat Sailo | Herat | 200 tonne wheat | 100% |
| Afghan Productive Factory | | 40,000 ton soap<br>7,500 tyres and shoes | 100% |
| Oxygen Plant | Kabul | 1.350 million ltr oxygen | 0% |
| Sailo Kabul | Kabul | 50,000 tonne wheat,<br>120,000 ton flour,<br>200 tonne bread | 10% |
| Ukab Shoe Factory | Kabul | 36,000 pairs | 0% |
| Afghan Carpenter | Kabul | | 40% |
| Baghrami Cott. Textile Mill | Kabul | 20 million mtr cloth | 0% |
| Guzarghah Textile | Kabul | 305 million mtr cloth | 0% |
| Marble Stone | Kabul | | 100% |
| Kandhar Fruit Factory | Kandhar | 300 tonne packing | 40% |
| Sailo Kandhar | Kabul | 20,000 tonne flour & wheat | 0% |
| Jungluck Steel Mill | Kabul | Machine's and engines | 0% |

## ECONOMIC SYSTEM

The present economic relations of the people, which constitutes the economic order of the country, is thoroughly built upon oppression and injustice. This economic order is the outcome of all corruptions, immoralities, cruelties and injustice of secular systems and regimes. The erroneous economic policies adopted by the non-Islamic regimes have actually developed these corruptions even further. Unless basic changes have been introduced in economic order of the country, the realisations and maintenance of fair justice and equity will never materialize. These basic changes or amendments should be brought about in the light of vital Islamic principles under the auspices of which the lawful rights of the people will be guaranteed. The life-restoring Islamic Guidance is very explicit regarding the economic order. Islamic jurisprudence has also explained the matter thoroughly.

The economic order which we want to materialize will be based on clear explanations of Islamic Jurisprudence and principles. The economic policy of Islamic order should possess the following merits:

a. Observance of justice and equity in all aspects of the economic order.
b. Complete eradication of various types of oppression and injustice and unlawful exploitation.
c. Creation of suitable conditions for the uniform and favourable work and profits for all.
d. Persistent struggle against hunger and poverty as well as indefatigable efforts for providing conditions so that nobody will be deprived of their natural and lawful rights.
e. Active and just possessions of national and social capitals.

In order to achieve the afore-mentioned aims, the working schedule of the Hezb in the economic field will sum-up as follows:

**AGRICULTURE**

1. For the last many years, as a result of despotic and secular regimes in the country, unlawful differences and privileges came into being regarding the ownership of agricultural lands and profiting from them. In an effort to eradicate any traces of such injustices and atrocities, the following steps will be taken:
2. Unlawful ownership which came to pass as a result of usurpation of ruling circles and which were misappropriate to the powerful landlords, will all be confiscated according to lawful principles and redistributed to their true owners.
3. State-owned fertile lands will be placed at the disposal of peasants who do not own land at all, (or do not have enough land in their ownership) either free of charge or on terms of easy instalment. When redistributing the land, priority will be given to the deserving local inhabitants.
4. Rules and regulations enacted by Islamic Religious code in connection with ownership of land and agricultural transactions of this nature will be completely stopped .
5. When distributing the state-owned lands it would be endeavoured as far as possible, that each family's share is such so as to ensure them a decent living standard.
6. Measures will be adopted so that reasonable and suitable prices of the products are directly paid to the owners and not through middle-men. This rule will particularly be applied to cotton harvests.
7. For maintaining a healthy development of agriculture, agricultural equipment and appliances, fertilizers and improved seeds of their own choice will be placed at the disposal of the peasants at a reasonable prices.
8. As a gesture of cooperation, the peasants and farmers will be supplied with interest-free loans.
9. For preservation, development and proper use of forests, necessary plans will be drawn out. Public pastures and grazing lands used by livestock owners shall, under no circumstances, be usurped.
10. Expect under conditions required by Islamic principles and/or economic policies, agricultural lands shall never be utilized for industrial or residential projects.

11. Attention will be drawn, as early as possible, to expand and better develop livestock breeders, there will be adequate and substantial facilities and incentives provided in this respect. The meadows and grazing lands will be thoroughly preserved and protected.
12. Difficulties emanating from food-grain deficiency will be overcome by the following fundamental plans:
    a. Lands which are suitable for cultivation but have been left barren for unknown reasons, will be made cultivable as soon as practicable.
    b. In order to further develop agricultural lands, hitherto barren lands will be reclaimed and prepared for cultivation.
    c. All-out efforts will be made for the construction of dams, dikes and canals for irrigation purposes of arid lands.
    d. Necessary steps will be taken in respect to food-grain transactions in an effort to curb price increase and scarcity of food supplies on the one hand, and on the other, the peasants and farmers will get a reasonable price for their products. This will also indirectly benefit the consumer.
    e. A balance will be maintained between food-grain production and commercial goods which will result in preventing shortage of food-grains.
13. In order to augment income of the peasants and, at the same time, put a stop to unemployment, the cottage industry will be further developed in the rural areas.

## COMMERCE AND INDUSTRY

Wealth and Capitals have been left stagnant in the hands of a limited few, because of unrealistic policies of secular regimes in the country. For reinvesting these for the realisation of national interests, the following lawful steps will be taken:

1. Transactions in usury, gambling, impermissible sales, hoarding and other means of earning which have been prohibited by Islam, will be legally banned. Lawful ways and means of becoming wealthy, will be recognized officially. Similarly, capitals that have found their way into private ownership will also be dealt with accordingly.
2. Administration of joint-stock companies and banks will be entrusted to elected representatives from among the share holders and partners.
3. In order to encourage, expand and develop small scale enterprises, beside supplying them with aid funds, other necessary measures will also be adopted.
4. To determine the rates of industrial products, measures will be adopted so that equally benefit both plant owners as well as consumers.
5. It will be required of the companies and industrial plants to manufacture or produce only necessary equipment and appliances and to refrain from producing articles of luxury.
6. As regards commercial transactions and production of industrial goods, stress will be laid on home requirements.
7. The state will oversee only that section of local industry which will be of vital importance and any interference in their affairs might prove harmful to national interests. We are in no way interested to nationalize local industries.
8. The present banking system will be converted to limited partnership and cooperation, according to Islamic principles.
9. In complete preparedness for the defence of the country, we attach great importance to the manufacture of armaments on a vast scale.
10. Heavy industry will be introduced whereas for the development and expansion of light industry, necessary measures will be adopted and maximum advantage will be taken in this respect from the experience of other nations.

11. We prefer to promote and expand industry in suitable regions and under no circumstances, will agree to keep it at special and predetermined areas.
12. In the course of activities taking place for the industrialization of the country, more importance will be given to requirements and job-creation rather than capital and investment.
13. The state will be duty-bound to place strict sanctions and bans on the import on the import of items that are already being manufactured at home. This state will be duty-bound to place strict sanctions and bans on import of items that are already being manufactured at home. This measure will only be taken for the promotion and development of local industries.

## WAGES OF LABOURERS AND LOW-RANKING CIVIL SERVANTS

1. The present system of payments which, because of various factors, are very unreasonable, will be adjusted gradually. When determining the salaries, prices of consumer items will always be considered. Accordingly, the minimum salary or wage will be such so as to suffice the purchase of essentials for a decent living of a family. With the rise in the price of basic food items or other consumer goods, the salaries will be readjusted proportionately.
2. Extra facilities will be provided for the labourers and low-ranking government employees to enable them to overcome their problems as regards housing, health-care and proper and healthy education and training of their children. As for allotting the salaries or wages of industrial officials and workers, measures adopted by the government will be such that according to the conditions of Art. 77 above, the officials and workers will have an incentive for further development and promotion of the country's industry.
3. Legalisation will be formulated and approved in connection with labour, workers and capital which should maintain a cooperative relation between the capital and the labour on the basis of cooperation. These would also ensure the legitimate rights of the workers. In the event of disputes arising between the worker(s) and propietor(s), an endeavour will be made to seek Islamic ways and means for a just and fait solution.
4. Child labour will be avoided by all possible means. Furthermore, necessary measures will be adopted for the healthy growth of children.
5. Co-working systems of men and women working together in the premises will be totally banned and Islamic principles will, strictly be adhered to in this respect.
6. When a worker gets sick while on duty, necessary arrangements will be made for his (her) treatment. If his injury is to such an extent that will be compensated for equitably and justly. When retired, however, he will receive a continuous and regular retirement benefit.
7. The law will also ensure individual's rights to demand what he is legally entitled to. The government will be duty-bound to hear the inhabitant's claims and to defend their rights. The government's programme of work regarding complaints of the people, will be prepared in such a way so that someone will be made available to attend to the matter in the shortest possible time.

## GENERAL ECONOMIC REFORMS

1. Preparations will get under way to collect alms, charities, tithes, donations etc. through government departments for redistribution in the proper and permissible channels. Products that have no legal basis, will be completely banned.
2. The economic policy of the country will be formulated by a committee of elected representatives of the nation and will be applicable after ratification by the parliament.
3. The treasury will be filtered from the least traces of unlawful shares, dividends or contributions.

4. Impermissible investments in unlawful cases will be prohibited, and wasteful expenditures will be prevented. The government will be, particularly, watchful in this respect over the construction of luxurious buildings.
5. Factors leading to higher prices of consumer goods, will be ended.
6. Effective and persistent efforts will be made to end unemployment.
7. Facilities will be provided so that a minimum of expenses will be required for medical examinations and treatment.
8. Wide and effective steps will be taken towards expansion and development of hospitals.
9. In order to prevent the disabled, the destitute and the blind from taking to streets for begging purposes, they will be supplied basic food items together with adequate allowance from the state treasury. They will also be provided with regular religious training.

## AFGHANISTAN LANDMINE

- Over 530 square kilometers of Afghanistan have now been identified as contaminated by Mines and UXOs (unexploded ordinance). Some 149 square kilometers have been identified as priority one, or areas which have immediate impact on people's lives (residential areas, commercial areas, agricultural land, irrigation canals, roads and grazing areas). Afghanistan has 10 million land mines. Figure provided by the United Nations Office for the Coordination of Humanitarian Assistance to Afghanistan.

- The capital Kabul is the most heavily mined capital city in the World. The UN estimated in 1993 that 162 of Afghanistan's 356 districts were affected by mines;177 districts were mine free;and 17 were still unsurveyed. Minefields constituted 466 sq km; 118 sq km were designated as high priority for mine removal. In that report by the MCPA Report of the National Survey of the Mine Situation, five provinces out of 29 surveyed had the largest amount of total mines: Helmand 26%; Kandahar 10.4%; Paktia 9.6%; Logar 8.6%; Herat 7.25%. The survey found that agricultural land accounted for 20.2% of mined areas, irrigation systems 6%, roads 2.4%, residential areas 1.2%, grazing land 75.6%. The survey broke down figures for the most affected provinces. Helmand: five high priority minefields; Kandahar: 47 high priority minefields; Paktia: 118 high priority minefields; Logar: 53 high priority minefields; Herat: 86 high priority minefields.

- Mine clearance teams in Afghanistan report finding literally dozens of types of landmines, mainly from the ex-USSR, but also from Belgium, Italy, US and the UK. The most infamous mine used during the Soviet Union's occupation period was the so-called 'butterfly' mine. Helicopter crews dropped untold numbers (figures range into the millions) of the small mines from the air. They were designed to flutter to the ground without exploding, and to thousands of children they resembled butterflys or toys. But one wing of the mine was filled with liquid explosive, designed to ignite and explode on contact, severing hands.

- Deminers have found the Valmara 69 mine, made in Italy in Afghanistan. The Valmara 69 is a bounding mine. When stepped on it leaps 45 cm into the air, and shatters into more than 1000 metal splinters, causing casualties within a 25 meter radius. There was also widespread use of Anti-tank mines, which have the capacity to destroy vehicles of any size and kill and injure dozens of victims.

- During the fighting an estimated 50% of Afghan villages were destroyed, and an estimated 25% of paved roads ruined. Crop harvests were seriously affected. Afghanistan is now rated by UNDP as 171 out of 173 countries in terms of poverty and development.

**1996**

- Cleared a total of 80 square kilometers of high priority area;
- Destroyed over 200,000 devices (mines and unexploded ordnance);
- Surveyed a total of 110 square kilometers;
- Provided mine awareness briefings to three million people;
- Trained and employed over 3,100 employees.

- Most of the high priority mined areas around the regional centres of Herat, Takhar and Jalalabad and other provinces and cities such as Badghis, Baghlan, Bamyan, Khost, Kunar, Laghman, Nimroz, Oruzgan and Wardak have been cleared. Hundreds of thousands of refugees waiting in the neighboring countries to return to these areas, especially to Beghlan, Herat, Jalalabad, Kunar and Khost either have returned or at least do not see mines as the main obstacle to their return, as they did in the early 1990s.

- Although the war in Afghanistan affected the whole country, the provinces bordering Iran and Pakistan (the western, southern and eastern parts) were the most heavily mined. Security belts were established around the major cities close to the Iranian and Pakistani borders, such as Herat, Kandahar, Jalalabad and Khost. The same tactic was followed in strategic places outside the cities, such as airports, government installations and power stations.

- Afghanistan, laden with an estimated 10 million mines, has been memorably described as resembling one big minefield. Grazing lands, waterways, schools, paths, villages and cities are infested with mainly Anti-personal mines. Mines are responsible for depopulating vast tracts of the countryside, affecting food supplies into the cities and crop harvests.

- The mine infestation affects both rural and urban populations. Kabul is the third largest mined area in the country, mainly due to the Taliban winter offensive of 1994/95, when many neighborhoods were mined after residents fled to safe havens outside the capital. The extent of the problem became apparent after government forces restored order and residents returned unaware of the danger. In Apr. 95 ICRC recorded 1,500 mine casualties.

- The Mine Clearance Programme (MCP) rushed 11 clearance teams into Kabul, in addition to seven survey teams and five dog teams. Halo Trust has four teams in Kabul. Demining in Kabul is slow because so much of the city is in ruins. Mined areas are full of metal fragments and shrapnel, rendering useless mine detectors. Mines have been found on rooftops and in underground passageways.

- In 1995 Vietnam Veterans of America Foundation (VVAF) reported that in a survey of households in 4,990 villages,277 refugee families, and 1,432 resettled families, mines severely impacted on agricultural activities. "In the rural villages surveyed, the food production of 43% of the families interviewed was affected by landmines. Landmine contamination prevents the cultivation of additional land totalling 150% of the agricultural land currently under cultivation." Eighty percent of families cited the presence of mines on their land, and 16% cited mines affecting their irrigation channels. Among the village families, 40,039 animals were killed by mines.

- The national infrastructure is seriously impacted by mines. UNOCHA estimated in mid-95 that 327 stretches of road still awaited clearance, a total of 14,731,114 sqm. The estimated cost of demining roads is .80 cents per sqm. Electrical pylons are mined. The country's largest dam,

Kajakai, was out of operation for ten years because it was mined. Power pylons linking that dam to Kandahar, and the Sarobi dam to Kabul, are mined.

- The repatriation of refugees back to Afghanistan is often contingent on landmines. In a 1995 VVAF field survey, 18% of refugee families in Pakistan said that mines were responsible for them leaving. Thirty-one percent reported mines preventing them from growing crops. Humanitarian organisations report mine incidents increasing after refugees have returned from exile. "During the mass return in 1992, casualty rates jumped to two or three times the rate recorded during the same period in the previous year," reports VVAF. "One study carried out during a six month period in Peshawar in 1992 indicated that 77% of mine victims were returnees."

## Casualties:

Oct 98 - A bus carrying a family from a wedding was overthrown by a landmine in the Kandahar city. 41 people died and 30 others were injured when the bus overturned.

Dec 96 - According to one official report, 600 Afghans are believed to be killed or wounded by mines every month.

Nov 96 - According to statistics collected by Save the Children, of all mine and UXO-related injuries and deaths in Kabul in the past six months, 37% occured in October. Furthermore, children account for the majority of victims - in October alone , 78% (66 of 85) people injured and killed were children. The surveys conducted by Save the Children reveal that UXOs, commonly known as unexploded bombs, are particularly deadly for children - 94% of all victims of UXO explosions in October were children.

October 1996 - In Afghanistan, *2,000-4,000* people die every year as a result of mines an UXO, with a far greater number of amputations. (Source: UN/MAC)

The ICRC's "Evolution of mine warfare" tables show two peaks of mine casualties: one in 1992 and another in 1995. The first corresponds to a large influx of returning refugees, many of whom unknowingly entered mined areas in their home regions. The second peak represents an upsurge in fighting between the Kabul government and the Taliban movement. This involved the widespread use of mines in the city of Kabul itself, resulting in heavy casualties among both combatants and civilians. (Source: ICRC News)

1993 - The International Committee of the Red Cross (ICRC) has compiled statistics of Afghan mine casualties from its hospitals in Pakistan. In a study of 5,189 registered mine injured patients, 29% had stepped on mines; 48% were hit by mine fragments; 5% were holding the mine; and another 18% were injured in other ways. Statistics confirm that recently returned refugees are at the highest risk from death or injury from mines.

Of 720 people admitted to an ICRC hospital in Peshawar in 1992, 66.1% had recently been repatriated and 36.8% of those had been back in Afghanistan less than three months. The study asked patients what they were doing when they were injured: 20% were working in fields or fetching water; 15% were traveling 13% were fighting; 8% were playing with a mine; 4% were demining.

Females were 7.3% of casualties; Males of 15 years or less were 19.8%; Males over 50 were 4.2%. The remainder were males between 16 and 50. ICRC estimated that 28.5% of all mine casualties lost one or both legs.

## LOCATIONS

May '97 - Estimate of suspected mined areas: 3,600 sq km or 2,600 fields.

*General Locations:* Mines and unexploded ordnance are located in almost every conceivable type of terrain in Afghanistan. Major military and civilian positions were mined, including the cities of Herat, Kandahar, Jalalabad and Khost. Mines pose a big danger to refugees returning home by passing through provinces bordering Pakistan and Iran. According to UNOCHA mines were most usually deployed along unused footpaths, tracks and roads; on the verges of tracks and roadways; in vehicle turn-around points; near culverts and bridge abutments; along damaged building walls; in the doorways and rooms of deserted houses; in and around wells and access points; around military posts; on or near destroyed vehicles; in areas where people might hide. "Minefields laid by the Soviets and the previous Afghan Government forces were generally recorded and catalogued according to military procedures," reported UNOCHA in 1994. "However the vast majority of mines laid by the mujahideen were not recorded or laid to any specific pattern. Moreover, the records lost much of their significance as the many areas were fought over, and won and lost by both sides during the war."

**Existing mines:**
**Anti-Personal Mines: 8,000,000**
**Anti-Tank Mines: 2,000,000**
**Total 10,000,000**
**Cleared mines:**
**Anti-Personal Mines: 150,900**
**UXO Cleared: 515,153**
**Land Cleared: 240,053,533**
**Total: 666,053**

**Table 1. Afghanistan: Area, Yield and Production of Main Crops: 1997/98 and 1998/99**

| Type of cereal | 1997/98 | | | 1998/99 | | | % Change in production |
|---|---|---|---|---|---|---|---|
| | Area ('000 ha) | Yield (MT/ha) | Production ('000 MT) | Area ('000 ha) | Yield (MT/ha) | Production ('000 MT) | |
| Irrigated wheat | 1,224 | 1.7 | 2,080 | 1,234 | 1.6 | 2,020 | (2.9) |
| Rainfed wheat | 900 | 0.7 | 631 | 952 | 0.9 | 814 | 29 |
| Rice (paddy) | 180 | 2.2 | 400 | 180 | 2.5 | 450 | 13 |
| Maize | 200 | 1.5 | 300 | 200 | 1.6 | 330 | 10 |
| Barley (for grain) | 200 | 1.3 | 250 | 200 | 1.2 | 240 | (4) |
| Total | 2,704 | 1.4 | 3,661 | 2,766 | 1.4 | 3,854 | 5.3 |

Source: FAO/WFP Crop and Food Supply Assessment – July 1998.

Table 2. Afghanistan: Livestock Production

| Type of animal | Headcount survey | Estimated figure for Afghanistan |
|---|---|---|
| Cattle | 1,694,024 | 4,555,311 |
| Sheep | 9,421,582 | 25,185,343 |
| Goat | 3,561,660 | 9,449,364 |
| Horse | 51,566 | 153,032 |
| Donkey | 417,183 | 1,122,526 |
| Camel | 147,879 | 463,675 |
| Poultry | 3,938,189 | 10,673,907 |
| Total | 19,232,083 | 51,603,158 |

Source: FAO – Livestock.
N.B. Data collected from 7,625 villages of 19 provinces and estimated country data for 1998

Table 3. Price of Wheat Flour October 1998 to March 1999 (in US$ per kilo)

| Province | October | November | December | January | February | March | % Change October-March |
|---|---|---|---|---|---|---|---|
| Kabul | 0.24 | 0.25 | 0.27 | 0.28 | 0.28 | 0.27 | 13 |
| Kandahar | 0.21 | 0.21 | 0.24 | 0.24 | 0.25 | 0.25 | 19 |
| Jalalabad | 0.24 | 0.23 | 0.25 | 0.26 | 0.27 | 0.26 | 8 |
| Herat | 0.18 | 0.17 | 0.18 | 0.19 | 0.19 | 0.18 | 0 |
| Mazar | 0.23 | 0.22 | 0.26 | 0.27 | 0.22 | 0.21 | (9) |
| Faizabad | 0.32 | 0.32 | 0.26 | 0.29 | 0.32 | 0.31 | (3) |

Source: WFP survey of food prices.

**Table 4. Daily Wages of Casual Labour from October through December 1998 (in US dollars)**

| Province | October | November | December | January | February | March | % Change October-March |
|---|---|---|---|---|---|---|---|
| Kabul | 1.38 | 1.30 | 1.19 | 1.21 | 1.11 | 1.14 | (17) |
| Kandahar | 1.40 | 1.34 | 1.69 | 1.71 | 1.59 | 1.61 | 15 |

| | | | | | | | |
|---|---|---|---|---|---|---|---|
| **Jalalabad** | **1.27** | **1.44** | **1.50** | **1.31** | **1.22** | **1.25** | **(2)** |
| **Herat** | **1.32** | **1.34** | **1.20** | **1.24** | **1.12** | **1.12** | **(15)** |
| **Mazar** | **1.76** | **1.53** | **1.34** | **1.00** | **1.00** | **1.00** | **(43)** |
| **Faizabad** | **3.00** | **2.16** | **1.81** | **1.79** | **1.63** | **1.59** | **(47)** |

Source: WFP survey of food prices.

**Figure 1: Afghanistan: Area and Food Production for 1997/98 and 1998/99 (in '000 MT)**

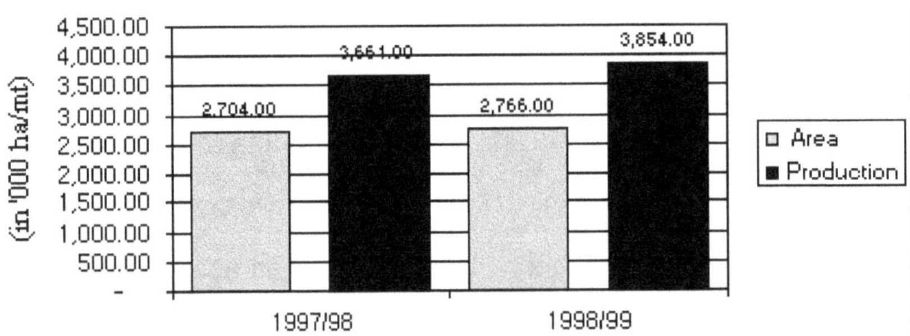


**Figure 2: Price of Wheat Flour from October 1998 to May 1999 (US$ per kilo)**

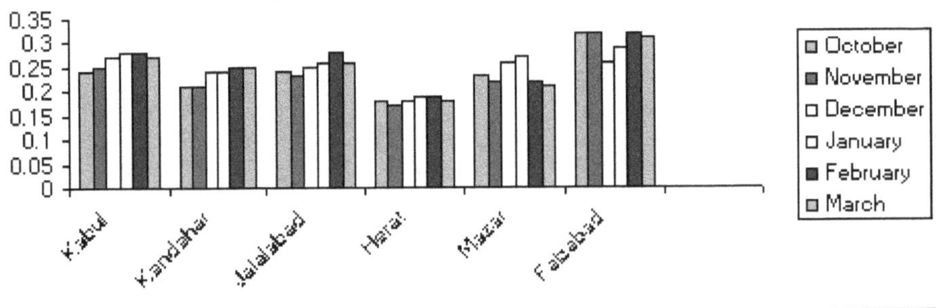

# MAJOR GOVERNMENT PROGRAMS AND BUSINESS OPPORTUNITIES

## NATIONAL SOLIDARITY PROGRAMME (NSP)

### RATIONALE

The chronic poverty in Afghanistan, exacerbated by years of neglect, accumulated effects of conflict and political instability and drought, has produced unacceptable levels of human suffering and deprivation. Over 50% of Afghanistan rural population live below the poverty line. While poverty reduction lies at the heart of the government's social policy, the objective can only be achieved by empowering poor communities to strengthen their social capital and bonds, make decisions that affect their lives and use public and their own resources in the best interest of their communities. Pursuing this objective, the NSP is mobilising community and public institutions, private sector, NGOs and UN agencies to support the Afghan poor communities in their struggle to make their way out of poverty.

### OBJECTIVES

The objectives of the programme are:

- To lay the foundations of community-level good governance.
- To support community-managed sub-projects for reconstruction and development to improve the access of rural communities to social and productive infrastructure and services.

### STRATEGY AND IMPLEMENTATION PLAN

NSP strongly promotes a unique development paradigm whereby communities can make important decision and control resources at all stages of their development. Through NSP, communities elect their legitimate leaders and representatives to form Community Development Councils (CDC).These CDCs formulate Village Development Plans through extensive consultation and participatory methods. To implement priority projects of the plans, CDCs mobilise community resources and receive block grants (average around USD 20,000) from the government. 21 NGOs and UN-Habitat as Facilitating Partners (FPs) have been contracted to provide technical assistance to communities in electing their leaders, establishing CDCs, formulating village development plans, design and implement development projects. The GTZ/DAI has been contracted as Oversight Consultant (OC) to supervise the entire process on behalf of the government, providing training and making sure that communities receive their block grants for eligible projects in a transparent manner. The MRRD is responsible for overall management and execution of the programme. A joint committee of government, donors, UN and the Afghan Human Rights Commission provides policy advice and strategic oversight. The villages are selected on the basis of three criteria, i.e. food & livelihood insecurity, return of refugees and IDPs and social targeting balance.

### SUMMARY OF ACHIEVEMENTS UP-TO-DATE

Today, NSP is the Afghan government's flagship programme for community development. This government's largest development program is gaining strong momentum with the following major achievements:

- NPS has covered 96 districts (3 in each of the 32 provinces). To date, over 5 million rural women and men have participated in electing 4,000 CDCs in 4,000 villages. 15% of these CDCs are special women councils and the rest are mixed.

- As of 31 March 2004, total amount of $4,694,629 of the block grants was disbursed (over USD 11 million obligated) for construction of roads and culverts (129 projects), water supply systems (89 projects), Gabion and irrigation canal (50 projects), for electricity (e.g., diesel generator and micro hydro-power, 50 projects), 27 public bathes, 20 schools, and 20 facilities for weaving and tailoring, 7 bridges, as well as other community facilities.

- NSP is now launching an intensive training program for more than 3,600 participants from MRRD, NSP, FPs as well as the elected representatives from communities across the country.

- 24 out of the planned 32 regional NSP offices are opened, equipped, staffed, and fully operational.

### PLAN FOR 1383

By the end of 1383, NSP will cover the planned 6,000 villages and start the initial phase of the programme in 6,000 new villages of the country. The objective is to reach all villages of the country (approx. 20,000) in 3 to 4 years.

From now on, it is projected that every month between 4 to 5 hundred villages will be receiving their block grants (estimated US$ 10 million in total).

### KEY BOTTLENECKS

- Inaccessibility to some of rural areas due to security situations.

- Weak capacity of MRRD engineering and management of FPs & OC.

- Insufficient communication and information infrastructure.

### INFORMATION ON FUNDING

Total contract value of the program is US$42,252,342 (with $20,319,700 disbursed as of 31st March 2004). The program has received contributions by IDA Grant-NSP component (SDR 18,650,000, approx.US$29,525,331), Denmark ($4,989,475), DFID ($5,723,000), and Canada ($10,985,000). The other funding that is committed but yet to be made available includes IDA NSP II Grant ($97,771,154), EC ($19,095,000) and USAID ($10,000,000) and Japan ($10 million).

## NATIONAL EMERGENCY EMPLOYMENT PROGRAMME (NEEP)

### RATIONALE

The livelihood insecure people including the returnees need productive work opportunities. Unemployment and under employment is widespread. The poppy growers and ex-combatants will have to be assisted with alternative livelihood opportunities. While economic growth is essential for a politically stable and prosperous Afghanistan, it is imperative to ensure that the vulnerable people benefit from such growth through special social safety nets.

On the other hand, physical inaccessibility exacerbates the poverty of our people, affecting their access to markets, health and education as well as hinders their participation in the political processes of the country. The NEEP is designed to address these challenges.

### OBJECTIVES

The objectives of NEEP include:

- To provide a safety net for the most vulnerable people by creating productive employment opportunities
- To establish effective mechanisms for developing public and productive infrastructure assets, through labour-based methods and a private sector-led approach
- To develop public sector capacity and systems for delivering various community services.

### STRATEGY AND IMPLEMENTATION PLAN

NEEP covers all 32 provinces of the country. Works are sub-contracted to private contractors through a bidding system. NEEP also provides training for the small local contractors to make sure that the construction works are of good quality. Labour-intensive methods are used in the construction to ensure that a maximum number of poor people can benefit from the NEEP projects. People with disability, destitute women, the elderly, refugees, and demobilized soldiers are also recruited by NEEP for the construction activities.

The NEEP National Inter-ministerial Board, composed of MRRD, MPW, MMD, Women's Affairs, Labour and Social Affairs, Returnees and Repatriation, Public Health, Education, Frontiers and Tribal Affairs, Reconstruction, and Finance, is responsible for steering the programme and managing resource allocation. A Joint Program Management Unit (JPMU) under the leadership of MRRD is responsible for the strategic management of the programme including the development of policies such as targeting and standards, etc. The Unit reports to the Inter-ministerial Board. Together with other ministries, MRRD coordinates all projects under NEEP.

### SUMMARY OF ACHIEVEMENTS UP-TO-DATE

NEEP completed its first phase in 2003 with great success, creating 5 million labour-days and reconstructing 1,050 km of roads. NEEP has also completed construction of 1,500 bridges and culverts, 3,000 shelter, 100 school, 15 clinics, 100 projects for irrigation, and 250 projects for water supply. Credit for the success of these projects goes to the Ministries Public Works, Water Resource, Irrigation and Environment, Rural Development and our partners such UNOPS, ILO and CARE.

Furthermore, draft guidelines and procedures for resource allocation/programming, planning, contracting, social targeting, monitoring & evaluation, and reporting, were developed for the NEEP staff to ensure smooth operation of the programme. A pilot Management Information System (MIS) has been established and operationalized to track physical and financial progress of the projects.

### PLAN FOR 1383

The target for NEEP in 1383 is to generate 13 million labour days through construction of work of 2,500 km of rural roads, 2,500 bridges, 50 irrigation projects, 150 water supply projects across the country. Plans are being reviewed to further scale up the NEEP delivery. The capacity of NEEP to implement and monitor the projects will be enhanced by expanding MIS at full-scale and recruiting more NEEP staff in the communities.

### KEY BOTTLENECKS

The implementation mechanisms for NEEP need to be strengthened further including the functioning of the Inter-ministerial Board. The engineering capacity of the organisations involved needs to be strengthened. Strengthening the capacity of the contractors for managing contracts is a key priority. Another priority is the development of national policies and technical standards and capacity for monitoring compliance.

### INFORMATION ON FUNDING

Total budget of the programme is US$126,738,670. NEEP has received contributions from WB, EC, USAID, UNHCR, and Japan. The budget requirement for continuation of the programme activities in 1383 is US$65,752,000, which is covered by WB, EC, USAID, UNHCR, and Japan. Yet, the programme requires an additional US$150million for expansion of the activities.

## RURAL WATER SUPPLY, SANITATION, AND HYGIENE PROMOTION

### RATIONALE

In addition to its impact on health, development of domestic water supply and sanitation is considered one of the most important factors for improving rural livelihoods. Safe drinking water is one of the biggest contributing factors to people's health, and reconstruction can only be accelerated through an active and healthy population. Afghanistan has some of the worst mortality figures in the world, for example, over 25% of children dying before the age of 5. Half of the deaths are caused by preventable waterborne diseases. Urgent action is necessary to improve rural livelihood and health in the communities.

### OBJECTIVES

The objectives of the programme are:

- To improve health and halve the child mortality and morbidity in the country within the next 5 years.
- To educate people on how to prevent waterborne diseases and stay on healthy.
- To reach all people with safe and sustainable drinking water.
- To improve public hygiene and environmental sanitation in the community.
- To equip all communities with a community environmental and sanitation plan to protect their health and local environment.

### STRATEGY AND IMPLEMENTATION PLAN

To reach all people with sustainable basic services for rural water supply and sanitation facilities, sustainability is developed with community ownership, based on the user demands as well as the willingness and ability to contribute and pay. The programme uses local technology and methods to provide safe water. The Government takes a regulatory and facilitating role while the private sector implements government-executed programmes, supervised and monitored by MRRD. A key strategy will be to collect information on the status of existing services nationwide to identify the community needs and implement activities accordingly.

To reach 15 million people over the next 5 years with enhanced capacity for basic services, the programme will develop 100,000 new water points providing 25 litres of safe water per day per person. In order to make people aware of the importance of safe drinking water and links to waterborne diseases, 2.5 million households will be educated on water, sanitation, and hygiene issues through a variety of approaches suitable for rural Afghanistan.

## SUMMARY OF ACHIEVEMENTS UP-TO-DATE

In 2003, National Policy Framework has been developed and approved. Also, the National 5-year targets and Millennium Goals in Afghanistan have been defined and the 5-year development plan was prepared. In order to achieve these targets, the programme has successfully implemented various activities in all 32 provinces. For example, approximately 1.5 million people have benefited from 204 projects with US$11 million in 2003 alone. Through those projects, 3,387 wells, 1,712 water tanks in schools, 1,042 sets of latrines as well as 600 family latrines, and 26 water supply networks were constructed. Furthermore, 7 hygiene education projects were implemented, 9 ozone solar systems were installed, and 704 hand pumps were repaired. A water pond was rehabilitated, and a chlorination project was also completed.

The project proposals have been prepared for sector investment, amounted to over $200 million for the next 5 years. Also, the project proposals, valued over $25 million, were drafted for the year of 2004. An agreement on implementation of these projects has already been signed between MRRD, UNICEF and UNHCR. A project proposal for $5 million supported by USAID is close to be finalized, and the $20 million-value proposal is already being appraised by Afghanistan Reconstruction Trust Fund.

## PLAN FOR 1383

Under the programme, the following activities are planned for 1383:

- Construction of 13,000 new water points.
- Construction of 40,000 household latrines.
- Hygiene education to 800,000 households.
- Establishment of a national training centre, later to be developed into a rural training academy.
- Provision of water supply and sanitation for more than 1,000 schools.
- Starting development of small scale private sector firms.

## KEY BOTTLENECKS

- Inaccessibility in rural areas.
- Lack of local engineers and staff to provide necessary technical services and supervision for the projects.
- Weak implementation mechanisms to ensure strengthening of community-based projects.
- The need to strengthen provincial government capacities.

## INFORMATION ON FUNDING

The total rural water supply and sanitation programme is budgeted around $205 million over the next 5 years. This does not include a special program for rural towns and peri-urban areas.

For 1383, the funds are now pledged by UNHCR ($2.3 million for support to MRRD), USAID ($5 million for support to 13 provinces), UNICEF ($5 million for total programme), Japan ($ 1 million) and Afghanistan Trust Fund ($17 million). Support from the government of Turkey ($ 2 million) is under discussion.

## NATIONAL AREA BASED DEVELOPMENT PROGRAMME (NABDP)

### RATIONALE

After the induction of the Afghanistan Interim Administration in December 2001, the Government identified ten priority geographical areas in the light of their severe war damages, large numbers of returning refugees and IDPs and earthquake damage. The NABDP was designed to support rebuilding essential functions of the state and civil society institutions, rehabilitating basic rural infrastructure, stimulating economic and income generating activities, and improving access to social services under the National Development Framework.

### OBJECTIVES

The objective of NABDP is to develop the capacity of the government at national and local levels to formulate and manage recovery and development strategies and programmes through a participatory process to address key social and economic challenges in the country.

### STRATEGY AND IMPLEMENTATION PLAN

NABDP has been implemented under the two different modalities executed by MRRD and UNDP in collaboration with UNOPS, FAO, and UN Habitat. NABDP is unique within the MRRD's program portfolio in that resources can be programmed flexibly in response to locally defined needs and availability of other program resources. The focus of the NABDP interventions is to support programme achieving results, ensure capacity development, and strengthen the MRRD and RRD provincial offices through skill enhancement of the staff, financial and material capacity, and system development.

### SUMMARY OF ACHIEVEMENTS UP-TO-DATE

- The programme enabled government officials, the Emergency Loya Jirga delegates, and local leaders to conduct a provincial planning process in all provinces of the country and identify over 1,500 key priority projects in all districts of the country. Of these, 317 sub-projects valued at over US$17.9 million have been implemented across 32 provinces, contracted through UN agencies, such as FAO, UN Habitat, UNOPS, NGOs, and private sector businesses, for immediate recovery in the areas of agriculture, building construction, education, heath, income-generation, irrigation, livelihood, rural development, shelter, transport, water supply, and public administration.

- NABDP has played the most important role in the institutional reform and strengthening of MRRD. Through provision of human and financial capitals, the programme has enabled the ministry to reform its mandate, policies and structures at both national and provincial levels, and develop new programmes that are relevant to the national priorities. Also, the programme has extended such a support to other ministries both at national and provincial levels.

- The feasibility study was conducted on macro-economic regeneration projects, particularly on the Spinzar Cotton Gin in Kudzu including scenarios for further operation of the Gin in the context of the government's privatisation law discussed with the Minister of MRRD, Light Industries and the Chairman of the Privatisation Commission.

### PLAN FOR 1383

In 1383, NABDP will intensify and expand its activities in the following areas:

- Continuation of the obligated NABDP Sub-projects for rural infrastructure and rehabilitation.

- Implementation of the remaining of the over 1,500 projects identified through provincial planning. Priority will be given to the projects not picked up by other national programmes.

- Continuation of support for further institutional reform and restructuring within MRRD and other LSP ministries.

- Re-organization of NABDP for resource mobilization and strengthening reporting and monitoring system in MRRD and NABDP.

- Provision of support for the Afghanistan's first National Human Development Report.

- Continuation of support for NRVA/NSS.

### KEY BOTTLENECKS

The progress of activities in the sub-projects is largely subject to severe security concerns. Social, political, cultural and economic implications needed to be carefully observed and measured before undertaking any intervention.

### INFORMATION ON FUNDING

Total budget of the programme amounts US$157 million. In 2003, NABDP received US$29.5 million from Italy ($10, 983,367), Malaysia ($500,000), Canada ($5,150,727), Japan ($1,854,000), UK ($1,562,500), USAID ($5,000,000), Sweden ($2,910,361), EC ($339,875), UNHCR ($161,410), and UNDP ($1,100,000).

Budget requirements for 1383 are estimated to be US$ 45 million and some donors have expressed their interest in contributing to NABDP in 1383, such as Italy ($7.2 million), Canada ($7.18million), Sweden ($2million), UNHCR ($0.5 million), UNDP ($0.5million) and EC ($0.5 million). This leaves US$27,107 as a shortfall.

## MICRO FINANCE INVESTMENT AND SUPPORT FACILITY IN AFGHANISTAN (MISFA)

As part of the needs assessment undertaken by the World Bank in early 2001, micro-finance was identified as one of the core needs for securing sustainable development at the micro and macro economic level. This was reaffirmed by the recent review of the needs assessment carried out by the World Bank under the Livelihoods and Social Protection program in December 2003 for and on behalf of the Afghanistan Transitional Government. Economic regeneration is an essential element in the reconstruction and stabilization of Afghan society. The provision of credit and finance generally is key to the development of the private sector economy.

### OBJECTIVES

The primary objectives of MISFA are:

- To improve the livelihoods and opportunities of the poor and vulnerable in Afghan society through the provision of credit.
- To develop a sufficient number of NGO micro finance institutions that have adequate capacity and infrastructure to implement sustainable credit programs.
- To develop MISFA as a long term independent wholesale financial intermediary for the micro finance sector (i.e., a bank to micro finance institutions) as well as an advocate for the sector and a vehicle through which the sector can co-ordinate activities and initiatives such as credit bureaus, and commercial law and regulation.

### STRATEGY AND IMPLEMENTATION PLAN

MISFA began operating in June 2003, and the programme now has around fifteen professional international and national staff. MISFA has its own premises and systems and operating procedures and is seeking to be formed as an independent entity by summer 2004. Also, the aim is to have MISFA management by national staff during 2005. MISFA has been working closely with NGOs as implementing partners. NGOs are identified through a selection process including a formal application together with a business plan prepared by the NGO. If selected, the NGO is subject to an assessment undertaken by MISFA's technical staff which results in the production of a work plan with deliverables and targets. Funding is disbursed in instalments and is subject to continuing satisfactory performance.

In relation to empowering livelihoods, MISFA focuses on vulnerable groups including women, the disabled, and the working poor, providing the credits ranged $50-1,000 for the term of 3-12 months.

### SUMMARY OF ACHIEVEMENTS UP-TO-DATE

Within as short as seven months, MISFA has already succeeded in funding five micro finance institutions (MFIs) or NGOs. Since the first disbursement made in July 2003, almost US$16 million has been contracted, and over US$5 million has been disbursed. More than 20,000 clients (mostly women-headed families) have received loans. The performance of the micro-credit loan has been remarkable with the average repayment rates of 98%. The MISFA loans have financed the activities for commercial services (e.g., carpentry, transportation, hairdresser, electrician, and plumber), craft (e.g., embroidery, carpets, and sewing), shops and retail sellers, and manufacturing.

### PLAN FOR 1383

MISFA aims to invest in at least twelve national and international institutions during 1383. The target is that at least 75,000 families will be receiving credit from those institutions by the end of

1383 and that another 14 provinces will be covered including Kunduz, Takhar, Laghman, Shibarghan, Samangan, Ghazni, Bamyan, Herat, Badakhshan, Wardak and some as yet unidentified western provinces. If, as hoped, other institutions can be incorporated under the MISFA projects then more provinces will be covered next year.

### KEY BOTTLENECKS

The limited number of competent micro-finance organisations in the country to implement the programme is a key constraint.

### INFORMATION ON FUNDING

Total budget of the programme is US$7.5 million for 1382, US$17.5 million for 1383, US$60 million for 1384. MISFA has been supported by World Bank ($5 million), CGAP ($1 million), CIDA ($10 million), USAID ($5 million), DFID ($ 1.8 million for 1382/83). MISFA requires additional US$5 million in 1383 to fill the financial gap. Because no commitments have been made for 1384, MISFA is looking for potential funding for the next year.

## LIVELIHOOD BASED FOOD SECURITY SURVEILLANCE SYSTEM

### RATIONALE

Most government agencies in Afghanistan have suffered significant decay and destruction of both physical infrastructure and human capital during the last 23 years. There has been little or no meaningful government data collection during this period. For example, the only census ever carried out in Afghanistan took place in 1979, but this was not completed due to security concerns. In order to identify priority development issues and design appropriate livelihood and social protection strategies, relevant informative data have to be collected and analysed regularly. Therefore, it is imperative that government reactivate its capacity to provide its own ministries and the wider development community with credible national statistics on poverty and vulnerability in both rural and urban settings.

### OBJECTIVES

This project aims to develop the capacity to provide timely relevant information in order to:

- Have a standardised and integrated surveillance system to which all agencies (government and non-government) wishing to develop policies and programmes addressing social protection, poverty and livelihoods can refer to as a primary data source of relevant and up-to-date information on livelihoods, risk and vulnerability.

- Identify early signs of change and deterioration in livelihoods, food security and nutrition in order to assist in the design of effective policymaking and programme responses.

- Collect data on aspects of rural livelihoods that inform targeting and programming for rural livelihoods, social protection and rehabilitation of rural infrastructure.

- Sharpen the capacity of Government to frame policies and make decision based on reliable quantitative information.

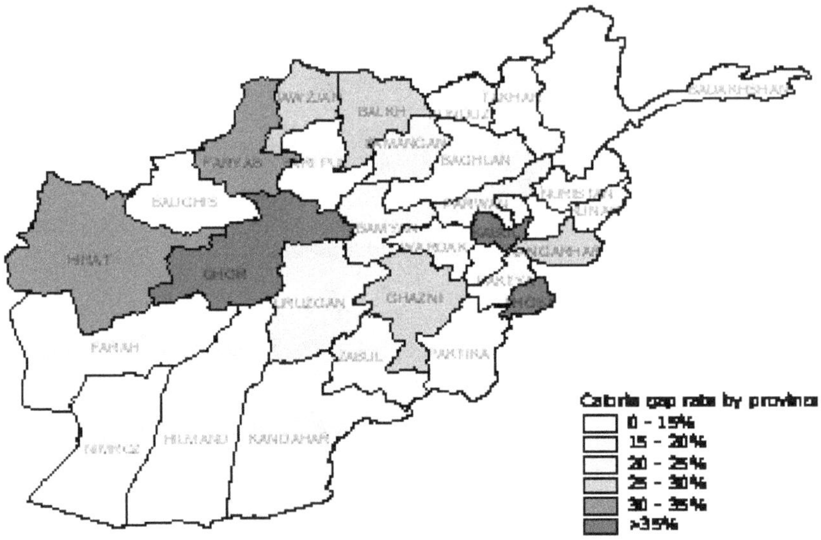


### STRATEGY AND IMPLEMENTATION PLAN

The project is centred in the Vulnerability Analysis Unit within the MRRD. It is currently going through a process of upgrading the staff of the unit to rise to the challenge of being able to take on analysis of national poverty and vulnerability data.
The roles and responsibilities of data collection and data analysis may separate. It is important that rural and urban analysis is conducted with the same methods, as well as having the data collected by an institution recognised by other government partners as the legitimate agency for this.

Therefore, engagement with the current process of developing a Statistical Master Plan of Afghanistan is on-going (the process whereby roles, responsibilities, and statistical law will be defined, programme of work for reactivation of government statistics sought) will result in Phase 2 of this programme, support going to CSO for the data collection activities, while continuing to strengthen capacity building within the Vulnerability Analysis Unit within MRRD for data and policy analysis .

Also, this project must support analytical capacity building in other key ministries such as Agriculture, Health and Urban Development to ensure value of the data is maximised. This project is beginning to produce results that can inform targeting programming and policy. As results emerge, advocacy and capacity building around their use in pro-poor planning processes will be embarked upon. The aim is to provide "pro-poor" policies that address people's needs through an understanding of their livelihoods with more effective targeting of marginalized and poor groups through improved livelihood and social protection programmes and instruments. The project aims to do this both in times of reconstruction and in an emergency, if severe drought returns.

### SUMMARY OF ACHIEVEMENTS UP-TO-DATE

Implementation of the first assessment of the rural population of Afghanistan designed to address multi stakeholder and government agency needs (National Risk and Vulnerability

Assessment (NRVA) 2003). This found that one in five households are still not meeting its basic food-energy needs despite the assessment taking place after one of the best harvest in many years in Afghanistan. Drought and water related stresses are still the major shocks that affect the rural population on a wide scale, whereas as household level health and unemployment shocks are the most frequently cited. The only pro-poor targeting that has been carried out through free food relief elements of the WFP program. Cash-for-work and food-for-work programmes have been poor neutral at best and by and large have excluded women. Not surprisingly, poor access to rural services emerges as a major issue, particularly to health facilities.

Managed data entry and cleaning, and currently in the process of producing an initial results.

Implementation of the pilot phase of National Surveillance System in collaboration with DFID.

## PLAN FOR 1383

The major activities planned for 1383 are:

Clarify institutional roles and responsibilities of various government agencies in relation to the collection of poverty and vulnerability data.

Strengthen the capacity of these departments to design, collect and analyse such data via recruitment of staff by embarking on long-term formal and informal training programme covering a range of topics from designing surveys and samples through to writing policy orientated reports.

Strengthen the ability of analytical units within key ministries to utilise this data to provide evidence based information and recommendations on targeting, programme then kneeling and policy.

Support the implementation of an open poverty and vulnerability assessment.

Conduct a workshop to promote the results of the NRVA for targeting, programming and policy among government ministries and other development agencies.

## KEY BOTTLENECKS

Although remarkable achievements have been made, the following issues need to addressed for further expansion of the programme:

Clarification on roles and responsibilities of government agencies for the collection of annual risk and vulnerability data and market price information.

Time needed to train Vulnerability Analysis Unit staff in database design, data management and analysis MRRD to perform required analysis on national datasets.

Demand from other government agencies and ministries for the use of policy and vulnerability data emerging from this initiative.

#### INFORMATION ON FUNDING

Phase I of this initiative is funded by the European Commission and with a small component of joint funding from UNDP (September 2003 –November 2004; $495,600). Phase II (November 2004 –October 2007) committed funds from European Commission €3.5 million and is open to competitive tender.

## REINTEGRATION AND IDP NATIONAL PLAN

#### RATIONALE

It is estimated that there are close to 190,000 IDPs in Afghanistan, the majority of whom are sheltered in Southern and Western Camps. The Government and its development partners have been supporting them in camps for the past few years. Returns have already taken place, but the key is for these to be sustainable and seen as successful to encourage further movements out of the camps and back to their homes. Through surveys and monitoring it is known that returnees face the same difficulties and issues as their receiving communities. The returnees in each area face problems with lack of water supply, employment opportunities and access to social services. MRRD plays a central role in inclusion of returnees through its national programmes, in addition to the activities of its Reintegration Unit, aiming to promote in particular the social and economic reintegration of the refugee and IDP returnees.

#### OBJECTIVES

- To increase the rate of IDP return
- To sustain IDP reintegration into areas of origin

#### STRATEGY AND IMPLEMENTATION PLAN

MRRD has decided not to design projects specifically for returnees but to mainstream their inclusion within the national development programmes. This inclusion in existing development programmes is aimed to facilitate their reintegration back into their villages of origin. It is understood that returnees are not the only prioritised beneficiary group, but the reintegration of over 3 million people (refugees returned) is a long-term objective that will require a sustainable commitment of resources. Within all of MRRD's national development programmes, returnees will be considered as a cross-cutting issue in planning, programming and implementation. The NSP will select its villages according to the criteria including the concentration of refugee and IDP returnees. NEEP will consider the levels of return within its social targeting and the Rural Water Supply programme will identify priority areas of high return where an increased population exacerbates scant resources.

The IDP National Plan is the initiative of the MRRD, Ministry of Refugees & Repatriation and the Ministry of Frontiers and Tribal Affairs, closely supported by UNHCR, UNDP, WFP, and UNAMA. This plan seeks an end to the perpetuation of care and maintenance in the IDP camps and strives toward durable solutions to facilitate return and a sustained reintegration.

#### SUMMARY OF ACHIEVEMENTS UP-TO-DATE

The activities within the IDP National Plan will start in 2004. At this stage there are a number of ongoing activities including an assessment of the feasibility of return by Kuchis to Registan and the establishment of provincial and central co-ordination mechanisms. The IDPs in the camps in the South are currently being profiled to determine those who wish to return and the obstacles to return and reintegration that must be addressed within the context of the plan. This plan also complements the activities of UNHCR, such as the Go and See Visits for IDP representatives to their areas of origin in the Northern provinces.

### Plan for 1383

For all IDPs, their return will only be sustained through area reintegration projects that benefit those who are returning, in addition to the receiving and neighbouring communities. The project activities of the National Plan in 1383 will include:

- Support the restocking of livestock herds and livestock bank
- Skills training in agricultural and livestock activities
- Rehabilitation of water supply systems
- Rehabilitation of dams, reservoirs and protection walls

### Information on Funding

Total budget of the programme over 3-years is an estimated $60m. UNHCR, WFP and IOM's programme activities are included within this Plan, but not included in the budget. The outstanding budget for 1383 is an estimated $19.5m, however, specific budgets will be proposed after technical assessments completed in July.

## HUMANITARIAN EMERGENCY RESPONSE

### Rationale

Afghanistan is a disaster prone country, with more than 70% of the inhabited area falling under medium to high risks caused by half a dozen natural disasters such as earthquakes, floods, landslides, avalanches, droughts and extreme winter conditions. These frequent natural disasters cause abject poverty and livelihoods, diminish income-generating opportunities, and contribute to poor state of infrastructure. Without prompt and appropriate responses, such natural and man-made disasters lead to the extremely vulnerable conditions of Afghan communities.

### Objectives

The overall objective of emergency response is to improve the sustainability of rural recovery efforts through reducing vulnerability of the rural population against natural disaster.

### Strategy and Implementation Plan

MRRD has been assigned to play a leading role in organizing and coordinating emergency relief assistances to the disaster-affected populations in the rural areas through Emergency Response Teams on various levels, such as province, district, and village. However, this role will be reviewed as the Disaster Preparedness Department is further strengthened.

### SUMMARY OF ACHIEVEMENTS UP-TO-DATE

The achievements in emergency response include:

- The response capacity of Provincial Department of MRRD was established and strengthened.

- 'Action Plan', 'Response Procedure', 'Assessment Guideline' and 'Surveyors Briefing Paper' were produced to facilitate smooth implementation of emergency relief activities.

- Relief assistance to more than 7,000 disaster-affected families was coordinated.

- A study on the rehabilitation of physical infrastructure damaged by disasters was conducted.

- Coordination of winter response with UNAMA was implemented.

### PLAN FOR 1383

The following activities are planned for 1383:

- Prepare a contingency response plan for 20,000 families.
- Develop and maintain a database for emergency stocks.
- Form provincial Emergency Response Teams.
- Build and improve capacities in disaster management.

### KEY BOTTLENECKS

The following constraints need to be addressed for effective responses:

- The need to undertake a serious institutional reform and restructuring to clarify the role of the key state institutions.
- Little coordination amongst relevant departments and agencies.
- Absence of early warning system at a national level.
- Lack of investment in the field of disaster management

### INFORMATION ON FUNDING

US$1,100,000 is required to support MRRD's planning activities for emergency response. No commitments have yet been made by our development partners.

## FOOD SECURITY-PROTRACTED RELIEF AND RECOVERY OPERATION

### RATIONALE

Chronic rural and urban poverty and food insecurity, malnutrition, and slow recovery from the impacts of severe droughts of 1998-2001 have been observed in Afghanistan. Absence of public safety nets (social policy) to protect the poor and the most vulnerable as well as poor socio-economic infrastructure further aggravate the situation. Furthermore, low school enrolment rates among children and teachers limit institutional capacity in Afghanistan.

### OBJECTIVES

The overall objective of the programme is to contribute to protection and re-establishment of livelihoods and household food security in the context of the National Development Framework.

### STRATEGY AND IMPLEMENTATION PLAN

The programme is executed by WFP and MRRD (the government counterpart) to ensure that the programme is coordinated with other government social protection programmes. The programme aims to support 9.2 million beneficiaries under various interventions with 619,000 MT of food through following mechanisms:

- Relief: Food assistance to returning refugees and internally displaced persons (IDPs), vulnerable rural and urban households, emergency assistance to disaster-affected populations, supplementary feeding for malnourished children and women, food assistance to patients in institutions, orphans, TB patients and their families.

- Recovery: Food assistance for school children, with a special focus on girls, teachers' salary supplement and instructors in training institutions, non-formal education and vocational training, food for work (employment based safety-net) and assistance to ex-combatants in the context of the Government's Disarmament, Demobilization and Reintegration (DDR) program.

- Capacity development of counterpart Government institutions, implementing partners and WFP national staff (training, provision of equipment, school construction, baseline surveys, food fortification, de-worming, etc).

### SUMMARY OF ACHIEVEMENTS UP-TO-DATE

- 6.9 million beneficiaries under various interventions of relief and recovery were assisted with 177,200 MT of food.

- Many assets were created or rehabilitated, including 4,203 km of roads and construction of 23 schools and 500 returnee houses.

- Capacity development of counterparts.

### PLAN FOR 1383

Under the programme, 269,065 MT of food commodities will be distributed to 5 million beneficiaries in closer cooperation with other national programs such as NEEP. Significant investments in capacity development will be provided in 1383.

### KEY BOTTLENECKS

The following issues need to be tackled for further implementation of the programme:

- Absence of a social safety net especially for the urban poor.
- Absence of a social policy framework to guide the most appropriate use of food and non-food interventions.
- Insufficient coordination between cash for work and food for work interventions between agencies.
- Limited capacity of counterpart government institutions and implementing partners.
- Inadequate baseline information to guide programming decisions.

### INFORMATION ON FUNDING

Total budget of the programme for two years (2004 and 2005) is estimated US$332.5 million. The programme so far received US$121.7 million (36.6% of the required fund) from Canada, Denmark, Europe Aid, ICRC, India, Italy, Japan, Luxembourg, Norway, Saudi Arabia, Switzerland, UK, UN, UNA-UK, USA, as well as the private sector. Yet, the programme still requires US$210.9 million for 2004 and 2005.

## NATIONAL HUMAN DEVELOPMENT REPORT (NHDR) FOR AFGHANISTAN

### RATIONALE

UNDP prepares Human Development Report every year and ranks the countries according to the value of the Human Development Index. Since 1995, Afghanistan does not have figures in the global HDR because of the lack of the data. Many countries of the world have started preparing NHDRs to study the regional, ethnic and other types of disparities in the country. NHDRs have proved an important tool in many countries for providing country–specific development indicators and promoting policy debate on the multi-dimensional development issues. With similar objectives in mind, it has been decided to prepare the first NHDR in Afghanistan.

### OBJECTIVES

- To create awareness among the policy makers and the public on human development and pro-poor development.
- To collect aggregated national data as well as disaggregated data according to gender, age, geographical location, ethnic, and other socio-economic groups and provide detailed analyses on the principal causes of poverty and the critical points of intervention.
- To give a thrust for the collection of quality data on various socio-economic variables in the country.

### STRATEGY AND IMPLEMENTATION PLAN

Because of the lack of the indigenous capacity for the preparation of the Report, UNDP is providing the necessary financial and technical inputs. Yet, in order to ensure that national issues are adequately represented in the Report, the Advisory Committee, consisting of the eminent people in their areas of expertise, has been constituted under the Chairmanship of Minister of MRRD. The report is to be written by experts of Afghan origin, while international experts are also providing the guidance. Background and thematic papers on selected topics have been contributed by experts, which provides the basis for the NHDR.

### SUMMARY OF ACHIEVEMENTS UP-TO-DATE

While preparation for the 1st NHDR is on-going, the following activities have already been completed:

- Background and thematic papers were produced.
- A team of authors has been appointed and operational.
- Three meetings of the Advisory Committee were organized.
- A study on data availability for the NHDR was conducted by an international expert.
- A workshop for the officers of the Central Statistical Office and other concerned Ministries was organized.

### PLAN FOR 1383

The report is tentatively scheduled to be released by September, 2004.

### INFORMATION ON FUNDING

The production of the first NHDR is funded through the UNDP Core-fund, amounted to US$600,000.

## MRRD REFORM & INSTITUTIONAL STRENGTHENING

## RATIONALE

After the establishment of the Transitional Islamic State of Afghanistan, the MRRD went through extensive review processes with assistance from UNDP, BRAC, EC and other partners. It was established that the old MRRD was not up to the challenge of poverty reduction in Afghanistan. The premise on which the old MRRD was based was outdated, neglecting new realities and best practices. Consistent with the government vision outlined in the National Development Framework, the leadership of the ministry has embarked on a phased institutional reform and restructuring.

### OBJECTIVES

The overall goal is to make sure that MRRD is not a liability for public budget and funds but an accountable and competent state institution to provide leadership to public, private and non-for-profit sectors as well as civil society organisations for poverty reduction and social protection in rural Afghanistan. The specific objectives therefore focus on MRRD mandate and policy reform, development of national social protection and poverty reduction programmes, structural reform, institutional and organisational development including staff competency development and reform of the institutional relationships.

### STRATEGY AND IMPLEMENTATION PLAN

An on-going strategic planning process involving the staff and the key stakeholders of MRRD has been the key approach to the reform process. Outside specialist agencies have been and will be contracted to undertake specific studies for policy, programme and structural review. The PRR (Priority Reform and Restructuring) is the key instrument drawn upon for the institutional reform and restructuring within the 7 central and 32 provincial departments. Donors' support to the process has been ensured through the PRR, NABDP/UNDP, WFP, UNICEF and national programmes such as NSP, NEEP and others. To increase the institutional capacity, the emphasis is on (a) investment in staff capacity development, (b) recruitment and deployment of national and international individual consultants in key areas, and (c) extensive reliance on contractors for programme oversight and implementation.

### SUMMARY OF ACHIEVEMENTS UP-TO-DATE

- The mandate, key policies and the national and provincial structures of MRRD have all been reformed in the light of the NDF and best practices.

- Development of new policies, e.g. peoples' ownership and empowerment in all programmes, full accountability and transparency, the focus of the MRRD on policy guidance and the establishment of regulatory frameworks, emphasis on private sector, a new partnership and labour division with NGOs and UN, policies on humanitarian aid and social protection, policy on food aid and cash-for-work, policy on wheat prices.

- Development and launching of six national programmes.

- Administrative procedures have been improved by streamlining the administrative structures and centralizing the procurement and recruitment systems connected with the province offices.

- A capacity development program was developed and various training programmes have been conducted. The majority of our staff members both in Kabul and provinces have gone through various types of training with over 50 trained overseas.

- An additional Deputy Minister position was created in line with new structure of MRRD.

- The Leadership Team, composed of the Minister, 3 Deputy Ministers, Director of Documentation, Legal Advisor, and 3 Senior Advisors, was instituted and is operational.

- Coordination mechanisms both within the Headquarters and with the province offices have been established with Information Coordination Team (ICT), Central Coordination Team (CCT), and Provincial Coordination Team (PCT) in all 32 provinces.

- Over hundred national and international advisors have been recruited for short and mid-term assignments.

### PLAN FOR 1383

The key activities planned for 1383 include:

- Complete the reform and restructuring of the PRR departments.
- Submit a new PRR proposal for the remaining departments of MRRD.
- Continue to implement the staff training in and outside the country.

- Submit the new MRRD Muqarara (legislation) for cabinet approval.
- Finalise the restructuring process.
- Recruit specialist staff on government consultancy contract for the functions such as procurement, finance, MIS, monitoring & evaluation and other technical areas.

### INFORMATION ON FUNDING

The MRRD reforms have been implemented with support from World Bank, Germany, Japan, Italy, Asian Development Bank, Finland, Denmark, Canada, Australia, UK, ICRC, OCO, EC, USA, the Netherlands, Norway, and Switzerland. The budget requirement for 1383 is estimated US$3.40 million, and out of which, US$1.78 million has already been pledged.

## AFGHANISTAN ASSISTANCE COORDINATION AUTHORITY

The Government has established a Consultative Group framework, within which the National Budget will be planned, financed and implemented. Twelve Consultative Groups, one for each of the National Development Programmes, will be convened by the chair Ministry (eg Ministry of Health of the Health and Nutrition CG), supported by a donor or donor/UN agency Focal Point. Other concerned ministries will participate, as will the major donors, UN agencies, and representative NGOs.

Advisory Groups are being established to ensure that cross-cutting issues are mainstreamed effectively in the work of the 12 CGs and reflected in the policy framework and budget. Arrangements are being finalised for Gender, Humanitarian Affairs, Human Rights and Environment Advisory Groups.

Each year, in March, the Afghanistan Development Forum will be held, to discuss the budget for the next fiscal year, review national priorities, and assess progress so far.

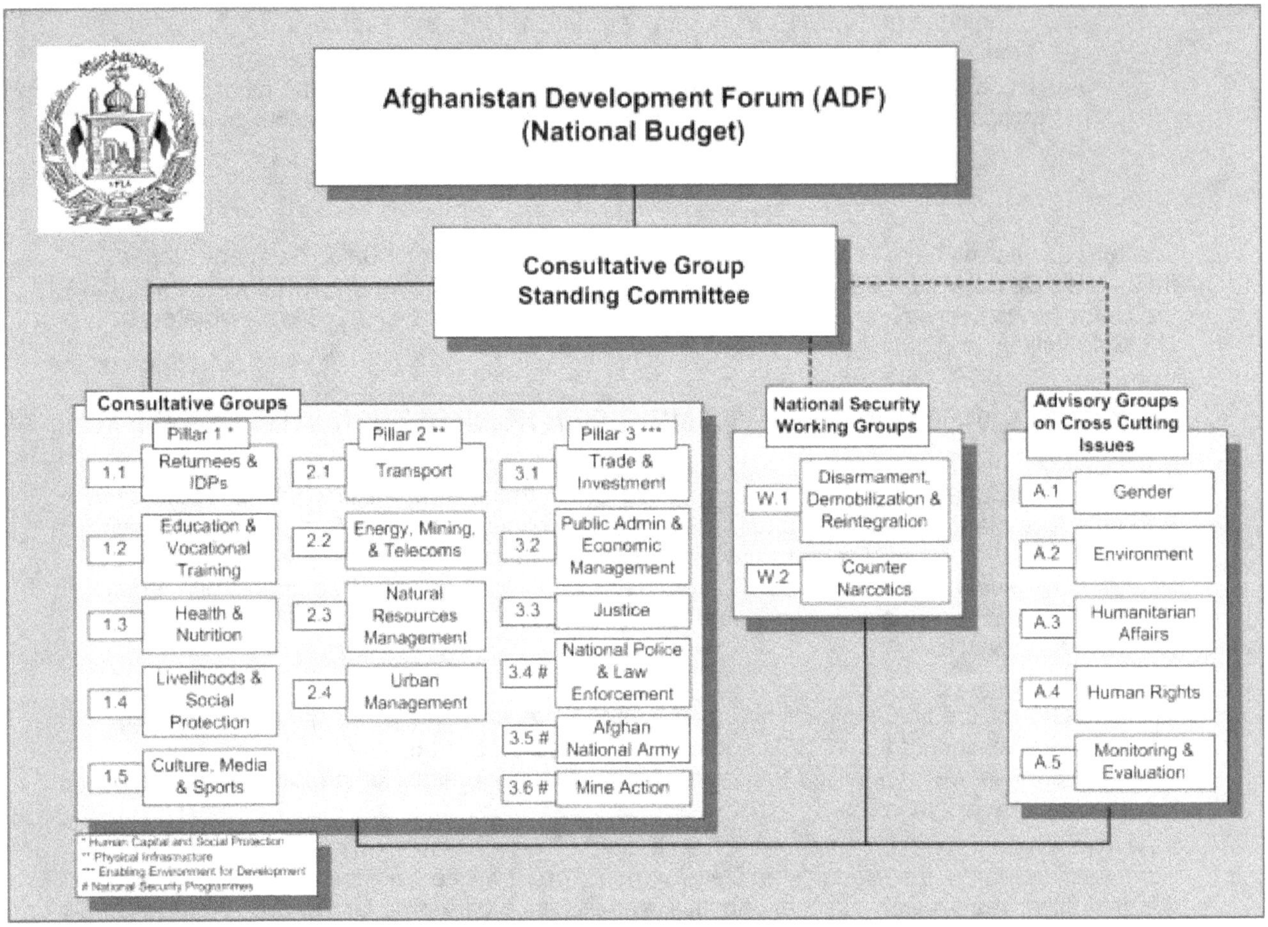


| Nationa Development Programs and Sub-programs | ToRs (none, draft, final) | TOR on Website | TOR Incorp Generic elements | Preparatory Meeting | First CG/AG Held | Next CG/AG Date | Next CG/AG Location |
|---|---|---|---|---|---|---|---|
| **1.1 Returnees & IDPs** | Draft | Yes | Yes | | 3 feb ,11 May | 23th July/3:00PM | Protocol Office , MoFA |
| **1.2 Education & Vocational Training** | Draft | | Yes | | 4 February | 06 July | MoE |
| **1.3 Health & Nutrition** | Draft | | | | 15 Feb,11 june | 11 Jun | MoH |
| **1.4 Livelihoods & Social Protection** | Draft | Yes | Yes | Held Jan | 5th Feb, 19th Feb, 8 Apr, 17th June | | MRRD |
| **1.5 Culture, Media & Sport** | Draft | | Yes | 8 February | | To be decided | MoIC |

| | | | | | | | |
|---|---|---|---|---|---|---|---|
| 1.5.1 Culture Sub-Group | Final | | | 8 February | | | MoIC |
| 1.5.2 Media Sub-Group | Final | | | 8 February | | | MoIC |
| 1.5.3 Sport Sub-Group | Final | | | 8 February | | | MoIC |
| **2.1 Transport** | Final | | Yes | 15th January | 27th January | 26 August, 03 /10:00 AM | MoPW |
| 2.1.1 Roads Sub-Group | Final | | | 15th January | 27th January,26th May | 2nd March | Embassy of Japan |
| 2.1.2 Civil Aviation Sub-Group | Final | | | | | | |
| **2.2 Energy, Mining & Telecoms** | None | | Yes | | 9 April | October 16.03 /10:00-12:0 | AACA conference room |
| 2.2.1 Energy Sub-Group | | | | 3rd February | Feb 05.03 | To be decided | |
| 2.2.2 Mining Sub-Group | | | | 3rd February | April 9.03 | | |
| 2.2.3 Telecoms Sub-Group | | | | 2nd February | August 16.03 | | |
| **2.3 Natural Resources CG** | Final | Yes | Yes | 10th February | 18th February,27th March,6th May,15th July | To be decided | Moag&L |
| **2.4 Urban Management CG** | Draft | | Yes | | 9 February ,3 June | 3 June | MUDH |
| **3.1 Trade & Investment CG** | Draft | None | Yes | 5th Feb/9th Feb | 23 Feb | 14 May | M. Commerce |
| **3.2 Public Admin & Economic Mgm CG** | Draft - waiting govt. response | Yes | None | None | None | 29 April | |
| **3.3 Justice CG** | | | | 1 Feb | 3 march | 11 August /15:30 PM | Italian Embassy |
| **3.4 National Police & Law Enforce CG** | | | | First CG 15th july | Auguest | To be decided | MoI |
| **3.5 Afghan National** | | | | | | To be decided | |

| | | | | | | | |
|---|---|---|---|---|---|---|---|
| **Army CG** | | | | | | | |
| **3.6 Mine Action CG** | | | | | | 30 August | MoFA |
| | | | | | | | |
| **Working Groups:** | | | | | | | |
| **W.1 Demilit., Demob.& Re-int. (TBC)** | | | | | | To be decided | |
| **W.2 Counter-Narcotics (TBC)** | | | | | 11 March | To be decided | |
| | | | | | | | |
| **Advisory Groups:** | | | | | | | |
| **A1. Gender Advisory Group** | Draft | Yes | None | Yes | Yes | 17 August /9-12Pm | IOM,JICA,AWN |
| **A2. Environment Advisory Group** | Draft | Yes | | 31st Janauary | 4 Mar ,4 May,19 July | | MIWRA |
| **A3. Humanitarian Affairs Advisory Group** | Final | Yes | Yes | 28 January | 2 February ,11 May | meeting No. 12 is planned for Monday, 13 October 2003, 14.00 h | SDC (switzerland)office |
| **A4. Human Rights Advisory Group** | Draft | | Yes | 25 Dec. 02 | 1 Feb,12 june | 12th August at 9:00 at | AIHRC office, Pul-i-Surkh, Kart-3 |
| **A5. Monitoring & Evaluation Advisory Group** | | | | | 2 june | 6 August,3pm | AACA |

## AFGHANISTAN: FINANCING PROPOSAL FOR AN INVESTMENT GUARANTEE TRUST FUND IN

### the Multilateral Guarantee Agency for Afghanistan

### PROPOSED PROJECT SUMMARY

| | |
|---|---|
| Recipient State | Afghanistan |
| Program Title | Investment Guarantee Trust Fund, Afghanistan |
| Description | The funds raised will be used to establish the |

| | |
|---|---|
| | "Investment Guarantee Trust Fund for Afghanistan", hereafter referred to as the 'Trust Fund'. The purpose of the Trust Fund will be to provide guarantees against political (non-commercial) risks of foreign investments in Afghanistan. The objective is to stimulate private investment and capital goods flows, thereby assisting in the reconstruction and revitalization of the economy. The political risks to be insured under the proposed project will include those covered normally by MIGA: war and civil disturbance, expropriation, transfer restriction and breach of contract. |
| Start Year and Commitment Period | 2003 – 2007 |
| Size of Fund | Up to $50 Million Contributed Over a Four Year Period |
| Requested Funding from Your Organization | Up to $10 Million |
| Potential Funding Sources | Multilateral Donors<br>Bilateral Donors<br>International Funds/ Foundations<br>Development Banks<br>The ARTF: Afghan Reconstruction Trust Fund |
| Implementing Agency | The Multilateral Investment Guarantee Agency, MIGA |
| Task Management | Special Projects Unit of MIGA |

## BACKGROUND

2. According to estimates by the World Bank and the Government of Afghanistan, Afghanistan will require up to $15 billion for its reconstruction over the next 10 years. This is a large amount of funding and the Government recognizes that there will not be sufficient donor funding to support the entire reconstruction effort. Most importantly, the government realizes that it must show real and tangible results of economic improvement, including employment creation, to further the prospects of lasting peace. In order to speed the pace of the reconstruction process, the private sector must be engaged. President Karzai has called on the Afghan Diaspora to return to Afghanistan with substantial private investments.

3. The National Development Framework (NDF) of the Government of Afghanistan identifies three main development objectives (pillars), related to Humanitarian Assistance and Human Social Capital (Pillar 1), Physical Reconstruction and Natural Resources (Pillar 2) and Private Sector Development (Pillar 3). In addressing Pillar 3's goal of Private Sector Development, trade and private investment is clearly stated in the NDF as one of the National Programs strongly supported by the Government. MIGA will be able to assist in implementing this objective through the establishment of the Trust Fund from which guarantees will be issued, aimed at mitigating the political risks of foreign private investment into Afghanistan. This will improve investor confidence

in Afghanistan and help to realize investments and allow for foreign transactions that otherwise would not take place.

4. There is strong support from the Government of Afghanistan for such a Trust Fund. Both the Ministry of Commerce and Ministry of Finance have publicly announced their support for such a program. The World Bank and other international donor organizations working in Afghanistan also recognize the need for the creation of a MIGA-administered Trust Fund. In September, 2002, in a meeting with Mr. Wolfensohn, Afghanistan's Finance Minister, Mr. Ashraf Ghani expressed the desire for MIGA's involvement in helping to attract Foreign Direct Investment (FDI) into Afghanistan. While MIGA originally intended to submit the proposal for a Trust Fund under the ARTF, the Government of Afghanistan has informed MIGA that it would like to fund this program outside the ARTF.

5. In the period of November, 2002 – January 2003, MIGA conducted an analysis of the potential level of FDI and trade into Afghanistan as a proxy for the potential demand for political risk insurance, and undertook a mission to Kabul. A preliminary investment analysis showed more positive results than initially anticipated.

6. Despite the difficult investment climate and barriers to doing business in Afghanistan, there is substantial interest from the private sector. The primary group currently consists of returning Afghan nationals who left Afghanistan as many as 25 years ago for Europe, Australia, North America, and countries in the region. The Diaspora has strong ties to Afghanistan and wishes to play a role in reconstruction of the country. Other countries interested in trade and investments are: Turkey, Iran, Pakistan, Uzbekistan and India, each of which has trade ties to the country. However, it is also expected that U.S. and European companies will show an interest when opportunities arise.

7. Many foreign investors view Afghanistan as a central business 'hub' and vital trade route, where the Middle East meets Southern and South East Asia. Results of interviews and in-country analysis indicate US$750 million of potential foreign investments over the next three years. In addition, there are many business people who want to take advantage of being the first one in Afghanistan to set up a business (Please see Annex I for details on the breakdown).

8. As indicated in Annex I, there is a wide spectrum of business sectors covered in these potential investments, creating many opportunities for down- and upstream business development:

- Power, telecommunications and internet services
- Banks, business hotels, housing and related infrastructure
- Food, agri-business, production of textile and steel, oil and gas mining

9. The majority of investors interviewed, and companies involved in substantial investment deals, indicate that they would need political risk insurance from an institution such as MIGA before going ahead with their projects. For larger investments in the country, investors will need to mobilize debt in addition to the equity contributions. International banks will not lend to projects in Afghanistan prior to obtaining political risk coverage for the investment. Of the $750 million in potential investments stated above, four formal applications have been received by MIGA in the areas of telecommunication, real estate/ land development, manufacturing and mining.

## THE ROLE OF MIGA IN ENCOURAGING FDI INTO AFGHANISTAN

10. As noted above, the long-term success for the economy of Afghanistan will depend on its ability to attract trade and investment both within the region and from abroad. While donor aid is

important for establishing sound conditions for a developing economy, aid alone cannot build long-term, lasting economic growth. It is more and more apparent that Afghanistan's prosperity and economic potential will evolve as its government and donors work to promote open, transparent and favorable conditions for investment.

11. MIGA covers eligible foreign investments against the risks of War and Civil Disturbance, Expropriation, Transfer Restriction and Breach of Contract (see also Annex III for a detailed description of MIGA's guarantee program). While there is real and substantial interest from foreign private investors in Afghanistan, the political risks are equally real and substantial, and will act as a major deterrent to foreign investment. The political risks emanate from physical damage or business interruption resulting from the possibility of renewed fighting or violence (including sabotage or terrorism), the risk of expropriation (including "creeping" expropriation) due to insufficient recognition of private property rights in a country that, for a long time, has seen little or no private ownership, and transfer risk, due to the fact that investors may not be allowed to repatriate profits or service the loans to their foreign creditors. Investors, and the financial institution lending to projects, are highly concerned about all of these risks. Without insurance for investment projects, many investors cannot do business in Afghanistan and must currently take a 'wait-and-see' approach.

### THE REASONS BEHIND THE TRUST FUND

12. There are three main reasons for the creation of this Trust Fund for Afghanistan.

(i) Afghanistan has not yet fulfilled all of its membership requirements with MIGA. Under the MIGA Convention, the Agency cannot guarantee investments until the country has become a full member. While this process should be completed in the near future, a Trust Fund would allow MIGA to start operating in Afghanistan now, without having to await membership;

(ii) More importantly, Afghanistan is a very high risk country for MIGA and without some form of risk sharing in the coming years, the scope of activities that the Agency could undertake would be very limited and, without the Trust Fund, could potentially be prohibitively expensive. Once the membership issue is resolved, the existence of a Trust Fund would allow MIGA to leverage Trust Fund money with MIGA's own resources, on a project-by-project basis. Depending on the actual risk of projects concerned, this leveraging could be higher or lower (see paragraph 15). In addition, MIGA will require investors to bear a certain amount of risk as well[1]. However, the aim would be to support as many projects as possible with a given amount of money in the Trust Fund. Therefore, MIGA will always try to minimize the amount that it requires from the Trust Fund, and will put as much risk on its own books as would be financially prudent. MIGA has previously used this particular formula of risk sharing with donor money with great success in Bosnia and Herzegovina. Over a period of four years, MIGA successfully leveraged its own resources at a ratio of around 6:1, and with modest donor funds from the European Union (EURO 10 million), the Agency issued more than US$70 million of guarantees for foreign investors in the banking, manufacturing and health sectors. Please see Annex II for further details with respect to the European Union Investment Guarantee Trust Fund for Bosnia and Herzegovina; and

(iii) Finally, a Trust Fund will allow MIGA to increase its flexibility with respect to the transactions that require political risk insurance. In the absence of other sources of insurance from most public and private insurers, it is important that the Trust Fund be allowed to cover not only FDI, but also the political risks associated with the financing of

[1] MIGA does not cover more than 90% of any investment (95% for shareholder and non-shareholder loans).

capital goods for productive purposes (e.g., tractors, machines, hospital equipment). Under MIGA's Convention, these types of transactions are not permitted unless they are also accompanied by an eligible equity investment .

## TRUST FUND PROPOSAL: TERMS OF OPERATION AND PROJECT ELIGIBILITY

Size and Terms of Operation

13. In view of MIGA's market analysis with respect to the number of potential projects, their individual size, the potential for leveraging donor money with MIGA's own resources, and taking into account the availability of donor money for Afghanistan, MIGA is of the opinion that up to US$50 million, contributed over a four year period, would be an appropriate target for the size of the Trust Fund. It is not proposed to cap the amount of Trust Fund resources used for individual projects. However, should donors require this, MIGA would suggest a cap of US$10 million per project. It is anticipated that, on average, 10 projects could be supported by the Trust Fund at any given time. One particular concern that donors may have is that funds would be tied up for long periods. However, these funds are supporting vital investments in the country and are necessary to backstop the guarantees issued. Moreover, the funds can be revolved and consequently each dollar could support multiple projects.

14. The Trust Fund will operate according to MIGA's Convention, Operational Regulations and other Agency policies, except for the fact that the Trust Fund will also be used to insure transactions that involve debt without an associated equity investment (please see paragraph 12 (iii) above). For each individual project, MIGA will seek prior Host Country Approval from the Government of Afghanistan, as it does for any of its projects world-wide. This means that only those investments that have the approval of the Government can be guaranteed by the Trust Fund.

15. The actual level of leveraging of Trust Fund resources with MIGA's own resources will be the decided on a project-by-project basis. Several factors will be taken into account, including the overall political risk of the country at the time of the proposed guarantee, the size of the investment and amount of guarantee required, the project sector, and the type of risk coverage requested by the investor.

16. The commitment period for the Trust Fund (i.e. initial period during which guarantees will be issued) is four years. Funds that remain uncommitted after this initial period will be returned to donors on a pro rata basis. During the operation of the Trust Fund, when guarantees expire or are canceled, MIGA would re-use the funds to support new projects. However, MIGA does not intend to recommit the funds indefinitely. The Agency therefore suggests that the continuation of the Trust Fund is discussed between the Government of Afghanistan, the donors and MIGA at the end of the seventh year of its existence, deciding whether:

to continue the re-use of Trust Fund resources as guarantees expire or are cancelled. This would be desirable and justified if the demand for political risk insurance in Afghanistan is considerable, but where the risks would still be of such magnitude that MIGA would be unable to book all the risks on its own account. The decision would include a renewed maximum period during which Trust Fund monies could be recommitted for projects; or

(ii) to refund the Trust Fund money on a pro rata basis to the donors concerned; or

(iii) to release the Trust Fund money to the Government of Afghanistan as guarantees expire and Trust Fund money is freed up.

The last two options assume that the risks in Afghanistan have decreased and MIGA can guarantee projects entirely from its own resources, or that there is not much further anticipated demand for political risk insurance. With regard to the last option, funds could be earmarked for use in priority development programs, as agreed between the Government of Afghanistan and Trust Fund donors. Returning the remaining funds (after the payment of any unrecovered claims) to the Government of Afghanistan would also have the benefit of providing a strong incentive for the Government not to cause any claims.

17. Investors would be charged guarantee premiums established in accordance with MIGA's normal procedures, but which will not be prohibitively expensive. MIGA would use part of the premium income to defray its administrative expenses of administering the donor funds.

**Project Eligibility**

18. Eligible investments will be restricted to new investments, the implementation of which begins after an application for guarantee has been filed with MIGA. New investment contributions associated with the expansion, modernization or financial restructuring of existing projects will also be eligible, as will acquisitions that involve the privatization of state enterprises. Up to 90% of the total investment can be insured by the Trust Fund (95% for debt transactions). The investor concerned would decide on the specific risks that it would need the Trust Fund to cover (please see Annex III for a detailed description of MIGA's coverages).

19. Eligible forms of foreign investment would include equity, shareholder loans, and loan guaranties issued by equity holders. Loans by unrelated lenders (such as a commercial bank loans) would also be insured if they are related to the supply of capital goods for productive purposes, including financial leasing. Other eligible forms of investment would include technical assistance and management contracts, and franchising and licensing agreements, etc., provided they have terms of at least three years and the investor's remuneration is tied to the project's operating results.

20. Projects will be screened for their development impact, using MIGA's standard methodology, including:

- The total value of investments and supplier inputs realized from assistance of the Trust Fund;
- Direct and indirect employment generated;
- Amount of taxes paid;
- Up- and down-stream impacts of the project;
- Foreign exchange generation.

In addition, all projects would have to comply with MIGA's normal risk evaluation, environmental standards, and social policies and safeguards.

21. The Trust Fund is also expected to have indirect benefits, in the sense that its existence will provide an incentive for the Government of Afghanistan to continue its reform efforts aimed at creating a more enabling environment for the private sector. Recent reform measures implemented by the Government include the following:

- In September 2002, the Government passed a new Law on Investment for both domestic and foreign investment. While there may be some small amendments to the law in the future, this is, overall, a liberal investment law for the country.

- As part of the new law, a special commission, Chaired by the Minister of Commerce, was created to simplify and speed the process of registering foreign companies in Afghanistan.
- The Government, with the assistance of German donor funding, is establishing a "one-stop-shop" for foreign investment. The office is designed to cut through the red tape of investment. The planned opening of the office is for April/ May, 2003.
- The Commercial Code is currently being revised by the Government with assistance from USAID and other donors.
- In early 2003, bi-lateral trade agreements were signed with Iran and India. Afghanistan has preferential trade status with the United States and the European Union.
- A new law on Banking is likely to be approved in the spring of 2003. The World Bank, IMF and other institutions are carrying out technical assistance programs to reform and revitalize the banking sector.

22. In addition, the following are a number of measures that the Government plans to undertake in the near future:

- The Government of Afghanistan will work toward finalization of the new banking law by the summer of 2003 which, in turn will allow for foreign banks to operate in Afghanistan and thus help to facilitate vital banking infrastructure reforms necessary to help attract foreign investors.
- Opening the 'One Stop Shop', the AISA project by summer of 2003. This project will be able to act as a liaison between the Trust Fund to inform foreign investors informing them of the possibility for investment guarantees, as well as act as a pre-screen to the Trust Fund on potential foreign investors.
- *Revision of the Commercial Code which will be vital for the successful advancement of domestic and foreign investment.*

## IMPLEMENTATION ARRANGEMENTS

### Framework Agreement

23. The implementation of the Trust Fund requires MIGA and the donors to execute a 'Framework Agreement' for the Trust Fund, which will outline the mode of operation of the Fund, the arrangements for the management and use of the funds, reporting requirements (every 6 months) and success criteria.

### Marketing:

24. Extensive marketing will be required on an ongoing basis to successfully implement the Trust fund. MIGA will produce a brochure and marketing materials for the Trust Fund, including in Dari. Press releases and public relations materials will be prepared to inform donors and the press on the achievements of the Trust Fund.

25. Furthermore, MIGA will recruit a special representative to implement the Trust Fund for Afghanistan. The need to have a person on a full-time basis has been one of the most valuable lessons of experience from the Trust Fund for Bosnia and Herzegovina. This person will spend approximately 10 days per month in Afghanistan to market the Trust Fund and the remainder outside the country to liaise with interested investors. In addition, the MIGA special representative will prepare operating procedures for the management of the Trust Fund.

26. MIGA will work with the World Bank in Kabul to establish a part-time office. Once operations are underway, the MIGA special representative will send potential Trust Fund guarantee applicants to MIGA for processing and approval.

## ANNEX I: ESTIMATES OF FDI FOR AFGHANISTAN IN US$ MILLION (JANUARY 2003)

Please note that this list is based on a survey and is not an indication of the current project pipeline. The list is in the process of being updated through a follow-up survey.

| Investor Country or Organization | Sector/ project | Accurate Project value in US$ millions as stated during interviews | High–Low Estimate: US$ millions | Totals, or average of hi/low estimates |
|---|---|---|---|---|
| Large power investor– Kabul | Power projects on a small scale: rehab | | 3-5 | 4 |
| Agha Khan Fund | Telecoms license, for all of country | 55 | | 55 |
| Agha Khan Fund | Hotel Serena, Kabul | | 40-60 | 50 |
| Austria/USA | Internet Service Provider – First ISP for country | | 20-25 | 22.5 |
| Australia with Afghan/Dubai Partner | Housing and Infrastructure PPP with Government | 100, as the initial investment | | 100 |
| Germany | Pharmaceutical plant | 0.2 with large in-kind contributions | | 0.2 |
| Germany | Metals smelting plant – rehabilitation | | 5-15 | 10 |
| India | Private Bank | | 10-20 | 15 |
| India | Mineral Water Bottling Plant | | 1-5 | 3 |
| Iran | Investments in all sectors as discussed via phone | 100, according to Iran Foreign Investment Co. (IFIC) | | 100 |
| Italy with Dubai partner | Rehabilitation of steel mill | | 20-40 | 30 |
| Pakistan | Investments in all sectors | | 40-100 | 70 |
| Turkey | Construction and Infrastructure. figures as of Oct, 2002. | Predicted to be highest foreign investor with 115 million USD | | 115 |

| Investor Country or Organization | Sector/ project | Accurate Project value in US$ millions as stated during interviews | High–Low Estimate: US$ millions | Totals, or average of hi/low estimates |
|---|---|---|---|---|
| | Likely higher by 2/ 03 | | | |
| USA | Hotel, Kabul | Project value not given | 40-60 | 50 |
| USA | Bank, Kabul | Project value not given; quoted as small bank | 10–15 | 12.5 |
| USA | Oil exploration and extraction in Herat | 40 | | 40 |
| USA | Small power station for Kabul | 2.5 | | 2.5 |
| USA | Agriculture – cultivation and packing of dried fruits and nuts | Estimate not given in interview | 1-10, depending on new or rehab of facility | 5.5 |
| Various countries | Privatizations of Govt owned factories | Not stated in discussion with the Minister | Possibly 20-80: Govt thinks these are higher | 50 |
| TOTALS | | 412<br>Stated investments | 210-436<br>Hi/Low Totals | 735<br>Stated & Ave of hi/lows |

## ANNEX II: The Case of the Trust Fund for Bosnia and Herzegovina

MIGA initiated the European Union Investment Guarantee Trust Fund (EUIGTF) for Bosnia and Herzegovina in the fall of 1997. The initial period of the EUIGTF was through 1999, however the Trust Fund was extended through the end of MIGA's fiscal year 2000 –June, 2001. *Overall the EUIGTF was a great success from many perspectives:*

**1) 10 million EURO in the Trust Fund was leveraged with US$61 million of MIGA's own capital for total investments guaranteed in the amount of US$ 71 million.**

**2) New jobs were created as a result of direct investments covered from the EUIGTF and countless more from down stream business effects, including from the lending operations of the commercial banks that the Trust Fund covered.**

**3) The investments covered provided training in areas of hi-tech production techniques, modern banking and the provision of healthcare services, thereby bringing much-needed employee training into Bosnia.**

**4) The EUIGTF was instrumental in helping MIGA to do business in Bosnia. After the EUIGTF had ended, MIGA has successfully continued to operate in Bosnia and Herzegovina on its own and has supported five additional projects worth US$38 million in guarantees.**

Over the years of operation of the EUIGTF *many lessons were learned on effective methods for managing such a Trust Fund.* These will be incorporated into new trust funds going forward:

- It is essential to have a full-time representative working on the ground to increase awareness and liaise with investors on a continuing basis. When the EUIGTF was initiated, the Trust Fund was managed by MIGA from Washington DC and by the European Commission in Brussels. Since no one was in Bosnia and Herzegovina for the EUIGTF, almost no one knew of its existence. Once a special representative was placed in-country, there was a steady flow of inquiries from foreign investors for guarantees.
- *Local representation gives foreign investors a positive psychological signal on foreign investment.* Once the investors are aware that an organization like MIGA are willing to place someone on the ground to cover investment issues, they are also more likely to regard the host country as investment-safe.
- Having someone in the field, in a country like Bosnia, *helps MIGA staff back in headquarters to better understand the risks involved in the country* since more detailed information can be provided. This greatly helps in the management of the risks in a high risk environment.
- It can be helpful for the special representative *to become engaged with issues related to investment and business reforms in the country*. In the case of Bosnia, the special representative of the Trust Fund worked with the Government, the World Bank, and others to raise issues hindering foreign investment. While the Trust Fund was initially a vehicle only for guarantees, the MIGA office was also used to promote reforms aimed at improving the investment climate.

## ANNEX III. DEFINITIONS OF MIGA COVERAGES

### 1. Transfer Restriction

Transfer Restriction Coverage protects against (i) the inability to convert, from local currency into guarantee currency, loan payments, dividends, profits, and proceeds from the disposal of the guaranteed investment, and (ii) host government actions that prevent the transfer of the guarantee currency outside the host country, including the failure of the government to grant an authorization for the conversion or the transfer of such currency. Compensation is based on the guaranteed percentage of any payments that cannot be converted or transferred.

### 2. Expropriation

Expropriation Coverage protects against losses attributable to measures taken or approved by the host government that deprive the guarantee holder of its ownership or control over its investment, or in the case of debt, results in the project enterprise being unable to meet its obligations to the lender. Both direct and indirect (creeping) expropriation are covered. Compensation for equity is based on the guaranteed percentage of the net book value of the guaranteed investment in the project enterprise. For debt, compensation is based on the guaranteed percentage of the principal and interest that is in default as a result of expropriation.

### 3. War and Civil Disturbance

War and Civil Disturbance Coverage protects against losses arising as a result of military action or civil disturbance in the host country, including sabotage and terrorism, that destroys or damages tangible assets of the project enterprise or interferes with its operations (business interruption), or, in the case of debt, results in the project enterprise being unable to meet its obligations to the lender. Compensation is based on the guaranteed percentage of the value of the assets destroyed or damaged or, in the case of business interruption, the net book value of the guaranteed equity investment. For debt, compensation is based on the guaranteed percentage of the principal and interest that is in default as a result of war and civil disturbance.

### 4. Breach of Contract

Breach of Contract Coverage protects against losses arising from a repudiation or breach by the host government of a contract entered with the guarantee holder, provided that a final and binding arbitration award or judicial decision has been rendered in favor of the guarantee holder and cannot be enforced against the host government. Compensation is based on the amount that the guarantee holder is entitled to recover from the host government in accordance with the terms of the arbitration award or judicial decision.

# AFGHANISTAN CUSTOMS SYSTEM AND TRADE REGULATIONS

## CUSTOMS ACTIVITIES ADMINISTRATION

Afghanistan is strategically placed between the Middle East, Central Asia and the sub-continent. As a land-locked country it is dependent on the transit of goods from its neighbors to develop trade. Pakistan and Iran are the two main countries from which Afghanistan can access sea ports. Afghanistan is a land bridge between these two major countries of Central Asia; on one side, the Port of Karachi on the Arabian Sea and on the other, the Port of Bander Abbas in the Persian Gulf.

The Pakistan corridor connects the Pakistani ports of Karachi, Port Qasim and a new port of Gwader with the Afghan border crossings at Torkham and Spinboldak. The Iran corridor connects the Iranian ports of Cha Bahar and Bandar Abbas with the Afghan border crossings at Zarang and Islam Qala.

In addition, the routes through the Central Asian Republics (CAR) connect Afghanistan to the Russian Federation as well as to European and Pacific ports via Tajikistan (border crossing at Sher Khan Bandar), Uzbekistan (border crossing at Hayratan) and Turkmenistan (border crossing at Torghundi).

Due to this strategic geographical position, Afghanistan also has the potential to become a link providing Pakistan and Iran with a direct route to the CAR and providing the CAR with its shortest distance to obtain access to the sea, in comparison with the routes to the Black Sea, Europe and China. The Trade and Customs Working Group (TCWG), in its meeting held at Bangkok (Oct 2004) under the Central Asia Transport and Trade Forum (CSATTF) organized by the Asian Development Bank, identified the following two corridors as the focal point for development:

South-North Corridor connecting the Pakistani ports of Karachi, Port Qasim and Gwader with Tajikistan, Uzbekistan and Turkmenistan while West-East Corridor connecting the Iranian ports of Cha Bahar and Bandar Abbas with Tajikistan, Uzbekistan and Turkmenistan.

Afghanistan understands its geographical importance and is aware of the responsibility which rests on its shoulders in regard to trade facilitation in the region. Keeping in view the gigantic task ahead, Afghanistan Customs has undertaken a substantial reform program with the sole aim of creating an environment conducive to trade and industry development, not only for itself but for all the countries in the region.

The Islamic Republic of Afghanistan has recognized that after war and civil strife there is now an enormous need for the reconstruction of infrastructure and the provision of basic services to the people of Afghanistan. Therefore, Afghanistan Customs Department (ACD) is working hard to fulfill their obligation to raise the current level of revenue collection and the scale of the trade volume and its potential for revenue maximization. Additionally, they are working on modernization of ACD to serve as a tool to facilitate trade and business to encourage investment and made a major contribution to the creation of a beneficial economic and social development.

In order to exercise best practices, Afghan customs Department made 5 year plan and started working on that since last 2 years, the plans are to enhance the current level of revenue collection and improve import and export clearance procedures. The simplification of Customs clearance procedures and the renovation and construction of physical infrastructure are started to have a standard Customs department which allows for proper and effective Customs control. The ACD also worked on reorganizing Headquarters and Regional Offices and enhanced their capacity to a level where senior management is fully in control of Customs activities. Functioning Customs offices, both in the centre and in the provinces, are seen as a prerequisite for a fully functional and modern Afghan Customs. Customs Training Academy is one of the major steps to enhance the customs officer's capacity up to international level.

Introduction of new technology to Afghan Customs, able them to fight corruption and to have full control on imports, exports and transit. The best technological introduction is ASYCUDA, by which you can track the shipments and his status. Afghan Customs are taking major steps to bring their data statistic to the international level by introducing internationally recognize data base experts to enhance the quality of import and export statistics.

Afghan customs is also active member of WCO (World Customs Organization) and has an observer status in WTO (World Trade Organization). Afghanistan customs is playing key role in regional organizations working for trade facilitation.

## CUSTOMS REFORM

Customs reform and modernization is a sine qua non for economic progress and security of Afghanistan. The reform process will ensure efficiency in collection of revenue and prevention of illicit, dangerous or undeclared goods from entering into the country. With better revenue realization, the Government will be able to meet its commitments to deliver its multiple objectives (better security, economic growth, democratic polity, pluralistic society and market based economy). Better quality of customs service will improve trade flows.

The Afghan Customs department has a lot of tangible achievement in last few years of reforms in the field of Automation, legislation, capacity development, control, infrastructure development and enforcement. The basic thrust of reforms is to develop a customs system that minimizes leakage in revenue collection through rationalization of laws, procedures and automated processes. This system will help facilitate clearance of goods and reduce contact of officers with trade, thereby reducing the scope of corruption. In addition adoption of automated processes and international best practices for international transit of goods through its territories will help make Afghanistan a land bridge of the region.

The reform process will see the strengthening of the enforcement machinery of department that will create deterrence to duty evaders and curb smuggling of goods including narcotics and environmentally hazardous goods. The department will take enforcement action against non-compliance by importers and exporters. By developing a strong intelligence network the department will be able to play a major role in coordination of intelligence with other security agencies.

The approach of the reform is not to confront the traders but to enter into a partnership with them for better voluntary compliance of laws and which will benefit the traders by reducing their transaction costs.

Customs due to its nature of operations has a large body of officers and the organizational issues are very important. The reform process aims at improving the organization so that it will have the correct structure, logical definition of roles, fair recruitment system, service conditions, Accountability, conduct and disciplinary rules, training support and a built-in mechanism for promotion of ethics in the staff.

Afghan Customs Department, like all other Customs Administrations is in the process of delivering on its core activities as mentioned above. However, ACD may carry out other essential activities such as protection of consumers, interdiction of dangerous goods, collaboration to fiscal audits and collection of other taxes at source.

Customs operations are spread over a large geographical area and many customs offices. There is a shortage of office buildings working space and equipment. The plan seeks to meet these requirements and their creation at an early date.

The Afghan Customs Department has been entrusted with the additional responsibility of creating and operating Customs Infrastructure facilities, though such activity is not within the core competence of any customs organization. In view of the existing poor facilities, creation of physical infrastructure of terminal buildings and cargo handling equipment assumes urgency in the interest of trade facilitation. The reform program addresses the need for such infrastructural development and suggests an autonomous body with necessary technical skills to assume the civil works procurement and management of these facilities.

# TRADE REGULATIONS AND STANDARDS

## IMPORT TARIFFS

Afghanistan maintains the lowest import tariffs in the region. A new tariff regime has significantly reduced and simplified the customs duty rates to six major categories: essential food and non-food products – 2.5%; raw materials and capital goods – 5%; petroleum products – 8%; semi-manufactured goods – 10%, and; luxury and non-priority products at 15% and 16% respectively. Further, planned customs rationalization will decrease the number of rates from six to four, increase the tariff rates charges on the bulk of imported products, and increase the weighted average tax rate from 3.9% to 6.9%. Even at these revised tariff rates, Afghan tariffs will remain the lowest in the region.

## TRADE BARRIERS

Afghanistan has few trade barriers for imported products. However, deficient infrastructure, a still evolving legal and commercial regime, high levels of corruption and a volatile security situation act as de facto trade barriers.

## IMPORT REQUIREMENTS AND DOCUMENTATION

All imported goods and products must have an original bill of lading and inventory documents. Transit permission is required for shipments transiting through Pakistan, which can be obtained from the Central Board of Revenue's Customs Division in Islamabad, Pakistan.

## U.S. EXPORT CONTROLS

In June 2002, the U.S. lifted most restrictions on exports and re-exports to Afghanistan. Such transactions are now subject to export control policies applicable to most countries who are not members of multilateral export control regimes. The majority of everyday commercial goods do not require specific U.S. government authorization for export or re-export to Afghanistan. However, certain items on the Commerce Control List do require a license from the Department of Commerce's Bureau of Industry and Security (BIS). These include items controlled for chemical and biological weapons, nuclear nonproliferation, national security, and missile technology reasons. There are also foreign policy controls in place for regional stability and crime control reasons. These requirements can be found in Part 742 of the Export Administration Regulations (EAR) http://www.access.gpo.gov/bis/ear/ear_data.html

The U.S. government generally reviews license applications to export controlled goods to Afghanistan on a case-by-case basis. Note that a license is required to export an item subject to the Export Administration Regulations even when one would not otherwise be necessary, if you know, have reason to know, or are otherwise individually informed by the Department of Commerce's Bureau of Industry and Security (BIS) with respect to a specific transaction that the item will be used in activities related to nuclear, chemical, or biological weapons or missile deliver systems as defined in part 744 of the Export Administration Regulations. In addition, certain restrictions administered by the U.S. Department of the Treasury's Office of Foreign Assets Control continue in effect with respect to transactions involving members of the Taliban. Detailed information on U.S. export policies can be found at the BIS website at www.bis.doc.gov. Specific guidance on U.S. export controls with respect to Afghanistan can be found at http://www.bis.doc.gov/policiesandregulations/RegionalConsiderations/Afghanistan.pdf (2.3MB PDF only)

You may also contact the BIS Export Counseling Division http://www.bis.doc.gov/licensing/ExporterFAQ.html at (202) 482-4811 for specific guidance.

## TEMPORARY ENTRY

Afghanistan currently has no laws or regulations governing products entering the country temporarily.

## LABELING AND MARKING REQUIREMENTS

Afghanistan currently has no laws or regulations governing labeling and marketing requirements for products.

## PROHIBITED AND RESTRICTED IMPORTS

The following items are prohibited from entry in Afghanistan:

- firearms, explosives, daggers
- obscene and subversive literature
- alcohol (2 liter exception for personal use for commercial air passengers)
- recorded VCR tapes and other movies
- parlor video games or parts thereof
- goods in commercial quantities

Although not prohibited from entry into Afghanistan, Pakistan currently maintains three items on its Negative List (cigarettes, cooking oil and auto parts) that are barred from transiting its territory for import into Afghanistan.

## CUSTOMS REGULATIONS AND CONTACT INFORMATION

Customs regulations and procedures in Afghanistan are neither transparent nor uniform. Coordination between customs and other government authorities is minimal; customs staff are untrained and infrastructure is degraded. Traders face unclear procedures at the borders, as well as extra-legal duties and bureaucratic obstructions.

Customs reform is a priority of the Government of Afghanistan. Large-scale reform efforts are underway to establish standardized fees and procedures for incoming goods and a trained cadre of professional staff. In December 2003 the Customs Department introduced a Single Administrative Document system pilot program, based on the European Union customs regime, for five key provinces. In March 2005, implementation of the Automated System for Customs Data (ASYCUDA) system began on a limited scale. Simplified exemptions processing documentation is being introduced and a new Customs Code is under consideration. A system of Licensed Customs Brokers is also being designed.

The Afghan Customs Department, a division of the Ministry of Finance, can be contacted at:
Telephone: +(93)(75)200-4199
Email: info@mof.gov.af

## STANDARDS

Afghanistan is currently in the process of developing a national standards regime. The Afghan National Standards Authority (ANSA) is an independent agency under the Ministry of Commerce and was established in 2005. ANSA is responsible for the establishment, maintenance, dissemination and enforcement of national standards and technical regulations. ANSA plans to have standards regulations in place for select goods and products in 2006.

ANSA can be contacted at:
Telephone: +(93)(70)151-696
Email: ansaafg@gmail.com

## TRADE AGREEMENTS

Afghanistan is a member of the Economic Cooperation Organization (ECO) and the Central Asia Regional Economic Cooperation (CAREC.) It will become a full member of the South Asian Association for Regional Cooperation (SAARC) in 2006.

Afghanistan has signed bilateral Trade and Economic Cooperation Agreements with Russia and Turkey, a bilateral Reciprocal Promotion and Protection of Investments Agreement with Turkey, a bilateral Preferential Trade Agreement with India and a bilateral Investment Treaty with Germany.

Afghan products enjoy duty free and quota free access under an LDC Market Access Initiative with Canada and a Generalized Preferences Treatment agreement with Japan. Afghan products also enjoy an "Everything But Arms" (EBA) agreement with the European Union, which allows duty free treatment for all other items manufactured in Afghanistan.

As a least-developed country, Afghanistan is eligible for duty-free access to the U.S. market for approximately 5,700 products under the Generalized System of Preferences (GSP) program. Afghanistan has signed a bilateral Investment Incentive Agreement with the United States to encourage and protect investment activities in Afghanistan through the provision of insurance and investment guarantees under the OPIC program. In 2004, a Trade and Investment Framework Agreement (TIFA) was also signed with the United States.

Afghanistan became an observer to the World Trade Organization in December 2004 and has announced its intention to complete the WTO accession process within the next five years.

## WEB RESOURCES

Department of Commerce's Bureau of Industry and Security www.bis.doc.gov,
http://www.bis.doc.gov/policiesandregulations/RegionalConsiderations/Afghanistan.pdf
(2.3MB PDF only) http://www.bis.doc.gov/licensing/ExporterFAQ.html

Export Administration Regulations http://www.access.gpo.gov/bis/ear/ear_data.html

Ministry of Finance http://www.mof.gov.af

South Asian Association for Regional Cooperation (SAARC) http://www.saarc-sec.org

Economic Cooperation Organization (ECO) http://www.ecosecretariat.org

Central Asia Regional Economic Cooperation (CAREC) http:// www.carec.kz

U.S. Department of Commerce http://www.doc.gov

Office of the U.S. Trade Representative http://www.ustr.gov

Overseas Private Investment Corporation http://www.opic.gov/

Canadian Department of Foreign Affairs and International Trade
http://www.dfait-maeci.gc.ca

United Nations Conference on Trade and Development (UNCTAD)
http://www.unctad.org/Templates/Page.asp?intItemID=2344&lang=1&print=1

Turkish Ministry of Foreign of Affairs http://www.mfa.gov.tr

Japanese Ministry of Foreign Affairs http://www.mofa.go.jp

Gateway to the European Union http://www.europa.eu.int

Indian Ministry of Commerce http://www.commerce.nic.in

# TRADE AND PROJECT FINANCING

## METHODS OF PAYMENT

Most local businesses operate on a cash basis. Import and export letters of credit are available at several banks, as well as electronic funds transfer. Due to wide mistrust and general underdevelopment of the banking system, many local businesses depend on the informal *hawala* system to make payments and transfer funds. The *hawala* system is an informal value transfer system, whereby money is transferred through a network of brokers, or *hawaladars*. Promissory instruments are not exchanged; the transaction is based on the honor system.

## BANKING SYSTEM

The Da Afghanistan (Central) Bank has licensed 12 commercial banks. Out of twelve, seven banks are full-fledged commercial banks:

- *Bank-e-Milli Afghan* or National Bank (parastatal bank)
- *Pashtany Tejarati* Bank or Pashtany Commercial Bank (parastatal bank)
- Export Promotion Bank (parastatal bank)
- First Microfinance Bank (an Aga Khan/IFC joint venture)
- Kabul Bank (a solely Afghan-owned bank)
- Afghanistan International Bank (an ING-affiliated enterprise with American equity)

- Arian Bank (joint venture of *Bank-e-Mille* "National Bank" of Iran and *Bank-e-Saderat* "Export Bank" of Iran)

**Five Branches of Foreign Banks:**

1. Standard Chartered Bank (UK)
2. National Bank of Pakistan (Pakistan)
3. Habib Bank Limited (Pakistan)
4. Punjab National Bank of India (India)
5. Bank Alfalah Limited (Pakistan)

Most of the twelve commercial banks licensed to operate in Afghanistan are concentrated in Kabul and provide services primarily to international donors and businesses, foreign NGOs and foreign government agencies. As of January 31, 2005, the Da Afghanistan (Central) Bank's main office in Kabul is no longer involved in commercial activities. However, in provinces with limited or no commercial banking services, the Central Bank continues to offer some commercial services. The banking system has limited capacity to provide credit and/or non-credit services.

There is no long term financing available from commercial banks in Afghanistan; most offer terms of a year or less, with a maximum tenure of three years. There is a small number of non-bank financial institutions (11 micro-finance institutions, one credit union and one leasing company), but these institutions meet only a small fraction of credit needs. There are no credit bureaus or credit rating agencies.

Because of widespread distrust of the banking system, many local businesses use the hawala system for short-term loans to finance working capital needs, or rely on family and friends.
The legal and regulatory framework of the financial sector is still under development.

## FOREIGN-EXCHANGE CONTROLS

Exchange rate policy is determined by the Central Bank, and is implemented through a weekly foreign exchange (USD) auction. No foreign exchange restrictions or multiple currency practices are currently in place.

## U.S. BANKS AND LOCAL CORRESPONDENT BANKS

There are currently no U.S. banks operating in Afghanistan. However, Afghanistan International Bank is an ING-affiliated enterprise with American equity.

## PROJECT FINANCING

Project financing is available from the following organizations:

**The Overseas Private Investment Corporation (OPIC)** is an independent agency of the U.S. government that offers specialty insurance (stand alone terror/sabotage and political risk coverage,) loans and guarantees to help U.S. businesses of all sizes invest and compete in more than 140 emerging markets and developing nations worldwide. A $100 million line of credit is available to projects that demonstrate substantial U.S. participation, promise significant benefits to the economic and social development of Afghanistan, and foster private sector competition in Afghanistan. OPIC gives preferential consideration to projects that significantly involve U.S. small businesses. OPIC is active in Afghanistan. Some examples include up to $35 million in financing and political risk insurance to support construction of a five-star international hotel in Kabul, managed by Hyatt International, and a direct loan of approximately $3 million to support construction of 1,200 homes near Kandahar by a small American company.

**The International Finance Corporation (IFC)** promotes sustainable private sector investment in developing countries and is the largest multilateral source of loan and equity financing for private sector projects in the developing world. IFC provides loans, equity finance and quasi-equity. It also offers financial risk management products and intermediary finance.

**The U.S. Trade and Development Agency (USTDA)** advances economic development and U.S. commercial interests in developing and middle-income countries. The agency funds various forms of technical assistance, feasibility studies, training, orientation visits and business workshops that support the development of a modern infrastructure and a fair and open trading environment. USTDA moved quickly to establish its program in Afghanistan and already has approved funding of about $5 million. USTDA has financed projects in telecommunications, civil aviation, oil and gas, higher education, private sector development, and power.

**The Export-Import Bank of the United States** provides financing for the sale of U.S. products overseas. Although Ex-Im is currently not open for business in Afghanistan, it will continue to survey future opportunities.

**Many business opportunities are connected to the reconstruction effort. The following agencies have large programs through which opportunities for interested businesses are available.**

**U.S. Agency for International Development (USAID)**

USAID has taken a leading role in Afghanistan's reconstruction effort, focusing on health clinics and basic health services, school construction and education programs, revitalizing agriculture through irrigation systems, farm-to-market roads, market centers, and infrastructure, including the Kabul-Kandahar-Herat highway. USAID is also funding programs that enhance the central government's capacity and provide it with the tools and technical assistance to govern effectively. Funding in 2005 exceed $1 billion. The USAID Web site, http:// www.usaid.gov , has a business and procurement link that lists upcoming procurements including solicitation documents, announcements, and other resources. This site is updated daily and offers e-mail notification when a new solicitation has been uploaded to the site. U.S. firms interested in bidding on USAID projects in Afghanistan can review requests for applications, proposals, quotations and invitation for bids on this web site. U.S. firms should also review the main portal for U.S. government procurements at http:// www.fedbizopps.gov.

**World Bank**

Since resumption of operations in April 2002, the World Bank has financed 19 projects in Afghanistan, committing around US $893.2 million in grants and interest free loans. World Bank projects primarily focus on improving rural livelihoods by rebuilding infrastructure and providing employment opportunities, education and basic health services. They are the largest international donor to the Government's National Solidarity and National Emergency Employment Programs, which offer cash-for-work on infrastructure projects. In addition, the World Bank administers the multi-donor Afghanistan Reconstruction Trust Fund, which provides coordinated financing of unfunded priority expenditures in Afghanistan's reconstruction program. The World Bank's website includes an information portal for the business community seeking to participate in opportunities that are generated from World Bank-financed projects at http://www.worldbank.org . Projects can be also be tracked at http://www.dgmarket.com/

**Asian Development Bank (ADB)**

ADB's latest Country Strategy and Program for Afghanistan was released in August 2005, covering the period 2006-2008. Since resuming operations in Afghanistan in 2002, ADB has approved seven public sector loans totaling $513.7 million (to the end of July 2005), $78.5 million in ADF grants (to two projects), and 25 technical assistance projects (both project preparatory and advisory or capacity development) totaling some $40.9 million (including $5.3 million in donor co-financing). In addition, ADB has approved $53.1 million in private sector loans, equity investments, and political risk guarantees. Contract awards in 2004 totaled $99.2 million, bringing the cumulative figure for 2002–2004 to $258.3 million. Public sector disbursements in 2004 totaled $43.2 million, with cumulative public sector disbursements totaling $199.8 million.

ADB projects focus in the areas of agriculture and natural resources, energy, gender, governance, financial and private sector development, transport and communications. A detailed description of their program can be found at http://www.adb.org/Documents/CSPs/AFG/2005/default.asp. The ADB website, http://www.adb.org, offers detailed information for companies interested in participating in upcoming procurements. Projects can be also be tracked at http://www.dgmarket.com/

In addition, there are also opportunities to bid on donor-funded projects administered by the Government of Afghanistan. **The Afghanistan Reconstruction and Development Service (ARDS)** manages the purchase of goods and services on behalf of the Afghan Government. Companies that wish to receive procurement notices can do so by registering through email. ARDS can be contacted at http://www.eafghanistan.gov.af/procurement/ or procurement@afghanistangov.org.

Political risk insurance is available both through OPIC and the Afghanistan Investment Guarantee Facility, a program of the World Bank's Multilateral Investment Guarantee Agency.

## WEB RESOURCES

OPIC http://www.opic.gov

International Finance Corporation http://www.ifc.org

U.S. Trade and Development Agency http://www.tda.gov

U.S. Agency for International Development: http://www.usaid.gov

Federal Business Opportunities http://www.fedbizopps.gov

World Bank: http://www.worldbank.org

Asian Development Bank: http://www.adb.org

Development Gateway Market Portal: http://www.dgmarket.com/

The Afghanistan Reconstruction and Development Service: http://www.ards.af/aaca/procurement

Multilateral Investment Guarantee Agency: http://www.miga.org

Export-Import Bank of the United States: http://www.exim.gov

Country Limitation Schedule: http://www.exim.gov/tools/country/country_limits.html

SBA's Office of International Trade: http://www.sba.gov/oit

USDA Commodity Credit Corporation: http://www.fsa.usda.gov/ccc/default.htm

## AFGHANISTAN REVENUE BY COLLECTION CUSTOM HOUSES.

In thousand Afs
Prepared by: Customs Statistics Unit..

| Provinces | 1385 | % | 1386 | % | 1387 | % | 1388 | % |
|---|---|---|---|---|---|---|---|---|
| Kabul | 603,898 | 4% | 1,084,547 | 6% | 1,125,123 | 6% | 1,668,247 | 5% |
| Airport | 616,378 | 4% | 838,698 | 5% | 942,241 | 5% | 1,177,660 | 3% |
| Post Parcel | 371 | 0% | 553 | 0% | 926 | 0% | 1,581 | 0% |
| Balkh | 2,366,130 | 15% | 3,250,598 | 18% | 3,550,174 | 18% | 8,346,803 | 23% |
| Herat | 5,723,904 | 37% | 4,428,418 | 25% | 5,168,897 | 26% | 9,491,516 | 26% |
| Kandahar | 1,617,197 | 10% | 1,898,791 | 11% | 1,466,278 | 7% | 2,229,408 | 6% |
| Ningarhar | 2,705,573 | 17% | 3,598,707 | 20% | 4,570,502 | 23% | 9,079,909 | 25% |
| Andkhoi | 490,940 | 3% | 549,407 | 3% | 633,329 | 3% | 1,057,236 | 3% |
| Kunduz | 78,994 | 1% | 132,591 | 1% | 281,162 | 1% | 568,199 | 2% |
| Takhar | 23,084 | 0% | 12,076 | 0% | 4,239 | 0% | 2,538 | 0% |
| Nimroz | 564,836 | 4% | 1,223,934 | 7% | 1,381,276 | 7% | 2,554,564 | 7% |
| Farah | 242,998 | 2% | 113,051 | 1% | 128,265 | 1% | 52,067 | 0% |
| Kunarha | 3,592 | 0% | 284,615 | 2% | 5,283 | 0% | 7,862 | 0% |
| Paktika | 27,463 | 0% | 45,019 | 0% | 42,909 | 0% | 33,255 | 0% |
| Paktya | 103,224 | 1% | 90,462 | 1% | 5,248 | 0% | 4,951 | 0% |
| Khost | 310,602 | 2% | 303,358 | 2% | 378,420 | 2% | 371,639 | 1% |
| Badkhshan | 0 | 0% | 0 | 0% | 0 | 0% | 1,237 | 0% |
| Total | 15,479,183 | 100% | 17,854,828 | 100% | 19,684,272 | 100% | 36,648,673 | 100% |

Email add:csu_revenue@yahoo.com
Ab.Hafiz Omari

## EXPORT FROM AFGHANISTAN BY HS SECTIONS.

In million Afs

| Section | | Annual |
|---|---|---|
| 01 | Live animal, animal products | 103 |
| 02 | Vegetable products | 8,279 |
| 03 | Animal and vegetable fats and oils | 15 |
| 04 | Prepared foodstuffs | 273 |
| 05 | Minerals products | 2,379 |
| 06 | Products of chemical or allied industries | 169 |
| 07 | Plastics, rubber and articles thereof | 23 |
| 08 | Raw hids and skins, leather, furskins and articles thereof | 726 |
| 09 | Wood and articles of wood, cork and wickerwork | 23 |
| 10 | Pulp of wood or of other fibrous cellulosic material | 45 |
| 11 | Textiles and textile articles | 719 |
| 12 | Footwear, headgear, umbrellas | 4 |
| 13 | Articles of stone, plaster, cement, asbestos, mica | 9 |

| | | |
|---|---|---|
| 14 | Natural or cultural pearls, precious stones or metal | 51 |
| 15 | Base metals and articles of base metal | 183 |
| 16 | Machinery and mechanical appliances | 123 |
| 17 | Vehicles, aircraft, vessels transport equipment | 180 |
| 18 | Optical,photograpic, cinematograpic, measuring checking precision | 12 |
| 19 | Arms and ammunition,part and accessories thereof | 4 |
| 20 | Miscellaneous manufactured articles | 9 |
| 21 | Works of art, collectors, pieces and antiques | 0 |
| Total | | 13,328 |
| Camulative | | |
| | | |

| Section | | Annual |
|---|---|---|
| 01 | Live animal, animal products | 111 |
| 02 | Vegetable products | 11,342 |
| 03 | Animal and vegetable fats and oils | 28 |
| 04 | Prepared foodstuffs | 230 |
| 05 | Minerals products | 1,870 |
| 06 | Products of chemical or allied industries | 119 |
| 07 | Plastics, rubber and articles thereof | 37 |
| 08 | Raw hids and skins, leather, furskins and articles thereof | 523 |
| 09 | Wood and articles of wood, cork and wickerwork | 21 |
| 10 | Pulp of wood or of other fibrous cellulosic material | 15 |
| 11 | Textiles and textile articles | 774 |
| 12 | Footwear, headgear, umbrellas | 1 |
| 13 | Articles of stone, plaster, cement, asbestos, mica | 6 |
| 14 | Natural or cultural pearls, precious stones or metal | 50 |
| 15 | Base metals and articles of base metal | 34 |
| 16 | Machinery and mechanical appliances | 343 |
| 17 | Vehicles, aircraft, vessels transport equipment | 284 |
| 18 | Optical,photograpic, cinematograpic, measuring checking precision | 9 |
| 19 | Arms and ammunition,part and accessories thereof | 5 |
| 20 | Miscellaneous manufactured articles | 7 |
| 21 | Works of art, collectors, pieces and antiques | 0 |
| Total | | 15,808 |
| Camulative | | |
| Email add:csu_trade@yahoo.com | | |
| Ab.Hafiz Omari | | |

# KEY U.S. GOVERNMENT AND DONOR ACTIVITIES

## U.S. AGENCY FOR INTERNATIONAL DEVELOPMENT (USAID)

Since October 2001, the United States has provided well over $1.8 billion in mostly humanitarian assistance to Afghanistan through the U.S. Agency for International Development. USAID has taken a leading role in the reconstruction effort, focusing on immediate relief including provision of food aid, wool blankets and quilts, shelter kits, and winterized tents. As part of rehabilitation and reconstruction efforts, USAID focuses on health clinics and basic health services, school construction and education programs, revitalizing agricultural through irrigation systems, farm-to-market roads, market centers, and better technology, and infrastructure, including the Kabul-Kandahar-Herat highway. USAID is also funding programs that enhance the central government's credibility and provide it with the tools and technical assistance to govern effectively.

The USAID Web site, www.usaid.gov, has a business and procurement link that lists upcoming procurements including solicitation documents, announcements, and other resources. This site is updated daily and offers e-mail notification when a new solicitation has been uploaded to the site. U.S. firms interested in bidding on USAID projects in Afghanistan can review requests for applications, proposals, quotations, and invitation for bids on this web site. U.S. firms should also review the main portal for U.S. government procurements at www.fedbizopps.gov.

## OVERSEAS PRIVATE INVESTMENT CORPORATION (OPIC)

OPIC has established a $100 million line of credit to support U.S. investment in this country.

OPIC, an independent agency of the U.S. government, offers specialty insurance (stand alone terror/sabotage and political risk coverage) and loans to help U.S. businesses of all sizes invest and compete in more than 140 emerging markets and developing nations worldwide. A $100 million line of credit is available to projects that demonstrate a substantial U.S. participation, promise significant benefits to the economic and social development of Afghanistan, and foster private sector competition in Afghanistan. OPIC gives preferential consideration to projects that significantly involve U.S. small businesses. OPIC is actively developing several projects in Afghanistan. For example, OPIC provided up to $35 million in financing and political risk insurance to support construction of a five-star international hotel in Kabul, managed by Hyatt International, and a direct loan of approximately $3 million to support construction of 1,200 homes near Kandahar by AFCO International, a Virginia-based small business. For more information, please visit www.opic.gov.

## U.S. TRADE AND DEVELOPMENT AGENCY (TDA)

TDA has moved quickly to establish its program in Afghanistan, and already has approved a number of activities, totaling about $200,000 and outlined here.

The U.S. Trade and Development Agency (USTDA) advances economic development and U.S. commercial interests in developing and middle-income countries. The agency funds various forms of technical assistance, feasibility studies, training, orientation visits and business workshops that support the development of a modern infrastructure and a fair and open trading environment. USTDA moved quickly to establish its program in Afghanistan, and already has approved funding of about $3 million for activities in that country.

***Telecommunications*** - USTDA is providing funding for a policy advisor to the Ministry of Communications, sponsored the September 2002 Orientation Visit to the U.S. by the Minister of Communications to meet with U.S. companies and appropriate U.S. Government agencies, and funding for a feasibility study on a fiber optic telecom backbone network.

***Oil and Gas*** - USTDA funded a Definitional Mission (DM) in the oil and gas sector (conducted by a USGS team), approved funding for a feasibility study on a gas pipeline/power plant project and the first phase of a petroleum resource assessment, and sponsored an Orientation Visit to the U.S. by the Minister of Mines and Industries in January 2003.

***Aviation*** - USTDA funded a DM in the civil aviation sector (conducted in part by FAA specialists), approved funding for technical assistance to develop a regulatory framework for the civil aviation sector and training for Afghan air traffic controllers, and sponsored an Orientation Visit to the U.S. of Afghan aviation officials in November 2002.

***Higher Education*** - USTDA approved funding for a feasibility study on establishment of a private university in Afghanistan, modeled after the American University in Beirut.

***Reconstruction Conference*** - USTDA cosponsored with the Commerce Department a conference on Afghan reconstruction in June 2003. This event, which attracted over 435 people, gave U.S. companies the opportunity to learn more about how they can participate in the reconstruction effort and to meet with Afghan officials to discuss specific projects.

***Power*** - USTDA sponsored an Orientation Visit to the U.S. by the Minister of Water and Power in December 2002 to meet with U.S. companies and relevant U.S. Government agencies.

***Hotels*** - USTDA funded an assessment of hotel opportunities in Kabul. Based in part on that assessment, two hotel projects are currently under development.

***Private Sector*** - USTDA is sending technical experts to Afghanistan to assist the government and growing private sector in identifying specific needs and in creating tailored strategies that will help guide the development of industry in Afghanistan, thereby stimulating trade and creating jobs for Afghan citizens.

## EXPORT-IMPORT BANK OF THE UNITED STATES

Export Import Bank is not currently open for business in Afghanistan.

## U.S. DEPARTMENT OF COMMERCE'S AFGHANISTAN RECONSTRUCTION TASK FORCE

To facilitate U.S. company participation in the Afghanistan reconstruction effort, the U.S. Department of Commerce created the Afghanistan Reconstruction Task Force to support U.S. private sector involvement in reconstruction and to contribute to U.S. government efforts to promote bilateral trade and investment. The Task Force has highlighted several industry sectors for business development, including electric power, water and sanitation, telecommunications, natural resource mining, transportation and construction. While Afghanistan reconstruction projects may provide U.S. companies with commercial opportunities, they also carry risks, not only financial, but also physical, due to the lack of security in many areas. Interested U.S. companies can call (202) 482-1812, visit the Web site www.export.gov/afghanistan, e-mail questions to AfghanInfo@ita.doc.gov for business counseling on opportunities in Afghanistan, or contact U.S. Embassy in Kabul. For more information, please see the key contacts section below.

## WORLD BANK

*World Bank Approves $100 million in Grants for Afghan Reconstruction*
In February 2002, the World Bank reopened its office in Kabul, where a country manager and a permanent staff of around 20 are now stationed. The Bank has been working closely with the government and bilateral and multilateral development agencies to help ensure that international assistance is well coordinated and efficient.

Since April 2002, the World Bank has committed $186.8 million in grants and an additional $128.4 million in no-interest loans, known as "credits", for development projects that are helping to meet urgent needs. The Bank is administering two grants, totaling $3.5 million from the Japan Social Development Fund (JSDF) for community rehabilitation and local infrastructure development, and a $1.5 million grant from the World Bank Post Conflict Fund to finance a number of refugee education projects being implemented by NGOs and United Nations-affiliated agencies. The World Bank is also helping the government develop its capacity to manage donor funds with transparency and accountability and to outsource program implementation to NGOs, the private sector, and communities.

In addition, the World Bank administers the multi-donor Afghanistan Reconstruction Trust Fund, which provides coordinated financing of unfunded priority expenditures in Afghanistan's reconstruction program. Projects can be tracked at www.dgmarket.com.

For more information, please visit www.worldbank.org/afghanistan or contact William Crawford, U.S. commercial liaison at the World Bank: tel (202) 458-0120, fax: (202) 477-2967, e-mail: wcrawford@worldbank.org.

## ASIAN DEVELOPMENT BANK

The ADB's Board of Directors endorsed a Country Strategy and Program (CSP) for Afghanistan for 2002-2004 on May 28, 2002, paving the way for delivery of a $200 million assistance package earmarked for 2002, and an allocation of $300 million during 2003-2004. The funds will support national reconstruction, including capacity building, rehabilitation of physical infrastructure, revitalizing agriculture and rural development, private sector development, social development, and gender empowerment.

ADB's 2002 assistance program for Afghanistan focused on capacity building, providing $14.6 million for reconstruction and development and $500,000 for disaster preparedness. ADB also initiated rehabilitation of the Kandahar-Spin Boldak road and community development activities in Kandahar with $15 million in grant funding. ADB is striving to ensure visible signs of progress on key reconstruction needs prior to the June 2004 elections.

For more information on ADB activities in Afghanistan, please go to www.adb.org/afghanistan and contact Frank Foster, U.S. Commercial Service Liaison Officer to the ADB at Frank.Foster@mail.doc.gov.

Given the major donor effort in Afghanistan, U.S. firms should also look to other potential project funding and contracting opportunities, including the United Nations, the International Finance Corporation, and non-governmental organizations.

# BEST PROSPECTS FOR U.S. SUPPLIERS

Commerce is growing almost daily on Afghanistan's streets, mostly confined to store front and informal roadside trading. Afghanistan's need to completely renovate its infrastructure will present opportunities for American firms. However, this will be severely hampered in the short-term by the very limited purchasing power of the Afghan population.

Based on an informal study of the market in Kabul, the following U.S. goods and services appear to have strong demand. This list is not prioritized. However it does convey the broad, extensive nature of the potential import market in Afghanistan. For more information on these opportunities, contact the U.S. Embassy's Economic Section or the Commerce Department's Afghanistan Reconstruction Task Force.

## SHORT-TERM OPPORTUNITIES

Based on an informal study of the market in Kabul, the following U.S. goods and services appear to have strong demand. This list is not prioritized, however it does convey the broad, extensive nature of the potential import market in Afghanistan.

- Architectural, construction, and engineering services
- Building materials for both residential and commercial properties
- Computer hardware, software and peripherals (to include Dari language capability)
- Telecommunications services and equipment
- Diesel generators for independent power supply
- Education/training Services
- Consumer electronics
- Heavy equipment, including trucks, trailers and buses; motor graders, concrete mixers, heavy duty dumpers, paver finishers, and bulldozers
- Security and safety equipment
- Automobiles/light trucks/vans and development of dealerships for 4x4 vehicles (sales, parts, and service)
- Translation services, including simultaneous, conference style translation products.
- Office furniture

## MEDIUM-TERM OPPORTUNITIES

- Aircraft/aircraft parts
- Airport/ground support equipment
- Electrical power systems
- Oil and gas field machinery, oil, gas and mineral exploration and production services
- Agricultural chemicals, machinery, equipment and services,
- Food processing and packaging equipment for nuts, raisins, and other fruits
- Irrigation planning and technologies
- Road upgrades, lighting and signage
- Transportation services (other than aviation)

Hard to maintain, expensive, high technology items will not sell well in Afghanistan. Competition from lower-quality, cheaper goods and services from Pakistan and Iran should be taken into consideration when preparing quotations. U.S. firms wishing to ship goods or equipment should look at quotes for consignment to Karachi, Pakistan. While trans-shipment through Bandar-i-Abbas, Iran, is common, U.S. citizens and entities are forbidden from doing so without written approval by the U.S. Department of Treasury's Office of Foreign Access and Control.

When considering opportunities in Afghanistan, keep the business plan simple, clear, and focused.

# TRAVEL WARNING FOR AFGHANISTAN

While the U.S. Embassy in Kabul encourages U.S. companies to review business opportunities in Afghanistan, it is important to keep in mind the fluid security situation in the country. Travelers should consult the State Department Web site (www.state.gov - see Consular Information Sheet and Travel Warning Page) prior to any travel.

There is currently a high-level of danger in the north of Afghanistan. Due to a growing number of attacks against United Nations and private humanitarian workers and non-governmental organizations in northern Afghanistan in and around the city of Mazar-i-Sharif, the U.S. government warns American citizens, including those with experience in the area, against traveling to or residing in the Mazar area. Those currently in the Mazar area should review their security arrangements, contact U.S. military forces in the region to register their presence, and make preparations to depart.

## U.S. EMBASSY KABUL

The United States Liaison Office in Kabul was officially inaugurated as an Embassy on January 17, 2002. The Embassy does not provide passport or visa services. The Embassy's ability to provide emergency consular services to U.S. citizens in Afghanistan is limited. Embassy officials in Kabul cannot travel outside the capital to provide assistance to Americans. Afghan authorities can provide only limited assistance to U.S. citizens facing difficulties. The U.S. Embassy in Islamabad, Pakistan, provides most routine consular services to American citizens traveling to Afghanistan. U.S. citizens who choose to visit or remain in Afghanistan are urged to pay close attention to their personal security and to take those actions they deem appropriate to ensure their well-being. Americans in Afghanistan should avoid rallies or demonstrations. All U.S. citizens remaining in Afghanistan or planning to travel to the country are strongly urged to register with and obtain updated security information from the American Embassy in Islamabad, Pakistan, the U.S. Consulate in Peshawar, or the Embassy in Kabul. Contacts are provided at the end of this overview.

## BUSINESS TRAVEL TIPS FOR KABUL

For a nuts-and-bolds guide to a successful start to business operations, read the U.S. Embassy's Business Primer.

Business meetings are usually conducted in English or Dari in the principal's office, often while sitting on couches. Green or black tea, nuts and raisins are served to greet guests. The form of greeting is Salam Aleykum (Peace be with you), followed by a firm handshake and then briefly placing your right hand over your heart. It is best to take several minutes initially to engage in pleasantries about each other's country, rather than going straight to business. Afghan interlocutors may appear vague and non-committal during meetings. In order to build trust and "get to yes," be patient, share meals and other social events, and discuss matters other than business. Capture the essence of your business meetings and agreements in a follow up letter to your Afghan interlocutor. Be clear about what you have committed yourself or your U.S. firm to do, or in many cases, have not committed to do. A promise to "look into" or "research" an issue, quote, or pricing policy is often interpreted here as a firm commitment.

Americans intending to travel to Afghanistan should carefully review the security situation and make travel decisions accordingly. Street crime against foreigners is still the exception rather than the rule, but foreigners make for easy targets given their prominence and perceived wealth. If out in the city, travel in pairs, be aware of your surroundings, and be in before dark.

Air transportation in and out of Kabul is spotty, and only is now beginning to take shape. Businesspersons can travel to Kabul on Ariana Afghan Airlines via Dubai, United Arab Emirates or Islamabad, Pakistan. Commercial air travel through Baku, Azerbaijan is also available through Azerbaijan Airlines (Azal). Finally, an American firm operating under the name of Swisskies, is planning to commence operations from the U.S. to Kabul via Geneva beginning in late 2003 or early 2004. Express mail services are offered by Federal Express, DHL and TNT.

Cash U.S. dollars and afghani are widely used as currency. Checks and credit cards are not accepted in Afghanistan. Hotel accommodations are spartan, with few acceptable hotels and minimal guesthouses. The Intercontinental Hotel is currently the only suitable hotel in Kabul for business travelers. However projects to build new hotel accommodations or renovate existing hotels are currently underway. Taxis around town should range between 20,000 to 40,000 afghanis ($0.50 to $1.00) per trip, but a dedicated car and driver are recommended. Afghanistan observes a five and a half day work-week, with Thursday afternoon and Friday as the days off. Saturday and Sunday are regular trading days.

Popular restaurants include Shandiz (Persian), Lai Thai, Golden Lotus, Marco Polo, B's Place, and Politano's. More restaurants are opening on a weekly basis to serve the growing expatriate population in Kabul. The tap water is not potable in Afghanistan; only bottled water, preferably sparkling, should be consumed. As Afghanistan is an Islamic country, alcohol is usually not sold or served in restaurants or hotels. Some restaurants catering to the expatriate population will sell alcohol to foreigners. As large parts of Kabul have been destroyed by war, acceptable housing is at a premium, with rents often going for several thousands of dollars per month.

The weather in Afghanistan is very dry, with summer highs into the 100s F and winter lows into the 20s F with snow. Kabul is very dusty, and shoes and clothes are difficult to maintain. Western-style medical care is not available in Afghanistan. Travelers should bring all necessary medications, both prescription and over-the-counter. Travelers with chronic medical conditions should defer travel to Afghanistan. Afghanistan is in a malarial zone. Afghanistan is on a 220v, 60 cycle electrical system, using European round, two-prong plugs. For more information on travel and medical conditions in Afghanistan, visit www.travel.state.gov and www.cdc.gov/travel.

## KEY CONTACTS

### U.S. GOVERNMENT CONTACTS

**Jana Nelhybel**
Afghanistan Reconstruction Task Force
U.S. Department of Commerce
Washington D.C. 20230
Tel: (202) 482-1812
Fax: (202) 482-0980
E-mail: afghaninfo@ita.doc.gov
Web site: www.export.gov/afghanistan

**U.S. Embassy Kabul**
Great Masood Road
Tel: [93](2) 29-00-02, 29-00-05, 29-01-54
Inmarsat Tel: [873](761) 83-79-27
Inmarsat Fax: [873](761) 83-73-74
E-mail: hawkinsjj@state.gov
E-mail: rosssm@state.gov
Zalmay Khalilzad, Ambassador
David Sedney, Deputy Chief of Mission
Jeff Hawkins, Political/Economic Counselor
Shannon Ross, Economic/Commercial Officer

Note: The U.S. Embassy in Kabul is staffed with an Economic/Commercial Officer, who works closely with U.S. government agencies and the Afghanistan Government on commercial matters. Phone and fax communications in Afghanistan continue to be unreliable. E-mail is usually the most reliable form of communication.

**U.S. Embassy Islamabad**
Consular Section
Ramna 5, Diplomatic Enclave
Islamabad, Pakistan
Tel: [92](51) 208-02700
Fax: [92](51) 282-2632
Web site: http://usembassy.state.gov/islamabad/wwwhcvsp.html

**Dan Stein**
Regional Director for Eurasia
U.S. Trade & Development Agency (USTDA)
Suite 1600
1000 Wilson Boulevard
Arlington, VA 22209
Tel: (703) 875-4357
Fax: (703) 875-4009
E-mail: dstein@tda.gov
Web site: www.tda.gov

**Abed Tarbush**
Overseas Private Investment Corporation (OPIC)
1100 New York Avenue NW
Washington, DC 20527
Tel: (202) 336-8400
Fax: (202) 408-9859
E-mail: atarb@opic.gov
Web site: www.opic.gov

**U.S. Agency for International Development**
Web site: www.usaid.gov/afghanistan

## AFGHAN GOVERNMENT CONTACTS

**Embassy of Afghanistan**
2341 Wyoming Avenue, N.W.
Washington D.C. 20006
Tel: (202) 483-6410

Fax: (202) 483-6487
E-mail: contact@embassyofafghanistan.org
Web site: www.embassyofafghanistan.org

**Hamid Karzai**
President
Transitional Islamic State of Afghanistan
Presidential Palace
Kabul, Afghanistan

**Abdullah Abdullah**
Minister of Foreign Affairs
Transitional Islamic State of Afghanistan
Kabul, Afghanistan
Tel: [93](20) 210-3064 (Protocol Dept.)
Inmarsat Fax: [873](762) 32-14-51
(Adib Farhadi is the Director for Business Affairs in the Ministry and oversees all commercial matters)

**Ashraf Ghani Ahmadzai**
Minister of Finance
Transitional Islamic State of Afghanistan
Kabul, Afghanistan
**Mohammad Masoon Stanakzai**
Minister of Communications
Transitional Islamic State of Afghanistan
Kabul, Afghanistan
Tel: [93](20) 210-1100
Web site: http://af-com.ministry.org

**TBD**
Minister of Mines and Industries (Across from the Ministry of Finance)
Transitional Islamic State of Afghanistan
Kabul, Afghanistan
Tel: [93](20) 210-0309

**Sayed Mustafa Kazimi**
Minister of Commerce
Transitional Islamic State of Afghanistan
Karti Sey
Kabul, Afghanistan
Mobile: [93](70) 27-62-90
Inmarsat Fax: [873](763) 090 711
Email: commerce@mail.gr

**Afghan Investment Support Agency**
Opposite Ministry of Foreign Affairs
Kabul
Tel: [93](20) 210-3220
Fax: [93](20) 210-3228
E-mail: invest@aisa.gov.af
Web site: www.aisa.gov.af

**Mohammad Amin Farhang**
Minister of Reconstruction
Transitional Islamic State of Afghanistan
Great Masood Road
Kabul, Afghanistan
Tel: [93](20) 210-0328 or 210-0329
E-mail: a.farhang@aia-afg.org

**Mirwais Saddiq**
Minister of Tourism and Civil Aviation
Transitional Islamic State of Afghanistan
Kabul, Afghanistan
Inmarsat Tel: [873](763) 09-06-11
Inmarsat Fax: [873](763) 09-06-10
E-mail: mocat@yahoo.com

**Saeed Mohammad Ali Jawad**
Minister of Transportation
Transitional Islamic State of Afghanistan
Kabul, Afghanistan
Tel: [93](20) 29-00-87
Tel: [93](20) 210-1371
Mobile: [93](70) 27-62-91

**Sayed Hussain Anwari**
Minister of Agriculture and Livestock
Transitional Islamic State of Afghanistan
Karti Sakhi,District 5 (Across from Faculty of Agriculture)
Kabul, Afghanistan
Tel: [93](20) 250-0315
Mobile: [93](70) 27-82-08

**Mohammed Shaker Kargar**
Minister of Water and Power
Transitional Islamic State of Afghanistan
Badan Bagh
Kabul, Afghanistan
Tel: [93](20) 240-1301
Mobile: [93](70) 84-48-44
Fax: [93](2) 29-00-85

**Rashid Janbaz**
Chairman of Planning and Finance
Kabul Municipality
Kabul, Afghanistan
Tel: [93](70) 27-56-78

## USEFUL CONTACTS

**Afghanistan Wireless Communication Corporation** (mobile telephone)
Address: c/o International hotel and ministry of communications building, Mohammad Jan Khan Watt Kabul Afghanistan
Tel: [93] (20) 20-00-00
Fax: [93] (20) 20-02-00

Web site: www.afghanistanwireless.com

**Intercontinental Hotel**
Address: Bagh-I-Balla Kabul Afghanistan
Inmarsat Tel: [873](761) 46-96-90
Inmarsat Fax: [873](761) 46-96-91
Afghan wireless: [93](2) 29-00-43

**Federal Express Mail Services**
Karte 3
Khai Street (North of Ministry of Commerce)
House #326
Kabul
Tel [93] (0) 20 250-0525
Mobile [93] (0) 70 286-028/29
Fax [93] (0) 20 250-0524

**DHL Express Mail Services**
Address: Wazir Akbar Khan next to Burhanuddin Rabani's house, behind the U.S. Embassy.
Mobile: [93](70) 27-63-62, 27-63-63 or 27-64-25
E-mail: shanlon@af.dhl.com

**TNT Express Mail Services**
Address: Cross road Turabaz Khan toward Charahee Sher Pur Rd. Kabul Afghanistan
Tel/Fax: [93](20) 29-02-18
Mobile: [93](70) 27-65-03

## PRACTICAL TIPS FOR SUCCESSFUL BUSINESS OPERATIONS

Businesses operating in Afghanistan face tremendous challenges. Transport and communications infrastructures are weak. Security conditions are fluid. Standard business-related institutions and infrastructure lack capacity, are poorly organized or, in some cases, do not exist. Kabul currently lacks appropriate hotel accommodations for international business, air links are still quite limited, and commercial banking facilities are extremely weak.

All of these shortcomings are, however, being addressed. The Afghan government has pledged to mobilize necessary resources and implement appropriate policies to make Afghanistan a more attractive destination for international and domestic business. During the past year, the new government of President Karzai has taken a number of important steps to improve the business climate. Moreover, the Afghan government has identified three construction-related sectors - Transport, Urban Infrastructure and Governance Infrastructure - as national development priorities and will devote an estimated $370m to such projects in the near future. Meanwhile the German-led Consultative Group on Trade and Investment - of which the U.S. is an active participant - is exploring comprehensive methods to enhance commercial activity in Afghanistan.

The Commercial Section of the American Embassy has worked closely with the Afghan Government, the small but critical Afghan private sector, and American firms to maximize business opportunities for qualified international and domestic commercial interests. Based upon experiences gained from these activities, the information contained in this primer is an effort to detail those approaches that have proven useful for all businesspeople conducting or considering business in Afghanistan, and are offered as recommendations to firms considering operations in Afghanistan.

**Ramin Asgard**
Economic/Commercial Officer
U.S. Embassy - Kabul
Afghanistan

## DO YOUR HOMEWORK BEFORE VISITING

The U.S. Government has been active in establishing the foundation for successful private sector operations in Afghanistan. The Department of Commerce's Afghanistan Reconstruction Task Force, working closely with the U.S. Embassy in Kabul and other U.S. government agencies, has set up the Rebuilding Afghanistan webpage as a link on their www.export.gov website. The site provides a wealth of updated information for firms interested in business opportunities in Afghanistan.

Of the items available on the website, it is essential to review the new Afghan Investment Law and Investment Application forms, which are both available in English on the site. Reading and understanding the law and the application will provide a good early barometer on the information you will need to prepare and the questions you might expect on a business visit to Afghanistan. Also available is the Country Commercial Guide [HTML, PDF], which provides an overview of commercial operations in Afghanistan. The current guide is undergoing updating and revision and a new version will be available in spring 2003.

Also ready to assist you in assessing commercial opportunities in Afghanistan are the representatives of the U.S. Department of State, U.S. Department of Commerce, USAID, U.S. Trade & Development Agency, Overseas Private Investment Corporation and other U.S. government agencies active in Afghan Reconstruction activities.

## MAKE YOUR FIRST STOP IN-COUNTRY THE U.S. EMBASSY

Many U.S. and international firms are operating in Afghanistan and have shared their diverse experiences with us. We use this general information and our extensive and close contacts with the Afghan government and private sector, as well as various other private and public organizations involved in Afghanistan's reconstruction, to comprehensively advise and support new or existing firms.

During our initial and any subsequent meetings, we generally update firms on the latest developments affecting their business prospects, identify sector-specific opportunities, and facilitate contacts and arrange meetings with and provide introductions to relevant government and private sector officials. Also, we are happy to arrange a meeting with senior Embassy officials to discuss your project(s) in Afghanistan and explore ways the Embassy can help support your business goals.
Being proactive in establishing a relationship with your embassy in Kabul carries many benefits, but none greater than the capacity to help guide your business operations to a profitable path from the very outset of operations. It is far easier to begin such a relationship early on, and reach a business decision later that it is no longer required, than it is to wait until major problems arise before contacting the Embassy for assistance.

## MAKE YOUR SECOND STOP THE MINISTRY OF COMMERCE

The Ministry of Commerce has worked closely with the U.S. Embassy and international and domestic business to improve the business climate in Afghanistan. According to the 2002 Investment Law, the Minister of Commerce serves as the Chair of the High Commission for

Investment. As the Chair, the Minister of Commerce is responsible for directing Afghan Cabinet consideration of proposed investment projects and helping approved projects advance through the licensing and permit approval process. By engaging early on with the Ministry of Commerce, firms interested in business operations in Afghanistan ensure that their concerns will be heard by the appropriate Afghan government officials and their need to engage with multiple Afghan government offices - and their bureaucracies - will be kept to a minimum.

Having the Ministry of Commerce "sell" your project within the government is the preferred approach for two main reasons: First, it is the process envisioned under the Afghan Investment Law, and will therefore be viewed as appropriate and authorized by all concerned. Second, the traditional method of locating influential local or expatriate Afghan "fixers" to sell the project within the government has led to numerous delays, conflicting webs of patronage and corruption and generally, to less than ideal results.

### MAKE YOUR THIRD STOP THE MINISTRY OF FOREIGN AFFAIRS

The Ministry of Foreign Affairs' Economic Affairs Department plays another key role in supporting international business seeking to establish operations in Afghanistan. By registering their project with the MFA Economic Affairs Department - as required by Afghan law - newly arriving firms ensure the continued support of this highly influential and international business-friendly Ministry during their operations in Afghanistan. This support will assist firms with issues concerning bilateral or multilateral agreements, international law, visas and regional trade and investment initiatives.

### VISIT THE RELEVANT SECTORAL MINISTRY

After visiting the Ministries of Commerce and the MFA, it is appropriate to meet with a senior official from the Afghan ministry or ministries most relevant to your firm's contemplated business activities. As discussed above, the Embassy will help set up appropriate meetings and provide useful guidance regarding ministerial policies and priorities in advance of the meeting.

### KEEP AFGHAN GOVERNMENT PRIORITIES IN MIND

The Afghan government faces tremendous challenges as it seeks to improve the Afghan business climate, attract investment and encourage private sector-led growth. For the government, a key issue is the need to demonstrate the benefits of private sector activity to the Afghan population. Therefore, the job-creation aspects of foreign business activities are a key factor in Afghan government assessments of their suitability. Another key concern of the Afghan government is building domestic managerial and technical expertise. This means that business proposals that include training and knowledge transfer, as well as opportunities for Afghans to meaningfully participate in project development, will be highly favored.

### REMAIN FLEXIBLE

Afghanistan is recovering from decades of instability and war. During this time, the Afghan private and public sectors deteriorated markedly. Most ministries now lack capacity below the Deputy Minister level. Further, many bureaucrats still harbor state-centric economic approaches derived from Soviet-era training. The private sector is small, lacks expertise, and is uncertain of its role. Most major Afghan businesspeople and firms, especially those with experience with international business practices, still remain outside Afghanistan (generally in neighboring countries). As noted above, Afghan physical and regulatory infrastructure is weak or in some cases non-existent, and attracting even expatriate Afghan investors will require substantial continued reforms.

All these factors mean that businesspeople accustomed to operating virtually anywhere else in the industrialized and even the developing world will often face novel and exasperating challenges in advancing their business goals in Afghanistan. By following the recommendations outlined above and maintaining a flexible approach, however, many firms will be able to navigate through these obstacles and find success during this early period of

Afghanistan's reconstruction. Those firms resilient and committed enough to do so will establish a lasting foundation for additional local and regional business success.

For further information please contact:

Ramin Asgard
Economic/Commercial Officer
U.S. Embassy Kabul
asgardrx@state.gov

Nasratullah Esmaty
Commercial Assistant
U.S. Embassy Kabul
esmatynw@state.gov

For business counseling on opportunities in Afghanistan, please call:

Afghanistan Reconstruction Task Force
U.S. Department of Commerce
(202) 482-1812 or 1-800-USA-TRAD(E) and press 2,
or e-mail questions to AfghanInfo@ita.doc.gov

## U.S. EMBASSY IN KABUL NOVEMBER 2002 BUSINESS ROUNDTABLE

The U.S. Embassy in Kabul's November Roundtable featured a presentation by Louis Berger, the contracting agent for the USAID Infrastructure Project. Louis Berger representatives Chief of Party in Afghanistan, Leroy Purifoy, and Contracting Officer, Douglas Bowlsby, presented how companies can apply as sub-contractors and suppliers to the project.

**Roundtable Highlights:**

• Project opportunities include:

° Roadwork
° Irrigation systems
° Water and sanitation
° Power transmission
° Construction of schools, medical centers, administration centers, and bridges

• Prospective contractors and suppliers to Louis Berger should complete the pre-qualification package:

° Notice available in HTML and PDF
° Instructions available in HTML and PDF

• Every contract beyond the one for the first 49 km segment of the Kabul-Kandahar road would be let through an open tendering process.

• All tender announcements will be publicized in the following:

° International Herald Tribune
° a U.S. publication (likely the Engineering News Record)
° in Turkey and in the UAE (in newspapers to be determined)

• International firms bidding on the tenders to include an Afghan partners or subcontractors in their proposals. This is in compliance with USAID's directive to build capacity among the local construction and contracting firms.

• The first few projects would be tendered in the next several months.

• There is no U.S. source requirement attached to the contracts.

• Some of the smaller projects, such as schools and clinics, might be set aside for NGOs to encourage community participation aspect in the program.

• While the United Nations had taken responsibility of clearing mines from the area around the road, each contractor was responsible for providing its own security.

• Vulnerable areas and populations would be particularly targeted for projects and the pace of program projects would be based upon the flow of available USAID funding.

• Company participants raised a number of questions that will require further clarification prior to the start of the tendering process. These included:

° Whether the tax-exemption granted by the Government of Afghanistan to USAID as a humanitarian organization would be extended to contracting firms. If not, the 25 percent import tax that currently applies to materials and equipment would hinder commercial viability of projects.

° Whether general transport of materials through Iran would be acceptable or if each individual sub-contractor would be required to obtain its own license from the U.S. Department of Treasury's Office of Foreign Access Control (OFAC). This was of particular interest to participants, as Afghanistan-Pakistan trade and transit trade relations are currently strained.

° Whether the required Afghan partner needed to be a joint venture partner or could also be a subcontractor. In a related vein, several companies asked what actually constituted an "Afghan partner."

## AFGHANISTAN USES RECONSTRUCTION TRUST FUND TO ADDRESS PRIORITIES

At the request of the Government of Afghanistan, the World Bank, as the administrator of the Afghanistan Reconstruction Trust Fund, signed agreements this week for three new projects designed to help improve the country's telecommunications system; repair its roads and drainage systems and provide credit and other financial services to low-income people.

### Rehabilitation of Telecommunications systems

A grant of US$ 3 million has been provided from ARTF to establish international connectivity between Afghanistan and the rest of the world, particularly with its neighboring countries. The funds will also begin investment in Afghan Telecom in preparation for its shift from a state-owned department to a corporation as a key step for future partnerships with the private sector.

"Today Afghanistan has one of the weakest telecommunications systems in the world. Only one out of every 625 Afghan citizens has access to telephone service," said Philippe Dongier, ARTF Manager. "The ARTF Management Committee approved Government's proposal for an investment in this project as it will generate funds from telecom services to strengthen Government's revenue base for contribution to the recurrent and development budget of the country."

The Ministry of Telecommunications will implement the project.

### Repair of Major Kabul City Roads and Water Drainage Systems

A grant of US$ 3 million has been approved from ARTF to improve transport services on important roads within Kabul city through the rehabilitation of high priority road sections, as well as the repair of drainage systems along these roads. The overall objective is to achieve effective and visible contribution to the economic recovery of Kabul. This project is the continuation of the ongoing German-funded project being implemented by KfW, Kreditanstalt für Wiederaufbau, in Kabul.

"As the capital of Afghanistan, Kabul has a population of about 3 million people including returnees, internally displaced people, female-headed households, disabled people and other vulnerable groups. One of the Government's priorities is to improve the situation here and the ARTF Management Committee felt it was critical to help the government finance activities to enable it to achieve its development goals for the city," said Mohammad Qahir Haidari, World Bank Operations Officer in Kabul.

As a result of this project, approximately 40,000 tons of asphalt will be produced and about 155 km of roads in Kabul will be repaired. The water drainage systems along these roads will also be repaired. This project will be implemented by KfW in cooperation with Kabul Municipality.

**Micro-finance Support for Poverty Reduction**

A grant of US$ 4 million has been provided from the ARTF to support access to credit and other financial services for poor and low-income people. These households can use the micro-finance to invest in business opportunities, meet emergency needs, reduce vulnerability and build assets. This project will specifically focus supporting the entrepreneurial spirit of the Afghan people to help them improve their livelihoods and make the transition from dependence on humanitarian assistance to economic independence. It will help the government establish the foundations of a strong, sustainable micro-finance sector and set up a national Micro-finance Investment and Support Fund for Afghanistan as an autonomous wholesale institution for long term development and the sustainability of the sector.

"War has devastated almost all basic services in the country, and has resulted in a significant increase in the level of poverty," said Mudassir Khan, a World Bank Senior Financial Specialist. "Micro and small business opportunities will generate livelihoods for the people of Afghanistan where lack of capital is the key constraint."

The Ministry of Rural Rehabilitation and Development will implement the project over an 18 month period.

**About the Afghanistan Reconstruction Trust Fund**

The multilateral Afghanistan Reconstruction Trust Fund (ARTF) was set up in May
2002 to provide support to Afghanistan for three main areas of expenditure: recurrent costs of the government, such as the salaries of teachers, health workers, and police; investments, including capacity building, feasibility studies, and technical assistance; and financing the return of expatriate Afghans.

Twenty-two donors including Bahrain, Canada, Denmark, European Commission, Finland, Germany, India, Ireland, Italy, Japan, Kuwait, Luxembourg, Netherlands,
Norway, Portugal, Saudi Arabia, South Korea, Sweden, Switzerland, Turkey, United
Kingdom, United States have pledged US$430 million to the Trust Fund, and US$276 million has been received. To date, US$188 million has been disbursed to the Government of Afghanistan. The fund has emerged as one of the main instruments for financing the country's recurrent budget deficit and is set to evolve into a major source of technical assistance and investment support for Afghanistan.

In addition, channeling support through the ARTF has helped the government to avoid addressing the distinct funding specifications of 22 different donors, allowing the assistance to be used more efficiently and effectively without the risk of duplication of work.

The ARTF is jointly managed by the Asian Development Bank, Islamic Development
Bank, United Nations Development Program, and the World Bank, which also administers the fund.

**Ongoing ARTF-supported Micro-finance Project**

The first phase of this US$1 million grant was signed in June 2003. The government requested this grant in order to hire a Project Manager to coordinate among donors interested in micro-finance investment and to analyze financing applications from micro-finance NGOs. Out of 14 applications, 10 NGOs which met the eligibility requirements were short listed. To date, an initial agreement has been signed with BRAC and financing arrangements with others are currently under discussions.

**Additional Information**

For more information contact:
In Kabul: Abdul Raouf Zia (93) 702 80800, E-mail: azia@worldbank.org
In Washington: Zita Lichtenberg (202) 458-7953, E-mail: Zlichtenberg@worldbank.org
For U.S. companies, contact Bill Crawford, U.S. Department of Commerce Commercial Liaison to the World Bank, (202) 458-0120, E-mail: wcrawford@worldbank.org

For more information on the World Bank's activities in Afghanistan, please visit: http://www.worldbank.org/af

For more information on the Afghanistan Reconstruction Trust Fund, ple

## U.S. to Seek New Afghan Aid Package Of $1 Billion

Planned Boost Comes Amid Criticism of Reconstruction

*By Vernon Loeb and Glenn Kessler*
Washington Post Staff Writers
Sunday, July 27, 2003; Page A01

The Bush administration will soon propose a $1 billion aid package for Afghanistan aimed at bolstering the government of President Hamid Karzai and countering criticism that U.S. officials have lost interest in rebuilding the country as their focus has shifted to postwar Iraq, senior administration officials said yesterday.

The $1 billion package, which more than triples the $300 million Afghanistan receives, represents new spending on Afghanistan and is designed to fund projects that can be completed within a year to have maximum impact on the lives of the Afghan people before scheduled elections in October 2004, the officials said, speaking on the condition of anonymity.

Among other things, the funds -- to be shifted from existing foreign and military aid accounts so as not to increase the deficit -- would go toward highway and school construction, other infrastructure initiatives, police training, beefed-up development of the Afghan national army, education projects and programs to help women enter the workforce, the officials said.

Defense policy officials, who developed the aid proposal, reasoned that accelerating ongoing initiatives and packaging them with new development programs are justified, in light of annual U.S. expenditures in Afghanistan of about $10 billion, most of which supports a military presence of 9,000 troops.

The proposed $1 billion in aid resulted from "a comprehensive, strategic update on Afghanistan," said Douglas J. Feith, undersecretary of defense for policy, who confirmed accounts of the program provided by other officials but declined to provide further details.

"We noted that there's a lot that we're spending in Afghanistan and there's a lot at stake strategically," Feith said. "And we asked ourselves are we investing enough, given the expense of everything that we're doing, the importance of success and the benefits, strategic and financial, of completing our mission there sooner rather than later."

In a speech in October, President Bush noted that the United States and 60 other countries had pledged $4.5 billion in aid to Afghanistan over five years at a donorsconference in Tokyo and said "America is delivering on our pledge; we're writing our checks. We're currently implementing more than $300 million worth of reconstruction and recovery projects."

The administration hopes to hold another donors conference as part of the September meeting of the World Trade Organization in Cancun, Mexico, with the expectation that the new $1 billion aid package will inspire other countries to increase their contributions as well, one senior administration official said.

As recently as May, Deputy Secretary of State Richard L. Armitage visited Kabul, the Afghan capital, and pledged that the United States remains committed to the reconstruction of Afghanistan, even as it pursues far larger postwar stability operations and reconstruction programs in Iraq.

Despite such promised support, the security situation in Afghanistan remains fragile, and the reconstruction of the country, devastated by decades of war, remains agonizingly slow. Numerous aid organizations, policy analysts and lawmakers have faulted the administration for its limited reconstruction efforts.

The administration, they argue, cannot adequately support Karzai's central government while maintaining de facto security agreements with a half-dozen or more regional military commanders who maintain their own forces and often work to undermine Karzai's central authority.

Remnants of the Taliban, which ruled Afghanistan until the United States and its allies toppled it in late 2001, continue to harass U.S. bases and patrols in Afghanistan, often from across the border in Pakistan.

Afghanistan also remains the world's largest opium producer, with a growing drug trade and associated corruption threatening the country's reconstruction and clouding its ongoing debate over such basic issues as law and governance. The country is to hold a constitutional convention this fall, with elections planned for next year.

Although Congress authorized $3.3 billion in financial and military assistance to Afghanistan in the fall of 2001, a relatively small part of that amount has been spent. Testifying in June before the House International Relations Committee, Barnett R. Rubin, former special adviser to the United Nations on Afghanistan, said that $200 million in construction projects have been completed.

Rep. Henry J. Hyde (R-Ill.), the committee's chairman, commented a month earlier, during a hearing on postwar Iraq policy, that it "would be a horrendous mistake for us to invest the blood and treasure we have in getting rid of Saddam Hussein and then making the same mistake we made in Afghanistan, leaving the scene."

At the same hearing, Rep. William D. Delahunt (D-Mass.), said that "it's been about a year and a half [since the war] in Afghanistan and President Karzai only has control, maybe, of Kabul, and we still have warlords all over that particular country. And I dare say that reconstruction in Afghanistan is a mess at this point."

One senior defense official, who recently returned from Afghanistan, conceded that serious problems remain but said far greater progress has been made than most critics and many commentators acknowledge.

"There's been tremendous progress in every field," the official said. "The doom and gloom in the media, both on Iraq and Afghanistan, is talked about by everyone who comes back. They say the coverage is incredibly negative. People in Afghanistan making bricks and repairing their houses is not news anymore."

Training of the first 4,500 soldiers of the new Afghan army by U.S. military personnel has been "an incredible success story," the official said, explaining that Afghans who see the well-disciplined troops in action think they are Western peacekeepers and are elated to learn that they are native Afghan forces.

## AFGHANISTAN JOINS WORLD BANK'S MIGA

### Agency poised to support reconstruction and economic progress

WASHINGTON, DC, July 3, 2003—Afghanistan took the final step to secure its membership in the Multilateral Investment Guarantee Agency with its subscription to the agency's capital base. The membership took effect June 16.

The move marks a critical step forward in the country's efforts to rebuild in the wake of two decades of conflict. The membership allows MIGA to provide political risk insurance for investments going into and out of Afghanistan, as well as to help the country develop its ability to attract investment. MIGA provides coverage against the risks of transfer restriction, expropriation, breach of contract, and war and civil disturbance (including terrorism).

After 23 years of conflict, the Afghan people are working to restore peace and prosperity. But daunting challenges remain: 70 percent of the population is malnourished, and only 23 percent have access to safe water, 12 percent to adequate sanitation, and just 6 percent to electricity. More than 70 percent of schools need repairs, as do most of the country's primary roads. Reconstruction alone is expected to cost about $15 billion over the next decade, underscoring the need for private sector help in meeting the challenge.

There are many areas in need of urgent attention, particularly basic infrastructure, says Afghan Finance Minister Ashraf Ghani. Investment priorities are primarily in the power, roads, telecommunications, industry, and tourism sectors. Agriculture, too, which has suffered due to an extended drought, is an area that stands to benefit from investment.

Since its inception, MIGA has supported 56 projects with guarantees worth nearly $1.5 billion in 16 conflict-affected countries. This represents 13 percent of the agency's gross portfolio. "MIGA can bridge the gap between investors' concerns and a country's desire to attract good investors to help reconstruct the economy," says Motomichi Ikawa, MIGA's executive vice president. "We have a healthy pipeline of inquiries from investors who are interested in doing business in Afghanistan, but are concerned about the safety of their investments."

MIGA is currently in the process of setting up a guarantee trust fund for Afghanistan, with donor and other outside funding. "This will allow us to more fully deploy our guarantee products in Afghanistan, as well as increase our flexibility in the types of deals and transactions we'll be able to support," says Ikawa.

"We are pleased to become a member of MIGA. We look forward to a fruitful relationship that will help us attract and retain more foreign investment, promote economic growth, and ultimately benefit the people of our country," says Ghani.

## AFGHANISTAN: WORLD BANK BOOSTS SUPPORT FOR JOB CREATION THROUGH PUBLIC WORKS IN RURAL AFGHANISTAN

**Washington, June 24, 2003**—The World Bank today, with the approval of US$39.2 million, has tripled its support for Afghanistan's successful program of labor-intensive public works, which is creating jobs and rehabilitating infrastructure across the country. The new financing will help supply jobs in road improvement, which will in turn increase rural access to necessities such as health care and food supplies.

The financing will support a **Rural Roads Access Project,** and includes a US$18.8 million grant and a US$ 20.4 million credit from the World Bank's International Development Association. The project is part of the Government of Afghanistan's **National Emergency Employment Program**, under implementation by the Ministries of Public Works and Rural Rehabilitation and Development.

Insufficient access to cities and markets has been a serious problem in Afghanistan's rural areas where there are few adequate health and education facilities or large markets for trade in commodities. More than two decades of conflict, combined with a prolonged lack of maintenance, has resulted in damage to long stretches of road and to many bridges and other critical structures, rendering the road network only partially usable and with significantly higher transportation costs.

People's livelihoods are also threatened by the continuing legacy of conflict, drought, and displacement, and vulnerable groups like returning refugees, displaced families and ex-combatants are in particular need of jobs in the short run. Border-crossing restrictions with Iran and Pakistan have reduced opportunities for Afghan migrant labor in those countries while returning refugees and internally displaced populations continue to stress the labor market.

*"Considering the fact that almost 80 percent of the rural population lives on subsistence-level incomes, the creation of employment opportunities will have an immediate impact on their livelihoods,"* said **William Byrd, the World Bank Country Manager in Kabul.** *"This program will support the creation of productive emergency employment opportunities in maintenance and rehabilitation of rural access infrastructure and will help build the capacity of the implementing ministries to oversee such programs. This program will also provide the rural population with easier access to the goods and services that they desperately need."*

The Government of Afghanistan launched a pilot project to test the effectiveness of providing employment opportunities under its National Emergency Employment Program(NEEP) in late 2002. This project was funded by the World Bank through the Emergency Community Empowerment and Public Works grant. Subsequently, the Afghanistan Reconstruction Trust Fund provided an additional grant in support of the NEEP.

The project will help the Government of Afghanistan target particularly vulnerable rural groups with employment opportunities that will both raise incomes and improve key rural access infrastructure in the countryside. It will create a minimum of 6 million unskilled labor days of employment—or around 300,000 temporary jobs of one month's duration—and rehabilitate some 2,000 km of rural roads and nearly 2,300 meters of bridges.

The credit portion of the project will finance the reconstruction of key infrastructure bottlenecks, primarily bridges. The grant will finance the rehabilitation and repair of tertiary rural access roads and technical assistance to the Government for implementing the project. The technical assistance includes general support for the NEEP as well as support for the development and implementation of a management information system that will be a useful tool for the government in road network management and maintenance planning.

The project will be implemented over a 39-month period by the Ministry of Public Works and Ministry of Rural Rehabilitation and Development. At the provincial level, government-led Technical Support Units will coordinate and supervise the implementation of the infrastructure works.

The IDA credit portion of this project is an interest-free loan which carries a 0.75 % service charge and has a 40 year maturity, with a 10 year grace period.

## U.S. GOVERNMENT ANNOUNCES MAJOR INFRASTRUCTURE CONTRACT FOR AFGHANISTAN

U.S. AGENCY FOR INTERNATIONAL DEVELOPMENT
PRESS RELEASE

WASHINGTON, DC 20523
PRESS OFFICE
http://www.usaid.gov
(202) 712-4320

Contact: USAID Press Office

**Kabul, Afghanistan** -- Today, U.S. government officials, including Frederick W. Schieck, Deputy Administrator for the U.S. Agency for International Development, announced the award of a multi-million dollar infrastructure development contract to the Louis Berger Group, taking another major step toward rebuilding Afghanistan's national infrastructure.

When meeting with Afghan President Hamid Karzai on September 12, 2002, President George Bush pledged $80 million in U.S. support to rebuild the road linking Kabul through Kandahar to Herat, in partnership with Japan and Saudi Arabia. All U.S. funds are subject to Congressional approval. This and other infrastructure projects are essential to revitalizing this country and creating a corridor of development.

"We'll help develop a modern infrastructure so that Afghan entrepreneur will be able to move product from one city to the next, and so that people will be able to find work, they'll be able to put food on the table," pledged President Bush.

"This is another major step in rebuilding Afghanistan's infrastructure. USAID is undertaking many important activities including irrigation, agriculture, and repairing schools, health facilities, municipal facilities and more," said Deputy Administrator Schieck, "but road reconstruction is one of the most important."

Afghan President Hamid Karzai has stated that reconstruction of the country's principle road system is key to Afghanistan's economic recovery. The journey from Kabul to Herat, about 600 miles, is an arduous trip that currently takes several days because much of the road surface and several bridges have been destroyed.

At the Tokyo Pledging Conference in January, 2002, the United States, Japan, Saudi Arabia and other donor nations pledged $4.5 billion in overall reconstruction funding. Rebuilding the transportation infrastructure enables the movement of people, aid resources, farm goods and trade goods, all essential to Afghanistan's development.

As the project manager, the Louis Berger Group will be responsible for the design and construction supervision of the road and a variety of other infrastructure projects. This project will generate significant employment for local laborers and contractors. The road is scheduled for completion in approximately 36 months. Initial survey work has already been completed and design work is expected to begin by mid-October.

## AFGHANISTAN, REP. LOAN: AFG 36673-01

**Project Name**
Emergency Infrastructure Rehabilitation and Reconstruction Project
**Executing Agency**
Ministry of Finance
Contact
: Mr A. S. Rahimy
Address
: Ministry of Finance
**Loan Amount (US$ million)**
150.00
**Sector/Subsector**
Multisector

---

**Objectives and Scope**

The main objective of the Project is to help the Islamic Transitional Government of Afghanistan restore key infrastructure in the transport (roads) and energy (power and gas) sectors. The project will have the following parts: Part A: Road Infrastructure; Part B: Power Infrastructure; and Part C: Gas Infrastructure.

**Procurement**

*Goods*

All contracts for civil works and supply of equipment and materials will be divided into suitable contract packages. The contracts have been mostly packaged as turnkey and design-build to ensure delivery within the project implementation period. The civil works contracts exceeding $1 million will be awarded following international competitive bidding procedures. The contracts for equipment and materials valued at $500,000 and below should be procured using international shopping procedures. For equipment and material contracts exceeding $500,000, international competitive bidding procedures will be followed

*Services*

Consulting services (280 person-months international and 500 person-months domestic) will be required to assist the EA and IAs in project implementation. All consultants financed under the project will be selected and engaged in accordance with ADB's Guidelines on the Use of Consultants with the flexibility, wherever essential, provided under emergency assistance projects.

**Environmental Category:** B

**Project Processing Stage**

Approved by the Bank
3 June 2003

**Project Officer**

Hasan Masood (632-6818)
South Asia Transport and Communications Division
hmasood@adb.org

## AFGHANISTAN RECONSTRUCTION CONFERENCE PROJECTS

These projects were presented at the Afghanistan: Rebuilding a Nation conference cosponsored by the U.S. Department of Commerce and the U.S. Trade and Development Agency that was held June 8-10, 2003 in Chicago.

**Transportation**

Kabul Airport Navigation Aid Rehabilitation
Ministry Project Presentation
Project Cost: $19.3 million
Financing Agency: World Bank

Kabul-Doshi Road and Salang Tunnel Rehabilitation Project
Ministry Project Presentation
Project Cost: $108.4 million
Financing Agency: World Bank

Kandahar-Spin Boldak Road Rehabilitation
Project Cost: $15 million
Financing Agency: Asian Development Bank

Priority Road Rehabilitation Projects
Project Cost: $305 million
Financing Agency: Various

National Roads Rehabilitation Projects
Project Cost: $410 million
Financing Agency: Not identified

**Construction**

Rehabilitation of Economic Facilities and Services (REFS) Program
Project Cost: $210 million
Financing Agency: U.S. Agency for International Development

Kabul Satellite City Construction
Ministry Project Presentation
Project Cost: $400 million
Financing Agency: Not identified

Rebuilding Afghanistan's Agricultural Markets Program
Project Cost: $150 million
Financing Agency: United States Agency for International Development

**Water, Sanitation, and Irrigation**

Emergency Water and Sanitation Project
Project Cost: $16 million
Financing Agency: World Bank

Kunduz Khanabad Irrigation System
Ministry Project Presentation
Project Cost: $25 million
Financing Agency: Not Identified

**Telecommunications**

National and International Satellite Network Installation
Ministry Project Presentation
Project Cost: $5.5 million
Financing Agency: Government of Afghanistan

Microwave Link to Pakistan Installation
Project Cost: $1.4 million
Financing Agency: Government of Afghanistan

Digital Switching Expansion Project
Project Cost: $25.6 million
Financing Agency: Government of Afghanistan

**Hotel**

Hotel Kabul Rehabilitation
Project Cost: $27.8 million
Financing Agency: Aga Khan Foundation

Hyatt Hotel Construction
Project Cost: $39 million
Financing Agency: Overseas Private Investment Corporation

ACATCO Hotel Construction
Project Cost: $29.8 million
Financing Agency: Not Identified

**Oil and Gas**

Sheberghan to Kabul Gas Pipeline and Generating Plant
Ministry Project Presentation
Project Cost: $333 million
Financing Agency: World Bank (partially)

Gas Regulatory Framework Study
Project Cost: $650,000
Financing Agency: Asian Development Bank

Energy Sector Review and Gas Development Master Plan
Project Cost: $950,000
Financing Agency: Asian Development Bank

**Power**

Secondary Cities Emergency Power Project
Ministry Project Presentation
Project Cost: $15 million
Financing Agency: World Bank

Pahwa Wind Energy Power Project
Project Cost: $4 million
Financing Agency: Not Identified

Priority Power Generation Projects
Project Cost: $400 million
Financing Agency: Not Identified

**Manufacturing**

Golbahar Textile Factory Rehabilitation
Project Cost: $2.5 million
Financing Agency: Not Identified

Kabul Plastics Factory Rehabilitation
Project Cost: $1.5 million
Financing Agency: Not Identified

Afghanistan Bottled Water Distribution
Project Cost: $1 million
Financing Agency: Not Identified

**Market Economy Transition**

Post Conflict Multi-Sector Program
Project Cost: $150 million
Financing Agency: Asian Development Bank

Pahwa Poultry and Dairy Production Project
Project Cost: $4 million
Financing Agency: Not Identified

Small-and Medium-Sized Enterprise Development Projects
Project Cost: $10 million
Financing Agency: Not Identified

State- Owned Industries Privatization Projects
Project Cost: $700 million
Financing Agency: Not Identified

Dried Fruit Processing Project
Project Cost: $500,000
Financing Agency: Not Identified

PVC Pipe Production and Plumbing Supplies Project
Project Cost: $500,000
Financing Agency: Not Identified

Cashmere Wool Washing and Spinning Project
Project Cost: $6 million
Financing Agency: Not Identified

Jams, Jellies, Juices, and Dried Fruits Processing Plant Project
Project Cost: $5 million
Financing Agency: Not Identified

Sugar Beet Production and Processing Project
Project Cost: $50 million
Financing Agency: Not Identified

Kandahar Cement Factory Project
Project Cost: $90 million
Financing Agency: Not Identified

Basic Industrial Production Project
Project Cost: $6 million
Financing Agency: Not Identified

Caustic Soda/PVC/Soda Ash Production Project
Project Cost: $40 million
Financing Agency: Not Identified

American University of Afghanistan
Project Cost: $553,000
Financing Agency: U.S. Trade and Development Agency

Plastic Window Frame Manufacturing Project
Project Cost: $500,000
Financing Agency: Not Identified

# MAJOR GOVERNMENT PROGRAMS AND BUSINESS OPPORTUNITIES

## NATIONAL SOLIDARITY PROGRAMME (NSP)

### RATIONALE

The chronic poverty in Afghanistan, exacerbated by years of neglect, accumulated effects of conflict and political instability and drought, has produced unacceptable levels of human suffering and deprivation. Over 50% of Afghanistan rural population live below the poverty line. While poverty reduction lies at the heart of the government's social policy, the objective can only be achieved by empowering poor communities to strengthen their social capital and bonds, make decisions that affect their lives and use public and their own resources in the best interest of their communities. Pursuing this objective, the NSP is mobilising community and public institutions, private sector, NGOs and UN agencies to support the Afghan poor communities in their struggle to make their way out of poverty.

### OBJECTIVES

The objectives of the programme are:

- To lay the foundations of community-level good governance.
- To support community-managed sub-projects for reconstruction and development to improve the access of rural communities to social and productive infrastructure and services.

### STRATEGY AND IMPLEMENTATION PLAN

NSP strongly promotes a unique development paradigm whereby communities can make important decision and control resources at all stages of their development. Through NSP, communities elect their legitimate leaders and representatives to form Community Development Councils (CDC).These CDCs formulate Village Development Plans through extensive consultation and participatory methods. To implement priority projects of the plans, CDCs mobilise community resources and receive block grants (average around USD 20,000) from the government. 21 NGOs and UN-Habitat as Facilitating Partners (FPs) have been contracted to provide technical assistance to communities in electing their leaders, establishing CDCs, formulating village development plans, design and implement development projects. The GTZ/DAI has been contracted as Oversight Consultant (OC) to supervise the entire process on behalf of the government, providing training and making sure that communities receive their block grants for eligible projects in a transparent manner. The MRRD is responsible for overall management and execution of the programme. A joint committee of government, donors, UN and the Afghan Human Rights Commission provides policy advice and strategic oversight. The villages are selected on the basis of three criteria, i.e. food & livelihood insecurity, return of refugees and IDPs and social targeting balance.

### SUMMARY OF ACHIEVEMENTS UP-TO-DATE

Today, NSP is the Afghan government's flagship programme for community development. This government's largest development program is gaining strong momentum with the following major achievements:

- NPS has covered 96 districts (3 in each of the 32 provinces). To date, over 5 million rural women and men have participated in electing 4,000 CDCs in 4,000 villages. 15% of these CDCs are special women councils and the rest are mixed.

- As of 31 March 2004, total amount of $4,694,629 of the block grants was disbursed (over USD 11 million obligated) for construction of roads and culverts (129 projects), water supply systems (89 projects), Gabion and irrigation canal (50 projects), for electricity (e.g., diesel generator and micro hydro-power, 50 projects), 27 public bathes, 20 schools, and 20 facilities for weaving and tailoring, 7 bridges, as well as other community facilities.

- NSP is now launching an intensive training program for more than 3,600 participants from MRRD, NSP, FPs as well as the elected representatives from communities across the country.

- 24 out of the planned 32 regional NSP offices are opened, equipped, staffed, and fully operational.

#### Plan for 1383

By the end of 1383, NSP will cover the planned 6,000 villages and start the initial phase of the programme in 6,000 new villages of the country. The objective is to reach all villages of the country (approx. 20,000) in 3 to 4 years.

From now on, it is projected that every month between 4 to 5 hundred villages will be receiving their block grants (estimated US$ 10 million in total).

#### Key bottlenecks

- Inaccessibility to some of rural areas due to security situations.

- Weak capacity of MRRD engineering and management of FPs & OC.

- Insufficient communication and information infrastructure.

#### Information on funding

Total contract value of the program is US$42,252,342 (with $20,319,700 disbursed as of 31st March 2004). The program has received contributions by IDA Grant-NSP component (SDR 18,650,000, approx.US$29,525,331), Denmark ($4,989,475), DFID ($5,723,000), and Canada ($10,985,000). The other funding that is committed but yet to be made available includes IDA NSP II Grant ($97,771,154), EC ($19,095,000) and USAID ($10,000,000) and Japan ($10 million).

### NATIONAL EMERGENCY EMPLOYMENT PROGRAMME (NEEP)

#### Rationale

The livelihood insecure people including the returnees need productive work opportunities. Unemployment and under employment is widespread. The poppy growers and ex-combatants will have to be assisted with alternative livelihood opportunities. While economic growth is essential for a politically stable and prosperous Afghanistan, it is imperative to ensure that the vulnerable people benefit from such growth through special social safety nets.

On the other hand, physical inaccessibility exacerbates the poverty of our people, affecting their access to markets, health and education as well as hinders their participation in the political processes of the country. The NEEP is designed to address these challenges.

### OBJECTIVES

The objectives of NEEP include:

- To provide a safety net for the most vulnerable people by creating productive employment opportunities
- To establish effective mechanisms for developing public and productive infrastructure assets, through labour-based methods and a private sector-led approach
- To develop public sector capacity and systems for delivering various community services.

### STRATEGY AND IMPLEMENTATION PLAN

NEEP covers all 32 provinces of the country. Works are sub-contracted to private contractors through a bidding system. NEEP also provides training for the small local contractors to make sure that the construction works are of good quality. Labour-intensive methods are used in the construction to ensure that a maximum number of poor people can benefit from the NEEP projects. People with disability, destitute women, the elderly, refugees, and demobilized soldiers are also recruited by NEEP for the construction activities.

The NEEP National Inter-ministerial Board, composed of MRRD, MPW, MMD, Women's Affairs, Labour and Social Affairs, Returnees and Repatriation, Public Health, Education, Frontiers and Tribal Affairs, Reconstruction, and Finance, is responsible for steering the programme and managing resource allocation. A Joint Program Management Unit (JPMU) under the leadership of MRRD is responsible for the strategic management of the programme including the development of policies such as targeting and standards, etc. The Unit reports to the Inter-ministerial Board. Together with other ministries, MRRD coordinates all projects under NEEP.

### SUMMARY OF ACHIEVEMENTS UP-TO-DATE

NEEP completed its first phase in 2003 with great success, creating 5 million labour-days and reconstructing 1,050 km of roads. NEEP has also completed construction of 1,500 bridges and culverts, 3,000 shelter, 100 school, 15 clinics, 100 projects for irrigation, and 250 projects for water supply. Credit for the success of these projects goes to the Ministries Public Works, Water Resource, Irrigation and Environment, Rural Development and our partners such UNOPS, ILO and CARE.

Furthermore, draft guidelines and procedures for resource allocation/programming, planning, contracting, social targeting, monitoring & evaluation, and reporting, were developed for the NEEP staff to ensure smooth operation of the programme. A pilot Management Information System (MIS) has been established and operationalized to track physical and financial progress of the projects.

### PLAN FOR 1383

The target for NEEP in 1383 is to generate 13 million labour days through construction of work of 2,500 km of rural roads, 2,500 bridges, 50 irrigation projects, 150 water supply projects across the country. Plans are being reviewed to further scale up the NEEP delivery. The capacity of NEEP to implement and monitor the projects will be enhanced by expanding MIS at full-scale and recruiting more NEEP staff in the communities.

### KEY BOTTLENECKS

The implementation mechanisms for NEEP need to be strengthened further including the functioning of the Inter-ministerial Board. The engineering capacity of the organisations involved needs to be strengthened. Strengthening the capacity of the contractors for managing contracts is a key priority. Another priority is the development of national policies and technical standards and capacity for monitoring compliance.

### INFORMATION ON FUNDING

Total budget of the programme is US$126,738,670. NEEP has received contributions from WB, EC, USAID, UNHCR, and Japan. The budget requirement for continuation of the programme activities in 1383 is US$65,752,000, which is covered by WB, EC, USAID, UNHCR, and Japan. Yet, the programme requires an additional US$150million for expansion of the activities.

## RURAL WATER SUPPLY, SANITATION, AND HYGIENE PROMOTION

### RATIONALE

In addition to its impact on health, development of domestic water supply and sanitation is considered one of the most important factors for improving rural livelihoods. Safe drinking water is one of the biggest contributing factors to people's health, and reconstruction can only be accelerated through an active and healthy population. Afghanistan has some of the worst mortality figures in the world, for example, over 25% of children dying before the age of 5. Half of the deaths are caused by preventable waterborne diseases. Urgent action is necessary to improve rural livelihood and health in the communities.

### OBJECTIVES

The objectives of the programme are:

- To improve health and halve the child mortality and morbidity in the country within the next 5 years.
- To educate people on how to prevent waterborne diseases and stay on healthy.
- To reach all people with safe and sustainable drinking water.
- To improve public hygiene and environmental sanitation in the community.
- To equip all communities with a community environmental and sanitation plan to protect their health and local environment.

### STRATEGY AND IMPLEMENTATION PLAN

To reach all people with sustainable basic services for rural water supply and sanitation facilities, sustainability is developed with community ownership, based on the user demands as well as the willingness and ability to contribute and pay. The programme uses local technology and methods to provide safe water. The Government takes a regulatory and facilitating role while the private sector implements government-executed programmes, supervised and monitored by MRRD. A key strategy will be to collect information on the status of existing services nationwide to identify the community needs and implement activities accordingly.

To reach 15 million people over the next 5 years with enhanced capacity for basic services, the programme will develop 100,000 new water points providing 25 litres of safe water per day per person. In order to make people aware of the Importance of safe drinking water and links to waterborne diseases, 2.5 million households will be educated on water, sanitation, and hygiene issues through a variety of approaches suitable for rural Afghanistan.

### SUMMARY OF ACHIEVEMENTS UP-TO-DATE

In 2003, National Policy Framework has been developed and approved. Also, the National 5-year targets and Millennium Goals in Afghanistan have been defined and the 5-year development plan was prepared. In order to achieve these targets, the programme has successfully implemented various activities in all 32 provinces. For example, approximately 1.5 million people have benefited from 204 projects with US$11 million in 2003 alone. Through those projects, 3,387 wells, 1,712 water tanks in schools, 1,042 sets of latrines as well as 600 family latrines, and 26 water supply networks were constructed. Furthermore, 7 hygiene education projects were implemented, 9 ozone solar systems were installed, and 704 hand pumps were repaired. A water pond was rehabilitated, and a chlorination project was also completed.

The project proposals have been prepared for sector investment, amounted to over $200 million for the next 5 years. Also, the project proposals, valued over $25 million, were drafted for the year of 2004. An agreement on implementation of these projects has already been signed between MRRD, UNICEF and UNHCR. A project proposal for $5 million supported by USAID is close to be finalized, and the $20 million-value proposal is already being appraised by Afghanistan Reconstruction Trust Fund.

### PLAN FOR 1383

Under the programme, the following activities are planned for 1383:

- Construction of 13,000 new water points.
- Construction of 40,000 household latrines.
- Hygiene education to 800,000 households.
- Establishment of a national training centre, later to be developed into a rural training academy.
- Provision of water supply and sanitation for more than 1,000 schools.
- Starting development of small scale private sector firms.

### KEY BOTTLENECKS

- Inaccessibility in rural areas.
- Lack of local engineers and staff to provide necessary technical services and supervision for the projects.

- Weak implementation mechanisms to ensure strengthening of community-based projects.
- The need to strengthen provincial government capacities.

#### Information on Funding

The total rural water supply and sanitation programme is budgeted around $205 million over the next 5 years. This does not include a special program for rural towns and peri-urban areas.

For 1383, the funds are now pledged by UNHCR ($2.3 million for support to MRRD), USAID ($5 million for support to 13 provinces), UNICEF ($5 million for total programme), Japan ($ 1 million) and Afghanistan Trust Fund ($17 million). Support from the government of Turkey ($ 2 million) is under discussion.

### NATIONAL AREA BASED DEVELOPMENT PROGRAMME (NABDP)

#### Rationale

After the induction of the Afghanistan Interim Administration in December 2001, the Government identified ten priority geographical areas in the light of their severe war damages, large numbers of returning refugees and IDPs and earthquake damage. The NABDP was designed to support rebuilding essential functions of the state and civil society institutions, rehabilitating basic rural infrastructure, stimulating economic and income generating activities, and improving access to social services under the National Development Framework.

#### Objectives

The objective of NABDP is to develop the capacity of the government at national and local levels to formulate and manage recovery and development strategies and programmes through a participatory process to address key social and economic challenges in the country.

#### Strategy and Implementation Plan

NABDP has been implemented under the two different modalities executed by MRRD and UNDP in collaboration with UNOPS, FAO, and UN Habitat. NABDP is unique within the MRRD's program portfolio in that resources can be programmed flexibly in response to locally defined needs and availability of other program resources. The focus of the NABDP interventions is to support programme achieving results, ensure capacity development, and strengthen the MRRD and RRD provincial offices through skill enhancement of the staff, financial and material capacity, and system development.

#### Summary of Achievements Up-to-Date

- The programme enabled government officials, the Emergency Loya Jirga delegates, and local leaders to conduct a provincial planning process in all provinces of the country and identify over 1,500 key priority projects in all districts of the country. Of these, 317 sub-projects valued at over US$17.9 million have been implemented across 32 provinces, contracted through UN agencies, such as FAO, UN Habitat, UNOPS, NGOs, and private sector businesses, for immediate recovery in the areas of agriculture, building construction, education, heath, income-generation, irrigation, livelihood, rural development, shelter, transport, water supply, and public administration.

- NABDP has played the most important role in the institutional reform and strengthening of MRRD. Through provision of human and financial capitals, the programme has enabled the ministry to reform its mandate, policies and structures at both national and provincial levels, and develop new programmes that are relevant to the national priorities. Also, the programme has extended such a support to other ministries both at national and provincial levels.

- The feasibility study was conducted on macro-economic regeneration projects, particularly on the Spinzar Cotton Gin in Kudzu including scenarios for further operation of the Gin in the context of the government's privatisation law discussed with the Minister of MRRD, Light Industries and the Chairman of the Privatisation Commission.

### PLAN FOR 1383

In 1383, NABDP will intensify and expand its activities in the following areas:

- Continuation of the obligated NABDP Sub-projects for rural infrastructure and rehabilitation.

- Implementation of the remaining of the over 1,500 projects identified through provincial planning. Priority will be given to the projects not picked up by other national programmes.

- Continuation of support for further institutional reform and restructuring within MRRD and other LSP ministries.

- Re-organization of NABDP for resource mobilization and strengthening reporting and monitoring system in MRRD and NABDP.

- Provision of support for the Afghanistan's first National Human Development Report.

- Continuation of support for NRVA/NSS.

### KEY BOTTLENECKS

The progress of activities in the sub-projects is largely subject to severe security concerns. Social, political, cultural and economic implications needed to be carefully observed and measured before undertaking any intervention.

### INFORMATION ON FUNDING

Total budget of the programme amounts US$157 million. In 2003, NABDP received US$29.5 million from Italy ($10, 983,367), Malaysia ($500,000), Canada ($5,150,727), Japan ($1,854,000), UK ($1,562,500), USAID ($5,000,000), Sweden ($2,910,361), EC ($339,875), UNHCR ($161,410), and UNDP ($1,100,000).

Budget requirements for 1383 are estimated to be US$ 45 million and some donors have expressed their interest in contributing to NABDP in 1383, such as Italy ($7.2 million), Canada ($7.18million), Sweden ($2million), UNHCR ($0.5 million), UNDP ($0.5million) and EC ($0.5 million). This leaves US$27,107 as a shortfall.

## MICRO FINANCE INVESTMENT AND SUPPORT FACILITY IN AFGHANISTAN (MISFA)

## Rationale

As part of the needs assessment undertaken by the World Bank in early 2001, micro-finance was identified as one of the core needs for securing sustainable development at the micro and macro economic level. This was reaffirmed by the recent review of the needs assessment carried out by the World Bank under the Livelihoods and Social Protection program in December 2003 for and on behalf of the Afghanistan Transitional Government. Economic regeneration is an essential element in the reconstruction and stabilization of Afghan society. The provision of credit and finance generally is key to the development of the private sector economy.

## Objectives

The primary objectives of MISFA are:

- To improve the livelihoods and opportunities of the poor and vulnerable in Afghan society through the provision of credit.
- To develop a sufficient number of NGO micro finance institutions that have adequate capacity and infrastructure to implement sustainable credit programs.
- To develop MISFA as a long term independent wholesale financial intermediary for the micro finance sector (i.e., a bank to micro finance institutions) as well as an advocate for the sector and a vehicle through which the sector can co-ordinate activities and initiatives such as credit bureaus, and commercial law and regulation.

## Strategy and Implementation Plan

MISFA began operating in June 2003, and the programme now has around fifteen professional international and national staff. MISFA has its own premises and systems and operating procedures and is seeking to be formed as an independent entity by summer 2004. Also, the aim is to have MISFA management by national staff during 2005. MISFA has been working closely with NGOs as implementing partners. NGOs are identified through a selection process including a formal application together with a business plan prepared by the NGO. If selected, the NGO is subject to an assessment undertaken by MISFA's technical staff which results in the production of a work plan with deliverables and targets. Funding is disbursed in instalments and is subject to continuing satisfactory performance.

In relation to empowering livelihoods, MISFA focuses on vulnerable groups including women, the disabled, and the working poor, providing the credits ranged $50-1,000 for the term of 3-12 months.

## Summary of Achievements Up-to-Date

Within as short as seven months, MISFA has already succeeded in funding five micro finance institutions (MFIs) or NGOs. Since the first disbursement made in July 2003, almost US$16 million has been contracted, and over US$5 million has been disbursed. More than 20,000 clients (mostly women-headed families) have received loans. The performance of the micro-credit loan has been remarkable with the average repayment rates of 98%. The MISFA loans have financed the activities for commercial services (e.g., carpentry, transportation, hairdresser, electrician, and plumber), craft (e.g., embroidery, carpets, and sewing), shops and retail sellers, and manufacturing.

### PLAN FOR 1383

MISFA aims to invest in at least twelve national and international institutions during 1383. The target is that at least 75,000 families will be receiving credit from those institutions by the end of 1383 and that another 14 provinces will be covered including Kunduz, Takhar, Laghman, Shibarghan, Samangan, Ghazni, Bamyan, Herat, Badakhshan, Wardak and some as yet unidentified western provinces. If, as hoped, other institutions can be incorporated under the MISFA projects then more provinces will be covered next year.

### KEY BOTTLENECKS

The limited number of competent micro-finance organisations in the country to implement the programme is a key constraint.

### INFORMATION ON FUNDING

Total budget of the programme is US$7.5 million for 1382, US$17.5 million for 1383, US$60 million for 1384. MISFA has been supported by World Bank ($5 million), CGAP ($1 million), CIDA ($10 million), USAID ($5 million), DFID ($ 1.8 million for 1382/83). MISFA requires additional US$5 million in 1383 to fill the financial gap. Because no commitments have been made for 1384, MISFA is looking for potential funding for the next year.

## LIVELIHOOD BASED FOOD SECURITY SURVEILLANCE SYSTEM

### RATIONALE

Most government agencies in Afghanistan have suffered significant decay and destruction of both physical infrastructure and human capital during the last 23 years. There has been little or no meaningful government data collection during this period. For example, the only census ever carried out in Afghanistan took place in 1979, but this was not completed due to security concerns. In order to identify priority development issues and design appropriate livelihood and social protection strategies, relevant informative data have to be collected and analysed regularly. Therefore, it is imperative that government reactivate its capacity to provide its own ministries and the wider development community with credible national statistics on poverty and vulnerability in both rural and urban settings.

### OBJECTIVES

This project aims to develop the capacity to provide timely relevant information in order to:

- Have a standardised and integrated surveillance system to which all agencies (government and non-government) wishing to develop policies and programmes addressing social protection, poverty and livelihoods can refer to as a primary data source of relevant and up-to-date information on livelihoods, risk and vulnerability.

- Identify early signs of change and deterioration in livelihoods, food security and nutrition in order to assist in the design of effective policymaking and programme responses.

- Collect data on aspects of rural livelihoods that inform targeting and programming for rural livelihoods, social protection and rehabilitation of rural infrastructure.

- Sharpen the capacity of Government to frame policies and make decision based on reliable quantitative information.

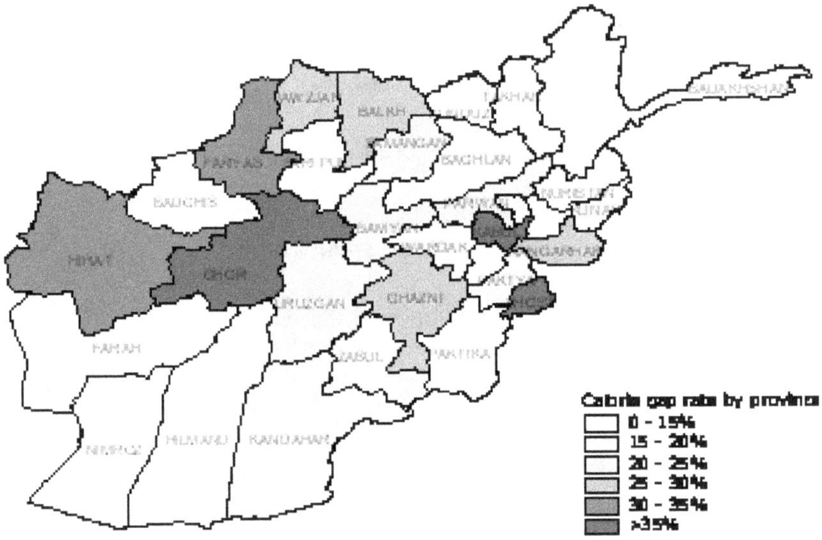


**STRATEGY AND IMPLEMENTATION PLAN**

The project is centred in the Vulnerability Analysis Unit within the MRRD. It is currently going through a process of upgrading the staff of the unit to rise to the challenge of being able to take on analysis of national poverty and vulnerability data.
The roles and responsibilities of data collection and data analysis may separate. It is important that rural and urban analysis is conducted with the same methods, as well as having the data collected by an institution recognised by other government partners as the legitimate agency for this.

Therefore, engagement with the current process of developing a Statistical Master Plan of Afghanistan is on-going (the process whereby roles, responsibilities, and statistical law will be defined, programme of work for reactivation of government statistics sought) will result in Phase 2 of this programme, support going to CSO for the data collection activities, while continuing to strengthen capacity building within the Vulnerability Analysis Unit within MRRD for data and policy analysis .

Also, this project must support analytical capacity building in other key ministries such as Agriculture, Health and Urban Development to ensure value of the data is maximised. This project is beginning to produce results that can inform targeting programming and policy. As results emerge, advocacy and capacity building around their use in pro-poor planning processes will be embarked upon. The aim is to provide "pro-poor" policies that address people's needs through an understanding of their livelihoods with more effective targeting of marginalized and poor groups through improved livelihood and social protection programmes and instruments. The project aims to do this both in times of reconstruction and in an emergency, if severe drought returns.

## SUMMARY OF ACHIEVEMENTS UP-TO-DATE

Implementation of the first assessment of the rural population of Afghanistan designed to address multi stakeholder and government agency needs (National Risk and Vulnerability Assessment (NRVA) 2003). This found that one in five households are still not meeting its basic food-energy needs despite the assessment taking place after one of the best harvest in many years in Afghanistan. Drought and water related stresses are still the major shocks that affect the rural population on a wide scale, whereas as household level health and unemployment shocks are the most frequently cited. The only pro-poor targeting that has been carried out through free food relief elements of the WFP program. Cash-for-work and food-for-work programmes have been poor neutral at best and by and large have excluded women. Not surprisingly, poor access to rural services emerges as a major issue, particularly to health facilities.

Managed data entry and cleaning, and currently in the process of producing an initial results.

Implementation of the pilot phase of National Surveillance System in collaboration with DFID.

## PLAN FOR 1383

The major activities planned for 1383 are:

Clarify institutional roles and responsibilities of various government agencies in relation to the collection of poverty and vulnerability data.

Strengthen the capacity of these departments to design, collect and analyse such data via recruitment of staff by embarking on long-term formal and informal training programme covering a range of topics from designing surveys and samples through to writing policy orientated reports.

Strengthen the ability of analytical units within key ministries to utilise this data to provide evidence based information and recommendations on targeting, programme then kneeling and policy.

Support the implementation of an open poverty and vulnerability assessment.

Conduct a workshop to promote the results of the NRVA for targeting, programming and policy among government ministries and other development agencies.

## KEY BOTTLENECKS

Although remarkable achievements have been made, the following issues need to addressed for further expansion of the programme:

Clarification on roles and responsibilities of government agencies for the collection of annual risk and vulnerability data and market price information.

Time needed to train Vulnerability Analysis Unit staff in database design, data management and analysis MRRD to perform required analysis on national datasets.

Demand from other government agencies and ministries for the use of policy and vulnerability data emerging from this initiative.

#### INFORMATION ON FUNDING

Phase I of this initiative is funded by the European Commission and with a small component of joint funding from UNDP (September 2003 –November 2004; $495,600). Phase II (November 2004 –October 2007) committed funds from European Commission €3.5 million and is open to competitive tender.

### REINTEGRATION AND IDP NATIONAL PLAN

#### RATIONALE

It is estimated that there are close to 190,000 IDPs in Afghanistan, the majority of whom are sheltered in Southern and Western Camps. The Government and its development partners have been supporting them in camps for the past few years. Returns have already taken place, but the key is for these to be sustainable and seen as successful to encourage further movements out of the camps and back to their homes. Through surveys and monitoring it is known that returnees face the same difficulties and issues as their receiving communities. The returnees in each area face problems with lack of water supply, employment opportunities and access to social services. MRRD plays a central role in inclusion of returnees through its national programmes, in addition to the activities of its Reintegration Unit, aiming to promote in particular the social and economic reintegration of the refugee and IDP returnees.

#### OBJECTIVES

- To increase the rate of IDP return
- To sustain IDP reintegration into areas of origin

#### STRATEGY AND IMPLEMENTATION PLAN

MRRD has decided not to design projects specifically for returnees but to mainstream their inclusion within the national development programmes. This inclusion in existing development programmes is aimed to facilitate their reintegration back into their villages of origin. It is understood that returnees are not the only prioritised beneficiary group, but the reintegration of over 3 million people (refugees returned) is a long-term objective that will require a sustainable commitment of resources. Within all of MRRD's national development programmes, returnees will be considered as a cross-cutting issue in planning, programming and implementation. The NSP will select its villages according to the criteria including the concentration of refugee and IDP returnees. NEEP will consider the levels of return within its social targeting and the Rural Water Supply programme will identify priority areas of high return where an increased population exacerbates scant resources.

The IDP National Plan is the initiative of the MRRD, Ministry of Refugees & Repatriation and the Ministry of Frontiers and Tribal Affairs, closely supported by UNHCR, UNDP, WFP, and UNAMA.

This plan seeks an end to the perpetuation of care and maintenance in the IDP camps and strives toward durable solutions to facilitate return and a sustained reintegration.

### SUMMARY OF ACHIEVEMENTS UP-TO-DATE

The activities within the IDP National Plan will start in 2004. At this stage there are a number of ongoing activities including an assessment of the feasibility of return by Kuchis to Registan and the establishment of provincial and central co-ordination mechanisms. The IDPs in the camps in the South are currently being profiled to determine those who wish to return and the obstacles to return and reintegration that must be addressed within the context of the plan. This plan also complements the activities of UNHCR, such as the Go and See Visits for IDP representatives to their areas of origin in the Northern provinces.

### PLAN FOR 1383

For all IDPs, their return will only be sustained through area reintegration projects that benefit those who are returning, in addition to the receiving and neighbouring communities. The project activities of the National Plan in 1383 will include:

- Support the restocking of livestock herds and livestock bank
- Skills training in agricultural and livestock activities
- Rehabilitation of water supply systems
- Rehabilitation of dams, reservoirs and protection walls

### INFORMATION ON FUNDING

Total budget of the programme over 3-years is an estimated $60m. UNHCR, WFP and IOM's programme activities are included within this Plan, but not included in the budget. The outstanding budget for 1383 is an estimated $19.5m, however, specific budgets will be proposed after technical assessments completed in July.

## HUMANITARIAN EMERGENCY RESPONSE

### RATIONALE

Afghanistan is a disaster prone country, with more than 70% of the inhabited area falling under medium to high risks caused by half a dozen natural disasters such as earthquakes, floods, landslides, avalanches, droughts and extreme winter conditions. These frequent natural disasters cause abject poverty and livelihoods, diminish income-generating opportunities, and contribute to poor state of infrastructure. Without prompt and appropriate responses, such natural and man-made disasters lead to the extremely vulnerable conditions of Afghan communities.

### OBJECTIVES

The overall objective of emergency response is to improve the sustainability of rural recovery efforts through reducing vulnerability of the rural population against natural disaster.

### STRATEGY AND IMPLEMENTATION PLAN

MRRD has been assigned to play a leading role in organizing and coordinating emergency relief assistances to the disaster-affected populations in the rural areas through Emergency Response Teams on various levels, such as province, district, and village. However, this role will be reviewed as the Disaster Preparedness Department is further strengthened.

### SUMMARY OF ACHIEVEMENTS UP-TO-DATE

The achievements in emergency response include:

- The response capacity of Provincial Department of MRRD was established and strengthened.
- 'Action Plan', 'Response Procedure', 'Assessment Guideline' and 'Surveyors Briefing Paper' were produced to facilitate smooth implementation of emergency relief activities.
- Relief assistance to more than 7,000 disaster-affected families was coordinated.
- A study on the rehabilitation of physical infrastructure damaged by disasters was conducted.
- Coordination of winter response with UNAMA was implemented.

### PLAN FOR 1383

The following activities are planned for 1383:

- Prepare a contingency response plan for 20,000 families.
- Develop and maintain a database for emergency stocks.
- Form provincial Emergency Response Teams.
- Build and improve capacities in disaster management.

### KEY BOTTLENECKS

The following constraints need to be addressed for effective responses:

- The need to undertake a serious institutional reform and restructuring to clarify the role of the key state institutions.
- Little coordination amongst relevant departments and agencies.
- Absence of early warning system at a national level.
- Lack of investment in the field of disaster management

### INFORMATION ON FUNDING

US$1,100,000 is required to support MRRD's planning activities for emergency response. No commitments have yet been made by our development partners.

## FOOD SECURITY-PROTRACTED RELIEF AND RECOVERY OPERATION

### RATIONALE

Chronic rural and urban poverty and food insecurity, malnutrition, and slow recovery from the impacts of severe droughts of 1998-2001 have been observed in Afghanistan. Absence of public safety nets (social policy) to protect the poor and the most vulnerable as well as poor socio-economic infrastructure further aggravate the situation. Furthermore, low school enrolment rates among children and teachers limit institutional capacity in Afghanistan.

### OBJECTIVES

The overall objective of the programme is to contribute to protection and re-establishment of livelihoods and household food security in the context of the National Development Framework.

### STRATEGY AND IMPLEMENTATION PLAN

The programme is executed by WFP and MRRD (the government counterpart) to ensure that the programme is coordinated with other government social protection programmes. The programme aims to support 9.2 million beneficiaries under various interventions with 619,000 MT of food through following mechanisms:

- Relief: Food assistance to returning refugees and internally displaced persons (IDPs), vulnerable rural and urban households, emergency assistance to disaster-affected populations, supplementary feeding for malnourished children and women, food assistance to patients in institutions, orphans, TB patients and their families.

- Recovery: Food assistance for school children, with a special focus on girls, teachers' salary supplement and instructors in training institutions, non-formal education and vocational training, food for work (employment based safety-net) and assistance to ex-combatants in the context of the Government's Disarmament, Demobilization and Reintegration (DDR) program.

- Capacity development of counterpart Government institutions, implementing partners and WFP national staff (training, provision of equipment, school construction, baseline surveys, food fortification, de-worming, etc).

### SUMMARY OF ACHIEVEMENTS UP-TO-DATE

- 6.9 million beneficiaries under various interventions of relief and recovery were assisted with 177,200 MT of food.

- Many assets were created or rehabilitated, including 4,203 km of roads and construction of 23 schools and 500 returnee houses.

- Capacity development of counterparts.

### PLAN FOR 1383

Under the programme, 269,065 MT of food commodities will be distributed to 5 million beneficiaries in closer cooperation with other national programs such as NEEP. Significant investments in capacity development will be provided in 1383.

### KEY BOTTLENECKS

The following issues need to be tackled for further implementation of the programme:

- Absence of a social safety net especially for the urban poor.
- Absence of a social policy framework to guide the most appropriate use of food and non-food interventions.
- Insufficient coordination between cash for work and food for work interventions between agencies.
- Limited capacity of counterpart government institutions and implementing partners.
- Inadequate baseline information to guide programming decisions.

### INFORMATION ON FUNDING

Total budget of the programme for two years (2004 and 2005) is estimated US$332.5 million. The programme so far received US$121.7 million (36.6% of the required fund) from Canada, Denmark, Europe Aid, ICRC, India, Italy, Japan, Luxembourg, Norway, Saudi Arabia, Switzerland, UK, UN, UNA-UK, USA, as well as the private sector. Yet, the programme still requires US$210.9 million for 2004 and 2005.

## NATIONAL HUMAN DEVELOPMENT REPORT (NHDR) FOR AFGHANISTAN

### RATIONALE

UNDP prepares Human Development Report every year and ranks the countries according to the value of the Human Development Index. Since 1995, Afghanistan does not have figures in the global HDR because of the lack of the data. Many countries of the world have started preparing NHDRs to study the regional, ethnic and other types of disparities in the country. NHDRs have proved an important tool in many countries for providing country–specific development indicators and promoting policy debate on the multi-dimensional development issues. With similar objectives in mind, it has been decided to prepare the first NHDR in Afghanistan.

### OBJECTIVES

- To create awareness among the policy makers and the public on human development and pro-poor development.
- To collect aggregated national data as well as disaggregated data according to gender, age, geographical location, ethnic, and other socio-economic groups and provide detailed analyses on the principal causes of poverty and the critical points of intervention.
- To give a thrust for the collection of quality data on various socio-economic variables in the country.

### STRATEGY AND IMPLEMENTATION PLAN

Because of the lack of the indigenous capacity for the preparation of the Report, UNDP is providing the necessary financial and technical inputs. Yet, in order to ensure that national issues are adequately represented in the Report, the Advisory Committee, consisting of the eminent people in their areas of expertise, has been constituted under the Chairmanship of Minister of MRRD. The report is to be written by experts of Afghan origin, while international experts are also providing the guidance. Background and thematic papers on selected topics have been contributed by experts, which provides the basis for the NHDR.

### SUMMARY OF ACHIEVEMENTS UP-TO-DATE

While preparation for the 1st NHDR is on-going, the following activities have already been completed:

- Background and thematic papers were produced.
- A team of authors has been appointed and operational.
- Three meetings of the Advisory Committee were organized.
- A study on data availability for the NHDR was conducted by an international expert.
- A workshop for the officers of the Central Statistical Office and other concerned Ministries was organized.

### PLAN FOR 1383

The report is tentatively scheduled to be released by September, 2004.

### INFORMATION ON FUNDING

The production of the first NHDR is funded through the UNDP Core-fund, amounted to US$600,000.

## MRRD REFORM & INSTITUTIONAL STRENGTHENING

## RATIONALE

After the establishment of the Transitional Islamic State of Afghanistan, the MRRD went through extensive review processes with assistance from UNDP, BRAC, EC and other partners. It was established that the old MRRD was not up to the challenge of poverty reduction in Afghanistan. The premise on which the old MRRD was based was outdated, neglecting new realities and best practices. Consistent with the government vision outlined in the National Development Framework, the leadership of the ministry has embarked on a phased institutional reform and restructuring.

### OBJECTIVES

The overall goal is to make sure that MRRD is not a liability for public budget and funds but an accountable and competent state institution to provide leadership to public, private and non-for-profit sectors as well as civil society organisations for poverty reduction and social protection in rural Afghanistan. The specific objectives therefore focus on MRRD mandate and policy reform, development of national social protection and poverty reduction programmes, structural reform, institutional and organisational development including staff competency development and reform of the institutional relationships.

### Strategy and Implementation plan

An on-going strategic planning process involving the staff and the key stakeholders of MRRD has been the key approach to the reform process. Outside specialist agencies have been and will be contracted to undertake specific studies for policy, programme and structural review. The PRR (Priority Reform and Restructuring) is the key instrument drawn upon for the institutional reform and restructuring within the 7 central and 32 provincial departments. Donors' support to the process has been ensured through the PRR, NABDP/UNDP, WFP, UNICEF and national programmes such as NSP, NEEP and others. To increase the institutional capacity, the emphasis is on (a) investment in staff capacity development, (b) recruitment and deployment of national and international individual consultants in key areas, and (c) extensive reliance on contractors for programme oversight and implementation.

### Summary of achievements up-to-date

- The mandate, key policies and the national and provincial structures of MRRD have all been reformed in the light of the NDF and best practices.
- Development of new policies, e.g. peoples' ownership and empowerment in all programmes, full accountability and transparency, the focus of the MRRD on policy guidance and the establishment of regulatory frameworks, emphasis on private sector, a new partnership and labour division with NGOs and UN, policies on humanitarian aid and social protection, policy on food aid and cash-for-work, policy on wheat prices.
- Development and launching of six national programmes.
- Administrative procedures have been improved by streamlining the administrative structures and centralizing the procurement and recruitment systems connected with the province offices.
- A capacity development program was developed and various training programmes have been conducted. The majority of our staff members both in Kabul and provinces have gone through various types of training with over 50 trained overseas.
- An additional Deputy Minister position was created in line with new structure of MRRD.
- The Leadership Team, composed of the Minister, 3 Deputy Ministers, Director of Documentation, Legal Advisor, and 3 Senior Advisors, was instituted and is operational.
- Coordination mechanisms both within the Headquarters and with the province offices have been established with Information Coordination Team (ICT), Central Coordination Team (CCT), and Provincial Coordination Team (PCT) in all 32 provinces.
- Over hundred national and international advisors have been recruited for short and mid-term assignments.

### Plan for 1383

The key activities planned for 1383 include:

- Complete the reform and restructuring of the PRR departments.
- Submit a new PRR proposal for the remaining departments of MRRD.
- Continue to implement the staff training in and outside the country.
- Submit the new MRRD Muqarara (legislation) for cabinet approval.
- Finalise the restructuring process.
- Recruit specialist staff on government consultancy contract for the functions such as procurement, finance, MIS, monitoring & evaluation and other technical areas.

### INFORMATION ON FUNDING

The MRRD reforms have been implemented with support from World Bank, Germany, Japan, Italy, Asian Development Bank, Finland, Denmark, Canada, Australia, UK, ICRC, OCO, EC, USA, the Netherlands, Norway, and Switzerland. The budget requirement for 1383 is estimated US$3.40 million, and out of which, US$1.78 million has already been pledged.

## ORGANIC AGRICULTURE

Agriculture is a fundamental means of livelihood in Afghanistan, generating 50% of the country's GDP and supporting 85% of its people. The climate of Afghanistan is well suited for the cultivation of horticultural crops and Afghanistan is the geographic origin of many high-end crops like raisins, pomegranates, pistachios and almonds.

There are approximately one million farms in Afghanistan and more than 2,000 wholesalers for horticulture products. Products are brought directly from the farms to five major wholesale markets located in Kabul, Mazar-e-Sharif, Kandahar, Heart and Jalalabad. Between farmers and wholesalers, there are thousands more employed as middle-men. The majority of private sector entrepreneurs in Afghanistan are farmers and the bulk of industrial sector processing is geared to providing services to farmers and farm related business. Because this sector contributes the most to national income and personal livelihoods, increased investment in the agro-business and agriculture areas will have a direct positive impact on the lives of thousands of Afghans.

Intensive commercial farming increases sustainable economic growth in rural areas, encourages competition, contributes to regional development and helps sustain the growth of private businesses. Afghanistan benefits from low labor and irrigation costs by regional comparison and high value cash crops provide vital food security and an alternative to poppy cultivation in the country. Between 1999 and 2002, Afghanistan experienced the worst drought in decades, which greatly damaged production levels of agricultural goods. Now Afghanistan is poised to increase these production levels, but it will take investment and government support to realize this potential. Part of this effort includes building capacity through training farmers on how to increase output and adopt modern techniques. In a recent survey (Maletta, Hector and Raphy Favre: Agriculture and Food Production in Post-War Ajghanistan), nearly 70% of farms interviewed (around 730,000 farms total) revealed they are too small to achieve self-sufficiency and are interested in farming higher value crops other than wheat. The NGO community is playing a strong role in this training and there is an encouraging willingness of local producers to receive technical assistance.

Agro-business and agro-processing provides an array of exciting investment opportunities. The industry has first-mover advantages for investors in modern processing techniques that involve cleaning, sorting and grading, and also packaging plants that incorporate quality control measures like hygiene and traceability. Improved transportation logistics for exports, including cold storage facilities, is one of the critical priorities. Adequate infrastructure, especially an improvement in road conditions, will alleviate the geographic constraints that accompany Afghanistan's position as a landlocked country. The involvement of the international community in Afghanistan's reconstruction process is playing an important role in building up the necessary infrastructure, but this takes time.

Investment in agro-business and agro-processing will make a positive impact on the economic development of Afghanistan and will give Afghans pride in producing and purchasing local Afghan products.

## OPEN REGIONAL MARKETS

Geographic proximity to large markets in India, China, Pakistan and the Middle East is an asset for Afghan agro-business and agro-processing. Pakistan is the main trading partner for fresh fruit exports and the two countries benefit from 'counter-season' market opportunities. Temperate fruits such as apples, apricots, peaches, grapes and almonds are among the most popular products for markets in India and Pakistan. India and Afghanistan have a preferential trade agreement (signed in March 2003) that places a high value on Afghan goods. With its rapidly growing income and population levels, the Indian market will continue to provide a profitable opportunity to sellers.

## THE MARKET POTENTIAL

Opportunities abound in agro-business and agro-processing and Afghanistan benefits from a number of comparative advantages that include a low labor cost, good surface water availability, a diverse range of produce, and an excellent reputation for good tasting and organic fruits and vegetables.

Over 600,000 farmers produce horticultural products in Afghanistan (FAO agriculture surveys conducted in 2003). Of these products, only five

(5) fruits and vegetables represent 90% of the area cultivated, which indicates a need for crop diversification. Afghanistan's climate is ideal for crop diversification and there is great investment potential for the private sector if they are willing take full control of the production, processing and distribution steps required.

## DRIED FRUITS AND NUTS

Climate and geographic proximity to rapidly growing markets dictate a huge potential for dried fruits and nuts (particularly the raisin, walnut, almond and pistachio). Increased dried fruit and nut exports alone are projected to reach $1 billion annually within ten years, which means there is a huge international export potential for Afghan horticulture crops (Ministry of Agriculture, Animal Husbandry and Food). The global export market for these products is estimated to be $2.2 billion for 1.3 million tons traded annually ((NDP/Altai Consulting Marret Sector Assessment in Horticulture (Phase 1, Market Research), June 2004).

Dried fruits from Afghanistan are exported through Central Asia, Iran and Pakistan to markets in the Middle East, Russia and beyond. Afghanistan's climate is ideal for drying fruits and there is a strong variety potential, specifically for raisins. In dried fruits and nuts, there are good opportunities for investment in existing factories as well as capitalizing on Afghanistan as a quality brand.

## RAISINS

Afghanistan is world famous for its superior quality raisins, due in part to its climate that provides optimal conditions for the organic production and drying of the crop. The Shomali, Parwan, Ghazni and Istalif areas have a reputation for producing the best quality harvests. Raisins are the largest part of the horticultural crop in Afghanistan and its primary export commodity. Afghanistan produces 520,000 MT annually of grapes and has more than 40 seedless grape varieties; the sultana, long green aftabi and currant varieties being most popular ((NDP/Altai Consulting Marret Sector Assessment in Horticulture (Phase 2-3, Feasibility studies and Business Plans), August 2004).

There once existed over thirty raisin-processing factories in Afghanistan, but only 8 of these are presently operational; two in Mazar, two in Parwan, two in Kandahar, one in Kabul and one in Herat (for more detailed information please refer Lister, Sarah and Tom Brown, "(nderstanding Markets in Afghanistan: A Case Study of the Raisin Market," ARE(, June 2004). These factories are using outmoded machinery from over 30 years ago and investment in updated machinery and newer and cleaner drying techniques is crucial. The raisin is a labor-intensive crop and because the manual sorting of raisins is preferred to the more expensive laser sorters, the raisin processing industry has the potential to employ many unskilled farm laborers.

To optimize raisin processing in Afghanistan, investment is most needed in the following areas:

-(pdated machinery and fruit drying technology;

-On-farm processing knowledge and skills training;

-(pgraded sanitary facilities;

-Packaging warehouses (which can be built directly next to processing and sorting facilities); and

-Rigorous marketing to successfully export raisins internationally.

In this industry, vertical control of the supply chain will ensure investors the best outcomes. This will include helping farmers increase production and sell dried raisins at a higher price, improving packing and processing, and facilitating export.There is currently little government control in the raisin trade and there is a high product loss due to transport problems. It is estimated that 5-10% of raisins are damaged or lost because they sit in rail cars for two or more weeks in Pakistan in high heat conditions.

The best export markets for Afghan raisins are currently in Russia and India, but the E( is likely to emerge as a lucrative market. There are opportunities on the Indian market, in particular, with India importing 6,000 MT raisins per year alone mainly because the aftabi raisin is considered a luxury product and commonly used in cooking. The aftabi also has a product preference on the Russian market.

Notably, Afghanistan is subject to a preferential import duty on its raisins, which is 52% instead of the usual 105% for other countries.

## RAISIN VALUE CHAINS

Value Chains: through Kandahar to India and Germany

1. Medium Quality Round Gieen Raisin

Afghan Wholesaler pays: (SD 0.91 / kg (sorts, packs, transports until border) Indian importer pays: (SD 1.22 / kg (takes delivery and pays at border) Indian retailer pays: (SD 2.61 / kg.

2. Medium Quality Lonh Gieen heedless Raisin

Afghan Wholesaler pays: (SD 2.87 / kg (sorts, packs, transports until border) Indian importer pays: (SD 3.48 / kg (takes delivery and pays at border) Indian retailer pays: (SD 6.00 / kg.

3.□iihQ□Quality□hQundukQani □Raisin□(specialty item)

Price at farmgate: (SD 4.50 / kg Afghan Wholesaler/exporter pays: (SD 6.26 / kg (sorts, packs, transports, duties until border) Indian importer pays: (SD 6.96 / kg (delivery at Pakistani border; later pays (SD 1.74/kg) Indian consumer pays: (SD 12.50 / kg.

4. Medium Quality Red Raisin

Afghan Wholesaler/exporter pays: (SD 1.22/ kg (sorts, packs, transports) German importer pays: (SD 2.96 / kg.

Value Chains: through Jalalabad to Pakistan

5.□hun □diied □hQomal□ □Raisin

Afghan Trader pays: (SD 0.52 / kg (sorts, packs, transports until border) Pakistani importer pays: (SD 0.70 / kg (takes delivery and pays at border)

6.□hun □diied □GQann□ Raisin

Afghan Trader pays: (SD 0.70 / kg (sorts, packs, transports until border) Pakistani importer pays: (SD 0.87 / kg (takes delivery and pays at border)

Value Chain: throughMazar-e-Sharif to Moscow

Price at farmgate: (SD 0.43 / kg; Traders buy from middlemen: (SD 0.47 / kg Paid to processors for processing inputs & packaging: (SD 0.02 / kg Customs tariffs at Russian border: (SD 0.10 / kg Traded price in Moscow: (SD 0.80 / kg

Sources: (C Davis study, also Kemal-(r-Rahim, Tom Brown and research interviews, (nderstanding the Raisin Market in Afghanistan.

## ALMOND

India currently imports 35% of the world supply of almonds ((NDP/Altai Consulting Marret Sector Assessment in Horticulture (Phase 2-3, Feasibility studies and Business Plans), August 2004). If Afghanistan increased its current production levels, it could be a major supplier to this market. There are a number of high quality varieties of almonds in Afghanistan and these are acclaimed in India for their taste and quality. Investment in this area, particularly aimed towards better packaging and processing, could expand Afghanistan's almond export potential.

## POMEGRANATE

The Afghan pomegranate is prized for its excellent quality and health benefits. Afghanistan was historically the leading producer of pomegranates and is host to numerous varieties. To meet the high demand of the world market, Afghanistan must increase production levels and improve productivity through better care of pomegranate orchards. The investment cost for starting up an orchard is (S $1,190 per hectare.

Iran is currently the lead producer and both demand and prices are increasing. From 2002-2005 alone, Iranian pomegranate prices increased by 15%. This is a clear indication that there exists a large potential for profitable entry into the world market.

## PISTACHIO

Afghanistan has comparative advantages in pistachio production due to low labor cost, available surface water, an ideal weather climate, product preference on the Indian market, inexpensive packaging, and experienced labor.

The potential for pistachio production in Afghanistan is enormous, with world demand increasing faster than current production supply. Iran alone supplies more than 66% of the world demand, but production conditions are declining due to salinity and irrigation problems (UNDP/Altai Consulting *Market Sector Assessment in Horticulture* (Phase 2-3, Feasibility studies and Business Plans), August 2004). Now is the time for Afghanistan to capitalize on these factors and become a major producer in this market. Moreover, the majority of pistachio farm laborers in Iran are Afghans, which can contribute to domestic technical knowledge, and there is a strong interest in partnership with the Afghan private sector.

## EDIBLE OIL

Edible oil processing is emerging as a profitable area of investment, as oil has a highly inelastic demand and is a necessity for every household. Afghanistan has access to high quality raw materials but current production is limited to cotton seed unrefined oil, pulp for animal feed and clothes washing soap. As a result, most edible oil is imported from the (nited Arab Emirates, Malaysia, Pakistan and other neighboring countries. Pakistan alone imports more than 70% of this supply and has over 70 factories specifically established for exporting edible oils to Afghanistan (International Trade Council Pakistan Report).

## LIST OF IMPORTED EDIBLE OIL AND THEIR RESPECTIVE VALUES

Name of oil Weight Price (Afs) Source

Gulab cooking oil 5 kg 220 Pakistan Gul cooking oil 5 kg 220 Pakistan Fawji cooking oil 5 kg 205 Pakistan Mujahid cooking oil 5 kg 200 Pakistan Sohail cooking oil 5 kg 200 Pakistan Yaadgaar cooking oil 5 kg 200 Pakistan Momin cooking oil 5 kg 270 (AE Shama cooking oil 14 kg 850

Pakistan Kohi Noor cooking oil 5 kg 203 Pakistan Al-Zahir cooking oil 5 kg 265 (AE Setara cooking oil 5 kg 265 (AE Bahari cooking oil 5 kg 265 (AE Sheaf cooking oil 5 kg 230 Malaysia Elfi cooking oil 5 kg 230 Malaysia

Source: (SAID/DAI/ALP-ER/PSD, Mini Subsector Assessment: Edible Oil.

To capitalize on opportunities in the edible oils area, investors will have to provide local factories with technical expertise, machinery and filtering systems to purify unrefined oil, making it suitable for consumption. Currently, domestic factories do not have access to a modern filtering system and the sale of unrefined oil is considered a health hazard.

With access to cheap labor and cultivatable land for raw materials, Afghanistan has the potential to locally produce peanut, pumpkin seed, walnut, wheat germ, cottonseed, poppy seed, sunflower and olive edible oils. There is a large market for these oils in restaurants and bakeries, as well as in the soap making industry.

## ORGANIC FOOD

This area is still marginal, but the trend is growing among western countries. Increased access to Western markets means that the production of organic fruits and vegetables will become a highly profitable area in the future.

Fruit Juices

Fruit juices are the fastest growing market for processed food in Afghanistan. The quality and variety of fruits could potentially make Afghanistan a leader in juices, nectars (fruit purees) and concentrates. The market value for juices in Afghanistan is approximately 20 million (SD with a yearly growth rate of around 15% ((NDP/Altai Consulting Marret Sector Assessment in Horticulture (Phase 1, Market Research), June 2004). In 2003 alone, Afghanistan imported 40 million liters of juices, mostly from Pakistan and Iran.

No herbicides, no pesticides and no artificial methods for agricultural production are used in Afghanistan

Local and regional demand in fruit juices, the potential for import substitution and growth given current consumption trends and rising income, and the many opportunities for production (such as bottling factories and sorting facilities) make fruit juice processing a booming market. Investment in this area will have high initial costs due to costly technology and machineries, but the potential for profit given demand and consumption is huge.

## FURTHER AGRO-BUSINESS OPPORTUNITIES

Fair-trade

This market is growing in popularity in the West and can provide an opportunity to Afghan farmers to market themselves as a country in transition through the sale of locally produced dried fruits, nuts and other products.

Logistics

Road transportation costs are high in Afghanistan despite low oil and labor costs. Air transportation is also very costly and is often accompanied by delays and cancellations or poor storage.

The most reliable air transport is currently through cargo services, but these companies are not cost-effective in the value chain.

Packaging and Cold Storage Transportation

These areas provide great opportunities for investors, as demand for Afghan agricultural goods is high, but current packaging procedures are outdated and damage fresh goods en route to markets. Some 20-40% of post-harvest horticulture products are wasted because of poor packaging ((NDP/Altai Consulting Marret Sector Assessment in Horticulture (Phase 23, Feasibility studies and Business Plans), August 2004).

Plastic tunnels could be used to extend the freshness of vegetables like cucumbers and tomatoes. Plastic as opposed to wooden crates would preserve freshness, maintain hygiene, and provide the highest quality products for international export beyond the immediate region. They are also easily re-useable and can be used creatively for product advertising.

Cold storage and transport is another advantageous opportunity for investment that will help farmers avoid losses and improve produce quality. The best opportunity for cold storage is at the end of the season when trading partners such as Pakistan are not yet ready for production. In cold storage transportation, there are currently less than 50 refrigerated trucks available around the country. An improvement in logistics would also help farmers obtain better prices for their exported products.

Processing

Afghanistan currently imports all processed products from Iran and Pakistan, including fruit juices and canned tomato products, which account for 75% of the trade and are growing rapidly. It is estimated that the processed fruits and vegetables market amounts around 1.4 to 2.5 billion Afghani ((S $28-60 million). The market potential for processed agricultural products including snack foods, packaged biscuits, fruits concentrates, pickles and fresh fruit jams is enormous.

Machinery

Domestic production of machinery related to the agro-business and agroprocessing industries is a lucrative opportunity for investors given rehabilitation efforts in rural Afghanistan. Agricultural and processing equipment in Afghanistan is currently imported from abroad, or from the Soviet era.

Demand for new machinery, such as grain cleaning and sieving equipment for flour, and tractor trolleys and plows, will continue to grow and be vital to the production of agricultural goods. In the long term, the manufacture of local machinery will be profitable to the agricultural industry and the establishment of repair centers for technical support will be crucial.

## RETAIL SECTOR

The retail sector is extremely limited in Afghanistan and its expansion would provide benefits to both consumers and producers, especially due to increased urbanization and increasing disposable income levels. Retail sector development would provide business opportunities to construction companies encourage competition and, in the long term, offer better quality products at lower prices for consumers. In the short run, it could provide a valuable opportunity for farmers to directly engage in business agreements with retailers, gaining commercial access to new consumer markets for their products.

## PRIVATIZATION PROJECTS

There are opportunities for investment in state-owned enterprises related to agro-business and agro-processing slated for privatization. The following is a list of several projects underway:

Pul-e-Khumri Silo

Presently barely operational due to lack of working capital, but silo and buildings are well maintained.

Kabul Silo

A silo and milling operation in Kabul city and two subsidiary silos in Herat and Kandahar of lesser capacity and without milling operation.

Balkh Silo

Silo and buildings and equipment are well-maintained. Limited production due to lack of working capital.

Cooperative and Commercial

Owns and operates six commercial retail venues in Kabul and Badakhshan.

Plants & Exports

Processes and packages flowers (e.g. hollyhocks, roses), seeds (e.g. cumin, caraway, and coriander), roots (e.g. liquorice, centaury) and leaves (e.g. dill, peppermint, tobacco) for export.

Slaughterhouse & Livestock of Herat

The slaughterhouse was badly damaged, but a dairy operation and livestock operation are currently working in the outskirts of Herat.

Slaughterhouse

Producing meat for the military with some limited sales in the bazaar.

Food Stuff Enterprise

Imports and distributes basic food stuffs. Has dozens of warehouses and storerooms around the country.

Medical & Technical Supplies

Currently produces alcohol for medical and technical purposes, although had been exporting wine and other potable alcohol in the past.

Samon Dried Fruits

Previously a processor of fruits, this enterprise is no longer operational.

Improved Seed

Currently being restructured to separate the quality control function from commercial seed production activities.

Kandahar Fruit

Previously it was processing fresh fruits but it is no longer operational.

North Power & Fertilizer

The Enterprise is the sole producer of fertilizers in Afghanistan. Plant and equipment are well maintained, but Enterprise is reliant on natural gas from Afghan Gas Enterprise as feedstock.

Fertilizer & Agro-Services

Currently being restructured to separate quality control functions from commercial operations of importing and distributing fertilizer and pesticides.

Helmand Bust

Cotton ginning factory. Located in Helmand.

Wool Weaving

This Kabul-based Enterprise's production of carpets and blankets are sold domestically, primarily to Government authorities, including the military. Raw materials, primarily cotton and wool, come from domestic sources.

Kandahar Textile Yarn

It is located in Kandahar province and has 2000 different sorts of textile machines but all of those are obsolete.

## GOVERNMENT ROLE

# A MASTER PLAN HIGHLIGHTS COMPARATIVE ADVANTAGES AND PROPOSES HUGE INVESTMENTS

The MAAHF Master Plan

The Government of Afghanistan recognizes the economic impact of the agricultural sector and has taken an active role in promoting sustainable development in this area. The Master Plan of the Ministry of Agriculture, Animal Husbandry and Food (MAAHF) outlines these current goals and proposes an investment of approximately uSD 1.6billion in the next five-year period (not including the funds needed for irrigation, which are projected at (SD 600 million over the same period).

This investment is expected to provide a 6% overall growth rate and double farm incomes in 12 years (Ministry of Agriculture, Animal Husbandry and Food (MAAHF), Executive Summary oj Ajghanistan Agriculture Master Plan, 1).

The MAAHF Master Plan recognizes the value and continued growth of the agricultural sector and aims to highlight the comparative advantages it has to offer by directing investment to the following key areas (numbers based on a five-year plan):

Cereals and Food security

Allocation oj $366 million to variousaspects oj productionoj basic jood

staples and raising jarmer incomes:

$167 million jor irrigation rehabilitation;

$49 million jor dietary-diversity and nutrition;

$30 million jor provision oj improved seed;

$42 million to cash crop alternative and sajety net program; and

Doubling oj wheat yields.

Poverty Reduction and Gender Initiatives

Activities to address unemployment and increase jarm incomes; Ejjorts to engage women in livestocr development; and Training jor rural woman in agro-business production and marreting.

Natural Resources

$45 million jor ajjorestation; $26 million jor watershed rehabilitation; and $40 million jor nursery development.

Research & Technology

$24 million to jood security and Horticulture-related research and $5 million in pest control and $3 million in disease control.

Financial Reform of the Sector

$30 million towards micro credit as a poverty alleviation measure jor small jarmers and non-jarmers; $1.9 million to stimulate the most agriculturally oriented commercial banrs; and $100 million jor middle jarmers in a rural credit system based on jarmers credit associations to be jarmer managed and jarmer owned.

Poppy Alternatives and Value Added Activities

$149 to $188 million towards: Technical support to jarmers on which crops possess the greatest marret opportunities; Establishment oj a marret injormation system with price and volume injormation; Formation oj regional and national jarmer and agribusiness associations; Assistance to businesses in accessing government land; and Support to agri-business through marret research) international jairs and trade missions.

Horticulture

$600 million in private investment; $900 million in public investment; $500 million oj capital needed by exporters over a 10-year period; and Increase in exports jrom over $100 million annually to nearly $1 billion.

Human Capital

Training programs to improve capacity oj local stajj; Expansion oj University education programs related to agri-business; and Targeting younger segments oj the population jor specialized training.

Infrastructure

Rehabilitation oj the rural road system; Development oj marret centers; and Irrigation rehabilitation.

Private Sector Assistance

The Master Plan identifies the private sector as a key player in agriculture. Private sector entrepreneurs and farmers require critical government support. The Master Plan provides this support not only through investment and financial resources, but also promotes institution building and guards against subsidies to the supply of goods that otherwise the private sector can provide. It also specifies regulations to foster private sector growth, primarily in exports. These measures foster local competition and enhance the private sector's ability to compete in international markets.

## CHALLENGES THAT CAN BE MASTERED

While Afghanistan offers many profitable opportunities in agro-business and agro-processing, formidable challenges remain. Some of these challenges include:

• Lo□ pioductivity □in commeicial ciops□faiminh

New installation of orchards and the adoption of modern farming methods would increase productivity and create employment opportunities in rural areas

• Pooi□infiastiuctuie

The supply of water and electricity vital to agro-processing and improvement in rural roads will reduce shipping time and costs

• Outdated oi non-opeiational ahio-piocessinh facilities

Many facilities are operating without sanitary floors and covered areas, proper drainage and clean water supply or waste collection systems

• Lack□of Food□safety□and□□eitification

There are no accredited food safety and certification laboratories in Afghanistan and these will be critical for export to international markets

• Lack□of□outdated faim macQineiy□and□tools

All machinery is imported and there is a high demand for machinery like tractor trolleys, plows, corn thrashers, drills, and electricity transformers

• ReseaicQ &□□evelopment

Research is currently 25 years behind and is crucial in improving cultivation practices and crop diversification

• Pooi pest□and□disease□manahement

Inadequate amounts of chemical fertilizer and lack of knowledge in disease and pest management

• Pooi intensive faiminh piactices

Problems include lack of pruning and soil testing, excessive irrigation and poor plant spacing

• Access to ciedit

Lending in agro-business is crucial so that farmers can build storage facilities, buy or lease equipment and purchase inputs

• Pooi□□uality□seedlinhs

Technical support and subsidized prices are necessary to promote commercial crops and high yield seed varieties

• Reduced access to iiiihation □atei in some aieas

Watersheds over-exploited in Kandahar and Ghazni regions and there is watershed insecurity in Northern and Western Afghanistan These problems present good potential for water reservoir development

Despite these challenges, progress is underway. Afghanistan has the potential to benefit from transfer of technology from neighboring countries and its location offers profitable access to large consumer markets like India and Pakistan. The Ministry of Agriculture is also doing its part to develop the sector and has identified key state-owned enterprises for privatization. The Ministry's five-year Master Plan demonstrates its commitment to the development of agriculture by supporting investment in key areas like value added activities, infrastructure and food security. Over time, the Government of Afghanistan will develop policies to regulate the import of agricultural products that can be produced locally. In the short term, investors can benefit from opportunities in agro-business and agro-processing that will help revive and make more profitable the most traditional sector in Afghanistan.

AISA Services

The Afghanistan Investment Support Agency (AISA) stands ready to provide investors with assistance and only the most up-to-date information available on Afghanistan's investment opportunities. AISA encourages you to contact us with your questions and concerns at:

Office address: Opposite Ministry of Foreign Affairs, Kabul, Afghanistan Phone: (93) (0) 20-210 3404; Email: info@aisa.org.af or invest@aisa.org.a□www.aisa.org.af

# CONSTRUCTION MARKET

Afghanistan offers a probusiness minded environment in a fast growing emerging market of strategic importance, receiving highlevel political attention from the international community. The country's major asset is twofold and stems from its geostrategic position right in the middle of a region rich in natural resources and close to some of the largest and fastestgrowing markets in the world. The country has become a transit link in the world energy game, strategically located between the energyrich republics of Central Asia and the major seaports in Pakistan and Iran. Afghanistan is also set to become a regional business hub over the next 10 to 15 years.

Afghanistan Demographics

Population: 29.9 million; male 16.4, female13.5 million Area: 652 thousands square kilometers (sqkm) Capital City: Kabul (population: 4.1 million) Population density (Kabul): approx. 10,000 per sqkm Population density (Country): approx. 50 per sqkm Population, urban: 21.7 % Population, rural: 78.3 %

Source: Government of Afghanistan

The rapid reconstruction of Afghanistan is visible in the whole country. Great progress is being made. Afghanistan is one of the world's largest building sites. Major roads like the Kabul – Kandahar – Herat are completed and the road from Kabul to the north over the famous Salang pass is mostly completed, but Afghanistan still needs many more houses, roads, commercial and production facilities and other infrastructure.

A trade crossroads and strategic transit hub

For centuries Afghanistan has been the hub connecting Asia, Europe, and the Middle East. Today, Afghanistan is ideally situated to again function as a strategic gateway, serving landlocked countries to the north and the Iranian and Pakistani seaports to the south. For the Central Asian republics and Russian industrial centers of western Siberia, Afghanistan is potentially the shortest route to the open sea. For Pakistan, Afghanistan offers a primary route for trade with Central Asia.

In fact, Afghanistan shares borders with six neighbors – Iran, Turkmenistan, Uzbekistan, Tajikistan, China and Pakistan – and is considered a "land bridge" connecting proximate country markets, as well as potentially large trading partners, such as Iran and India. Afghanistan offers a point of access to an extended regional market of more than two billion people, linking the Middle East to Southern, Central and Southeast Asia.

New and expanding trade routes

The improving transport infrastructure supports Afghanistan's trade nexus, both incountry and across its borders. It is estimated that 60% of overland transportation comes to or from Pakistan, 30% to or from Iran, and a combined 10% through borders with the Central Asian republics. To the north, in Turkmenistan, Uzbekistan and Tajikistan, goods and commodities flow on main transit routes (and by rail in Turkmenistan and Uzbekistan) south through Afghanistan to the ports of BandareAbbas and Chah Bahar in Iran, and Gwadar and Karachi in Pakistan. A new bridge links Afghanistan and Tajikistan over the Amu Darya (Oxus) River, which carries barge traffic along the borders with Turkmenistan, Uzbekistan and Tajikistan. Within Afghanistan, the main roads connecting Kabul to Kandahar and Herat in the south and the "Ring Road" in the north and east form a developing major network of highways that links the country's key commercial centers, and extends to the border crossings with Iran, Pakistan and other neighboring countries.

City of Kabul (The Ministry of Urban Development and Housing is planning 20–25 satellite cities in Afghanistan for 50,000 families); Photo: Dr. Q. Dallalzada

Construction Activities

Construction has been a main driving force behind Afghanistan's recovery and the construction materials industry is expanding rapidly. The variety, quality and quantity of production materials is increasing. This reflects the considerable business opportunities in the construction materials industry. The continued reconstruction process, increasing income, and increasing population imply that construction will remain strong over the next years. Demand comes from different types of construction activities:

-Major militaryrelated projects -Government reconstruction projects, such as roads, power and water infrastructure, irrigation systems, etc. -Large scale private and business construction fuelled by business opportunities -Small scale development of retail and residential construction

Although the third and fourth categories of building are the most visible when driving around the major cities in Afghanistan, construction in the first two categories actually dwarfs the private construction activities in value several times over.

In 2005 the total investment in private buildings was 2.4 billion USD. No downturn is expected.

Infrastructure is a key area in the government's national development framework and its mediumterm economic plan. Infrastructure projects will be designed to meet the growing regional demand for transit and business services, strengthening the country's position as a regional transit link and business hub. A minimum of USD 13.9 billion will be invested in a first phase up to the year 2010, largely to be raised through reliance on international technical assistance, concessional loans, privatepublic partnerships, and access to international capital markets.

## INFRASTRUCTURE TARGETS

Transport

Paved roads 16% 32% 48.1% Paved roads (km per 1000 people) 0.15 0.19 0.23 Number of airports ICAO standard 20 30 International airports ICAO standard 0 4 5 Number of tourist sites opened 0 20 30 Motor vehicles per 1000 people 14 27 40 Number of busses per 1000 urban people 0.06 0.15 0.3 Number of railway stations 0 5 5

Energy and telecommunications

Countrywide electricity access 6% 24% 33% Urban access ratio 27% 77% 89% Countrywide gas access ratio 8% 23% 42% Teledensity (phones/1000 people) 1.6 49 120

Urban management

Population with basic services 10% 100% 100% Paved coverage of urban roads 59% 100% Informal plots with tenure – Kabul 100% 100% Informal plots with tenure – other 100% 100% Kabul water supply coverage 20% 64% 80% Kabul sanitation coverage 20% 64% 80%

Source: Government of Afghanistan

By the end of 2010 all municipal governments in Afghanistan should be able to manage urban development and to ensure that municipal services are delivered effectively, efficiently and transparently.

Basic services such as electric power, water and sewage infrastructure are still very limited in Afghanistan. Most companies use their own power generators, and even when state or municipal services are available, companies rely heavily on their own equipment due to frequent breakdowns of the network. There are no fixed rates for power to date, with prices between companies and the government being negotiated on a casebycase basis. Similar conditions apply to water. Companies generally drill their own wells and then pump for free. They may also purchase water from another company or locate near rivers and other sources of natural water. No waste water services are available in Kabul for the time being. Reliable infrastructure for businesses will be available, however, in the 20 new industrial parks which are being set up throughout the country.

State investments in water supply

Water supply is an important priority of the Ministry of Urban Development and Housing. The investments in water supply systems of the Ministry will be 120 million USD in the next two years. Additionally, the Ministry is preparing the renovation of existing dams in the country and a new dam for the water supply of Kabul is planned.

State investments in new satellite cities

The Ministry of Urban Development and Housing is planning 20–25 satellite cities across the country to house approximately 50,000 families. The total investment will be more than 1.2 billon USD.

Selected state construction projects in the next two years

- Rehabilitation of the Historic Old Town of Kabul
- Provincial town water supply System in 14 Afghan towns
- Ten thousand housing unite in Qasaba Kabul
- Construction of 12 thousend houses in Dah Sabz
- Review and update of Kabul Master Plan 1978 with Kabul Municipality
- Feasibility study of then small towns less than 10,000 population
- Rehabilitation of historical bazaar in Tashqorghan
- Construction of uncompleted blocks No. 22 in Fourth Macroyan
- Guide planning for old cities of Heart province
- Rehabilitation of historical Kharabat Gozar in old city of Kabul
- Reconstruction of uncompleted block No. 15 in Macroyan 4
- Increasing the level of water supply, garbages transfer of Macroyan
- Construction of uncompleted block No. 15 located in Qasaba area
- Rehabilitation of Hendo Gozar in Kabul
- Rehabilitation of Kabul Machine House
- Rehabilitation of Bagrami bricks factory
- Rehabilitation of Dah Sabx Bricks factory in Kabul
- Building of dumping sites and solid waste management in different cities
- Design and construction of an institution for dust testing and construction material testing
- Rehabilitation of Baghe Qazi Park
- Rehabilitation of Balahesar Park in Kabul
- Rehabilitation of the buildings around Kabul rivers
- Rehabilitation of heating system in Macrorayan
- Technical infrastructure for the old city of Kabul

Source: Ministry of Urban Development & Housing

Privatization Projects

There are opportunities for investment in stateowned enterprises related to construction slated for privatization. The following is a list of several projects underway:

Banaye Construction: Together with Afghani Construction and Housing Construction, these three enterprises have what remains of the construction engineering expertise and the construction equipment which previously served the Government of Afghanistan's construction needs. Owns two brick factories, not currently operational.

Afghani Construction: Together with Banaye Construction and Housing Construction, these three enterprises have what remains of the construction engineering expertise and the construction equipment which previously served the Government of Afghanistan's construction needs. Currently operating in Kabul and Herat.

Housing Construction: Together with Afghani Construction and Banaye Construction, these three enterprises have what remains of the construction engineering expertise and the construction equipment which previously served the Government of Afghanistan's construction needs. Some marble cutting and wood working operations.

Spin Ghar Construction: Specializing in irrigation and dams, Spin Ghar has limited operations and limited capacity at present.

Construction Materials Production: Currently operating and working under a cooperative agreement with a foreign firm to produce concrete blocks.

Afghan Carpentry: The Enterprise has limited operations, but is operating profitably.

Helmand Construction: Specializing in irrigation and dams, as well as erecting buildings, Helmand Construction operates in twelve provinces in Afghanistan.

Metal Components: Production of hydrotechnical equipment for water supply and irrigation.

## DEVELOPMENT OF NEW INDUSTRIAL PARKS

Twenty new industrial park areas are being set up in three phases at different locations in the country, providing a combination of high quality infrastructure and services unavailable elsewhere in Afghanistan, including clean land title, reliable electrical power supply, 24 hour security, paved roads, central water and sewage system, and professional management.

Afghanistan is providing investors access to developed land to set up in professionally managed industrial estates. These modern parks offer investors the benefits of highquality infrastructure and reliable power supply in "build to suit" sites, strategically located in several key industrial areas. Designed to accommodate small, medium and largesized firms, the parks help investors avoid costly title disputes and reduce risks and delays associated with land acquisition, zoning and permitting.

The first phase of construction initiated by AISA Industrial Parks Development Department is for three parks:

1. Bagrami Industry Park: more than 24 hectares 7 km east of central Kabul. The "Phase One" of Bagrami Industrial Park is completed and contains 34 lots. "Phase Two" is expected to start soon and will include 38 lots.
2. MazareSharif Industrial Park: 26 hectares 7 km north of downtown. This park will have a total of 48 plots and is expected to be ready for settlement at the end of 2006.
3. Kandahar Industrial Park: 15 hectares 10 km east of the city. Kandahar Industrial Park is expected to accommodate 58 lots and be completed by June 2006.

The second phase of Park Development, for which survey and design of the sites have started, includes 100 hectares Kamari Industry Park near Kabul which is expected to have around 140 lots, and the 200 hectares HisareShahi Industry Park, 22 km southeast of Jalalabad city with 180 expected lots.

Contact and further information about investment and reservation:

Mr. Zubair Ahmad, Director AISA Industrial Parks Development Department (IDP); Mobile: 0093 (0) 799652153, Email: zubair@aisa.org.af

A selection of helpful addresses for construction companies

Afghanistan Investment Support Agency (AISA), President Dr. Omar Zakhilwal and Vice President (Investment Promotion) Suleman Fatimie, Opposite to Ministry of Foreign Affairs, Kabul, Afghanistan, Phone 0093

(0) 20 210 3404, Email: josigl@aisa.org.af
Ministry of Urban Development and Housing, Minister Eng. Mohd. Yosuf Pashtoon and Deputy Minister Dr.–Ing. Q. Djallalzada, Microrayan 3, Opposite to Azadi Press, Kabul, Afghanistan, Phone 0093
(0) 752015393, Email: djallalzada@gmx.de

Ministry of Finance, Minister Dr. Anwar ul Haq Ahadi, Pashtunistan Watt, Kabul, Afghanistan, Phone 0093 (0) 20 210 3157

ICS International Consulting Service for Construction, Kartee3, House 235, near Darul Aman Street, Kabul, Afghanistan, Mr. Joerg Reich, Dipl. Ing. Architect, President and Wolfgang Everts, Dipl.Ing. Architect, Vice President, Phone: 0093 (0) 79 553558 or 0049 (0) 179 4951660,

Email: w.everts@ICS Kabul.com, Internet: www.ICSKabul.com; The activities of ICS spans all parts of architectural and engineering services, supervision and project development for construction projects, like residential buildings, hotels, offices, hospitals, airports, industrial facilities and infrastructure.

AfghanYar Construction Company Ltd (ACCL), Mr. Shah Mohammad Peerzada, President, Shahrenow, Charahi Shahid, beside Zarghuna High School, Kabul, Afghanistan, Phone: 0093 (0) 70290504, Email: Habib_peerzada@yahoo.com; ACCL is specialized in reconstruction, renovation, new construction, containerized construction and construction material procurement. ACCL is the sole registered agent in Afghanistan for high quality gypsum and drywall products from Germany.

EDBRCC Emam Dara Building & Road Construction Company, Mr. M. Tahus (MIR), Eng., Director, Darlaman Road, next to old Russian Embassy, Kabul, Afghanistan, Phone: 0093 (0) 202103303, Email: tahusmir@yahoo.com; EDBRCC is specialized in building and road construction. Besides them the company has production facilities for the manufacture of glass and aluminum products as well as PVC pipelines.

## CONSTRUCTION MATERIALS

## BOOMING DEMAND AND PROFITABLE INVESTMENT OPPORTUNITIES

The construction material sector at a glance:

The construction and construction materials sector is booming! Materials of different quality, origin and price can be found in different marketplaces across the cities of Afghanistan. At first glance, it appears that this sharp rise in demand has also brought an increasing number of traders and trading companies into the market. However, there still remains many opportunities for potential industrial investors in this sector.

Considerable growth potential

Afghanistan has a wide array of known mineral resources as well as vast areas where the potential is unknown. Few reserves are being commercialized presently, creating a vacuum that can be filled by private investment.

High demand for construction materials

As a result of the reconstruction boom that Afghanistan is presently undergoing, there is significant local demand for mineralbased construction materials, including paving stones, cement and cement blocks, bricks, gravel, wood, steel, sand, glass, and tile. No downturn is expected before 2010. Presently, even basic materials like cement are imported from Pakistan and Iran, offering great potential for import substitution.

Costs associated with transport provide advantages to locally produced construction materials

Assuming mineralsbased products such as construction materials can be produced at a quality on par with imports, the costs associated with importing such materials confers an advantage to companies that produce locally.

Source: Investment Horizons: Afghanistan, Benchmarking FDI Opportunities, conducted by the Multilateral Investment Guarantee Agency (MIGA) of the World Bank Group

Construction materials and their supply

There is very little manufacturing capacity in Afghanistan. Most cement and wood, and all steel, sanitary fixtures and other manufactured goods are imported. The main sources of import of construction materials are Pakistan, Iran, Russia and, to a lesser degree, China. Pakistan and Iran have road networks connected with Afghanistan, while railway and air freight are used for import from Russia and China.

Investors taking up the production of construction materials are experiencing excellent business opportunities in this dynamic environment. Afghanistan invites investors to take the opportunity and participate in the development of this industry. Afghanistan is rich in natural resources that provide an excellent base for the production of construction materials. The Afghan people are hardworking and possess a spirit of entrepreneurship and resilience. They are eager to learn and engage in the production of many products that are currently being imported. As policy influencers, the Afghan Investment Support Agency (AISA) is working to create a framework that allows private activity in construction and in construction materials industries to flourish. AISA invites you to invest in its rebuilding efforts and to participate in the business opportunities that exist in the construction and construction materials industry.

Infrastructure investments: more than 13.9 billion up to 2010, Photo: AISA

Average cost structure of a construction material company

| | |
|---|---|
| Total property cost | 58% |
| Annualized construction cost | 26% |
| Total utility cost | 12% |
| Total labor cost | 4% |

This shows the average cost structure in percentage for investments in Afghanistan from the investor's perspective.

## DEMAND FOR CONSTRUCTION MATERIALS IS BOOMING

With the reconstruction process continuing at high speed, demand for all kinds of construction material is booming. Demand comes from different types of construction activities. Most construction materials are being imported, but the share of domestically produced materials is rising rapidly. Given the nature of many construction materials, transportation costs are an important cost factor for imported goods. This opens up important business opportunities for investors, since many construction materials can easily be produced in Afghanistan. Given the abundance of raw materials, mining activities also offer great business opportunities. Even more promising is the processing of these local resources.

The combination of strong demand for construction materials, existing raw materials and the foreign competition's high transportation costs give rise to many profitable investment opportunities. Afghanistanbased businesses can outcompete their foreign rivals with modest investment and well established technology. The construction industry is booming. Exports grew 60%

## MANUFACTURING OF FINAL CONSTRUCTION PRODUCTS

Profitable investment opportunities also exist in the manufacturing of final construction products from intermediate inputs such as doors or windows. Often these activities are carried out on a small scale basis, but many opportunities exist to expand these activities to mass production.

There is also mediumterm potential for exporting construction materials. This is clear for the marble and marble cutting industry, but also for some lowvalue goods where Afghanistan possesses good natural resources and enjoys a comparative advantage over its neighbouring countries. The national market for construction materials is already wellintegrated. Prices across regions are comparable. This allows producers to serve the entire national market. Wholesaling and retailing is quite competitive, providing sufficient distribution channels for producers of construction materials.

Comparison of provincial prices for selected construction goods in three Afghan Cities and in Peshawar, Pakistan

| Item | Kabul | Mazar | Jalalabad | Peshawar |
|---|---|---|---|---|
| Pakistani white toilets | 28 | 39 | 27.80 | 27.80 |
| Plastic pipe 4ins/6m | 8.5 | 8.6 | 11 | 9.6 |
| Plywood 120 to140 (12mm) | 11 | 12.5 | 11.5 | 5.9 |
| Wooden bars localqury (20) | 265 | 232 | 442 | n/a |
| Wooden bars importqury (20 | 135 | 186 | 120 | 43 |
| Steel rebar 8 mm/kg (Russian) | 0.7 | 0.7 | 0.6 | 0.5 |
| Uchannel (Russian) 12m | 102 | 125 | 121 | 121 |
| Ibeam 12m | 102 | 92 | 85 | 121 |
| Red baked bricks (1000 pieces) | 58 | 41 | 32 | 39 |
| Coarse aggregate/truck | 33 | 62 | x | n/a |
| Crushed aggregate/truck | 40 | n/a | x | n/a |
| Sand/truck | 38 | 40 | x | n/a |
| Cement/50 kg bag | 4 | 4 | 4 | 4 |

All prices in USD (Exchange rate: one USD = 50 Afs), n/a = goods not available, x = price not collected; Source: Sarah Lister and Zainiddin Karaev, Understanding markets in Afghanistan: A case study of the market in construction material, June 2004. The above figures give only a rough indication of the regional price differences.

## THE MARKET POTENTIAL

There are many exciting investment opportunities in construction materials. The following is a sample, but by no means exhaustive list of opportunities for investors:

Cement

Currently, most cement is imported. All necessary conditions for cement production (adequate limestone, energy) can be found in various locations in Afghanistan. Given the high transport costs for the product, Afghanproduced cement is highly competitive with imported cement. Demand for cement has been strong and is forecasted to grow substantially. Cement prices have been increasing and the neighbouring countries' cement industries are operating at full capacity levels. Growth in South Asia and demand for cement in the region are forecasted to remain strong.

AISA and other government agencies are looking for various international investors to establish new cement plants or take over nonoperational former cement production facilities in Afghanistan.

However, given the size and projected growth of the market, many additional opportunities for investors in this sector exist.

Cement imports, value in million USD

Bricks

There are two kinds of bricks that are used for construction, baked and unbaked. While all mud bricks are made in Afghanistan, baked bricks are imported from Pakistan as well as produced locally. In the higher quality segment of the market, Afghan firms are still under represented. With the high quality demand by the construction projects of international agencies and rising incomes of the population, this segment is expected to grow rapidly.

Sand, gravel and aggregate

These materials are easy to mine and produce in Afghanistan. Many production sites exist, but quality is mixed due to insufficient investment in appropriate equipment. Investment opportunities exist to upgrade the quality of the production as well as in the exploitation of new mining sites.

Cement blocks

Cement blocks are a popular construction material in Afghanistan. Upgrading, extending or establishing new production facilities offer good investment opportunities, as the current local production is insufficient.

Wood

Some of the large demand for wood in Afghanistan is met by domestic production, but most wood is imported from either Pakistan or Russia. However, overall quality tends to be poor, because it has not been dried properly, and facilities do not exist in Afghanistan for the artificial drying of wood. The biggest markets for wood are in Kabul, MazareSharif and Kandahar.

Doors and windows

Demand for doors and windows is strong. Traditionally, locally produced windows are made from wood and glass on a very small scale. Many construction businesses could profit from expanding the production they use for their own needs and sell the excess on the market. Driven by the surge in demand, some construction companies have started producing windows from imported plastic and glass.

Glass

The demand for construction glass is increasing significantly in Afghanistan, due to the current style of major buildings in large cities. Construction glass comes from Uzbekistan, Russia, Iran, Belgium, Pakistan, China and Kyrgyzstan. Import of Chinese construction glass has increased. Domestically, Afghanistan provides opportunities for smallscale productions of glass recycling. Afghanistan also provides an abundance of natural sand essential for the production of high quality construction glass. A good business opportunity would be the establishment of a new float glass line given the high demand for such materials in the local construction industry.

Marble

There are substantial quantities of marble deposits within Afghanistan. The marble mined in Afghanistan is typically exported and only a tiny fraction is processed locally. The processing is done primarily for handicraft activities or local construction use. Most of production is exported as uncut marble to Pakistan, where it is cut and polished into blocks and slabs. Investing in cutting activities in Afghanistan has a high profit potential, since doing these activities closer to the quarry reduces transport costs substantially.

Tiles

There is strong local demand for ceramic tiles. Necessary raw materials for ceramic tiles as well as for other ceramics production can be found in Afghanistan. This offers great business opportunities for investors possessing the necessary skills for ceramics production. Roof tiles could also be produced in Afghanistan and demand for these products is likely to increase as income is growing.

Tubes and appliances

Some businesses have started the production of simple products such as tubes, which can be produced from PVC or imported sheet metal.

Asphalt

Some asphalt production capacity has been established given the demand from the construction and reconstruction of roads. As road construction remains a priority over the next years, there is room for further activities in the business.

Natural stone

Natural stone can be mined and processed at various locations and is in high demand.

Other construction goods

The import of other construction goods such as steel, sanitary and plumbing products vary in quality and price levels. Such materials are sometimes imported from as far as Germany. Most arrive from Pakistan, Iran and China and usually with poor quality. Domestic production of these goods would be a profitable opportunity for investors.

## MINING SECTOR OPPORTUNITIES

The mining and energy sectors are crucial to the reconstruction and rehabilitation of Afghanistan, yet they remain virtually absent of foreign investment due to historic state control of natural resources. Today, many mining resources remain under the control of failed stateowned enterprises (SOE's). Other mining activities are conducted on a smallscale, mostly illegal, basis. Because smallscale mining has continued over the years unregulated and with outdated methods, it has had severe consequences for the environment and threatens the quality of existing mineral reserves. Experience in other countries shows that private operators are, for the most part, more effective in the exploitation and exploration of natural resources and mining.

Currently more than 1,400 mineral deposits in Afghanistan

Afghanistan is a country abundantly rich in natural resources. There are currently more than 1,400 mineral deposits that have been identified including energy minerals such as oil, gas and coal and other metallic and nonprecious minerals such as lead, cementgrade limestone, gemstones, copper, iron, gold, salt, and industrial minerals (for use in the glass, ceramic, construction, chemical and fertilizer industries). Known precious and semiprecious stones include emerald, jade, amethyst, alabaster, beryl, lapis lazuli, tourmaline, ruby, quartz, and sapphire. Afghanistan's iron and copper deposits are of worldclass quality and its famous blue lapis lazuli mines are reported to date back to 5,000 B.C., which might arguably make these mines among the oldest in the world.

The hydrocarbons (petroleum and natural gas) industry provides great investment potential for Afghanistan, both financially and as a means for energy production. Recent findings in March 2006 indicate that the AfghanTajik and Amu Darya Basins contain 18 times the oil and triple the natural gas reserves previously determined. In response to this promising news, President Karzai stated, "Knowing more about our country's petroleum resources will enable us to take steps to develop our energy potential, which is crucial for our country's growth."

The Government of Afghanistan ratified the Minerals Law in 2005 and is presently working to ratify the Hydrocarbons Law (2006), which will govern the natural gas and petroleum industries in the energy sector. These two laws are major initial steps in addressing how to create a regulatory framework for the development of these sectors and, most importantly, enable a suitable environment to attract and retain private investment.

The development of the mining and energy sectors has clear benefits to the economy of Afghanistan and provides firstmover advantages to investors. Development of these sectors would decrease Afghanistan's reliance on foreign energy imports, create government revenue from natural resource discoveries, stimulate employment, provide tax revenues to local and central governments, and discourage imports of certain mineral resources since many of these can be produced locally. The construction sector is currently the largest beneficiary of this advantage because of the availability of local raw materials such as limestone, sand and gravel.

### SUBSTANTIAL GROWTH POTENTIAL

At present, the minerals industry comprises around one percent of Afghanistan's GNP. This percentage is not at all indicative of the potential value of Afghanistan's mineral wealth. Afghanistan possesses an abundance of mineral resources including rare metals, oil, natural gas, precious and semiprecious stones, industrial minerals and precious metals. These mineral resources are largely undeveloped and the potential to discover new and larger mineral reserves in Afghanistan is enormous. Investment, particularly from overseas, would provide the expertise, capital and technology essential to the development of this sector.

The mining and energy sectors can play a key role in Afghanistan's postwar reconstruction. The World Bank estimates that the annual value of Afghanistan's minerals reserves could reach US $253 million up from the current value of US $60 million if the Government of Afghanistan enacts the necessary reforms. This would require approximately US $100 million in public investment and around US $360 million in private sector investment. The annual economic benefits streams would include the creation of nearly 6,000 jobs, US $17 million in taxes and royalties, and US $100 million in value added activities.

Economic Indicators

| GDP (excluding opium) forecast 2006: | 8,500 million USD |
|---|---|
| Real GDP growth rate; forecast 2006: | 12% |
| GDP per capita; forecast 2006: | 340 USD |
| Area in square kilometres: | 652,000 |
| Number of current available mineral deposits: | more than 1,400 |
| Current annual value of used mineral reserves: | 60 million USD |
| Estimated annual value of usable mineral reserves (next years): | appr. 250 million USD |
| Required public investments in mineral reserves (next years): | appr. 100 million USD |
| Estimated private investment in mineral reserves (next years): | appr. 360 million USD |

Sources: International Monetary Fund, Government of Afghanistan, and World Bank Group/Multilateral Investment Guarantee Agency (MIGA)

The minerals sector has great potential in the mid to longterm. There are vast areas where the potential for minerals is unknown and investment in exploration is a good shortterm opportunity for mining investors to ensure longterm profits from exploitation and extraction. Mining companies report an average initial investment of US $122,500 with average annual sales of US $11,000.

Despite the potential for growth in mining and energy, investors are still expected to have concerns. Of particular importance to investors in this sector are the following criteria:

- Mining legislation, which includes clarity of ownership and terms of operations
- Clear criteria for granting private mining rights and title
- Competitive and transparent taxation system that adheres to international standards and best practices
- Security and political stability
- Mining potential and geological research and information to support these claims

Mining is considered a 'highrisk' industry and has a finite life, which means that companies will only have a limited number of years to explore and develop mineral reserves, as well as ensure a competitive return on their investment.

## MINERAL OCCURRENCES IN AFGHANISTAN

Source: Natural Resources Maps, Afghan Geological Survey

## SURVEYING MINERAL RESOURCES IN AFGHANISTAN

The mapping of Afghanistan's natural resources began in the 1960s and 70s. It was primarily taken over by Soviet and Afghan geologists, but then abandoned over the decades of conflict that ensued thereafter. Given the country's abundance of natural resources, there is presently renewed interest in the area.

The Government of Afghanistan, in collaboration with the Afghan Geological Survey and community, realizes that a crucial step in assessing investment potential in mining and energy is gathering reliable information for investors. Since 2002, experts from the British and U.S. Geological Surveys have been building local capacity to initiate new research in this area and provide the most accurate and updated information to the public.

An ongoing part of this process is to create an updated comprehensive written and mapped inventory of Afghanistan's known mineral resources. Updated mineral resource maps and the use of modern exploration equipment and methods will likely contribute to the rapid discovery of new mineral reserves in the country. The newly rehabilitated Afghan Geological Survey is also working to assist the government in identifying new areas of minerals exploration, as well as to advise on land use and environmental protection.

## CONSTRUCTION MATERIALS

Afghanistan's material deposits of marble, sand, gravel, clay, and limestone places it at a comparative advantage for supplying local raw materials to the construction sector. Sand and gravel are currently the most commonly exploited minerals and demand for these aggregates will continue with planned infrastructure projects such as major highways. The demand for clay to produce fired bricks is enormous, and Afghanistan's large coal reserves assist in the industrial manufacture of these goods. Limestone is another essential construction mineral in high demand and reserves in Badakhshan are estimated to be several hundred million cubic meters total.

The construction sector has attracted foreign entrepreneurs from around the world and will likely to continue to generate high growth and profits as the reconstruction process continues.

Average cost structure of a construction material/mining company

| | |
|---|---|
| Total property cost | 58% |
| Annualized construction cost | 26% |
| Total utility cost | 12% |
| Total labor cost | 4% |

This shows the average cost structure for investments from investor's perspective.

## MARBLE

Afghan marble is good quality and in high demand. There are currently 35 types of marble in Afghanistan and 40 different colours. World marble imports are estimated at US $2.5 billion and there is a huge market potential for finished Afghan marble in the Gulf. With sufficient investment in knowledge and equipment, the marble industry in Afghanistan has the potential to be a major supplier in the region.

In 2005, the Afghan marble industry produced approximately 720 thousand feet of marbles tiles. This industry has vast potential for growth and development and it is estimated that production volume in 2006 will reach up to 1 million feet.

Currently, Afghanistan exports raw marble that is primarily processed and reexported from Pakistan. This fails to maximize the potential value of the marble, which would capture higher export prices if cut into slabs and polished. Presently, there is no equipment in the country that can cut slabs to international standards and outdated processing methods and machinery leads to a high degree of wastage, in some cases as high as 80%. Additionally, the use of explosives in marble quarries, which is dangerous for labourers and crushes the stone into less valuable smaller pieces, wastes around 25% of the total value of production.

Since Afghanistan has not yet developed a strong export market for marble, it has a first mover advantage for investors and high potential for growth given regional and global demand.

Current market prices for marble products in Afghanistan

| Item name | Size | Price (Afs) |
|---|---|---|
| Kabul Green | one foot | 70 |

| | | |
|---|---|---|
| Kabul Green | half foot | 25 |
| Kabul Black | one foot | 80 |
| Kabul Black | half foot | 25 |
| Kabul Pink | one foot | 75 |
| Afghan White | one foot | 100 |
| Afghan White | half foot | 45 |
| Afghan Black | one foot | 115 |
| Afghan Tiger | one foot | 100 |
| Afghan Tiger | half foot | 35 |

Source: USAID/DAI, Marble Sub Sector Production and Market Analysis, July 2005

## COPPER

The regional demand for copper is growing rapidly, particularly in China and India. Afghanistan is positioned to meet this demand if the proper investments are made for the development and exploitation of its copper reserves. There are also investment opportunities for copper smelting facilities, which would reduce the volume and cost of transportation to domestic and regional markets.

Afghanistan has sizeable reserves of copper that extend located in the KabulLoghar province. The three major reserves that have been identified are Jawkhar, Darband and Aynak, but there are around 300 known deposits in the country. Exploration has not been conducted for some 30 years and is vital to demarcate new deposits. The Aynak copper deposit in Loghar has a declared estimated reserve of 240 million tons of superior quality copper. If developed properly, could produce annually US $100 million, with US $15 million in taxes and royalties and US $56 million in value added. With this potential, Aynak is expected to attract interest from major international mining companies.

## GOLD

There is significant potential for gold exploration throughout Afghanistan. Gold is an excellent opportunity for investors because it has a high unit price and a relatively low capital cost for development. Afghanistan's major gold deposits are located in the northern provinces of Ghazni, Badakshan and Takhar and utilized mainly by artisanal miners. The Zarkashan and Samty deposits are best known, with the latter having an estimated supply of 20 to 25 tons.

Afghanistan's gold deposits are fairly unexplored since the Soviet withdrawal and require further investigation.

## IRON ORE

Afghanistan has major iron ore deposits located primarily between Herat and the Panjsher valley. The most famous deposit is Hajigak in Bamyan Province, which is the largest reserve in the Middle East, containing 110 million tons total of highgrade iron. There are also occurrences in Badakhshan and Baghlan provinces. Since Afghanistan's iron ore deposits have not been reviewed for over thirty years, they require further exploration and assessment.

Afghanistan's iron deposits have great potential given the practical use of iron in heavy industry and there exists a growing demand for the resource in China and Southeast Asia. A profitable value added activity would be to combine iron mining with steel production facilities for local and international markets.

## SALT

Afghanistan has at least 13 large known salt deposits in the Herat and Balakh provinces, but the majority of salt is still imported from Iran and Pakistan. Afghans have a very high salt consumption and consume an average of two kilograms of salt per person per year, which equates to an estimated US $21.6 million annually.

Salt mining requires minimal investment and would be a profitable opportunity for investors. Locally produced salt would also provide good health benefits to Afghans if iodine were added.

## PRECIOUS AND SEMIPRECIOUS STONE INDUSTRY

Afghanistan is blessed to have some of the most plentiful reserves of gem and semiprecious stones in the world, including emeralds, rubies, tourmaline, lapis lazuli, kunzite and aquamarines. Smallscale miners dominate the gemstone industry and good quality stones have a high demand, both for the domestic handicrafts industry and export markets. The total annual value of exported gemstones is approximately US $2.8 million, though most of these are exported illegally.

There are several potential areas for investment in this industry. These include:

- The Panjsher valley, where emeralds are best known and the quality is comparable to the finest emerald mines in South America The current annual production of emeralds is estimated to be worth more than US $912 million.
- Nuristan, where there are known deposits of kunzite, tourmaline, beryl, and aquamarine;
- SareSang lapis lazuli mines located in northeast Afghanistan, where production and inventory are still strong;
- Jegdalek ruby mines near Jalalabad, where stones display a vivid range of red hues and deposits are expected to be large. The British Crown Jewels, namely the Black Prince's Ruby, are reported to contain stones from Jegdalek.

The vast majority of gemstones are currently cut and polished in Pakistan. A key value added activity for gemstones would be the establishment of cutting and polishing centers in major urban centers. Stone finishing could also be a good source of employment for Afghans.

## PRIVATIZATION PROJECTS

There are opportunities for investment in stateowned enterprises slated for privatization. The following is a list of several projects underway:

North Coal: Currently operating and supplying the Ghuri Cement Enterprise and the region in general, with coal for electricity generation. There may be considerable reserves of good quality coal, which have to be confirmed.

Power Construction: Producer of transformers, electric networks and pylons for electric wires.

New Energy: Currently producing solar water heaters and cookers for the local market.

Afghan Gas: The Enterprise has estimated reserves of gas exceeding 100 billion m3 and is presently delivering gas to North Power & Fertilizer Enterprise and the cities of Shibarghan and MazareSharif. New investments will be required to develop the Enterprise's potential.

North Coal: Currently operating and supplying the Ghuri Cement Enterprise and the region in general, with coal for electricity generation. There may be considerable reserves of good quality coal, which have to be confirmed.

Global demand for natural resources and its expected benefits for Afghanistan's economy are the main drivers towards regional integration and will help the country to become a leading business hub for the region.

## ENERGY SECTOR

Unmet demand for energy

The development of domestic energy, through electrical power generation, petroleum and natural gas drilling, and hydropower are vital components in Afghanistan's reconstruction. Domestic energy needs are currently reliant on energy sharing with Afghanistan's Central Asian neighbours, which is only a shortterm solution given increased industrial and commercial demand. The Government of Afghanistan, with technical and financial assistance from the international donor community, is working to address the country's shortfall in domestic energy production. The following outlines some of the major areas for development, including power generation facilities and the development of fossil fuel supplies (namely coal and hydrocarbons).

Power Generation

Power and energy represent the largest existing infrastructural impediment in presentday Afghanistan. The Government and more specifically, the Ministry of Water and Power, is in the process of addressing these concerns and helping restructure the energy sector to include more private sector participation on the supply side, while strengthening their own regulatory role.

Afghanistan currently produces a domestic total power supply capacity of 454 MW. This supply comes from 11 installed hydropower plants and 4 diesel power plants in the country. Afghanistan imports a total of 64 MW from its neighbors, but this will likely increase to over 900 MW in the future, with increased hydropower energy from Tajikistan and thermal power imports from Turkmenistan and Uzbekistan. There are current plans to create 10 more domestic hydropower plants and an increase in capacity of an existing diesel power plant.

The Government of Afghanistan, with the financial support of the World Bank, is also restructuring the existing state owned power enterprise "DABM," which owns and operates all existing power plants, distribution systems and transmission lines in Afghanistan. The restructuring will focus on technical improvement, as well as institutional and administrative capacity building. With assistance from USAID, the Government is establishing a Bilateral Cooperation Agreement for Power Trade with Central Asian nations bordering Afghanistan. This will be an integral part of the NorthEast Transmission System (NETS). USAID is also assisting in the creation of future

power utility companies in Afghanistan that will revitalize the NorthEast and South West Transmission Systems. Investment possibilities in the power sector include the creation and development of local utility companies, the construction and maintenance of electrical systems, and the development of generation systems (electrical, wind and solar).

Fuel Supply

The main fossil fuel resources in Afghanistan include coal, natural gas, and petroleum. Investments in these areas have not been made for many years and the industry was at a virtual standstill until recently. In oil and gas, old technologies and lowcost approaches to developing the sector failed to provide the industries with arrangements to support the demands of an open market economy in Afghanistan. With today's steadily increasing demand for energy domestically and regionally, development of the sector is critical.

Afghanistan is strategically positioned to provide a route for hydrocarbons from Central Asia to the Arabian Sea. This role was most apparent in plans to utilize Afghanistan as a transit route for the construction of a pipeline from Turkmenistan through Afghanistan to natural gas markets in Pakistan. This pipeline was proposed in the late 1990s by the U.S. Unocal Corporation, in cooperation with the Central Asia Gas Pipeline Consortium, but at present no decisions have been made on which companies will take over and implement this project. In the future, the probable discovery of new hydrocarbon reserves will likely provide greater interest in similar high profile pipeline construction projects.

Coal

Afghanistan uses coal primarily for domestic heating/energy during the winter months and for electricity generation and industrial uses. Coal reserves are estimated to be nearly 70 million tons and are primarily located in the north of the country between Herat and Badakhshan. It is estimated that Afghanistan currently produces around 120,000140,000 metric tons of coal annually. The Ministry of Mines and Industry approximates that the country requires a domestic consumption of 500,000 tons per year, which could easily double to over 1 million tons. It is predicted that if the cement and thermal power industries are further developed, several million tons of coal could be utilized in these two areas alone.

The price of coal has increased considerably in the past several years, from around US $12/ton to US $6080/ton on the Kabul market. This is mainly due to demand for fired bricks to be used in construction projects. The estimated total value of coal production in Afghanistan is US $10 million annually. With adequate government regulation, the restoration of existing coal mines including machinery replacement, and an influx of private investment, this value could easily increase several fold annually.

Hydrocarbons

Afghanistan's main energy resource is natural gas. These deposits are located in the Gelmend, KundarUrgun, Tirpul and Karakum and AfghanTajik basins. Historically, these reserves were exported to the former USSR and Sovietcontrolled Central Asia. As of 1985, the largest discoveries were the KhojaGugerdag and Djarkuduk gas fields, and the Kashkari oilfields.

In March 2006, scientists from the U.S. Geological Survey and the Ministry of Mines and Industry released new findings that indicate that the AfghanTajik and Amu Darya Basins contain 18 times the oil and triple the natural gas reserves previously determined. The AfghanTajik basin was found to have around 1.6 billion barrels of oil and 15.7 trillion cubic feet of natural gas has been discovered in the Amu Darya basin. Previous exploration studies by Soviet and Afghan scientists estimated Afghanistan's total oil reserves at 88 million barrels and natural gas reserves at 5 trillion cubic feet.

The area covered by the study was only roughly onesixth the size of the two basins, which cover nearly 200,000 miles total. Given these findings and the relatively small area covered in total, further discovery of resources using modern exploration techniques is probable. With these new discoveries and renewed interest in the sector, competition among multinational hydrocarbon companies is expected to be fierce in the coming years.

Since Northern Afghanistan is a prime area for hydrocarbon exploration, the Asian Development Bank has pledged US $24.5 million to rework gas wells and refurbish pipelines in the north. ADB is also working to develop a gas strategy and gas regulatory secretariat.

Existing natural gas pipelines in Afghanistan are as follows (as provided by the Ministry of Mines and Industry):

- From Jarquduk to Khwoja Gogerdak (40 km)
- From Acha to Acha City (10 km)
- From Sheberghan to Jarquduk (13 km)
- From Khwoja Gogerdak to Cleft (100 km)
- From Khwoja Gogerdak to Fertilizer Company (89.1 km)
- From Yatimtaq to Jarqo Doq (28 km)
- From Acha Roundabout to MazareSharif (63 km)

Notably, Afghanistan also has some 1.5 million tons of barytes, an industrial mineral used as a weighting agent in the manufacture of oil well drilling. This deposit will play a strong support role in the development of the hydrocarbons industry in Afghanistan and other Central Asian countries.

Afghanistan's main energy resource is natural gas.

Main Energy Infrastructure at a Glance Oil

Angot Oilfield Produces a small quantity of crude oil; located in SariPol province. Primitive retorts used at the field and near Sheberghan to refine produced oil.

Natural Gas

| | |
|---|---|
| Sheberghan Area Gas Fields | The Djarquduk, Khowaja Gogerak, and Yatimtaq natural gas fields are all located within 20 miles of Sheberghan. |
| Pipeline to MazariSharif | A pipeline connects these natural gas fields to MazareSharif. Limited amounts of gas currently is supplied to a 48MW power plant near MazareSharif (which is operating at less than onethird full capacity) and for the 100,000 mt/y fertilizer plant, which is partially operational. |
| Local pipelines | Smalldiameter pipelines supply gas to the Khwaja Gogerdak and Djarquduk gas fields with Sheberghan and nearby villages . |

Electricity

| | |
|---|---|
| Kajaki Dam | Located in Helmand province near Kandahar; transmission lines to Kandahar repaired in early 2002, after being damaged by airstrikes in November 2001. Upgrading and expansion program is underway. |
| Mahipar Dam | Installed capacity of 66 MW. Near Kabul. Operational only two to three months out of the year (springtime) but currently lacking adequate water. |
| Naghlu Dam | Installed capacity of 100 MW. Operational. Provides most of the electricity used in Kabul. |
| Darunta Dam | Installed capacity of 11 MW. Operational. In Nangarhar province near Jalalabad. |
| Sarobi Dam | Installed capacity of 22 MW. |
| Dahla Dam | Kandahar province. Operational. |
| MazareSharif Power Plant | Small natural gasfired power plant near MazareSharif, partially operational at under 30 MW. |

Source: Energy Information Administration (EIA) on Afghanistan, Afghanistan Fact Sheet: Energy Overview

## MACHINERY

Domestic production of machinery related to the mining and energy sector presents yet another opportunity for investors. All mining equipment in Afghanistan is currently imported from abroad, or from the Soviet era. In the long term, the manufacture of local machinery will be profitable to the mining and energy industries and the establishment of repair centers for technical support will be crucial.

## GOVERNMENT ROLE

### CREATING A SUITABLE ENVIRONMENT FOR INVESTORS

The Government of Afghanistan realizes that the development of mineral resources will mean creating an enabling environment for attracting investment. As this industry is at the beginning of its development process, the Ministry of Mines and Industry has not yet issued any private licenses or permits for minerals extraction or exploration. Gas exploration is operating under similar conditions, but this is likely to change with the recent discoveries of large gas and oil reserves in the AfghanTajik and Amu Darya Basins. The following details show the existing regulatory and legal framework for the mining and energy industries in Afghanistan.

Mining

The Government of Afghanistan faces many challenges in reestablishing control over the mining sector, but is aware the longer the mining industry goes unregulated, the more threatened Afghanistan's natural reserves become. As a result, the responsible Ministry is working with the Geologic Surveys and donor community to develop a strategy that will encourage private sector development in mining. Some of the major functions and responsibilities include, but are not limited to:

- Development of infrastructure for mining;
- Administration of mineral rights and concessions;

- Control and regulation of industry (this would include measures to reduce smuggling and encourage official channels for trading in precious and semiprecious minerals);
- Assistance to environmental permitting of operations; and
- Creation of an Inventory of Mineral Activities currently conducted by the State.

Legal Framework: Mining

Competitive mining legislation is a key component in creating a suitable environment for investment. Experience in other countries has shown that a strong regulatory framework can successfully attract and retain investment and achieve sustainable growth. Article 1 of the new Minerals Law, passed in July 2005, states that "All naturally occurring Mineral Substances and all Artificial Deposits of Mineral Substances on or under the territory of Afghanistan or in its water systems are the exclusive property of the State." The Article also endows the State, most specifically the Ministry of Mines and Industries, as the only legal entity permitted to grant authorization "by any Person other than the State" to Mineral Rights.

Eligibility for Mining

Those individuals eligible to obtain Mineral Rights include "any legal entity organized or incorporated under the laws of Afghanistan" or "any legal entity organized or incorporated under foreign law that is legally entitled to reside or do business in Afghanistan." However, such persons are required by law to establish an administrative presence in Afghanistan or appoint an Agent duly responsible for reporting to the appropriate governmental authorities.

Key administrative provisions of the Minerals Law are as follows:

- The administration of tenders for Mineral Rights;
- Eligibility criteria to obtain Mineral Rights;
- The establishment of a Mining Cadastre to process applications for Mineral Rights;
- The establishment of a Mining Inspectorate to enforce compliance and conduct inspections;
- The establishment of an Environmental Protection Department to enforce regulations concerning environmental and social protection with regard to Mineral Activities;
- The establishment of the Geological Survey to conduct research activities and studies.

Key implementation provisions of the Minerals Law (critical to Investor rights and responsibilities) include:

- Description and differentiation between different types of permits (Exploration Licenses, Exploitation Licenses, Quarry Exploration Authorization, Quarry Exploitation Authorization, Artisanal Exploitation Authorization, and Authorization for Construction of Infrastructure);
- Duration, surface area and obligations provisions of various permits;
- Description of Surface Rights Fees for various permits;
- Article 19 states that a Person may hold one or more Licenses and/or Authorizations simultaneously;
- Perimeter of Mining Operations and occupation of land;
- Permit/License Renewal Procedures;
- Transferability of Title (ability of Holder to transfer Mineral Right to a third party or inheritance provisions);
- Withdrawal or Termination of Mineral Right;

- Sale of Minerals and Mineral Substances;
- Protection of Investments (state guarantees, foreign exchange rights and import/export provisions);
- Assurances of protection against financial consequences of legislation which becomes effective after the issuance of the Mineral Right;
- Detail of Penalty provisions enforced by the Mining Inspectorate;
- Health and safety provisions (Holders of Mineral Rights are required by law to publish a Health and Safety Plan to the Mining Inspectorate);
- Environmental Impact Statement (required by law for Holders of the Exploitation License or Quarry Exploitation Authorization); and
- Arbitration and dispute resolution.

Taxation and Mineral Royalties

The Minerals Law grants authority to the Ministry of Finance for collection of application taxes and customs laws. Moreover, the Holders of Mineral Rights are "entitled to the rights and privileges available to Investors under the Investment Law."

The collection of Mineral Royalties falls under the jurisdiction of the Ministry of Mines and Industries and Holders subject to such royalties are legally bound to submit quarterly operations reports to the Mining Inspectorate. Royalties differ for various minerals and these rates can be obtained from the Ministry.

Legal Framework: Hydrocarbons

The Government of Afghanistan is currently working within the Ministry of Mines and Industry to ratify the drafted Hydrocarbons (Petroleum and Gas) Law (2006). Similar to Article 1 of the Minerals Law, the Hydrocarbons Law declares all petroleum and gas located on the territory of the State exclusive property of the State. The State designates the Ministry of Mines and Industry as the appropriate authority to grant petroleum and gas operations licenses.

Some of the major administrative functions and responsibilities of the Ministry in this respect will include:

- Organize bidding rounds;
- Divide territory into exploration 'blocks' to invite bidding;
- Creation of an InterMinisterial Committee to approve and evaluate bidding procedures for hydrocarbons contracts;
- Register all hydrocarbons operations (an office specifically for this purpose will be established in the MMI);
- Delineate areas closed to or prohibited from hydrocarbons activities;
- Supervise contract implementation;
- Fix surface rentals;
- Authorize inspection of operations at any time;
- Terminate contracts in conjunction with the InterMinisterial Committee;
- Determine percentage of minerals royalties and collection procedures;
- Propose regulations; and
- Issue reports of financial revenues.

Eligibility for Hydrocarbons

Eligibility for hydrocarbons licenses has similar criteria as for mineral rights. Those individuals eligible to obtain petroleum and gas operations licenses include foreigners legally permitted to reside in Afghanistan and "any foreign legal entity established according to external law or is a collaborator and has the right to reside in Afghanistan legally and embark upon investment and trade." (Minerals Law, Article 4). Foreign persons are required by law to establish an administrative presence in Afghanistan or appoint an Agent duly responsible for reporting to the appropriate governmental authorities. Other key provisions of the Hydrocarbons Law will include:

- An updated Petroleum and Gas Data Bank monitored by the Afghan Geological Survey;
- Differentiation between two types of hydrocarbons contracts: Exploration and Production Sharing and Services and Production Sharing;
- Tenure of contracts for Exploration (10 years, but with possibility of extension) and Production (25 years maximum from the date of discovery);
- Environment Protection and Management Plan (mandatory for contracts);
- Abandonment and Decommissioning Plan;
- Health and Safety Plan;
- Legal Provisions for Pipelines (including construction, use, and transportation terms);
- Payment of Royalty Fees as determined by the InterMinisterial Committee;
- Transfer of Foreign Exchange; and Dispute settlement.

Challenges that can be mastered

While Afghanistan offers many profitable opportunities in energy and mining, formidable challenges remain. Some of these challenges include:

• Transition to a market economy

Government control over mineral resources burdened the central government with subsidies for inefficient production at state owned mines and also resisted the adoption of new modern mining methods

• Security

Ineffective government control over mineral rich areas; many mines are in rural areas out of central government control or located in unstable areas i.e. the border of Pakistan

• Lack of infrastructure (power, water and transport)

Poor rural roads make shipping materials more expensive relative to other countries

• Obsolete mining practices

Methods dating back to the 1980s and before

• Lack of investment in Modern Machinery

Replacement of outmoded machinery will increase startup costs for investors; Uptodate quarrying & processing technologies/facilities crucial

• Unexploded ordinance

Afghanistan remains one of the most heavily landmined countries in the world and security precautions are essential for exploration

• Shortage of skilled workforce

The shortage of skilled labor will increase startup costs for investors, as more expensive labor (engineers, managers and machinists) will have to be imported until local workers receive appropriate training

• Landlocked Location

Cost of transport to markets higher

• Research & Technology

Efforts are underway, but geological clarity of reserves will be vital in directing investment

• Legal & Regulatory Framework

Implementation of the new Minerals and Hydrocarbons Law will be a challenge capacitywise for the Government

• Access to Credit

Mining is high risk and capitalintensive; Lack of financing possibilities most detrimental to SME's (small and mediumsized enterprises)

Despite these challenges, progress is underway. The Government of Afghanistan has identified key stateowned enterprises for privatization (see paragraph before) and financial institutions are building capacity and working alongside investors to provide reliable credit facilities. Security and demining is gradually improving. Most importantly, the Afghan Government has begun establishing the appropriate legal framework for mining and energy through the Minerals and Hydrocarbons Laws, demonstrating its commitment to the development of these sectors. Lastly, the international community is making every effort to provide technical and financial expertise in these areas and is helping Afghanistan reconstruct the physical infrastructure that will be vital to sustaining investment in its mining and energy sectors.

AISA Services

The Afghanistan Investment Support Agency (AISA) stands ready to provide investors with assistance and only the most uptodate information available on Afghanistan's investment opportunities. AISA encourages you to contact us with your questions and concerns at:

Office address: Opposite Ministry of Foreign Affairs, Kabul, Afghanistan Phone: (93) (0) 20210 3404; Email: info@aisa.org.af or invest@aisa.org.af; www.aisa.org.af

# INVESTMETN PROJECTS

## AGRICULTURE

Being central to Afghanistan's economy, agriculture is an important area in need of further financing. The sector accounts for 31 percent of GDP but provides employment to 59 percent of the labor force. This is therefore a critical sector for ARTF support. In an arid country like Afghanistan irrigation is of particular importance to foster growth in the agriculture sector. Water resources and development is therefore a key area for ARTF support. The ARTF is supporting irrigation rehabilitation through the Irrigation Restoration and Development Project which would include an increase of about 10-15 percent in the irrigated area and about a 10-15 percent increase in crop yields in rehabilitated areas. The pilot On-Farm Water Management Project will build the link between the irrigation channels, bringing the water more efficiently to the farms themselves to improve yields.

### ON FARM WATER MANAGEMENT PROJECT

Grant Amount: $70 million

Approval Date: January 11, 2011

Closing Date: December 31, 2019

**Project Objective:**

The development objective of the On Farm Water Management is to improve agricultural productivity in project areas by enhancing the efficiency of water used.

#### PROGRAM SUMMARY

**The Project**: Over 70% of Afghanistan's population lives in rural areas and a major part of Afghanistan's population is dependent on the agriculture sector (defined as annual crops, horticulture and livestock), which on average has accounted for nearly 40 percent of the total Gross Domestic Product during the past decade. Agricultural development is recognized by the Government as a major driver of economic growth and food security. However, most of the modern irrigation systems in Afghanistan were damaged during years of warfare and are in a state of disrepair as a result of long-term neglect.

The project is providing farmers with improved, reliable, and equitable distribution of irrigation water to increase agricultural productivity. While primary and secondary conveyance infrastructure is being restored and rehabilitated under various other projects, physical improvements of tertiary irrigation facilities are equally important to complement effectiveness of the upstream developments. The latter is thus crucial for enhancing farm incomes and improving food security.

### EXPECTED RESULTS

Productivity of agricultural crops in project areas increased by 30%

Water User Organizations capable to adequately perform O&M tasks

Water use efficiency in project areas improved by 25%

MAIL staff in project areas capable to plan, implement and monitor OFWM programs

Effective and efficient project organization established.

The OFWMP is implemented by the Ministry of Agriculture, Livestock and Irrigation (MAIL).

## IRRIGATION REHABILITATION AND DEVELOPMENT PROJECT

Grant Amount: $118.40 million

Approval Date: February 28, 2012

Closing Date: December 31, 2017

**Project Objective:**

The development objective of the Irrigation Rehabilitation and Development Project (IRDP) is to increase agriculture productivity and production in the project areas.

### PROGRAM SUMMARY

**The Project:** With only 12 percent of the total land being arable and the country's arid climate, irrigation is essential for reliable agricultural production in most parts of the country. Notwithstanding the achievements of the preceding IDA-financed Emergency Irrigation Rehabilitation (EIRP), there is a huge unmet demand for irrigation rehabilitation. The total irrigated area in the country prior to 1979 (the year of USSR invasion) was about 3.2 million ha, but in 2007 it was only 1.8 million ha. As of April 2011, irrigation systems serving an irrigated area of about 0.9 million ha had been rehabilitated; while irrigation systems covering about one million ha remained to be rehabilitated.

The project provides support for: (a) rehabilitation of irrigation systems covering about 300,000 ha of irrigated areas; (b) the design and construction of a limited number of multi-purpose small dams and appurtenances, and associated irrigation conveyance and distribution systems in closed river basins; (c) establishment of hydro-meteorological facilities and services; and (d) project management and capacity building of MEW and beneficiary communities.

The IRDP is co-financed with IDA (US$97.8 million).

### EXPECTED RESULTS

A 15 % increase in the irrigated area;

At least 20 % increase in crop yields in rehabilitated schemes;

Availability of improved hydro-meteorological data to support planning and preparation of irrigation and water resources development investments; and

Improved capacity of MEW staff in various fields.

## NATIONAL HORTICULTURE AND LIVESTOCK PROJECT

Grant Amount: $190 million

Approval Date:December 22, 2012

Closing Date:December 31, 2018

**Project Objective:**

The development objective of the National Horticulture and Livestock Project is to promote adoption of improved production practices by target farmers, with gradual rollout of farmer-centric agricultural services systems and investment support.

### PROGRAM SUMMARY

**The Project:** The ARTF funded NHLP is a follow-on project to the Horticulture and Livestock Project. The National Horticulture and Livestock Project (NHLP) was approved by ARTF Management Committee to provide support in an amount of US$ 100 million, with an initial allocation of US$ 50 million, to the Islamic Republic of Afghanistan. The project contributes to the overarching goal of increased productivity and overall production of horticultural products and improved animal production and health. The technical strategy for achieving this objective is based on the delivery of extension and investment support through strengthened systems. The National Horticulture and Livestock Project (NHLP) has three components: (1) Horticultural Production, (2) Animal Production and Health, and (3) Implementation Management and Technical Assistance Support. These activities are implemented in 100 focus districts spread over time as conditions warrant in up to 22 target provinces.

The Project contributes to the Agriculture Production and Market Development Program –the National Priority Program 2 (NPP2).

### EXPECTED RESULTS

97500 Target farmers exposed to a horticulture production practice and understand it and its benefits;

6000 Orchards rehabilitated (ha) directly and indirectly, benefiting 30,000 people;

8000 New Orchards (including vineyards) established with at least 70% survival rate;

133,000 Target farmers exposed to a practice and understand it and its benefits;

50% of the target farmers adopting regular livestock inoculation (or VFUs stocking inputs recommended in extension messages).

## AFGHANISTAN AGRICULTURE INPUTS PROJECT

Grant Amount:

$74.75 million

Approval Date:

June 17, 2013

Closing Date:

June 30, 2018

**Project Objective:**

The Project Development Objective of the Afghanistan Agriculture Inputs Project (AAIP) is to strengthen the institutional capacity for safety and reliability of agricultural inputs and sustainable production of certified wheat seed.

**PROGRAM SUMMARY**

**The Project:** The project objective is being achieved through: (i) strengthening capacity in the value chain for producing certified wheat seed; (ii) preventing marketing of banned, hazardous, sub-standard, and unreliable pesticides and fertilizers; (iii) lowering the risk of introduction and spread of plant quarantine pests into the country; and (iv) improving farmers' access to agricultural inputs of reliable quality.

**Expected Results**:

- Increased wheat seed multiplication factors, ratio of foundation seed to breeder seed increased from 14 to 26, and ratio of registered seed to foundation seed increased from 9.6 to 23;
- Increase annual production of certified seed by Private Seed Enterprises from 24,000 to 30,000;
- Improved listing of plant quarantine pests and diseases;
- 180 product samples tested for pesticides residues;
- 105 bad pesticide samples intercepted by the end of the project.

# RURAL DEVELOPMENT

Rural development is critical in Afghanistan where poverty rates in rural areas are high. As a result the Rural Development Sector is a key recipient of funds from the ARTF. This is first and foremost due to the flagship project the National Solidarity Program, which started its implementation in 2002 and is now in its third phase. About 80 percent of the community subprojects involve infrastructure such as irrigation, rural roads, electrification, and drinking water supply, all critical for the recovery of the rural economy, stability, and governance. But more importantly, NSP is about mobilizing communities to organize themselves to receive direct government assistance to meet their most pressing needs. NSP is seen as an equitable program following the same guidelines across the country and ensuring that all communities which are willing to adopt the NSP principles, even those in the conflict areas, are eventually reached. Other projects include the Rural Access Program (NERAP/ARAP) which funds rural roads and the Rural Enterprise Development Project focusing on support for small scale private businesses. Through NERAP more than 10,000 km of rural access roads have been constructed or repaired, providing for 13 million labor days in rural areas and enhanced access to markets, employment and social services. Rehabilitation of these village roads has given some 9000 villages access to all-season roads.

Project Title:

**RURAL ENTERPRISE DEVELOPMENT PROGRAM**

Grant Amount:

$39.2 million (ARTF Grant: $10.97; IDA: $28.2 million)

Approval Date:

March 9, 2010

Closing Date:

31 Dec, 2015

**Project Objective:**

The development objective of the Rural Enterprise Development Program is to improve employment opportunities and income of rural men and women, and sustainability of targeted local enterprises.

**PROGRAM SUMMARY**

Over 75% of the people of Afghanistan live in rural areas where agriculture is the primary activity and contributes about one third of the GDP (excluding the opium economy). However, poor governance, weak factor markets, inadequate marketing infrastructure and business development services, and poor post-harvest practices are limiting the economic development potential of this sector and constraining on-farm and non-farm employment opportunities, thus perpetuating poverty in the rural areas. The following are the key issues and challenges: (a) Poverty and Vulnerability; (b) Economic Slowdown and Increasing Insecurity; (c) Spread of Opium Poppy; (d) Weak Institutions; (e) Lack of Access to Finance and Poorly Functioning Factor Markets; and (f) Shortage of Business Expertise.

The Afghanistan Rural Enterprise Development Project (AREDP) seeks to enhance the participation of the rural poor in economic activities by supporting them through business development services, access to finance, and improving market linkages and value chains. The project is supporting the establishment of 13,000 Savings Groups (SGs), 6,500 Enterprise Groups (EGs) and 1,300 Village and Savings Loan Associations.

**EXPECTED RESULTS**

40% of the Enterprises Enterprises include EGs, SMEs, micro enterprises and individual entrepreneurs will have increased their net revenues, by at least 20%. 35% of these will be female Enterprise

At least 20% of participating enterprises will have increased direct and/or indirect employment by at least 30%; Of these at least 35% will be women

Number of direct beneficiaries of which 35 % are female

At least 60% of project beneficiaries have access to financial services

40% of enterprises Enterprises include EGs, SMEs, micro enterprises and individual entrepreneurs supported by the Project will still be operating 2 years after start-up. At least 35% of these will be female Enterprises.

Project Title:

**NATIONAL SOLIDARITY PROGRAM III**

Grant Amount:

1107.26 million

Approval Date:

January 24, 2011

Closing Date:

March 31 2017

**Project Objective:**

The development objective of the National Solidarity Program III is to build, strengthen, and maintain community development councils (CDCs) as effective institutions for local governance and social-economic development

**PROGRAM SUMMARY**

**The Project:** The National Solidarity Program (NSP) is now in its third phase, known as NSP III. NSP III is funding activities for; (a) establishment and capacity building of Community Development Councils (CDCs) and their federations (cluster CDCs); (b) continuing roll-out of the NSP to the remaining 1107.26 communities not yet covered by the program and scaling up support for local economic and social development through provision of repeater block grants to 17,400 rural communities; and (c) program implementation management support, including program monitoring and evaluation.

NSP III is co-financed by an IDA grant of $40 million.

**EXPECTED RESULTS:**

Minimum of 70 % sampled communities recognize CDCs as the legitimate institution and respresentative of communities

Minimum of 60 % of CDCs perform their functional mandates in the areas of community development and coordination, project implementation and conflict resolution

Minimum of 70 % of sampled communities have improved access to services.

Minimum of 70 % of sampled women representatives in the CDCs take active part in decision-making related to community development

At least 50 % of total beneficiaries are female

Project Title:

**CASA COMMUNITY SUPPORT PROGRAM**

Grant Amount:

$ 40 Million

Approval Date:

March 4, 2014

Closing Date:

May 30, 2017

**Project Objective:**

The proposed Project Development Objective is to provide access to electricity or other social and economic infrastructure services to communities in the project area in order to strengthen community support for CASA-1000 transmission line.

**PROGRAM SUMMARY**

The project will benefit all those communities that live along a 2 kilometer 'Corridor of Influence' each side of the CASA-1000 transmission line. It is expected that there will be approximately 700 communities spread over 23 districts in 6 provinces, with a total of over 152,000 families along the corridor of influence (COI).

The project consists of four components and an unallocated category, which if applied will be allocated across all four components. The key features of each component are: i) Community Grants for sub-projects fund economic infrastructure, with preference given to power-sector sub-projects; ii) Community Mobilization to engage communities to increase the shared prosperity associated with the CASA-1000 transmission line which will pass through their villages; iii) Project Implementation Support through a cost sharing mechanism with NSP; and iv) Communications and Outreach campaign and information-sharing activities as well as ensuring feedback loops between the corridor communities and the implementing agencies.

## EXPECTED RESULTS:

50 % of communities within the CoI are provided with access to electricity through the CSP grant funded subprojects;

Minimum of 70% of communities in project areas, have improved access to social and economic infrastructure services;

At least 50% of total beneficiaries are female;

Project Title:

## CITIZENS CHARTER AFGHANISTAN PROJECT

Grant Amount:

$500 Million (ARTF Grant amount: $400 million; IDA grant: $100 million; Government financing: $128 million)

Approval Date:

27 October 2016

Closing Date:

31 October 2020

**Project Objective:**

To improve the delivery of core infrastructure and social services to participating communities through strengthened community development councils (CDSs). these services are part of a minimum service standards package that the government is committed to delivering to the citizens of Afghanistan.

### PROGRAM SUMMARY

The Citizens charter is a National Priority Program (NPP) of the National Unity Government (NGU) that is currently in its design phase and is expected to lunch on October 1, 2016. The Citizens Charter is the first ever inter-ministerial, multi-sectorial NPP, where Ministries will collaborate on a single program using a programmatic approach. The key services delivery ministries involved are: MRRD, MoE, MoPH and MAIL. The Citizen' Charter will go one step further than NSP and bring the CDSc to the forefront of program delivery and all development activities thereafter. The Community Development Councils (CDCs) will be linked to sub-national government to improve communications and coordination from the community to the district, provincial and national levels, which will increase Government visibility and accountability. The Citizens' Charter is an important foundation for the Government's reform agenda, contributing to a number of priority areas including; Ensuring Citizens' Development Rights; Building Better Governance; Reforming Development Planning & Management and Developing partnership.

**EXPECTED RESULT:**

Minimum of 8.5 million direct and indirect beneficiaries reached by CCAP;

Minimum of 50 percent of direct and indirect beneficiaries will be women;

Minimum of 9,000 communities in rural and urban areas receiving the stated minimum services standards. The minimum target is estimated at 9,000 communities (8,600 rural and 400 urban) due to high risks of insecurity and fluctuating conditions. However, the overall coverage target is planned for 12,600 total communities (12,000 rural and 600 urban communities); and

Minimum of 10,500 CDSs/clusters/Gozars able to plan, implement, monitor and coordinate development activities as measured by an institutional maturity index.

# INFRASTRUCTURE

The Afghan economy needs sustainable sources of long-term inclusive growth. Resources and agriculture are the only sectors with the potential to significantly drive such growth. Support for infrastructure is key in this regard. While the ARTF is not involved in large-scale infrastructure like highways or railroads, significant support is provided for rural roads (see Rural Development), irrigation (see Agriculture), power projects, urban development and resource corridors. Through the Resource Corridors Project, the ARTF also supports the preparation of a platform of "hard" and "soft" infrastructure that will enable Afghanistan to derive broader economic benefits from the development of its extractive industries (i.e. mining). The ARTF aims to support the accelerated realization of private sector anchor investments in the resource sector, and leverage those investments for broader benefits. Mining sector growth will not be inclusive unless it is leveraged to create broader benefits and growth breaks out of "enclave" investments. The Government of Afghanistan's resource corridor strategy (building on the National and Regional Resource Corridor National Priority Program) seeks to achieve this, leveraging the resource sector for transformation – prioritizing public and private investments through the four dimensions of governance, livelihoods, environmental and social impact (referred as "soft" infrastructure), and ("hard") infrastructure. .

Project Title:

**AFGHANISTAN POWER SYSTEM DEVELOPMENT PROJECT**

Grant Amount:

$75 million

Approval Date:

March 19, 2009

Closing Date:

31 May, 2017

**Project Objective:**

The development objective of the Afghanistan Power System Development Project is to increase access to grid power and the quantity of available power to the consumers in the target areas of the urban centers at Pul-e-Khumri, Charikar, Gulbahar, and Jabul-Seraj.

### PROGRAM SUMMARY

**The project:** Following a programmatic approach to rehabilitating and expanding the Afghanistan power system, the Afghanistan Power System Development Project builds and complements the investments made under the ARTF funded Kabul-Aybak-Mazar-e-Sharif Power Project and the Emergency Power Rehabilitation Project.

The project supports the Government of Afghanistan in increasing: (i) access to grid power; and (ii) the quantity of power available to consumers in the target urban centers of Pule-Khumri, Charikar, Gulbahar and Jabul-Seraj. The project is also supporting the establishment of a unit within MEW to promote energy efficiency and saving.

### EXPECTED RESULTS

Increase in electricity access rate in Charikar, Doshi, Gulbahar and Jabul-Seraj (% of households).

Increase in power supply quantity to project areas in Pul-e-Khumri; Charikar, Gulbahar and Jabul-Seraj (in MWh).

Initiation of the energy efficiency promotion activities in Afghanistan.

Project Title:

### KABUL MUNICIPAL DEVELOPMENT PROGRAM

Grant Amount:

$110 Million

Approval Date:

March 25, 2014

Closing Date:

December 31, 2019

**Project Objective:**

The Project Development Objectives are to: (i) increase access to basic municipal services in selected residential areas of Kabul city; (ii) redesign KM's Financial Management system to support better service delivery; and (iii) enable early response in the event of an eligible emergency.

### PROGRAM SUMMARY

THE PROJECT: The Kabul Municipal Development Program (KMDP) is expected to deliver welfare and human development benefits to approximately 777,380 people through services provided in 1773 hectares of government owned land. Equipment for the Roads and Sanitation departments of Kabul Municipality will combat pollution and improve service delivery as well as the city environment. Project support to develop a plan for improving the municipality's financial management and planning capacity to deliver improved services to its people, will enhance KM's legitimacy when implemented.
The project is being implemented by Kabul Municipality.

The project will be implemented by Kabul Municipality.

EXPECTED RESULTS:
(i) 775,000 beneficiaries from upgrading of basic municipal infrastructure.
(ii) Number of people in urban areas provided access to all-season roads within a 500 meter range of project supported roads.
(iii) Report on Financial Management reforms.

Project Title:

### KABUL URBAN TRANSPORT EFFICIENCY IMPROVEMENT PROJECT

Grant Amount:

$ 90.5 Million

Approval Date:

March 25, 2014

Closing Date:

December 31, 2019

**Project Objective:**

The Project Development Objective (PDO) is to improve road conditions and traffic flows in selected corridors of Kabul City.

Unprecedented population growth in Kabul, large-scale destruction of the city's infrastructure during the war, followed by a growing concentration of security related activity has exacerbated the backlog of infrastructure deficiency. The capacity of the existing road network is diminished further by an astronomical growth in the number of motor vehicles that is today double the 300,000 vehicles the network was designed for.

### PROGRAM SUMMARY

THE PROJECT: Kabul Urban Transport Efficiency Improvement Project (KUTEI) targets transport services improvement through a package of interrelated interventions, to build Kabul Municipality's capacity. The project focuses on improvement of road infrastructure and provision of technical assistance to the Kabul Municipality in specific areas.
Investments in key road infrastructure will improve connectivity and make Kabul more inclusive, while technical and knowledge support will gradually transform Kabul Municipality into a modern planning and implementing agency by adopting best international practice.
Kabul Municipality is responsible for implementation of the project, including procurement and financial management.

EXPECTED RESULTS:
i. Traffic capacity improvements will be measured by average vehicle speed during off peak hours.
ii. Number of people (within a 500 meter range under the project) in urban areas provided with access to all season roads.
iii. Rating of surface condition of major urban road network improved.

Project Title:

### AFGHANISTAN RESOURCE CORRIDORS - PROJECT PREPARATION GRANT

Grant Amount:

$2,700,000

Approval Date:

29-May- 2013

Closing Date:

31-December-2017

**Project Objective:**

The Project Development Objective is to prepare a platform of "hard" and "soft" infrastructure that will enable Afghanistan to derive broader economic benefits from the development of its extractive industries.

### PROGRAM SUMMARY

The Afghanistan Resource Corridors Project aims to: (a) support the accelerated realization of private sector anchor investments in the resources sector, and (B) leverage those investments for broader benefits, through: (i) preparing incremental investments that can create public goods; and (ii) investing in soft infrastructure that builds the capabilities of national and local firms, communities and job seekers to benefit from the resource sector.

### EXPECTED RESULT:

ID cluster Secretariat established, demonstrating its ability to effectively coordinate the review process of ID cluster NPPs.

Resource Corridor Secretariat has initiated the required preparatory work (Elaboration of Terms of References, launch of procurement process) for the project components for which it is responsible.

Project Title:

## NAGHLU HYDROPOWER REHABILITATION PROJECT

Grant Amount:

$83 MILLION

Approval Date:

December 14, 2015

Closing Date:

September 30, 2022

**Project Objective:**

The project development objective (PDO) is to improve dam safety and to increase the supply of electricity at the Naghlu Hydropower Plant.

### PROGRAM SUMMARY

The Project: The Project aims to improve dam safety and sustainability of hydropower and to increase the supply of domestically generated hydroelectricity at the Naghlu Hydropower Plant (NHPP). The following areas comprise the main project activities: will comprise three components: (a) mechanical, electrical, and electromechanical works; (b) dam safety and power generation improvement; and (c) environmental and social sustainability, project management support, and future project preparation. This will contribute to enhancements in the reliability of the electric power system and help benefit both households and industries, hence stimulating economic development and growth. The local population is also expected to benefit from employment opportunities during the project repair and rehabilitation phase. The Project will also have important climate change impacts through the enhancement of hydropower which has almost zero green-house gas emissions.

Expected Results: (a) Improvement in the generation capacity (in MW) of Unit 1 in the NHPP

(b) Reduction in the total number of forced power outages in the NHPP

(c) Establishment of dam safety plans and periodic audits in accordance with international best practices

(d) Implementation of dam safety measures as recommended in dam safety audit reports

(e) Development of O&M procedures and guidelines that are in line with international best practices

Project Title:

## DABS PLANNING AND CAPACITY SUPPORT PROJECT

Grant Amount:

$6 million

Approval Date:

February 10, 2016

Closing Date:

July 31, 2020

**Project Objective:**

The project development objective is to improve DABS capacity in distribution investment planning, implementation, operation and maintenance.

### PROGRAM SUMMARY

The Project: The Project aims to improve DABS capacity in distribution investment planning, implementation, operation and maintenance. The Project is part of the core of the World Bank's strategy in energy sector interventions in Afghanistan, as it will contribute to DABS ability to sustainably maintain and expand the distribution networks. Project activities will focus on supporting the capacity of DABS staff by: (a) Developing a core training curriculum and providing general and task-specific training to managers and staff on distribution investment selection, planning and implementation, specifically on the preparation of pre-feasibility and feasibility studies, procuring design, supply and installation contractors, and supervising such contractors; b) Providing general and task-specific training to managers and staff on distribution operation planning and implementation, specifically on the preparation and execution of annual O&M plans; and (c) establishing a training center in DABS.

Expected Results: (a) 50% of Distribution Operations staff in DABS with improved skills in investment planning, implementation, operation and maintenance through the project supported training and use of new training facility;

b. Annual O&M plans for six major load centers prepared and implemented using new standards and procedures based on good international practice adjusted for local conditions

Project Title:

## DIGITAL CASA

Grant Amount:

$5.000 million

Approval Date:

09-September 2016

Closing Date:

31-December 2017

**Project Objective:**

To facilitate the preparation of the proposed Digital Central Asia South Asia Project to increase access to and reduce costs of regional and domestic internet traffic, improve public service delivery through the development of e-government services, and promote access to Digital Job opportunities.

### PROGRAM SUMMARY

Through Digital CASA PPG project (a) carrying out of feasibility studies for fiber optic connectivity options, networks, automation of e-services delivery, e- procurement, enhancing national data center and options for backup disaster recovery center, and preparation of related biding documents through the provisions of technical assistance and advisory services, (b) provision of technical advisory services designed to prepare a national broadband strategy; and environmental and social management framework; IT/IT- enabled services industry development strategy and roadmap; and geographical information system mapping and database development for national infrastructure an asset mapping, (c) capacity building activities to strengthen MCIT and ATRA to facilitate preparation of the project; identification of information and communications technology skills development requirement and implementation plan; and advisory services for national cyber security. (d) Provision of training and workshop in connection with above activities.

### EXPECTED RESULT:

Digital Central Asia South Asia Project is approved and effective

Bidding documents for major contract are prepared

Project Title:

### SUPPORT TO AFGHAN LAND AUTHORITY PROJECT

Grant Amount:

$4,950, 000 million

Approval Date:

9-September-2016

Closing Date:

30-June-2018

**Project Objective:**

The objective of the activities is to facilitate the preparation of the proposed support to Afghan Land Authority Project which has the objective of supporting the Recipient to develop the policy and regulatory framework and build capacity to deliver transparent, pro-poor land services.

**PROGRAM SUMMARY**

Through Afghan Land Authority project, (a) technical advisory services, training, and other material support to update the land policy paper for consultation with the stakeholders, and to develop law on land expropriations' procedure for land rights identification and land clearance; regulations for registration customary mechanism; by-law in support of the implementation of AILA's 5-year strategic development plan. (b) carrying out of an environment and social assessment to take stock of earlier analytical work and pilots in dispute resolution, land registration, as well as identification of major stakeholder and political economy dimensions of land governance reforms; to assess potential downstream impacts; and to ensure compliance with policies, laws and procedures with applicable safeguard provisions and facilitate a pro-poor orientation of all approaches and documents prepared under the project. (c) Carrying out the review of the land survey system and developing new strategy for mapping surveying and registration land, development of a strategy and procedure for transfer from court based to administrative land registration, including the provision of technical advisory services. (d) Carrying out set activities to disseminate and raise awareness, training (local and international) and capacity building activities in connection with the revised laws, regulations and procedures, at national and provincial level, and upgrading of ALAA's office facilities.

Expected Result:

An updated version of the land policy paper has been prepared.

A strategy for mapping, surveying and registering has been drafted.

An updated implementation plan for AILA's 5- year development strategy has been prepared.

Project Title:

**URBAN DEVELOPMENT SUPPORT PPG**

Grant Amount:

$2,900,000

Approval Date:

7-November-2016

Closing Date:

21-September-2017

**Project Objective:**

The Objective of the activities is to facilitate the preparation of the proposed Urban Development Support Program which has the objective of creating an enabling policy framework and capacity at the national and local level to strengthen local city planning, management and service delivery.

### PROGRAM SUMMARY

The Urban Development Support Program (UDSP) will finance technical assistance, capacity building and system development at the Ministry of Urban Development and Housing (MUDH) and in 6 participating municipalities. The program will promote effective transversal urban management in the context of rapid urbanization and increased urban poverty and will finance spatial planning and feasibility studies at the city level to facilitate catalytic investments. These will be aimed at promoting local economic development and improved municipal service delivery. The proposed UDSP preparation grant will assist MUDH in mobilizing a core coordinating team to plan and manage the project, help prepare draft terms of reference for assignments, initiate date collection that will contribute to project design, and facilitate project preparation necessary to move swiftly into the implementation phase.

### EXPECTED RESULT:

Enhanced system of urban data collection and information management established at MUDH and participating cities informing policy decisions;

Strengthened institutional capacity of MUDH to exercise its regulatory oversight functions;

Improved urban development policy framework at MUDH;

Number of participating municipalities with updated detailed spatial plans;

Number of hectares of land that have been incorporated into updated spatial plans.

## HUMAN DEVELOPMENT

The Human Development Sector covers support for service delivery within essential areas like health and education. Important progress has been made: Enrolment in primary schools for both girls and boys has increased significantly by at least 60 percent and 75 percent respectively and the number of female teachers has increased by 50 percent. Within the health sector results are equally impressive, particularly in reducing infant and under five mortality rates. The health program has made good use of non-governmental organizations (NGOs) as service providers by building contracting capacity in the public sector, increasing access and coverage of essential services and enhancing the availability of health care workers particularly female health care workers. This has allowed a rapid roll-out of a basic package of health services across the country. More work needs to be done to strengthen and solidify results and the ARTF therefore continues to provide service to these critical areas through Government's national priority programs.

Project Title:

**SYSTEM ENHANCEMENT FOR HEALTH ACTION IN TRANSITION**

Grant Amount:

$300 million

Approval Date:

June 17, 2013

Closing Date:

June 30, 2018

**Project Objective:**

The development objective of the System Enhancement for Health Action in Transition (SEHAT) project is to expand the scope, quality and coverage of health services provided to the Afghan population, particularly to the poor in the project areas, and to enhance the stewardship functions of the Ministry of Public Health.

**PROGRAM SUMMARY**

<a data-cke-saved-href="https://finances.worldbank.org/Trust-Funds/ARTF-System-Enhancement-for-Health-Action-in-Trans/x34k-qbiy" href="https://finances.worldbank.org/Trust-Funds/ARTF-System-Enhancement-for-Health-Action-in-Trans/x34k-qbiy" title="ARTF System Enhancement for Health Action in Transition - Allocations & Disbursements" target="_blank">ARTF System Enhancement for Health Action in Transition - Allocations & Disbursements</a>

The chart above represents total allocations and disbursements during the lifetime of the project. To see the raw data behind this chart, go to the dataset and you will be directed to the World Bank Group Finances website. Once there, you can build your own views, share, embed, and download the data or your work. Read the instructions on how to build this chart from the raw data.

**The Project:** The SEHAT project is the second and scaled-up phase of the ARTF and IDA-financed Strengthening Health Activities for Rural Poor (SHARP). The project supportings the implementation of the Basic Package of Health Services (BPHS) and Essential Package of Hospital Services (EPHS) through contracting arrangements both in rural and urban areas covering a total of 22 provinces, including Kabul urban (out of 34 provinces) in the country, expanding from 11 provinces under SHARP to 22 provinces under SEHAT.

The project is also strengthening the national health system and Ministry of Public Health's (MOPH) capacity at central and provincial levels, so it can effectively perform its stewardship functions in the sector.

The program, which is estimated for a total value of US$407 million, is jointly supported by the Government of Afghanistan with US$30 million, IDA Grant of US$100, Health Results Innovation Trust Fund (HRITF) of US$7 million, and ARTF of US$270 million.

### EXPECTED RESULTS

• Increase births attended by skilled health personnel among lowest income quintile
• Increase PENTA3 immunization coverage among children aged between 12 and 23 months in lowest income quintile
• Increase contraceptive prevalence rate (using any modern method)
• Increase the proportion of children under 5 years of age with severe acute malnutrition receive treatment
• Improve the score on the examining quality of care in SCs, BHCs, and CHC on the balanced scorecard.

Project Title:

### EDUCATION QUALITY IMPROVEMENT PROGRAM II

Grant Amount:

$408 million

Approval Date:

August 14, 2009

Closing Date:

December 31, 2016

**Project Objective:**

The development objective of the Second Education Quality Improvement Program is to increase equitable access to quality basic education especially for girls through school grants, teacher training and strengthened institutional capacity with support from communities and private providers.

### PROGRAM SUMMARY

<a data-cke-saved-href="https://finances.worldbank.org/Trust-Funds/ARTF-Second-Education-Quality-Improvement-Program-/x64c-5nur" href="https://finances.worldbank.org/Trust-Funds/ARTF-Second-Education-Quality-Improvement-Program-/x64c-5nur" title="ARTF Second Education Quality Improvement Program - Allocations & Disbursements" target="_blank">ARTF Second Education Quality Improvement Program - Allocations & Disbursements</a>

The chart above represents total allocations and disbursements during the lifetime of the project. To see the raw data behind this chart, go to the dataset and you will be directed to the World Bank Group Finances website. Once there, you can build your own views, share, embed, and download the data or your work. Read the instructions on how to build this chart from the raw data.

**The Project:** Improving the quality of education is a critical ingredient for human capital development, poverty alleviation and economic growth in Afghanistan. While major achievements have been made since 2002, enrolling more than seven million children in school, the challenges remain daunting. A massive skills deficit cuts across all institutions in Afghanistan, from principals to teachers, and from managers to skilled labor force needed for the bulk of the reconstruction work and its maintenance. Increasing conflict in the country undermines further education access, quality and institutional capacity.

The Second Education Quality Improvement Program (EQUIP II) is a follow-on program to the Education Quality Improvement Program (EQUIP I). The Program is fully aligned with the Afghanistan National Education Strategic Plan and supports the institutional development of the program staff of the Ministry of Education.

EQUIP II is seeking to: (i) increase access to schooling from Grades 1-12; (ii) strengthen the management capacity of communities to better manage teaching-learning activities; (iii) promote institutionalized district based teacher training activities nationwide; and, (iv) prioritize education for girls through a household scholarship scheme and the provision of high school teachers in underserved schools. Institutionally, EQUIP II is consolidating the following implementation systems: (i) the community and school-based management education system; (ii) the supervision and monitoring systems through the Provincial and District Education Departments teams; and (iii) the systems, procedures and skills within key departments of the MOE to continue to guide education services in a systematic and result-oriented approach.

## EXPECTED RESULTS

- Increase in girls enrollment;
- Increase in boys enrollment;
- Number of additional qualified primary teachers resulting from project interventions;
- Number of additional classrooms built or rehabilitated at the primary level resulting from project interventions;
- System for learning assessment at the primary level.

Project Title:

**NATEJA**

Grant Amount:

$ 15 MILLION

Approval Date:

February 20, 2014

Closing Date:

December 30, 2018

**Project Objective:**

The Project Development Objective is to increase the potential for employment and higher earnings of targeted young Afghan women and men in rural and semi-urban areas through non-formal skills training.

### PROGRAM SUMMARY

The project is based on the lessons learnt during the implementation of the ongoing ASDP and is composed of the following components: i) improving the Quality of Non-formal Training and the Labor Market Outcomes of Trainees to incentivize non-formal training providers to provide quality training and increase their job placement rates; ii) Project Management, Capacity Building of MOLSAMD and M&E; and iii) Piloting Entrepreneurship among Unskilled and Illiterate young Afghans to promote entrepreneurship among them to help improve their welfare status.

### EXPECTED RESULTS:

1. Share of trainees who find employment within 6 months of graduation, with respect to control groups.
2. US$ 4 million in incentives disbursed to training providers.
3. 445,000 training providers, trainees, graduates, saving group members and recipient of competitive grants benefit from the project. Of these, 30% are women.
4. Increase in trainees' earnings, with respect to control groups.

Project Title:

### HIGHER EDUCATION DEVELOPMENT PROJECT

Grant Amount:

$50 Million

Approval Date:

July 7, 2015

Closing Date:

December 31, 2020

**Project Objective:**

The Project development objective is to increase access to, and improve the quality and relevance of, higher education in Afghanistan.

**PROGRAM SUMMARY**

The Project: An estimated 500,000 higher education students, and 10,000 university academics, managers and technical staff members will benefit from the HEDP over its life-span. As the universities are directly contributing to economic base of Afghanistan, the project will have a positive impact on economic development in the country.

The HEDP is organized under two components. Component one is the Higher Education Development Program and will support five key themes; Increasing Access to Priority Degree Programs for Economic Development, Modernizing and Enhancing the Quality of Teaching and Learning, Improving the Qualifications and Skills of University Staff Members, Strengthening Governance, Quality Assurance and Accreditation and Stimulating Development Oriented Research. Component two is the Program Operations and Technical Support which aims to strengthen the capacity of MoHE and universities to implement the reforms. Support under this component will cover coordination, capacity building, innovations, monitoring and evaluation, research and communication.

**Expected Results:**

· Increased student enrollment in universities in priority degree programs for economic development.

· Expanded number of universities implementing and monitoring strategic institutional development plans consistent with the National Higher Education Plan.

· Increased number of full-time academic staff members with at least a Master's degree in priority degree programs for economic development.

# PUBLIC SECTOR CAPACITY/GOVERNANCE

The importance of institution building to the long-term sustainable development of Afghanistan is immense. The ARTF is providing support for critical areas for key institutions that will, ultimately, provide legitimacy to the State at both central and local levels. The ARTF in particular focuses on the civil service in key development ministries. The rules for civil service have been created and modest capacity has been injected through prior programs. The next phase will focus on deepening of capacity and creation of platforms for larger scale interventions that can be sustained over a longer time frame. The ARTF is supporting a second phase of the successful Public Financial Management Reform Project (PFMRP II). The goal of this 3-year project is to continue to build robust public financial management in central control agencies (Ministry of Finance, Control and Audit Office) and extend support to executing agencies both in Kabul and provinces. The ARTF is also providing financing for the justice sector through the Justice Service Delivery Project II and the new Capacity Building for Results focusing on a comprehensive, incentive-based approach to capacity building of the public sector. The ARTF thereby supports a strategic approach of working within, rather than outside government systems. This is the only way to build capacity within Government.

Project Title:

**CAPACITY BUILDING FOR RESULTS FACILITY**

Grant Amount:

$100 million

Approval Date:

December 31, 2011

Closing Date:

December 31, 2017

**Project Objective:**

The development objective of the Capacity Building for Results Facility project is to assist the Government in improving the capacity and performance of select line ministries in carrying out their mandates and delivering services to the Afghan people. This is achieved through the implementation of specific capacity and institution building programs, which include systematic monitoring of and reporting on results.

## PROGRAM SUMMARY

**The Project:** The Government faces significant challenges in managing these reform processes as transition moves forward. Enhancing capacity of the core civil service, with an emphasis on strengthening budget execution and service delivery, is critical to mitigate the substantial fiscal challenges that will unfold during transition. As donors begin to reduce their funds for technical assistance and project support, the Government will face an increasing responsibility for delivery of services in the context of a shrinking envelope of support. Government must have the skilled staff at the central and sub-national levels to be able to absorb and manage increasing amounts of donor funding provided through the Afghan budget. The task of building more sustainable, strategic and longer term capacity is therefore more urgent than ever.

The 5-year CBR project supports the Government's effort to significantly increase the capacity of ministries to delivery essential services and implement national priority programs. CBR and its components are structured as a facility that allows for adaptation based upon experience in the initial years. The Facility is operated on a demand-driven approach with each participating line ministry demonstrating its ownership and commitment through formulation of a prioritized capacity building program to execute its mandates with concrete and monitorable results. All ministries are supported to complete essential reforms, such as the implementation of pay and grading. More extensive support will be contingent upon the ministry fulfilling certain criteria, such as having completed basic public administration reforms, and having an approved strategic plan. This is to set a ministry on a reform path that helps it function more effectively.

## EXPECTED RESULTS

- Development budget execution rate improvements,
- Business process improvements;
- Service delivery improvements, in participating line ministries.

Project Title:

## SECOND PUBLIC FINANCIAL MANAGEMENT REFORM PROJECT

Grant Amount:

$114.125 million

Approval Date:

June 29, 2011

Closing Date:

June 30, 2017

**Project Objective:**

The Project's development objective is to strengthen public financial management through effective procurement, treasury and audit structures and systems in line with sound financial management standards of monitoring, reporting and control.

### PROGRAM SUMMARY

**The Project:** The Second Public Financial Management Reform Project (PFMRII) constitutes a second phase of support for public financial management (PFM) and builds on the outcomes of a series of IDA operations and bilateral donor technical assistance projects that have assisted the Government of Afghanistan (GOA) in establishing the legal framework for PFM and put in place the capacity at the central government level to operate PFM systems and processes for budget planning, execution and monitoring. PFMR II is entirely financed with ARTF donor financing. The objective of the new program is to strengthen public financial management in line with sound financial management standards of monitoring, reporting and control.

PFMR II is specifically designed around the new PFM Roadmap and National Priority Program. Like the first program, it continues to focus on three core areas: treasury, procurement and audit. In addition, it looks to establish the basis for an accounting profession in Afghanistan. While the project continues to support good public financial management performance developed in central control entities under the first program, support is during the second phase being extended to line ministries both at the central and the provincial levels to improve their financial management capacity.

### EXPECTED RESULTS

- Donors shift 20 % of their off-budget official development assistance to Afghanistan to on-budget;
- PEFA ratings for internal audit (P-21) improve to B;
- PEFA ratings for internal audit (P-26) improve to B;
- At least 50 % of procurement under the budget is done by line ministries;
- Conducting stand-alone procurement;
- Increased number of functions carried out by regular ministry staff that were previously carried out by contracted staff.

Project Title:

**JUSTICE SERVICES DELIVERY PROJECT II**

Grant Amount:

$40 million

Approval Date:

May 19, 2012

Closing Date:

June 1, 2017

**Project Objective:**

The development objective of the project is to increase the access to and use of legal services. The project seeks to help implement the Government's National Priority Program, mitigate the impact of the Transition, put the system on a sustainable path for long term results and improve service delivery. It will focus on achieving this through improvements to the scope and quality of legal services and to the productivity and accountability of legal service providers.

**PROGRAM SUMMARY**

<a data-cke-saved-href="https://finances.worldbank.org/Trust-Funds/ARTF-Afghanistan-Justice-Service-Delivery-Project-/hwh4-us99" href="https://finances.worldbank.org/Trust-Funds/ARTF-Afghanistan-Justice-Service-Delivery-Project-/hwh4-us99" title="ARTF Afghanistan Justice Service Delivery Project - Allocations & Disbursements" target="_blank">ARTF Afghanistan Justice Service Delivery Project - Allocations & Disbursements</a>

The chart above represents total allocations and disbursements during the lifetime of the project. To see the raw data behind this chart, go to the dataset and you will be directed to the World Bank Group Finances website. Once there, you can build your own views, share, embed, and download the data or your work. Read the instructions on how to build this chart from the raw data.

**The Project:** The Justice Service Delivery Project (JSDP) II is an $85.5 million, 5-year investment operation funded by the ARTF. JSDP will assist the Government in the implementation of the National Priority Program (NPP) in the justice sector, the 'National Program for Law and Justice for All'. The project supports the Supreme Court, the Ministry of Justice and the Attorney General's Office in balancing the demand for and supply of core legal services, and in increasing the productivity of legal service providers. The project aims to encourage specialization and close collaboration between various service providers; to align the structures, processes and capacity of justice institutions to the needs of users; and to improve access to legal information for legal professionals, justice institutions and the public. The project builds on and expands reforms which were supported by the $27.75 million, Phase I Justice Sector Reform Project which closed on December 31, 2011.

The current JSDP seeks to mitigate the impact of the Transition, put the justice system on a sustainable path for long term results, and improve service delivery. The project consists of four interrelated components: (a) Partnership for Justice; (b) Legal Empowerment; (c) Organization and Capacity of Justice Institutions; and (d) Implementation Capacity.

# PRINCIPAL SECTORS FOR DEVELOPMENT AND BUSINESS OPPORTUNITIES

Afghanistan needs a new source of growth as the country seeks to develop with a rapidly growing workforce and declining aid.

A Resource Corridor is a means to develop infrastructure and services around the area of a large mine or oilfield while using these for other economic activities that will promote growth. Its growth approach seeks to make mining and gas/oilfield activities more socially inclusive.

Afghanistan's resource base is large and uniquely undeveloped. The huge untapped mineral resources of copper in Aynak, iron ore in Hajigak, oil & gas deposits in Amu Darya are examples of the potential to drive growth and create jobs in the long term while producing viable economic development and diversification.

As part of the Afghanistan Reconstruction Trust Fund actions, The World Bank and Australian Aid commissioned a series of reports to understand the many options and features of each intervening sector in the Resource Corridor. The Resource Corridor Strategy is the outcome of their research.

The pages following the Strategy will lead you through the background documents covering the sectors involved for the mining and gas/oil field industries development. These pages will be released in the weeks to come.

### MINING AND WATER SECTORS

One of the main industries around which the Resource Corridor notion revolves is mining. Aynak copper mine involves the development not only of the mine itself but also an ore processing plant.

According to the most recent available information, Aynak would have a capacity of 30 ktpd of ore for phase I and 60 ktpd in phase II1.

The main natural resource inputs in the copper extraction process are water and energy.

Based on benchmark parameters, it is estimated that Aynak will require fresh water consumption at 225 l/s for phase I and 723 for phase II. In terms of power, the project would demand 52MW during phase I and an approximate 145MW during phase II2 .

The Kabul river basin serves the needs of Kabul city, its surrounding agricultural areas and Aynak mine.

The key challenge facing the basin is that although recycling process water can minimize water consumption at the mine, the aquifer under Kabul itself cannot supply the city's needs. The upper and middle Logar aquifers might be sufficient to supply the city, irrigate the area, and satisfy Aynak, if security stabilizes, allowing access to them.

However, under extreme scenarios of Kabul's growth or of low or inaccessible supply from the aquifers water will not be sufficient. The win- win solution to mitigate this risk lies at the construction of a dam in the river basin, if dam is cross-subsidized by Aynak's tariffed use of water from its aquifer.

The approach of the project design values a criterion of flexibility as risk and uncertainty conditions are deeply present.

1For the moment these figures provide the soundest basis for estimating the mine's input requirements. . A bankable feasibility study as well as contract changes have to confirm them.

## POWER AND GAS SECTORS

Significant coal and gas reserves and hydropower potential make domestic electricity generation possible. The large power generation projects needed for mining purposes can be readily sized to meet demands for other industrial, commercial and household use. Such an approach also brings also an opportunity to utilize and extend the transmission system to provide alternative routings of power across the Hindu Kush and to form the basis for a 220 kV ring around Kabul.

While coal fired power generation will increase carbon emissions, greenhouse gas (GHG) emissions per capita or per $ of GDP will remain among the world´s lowest. Efficiency can be incentivized by a normative heat rate requirement. In addition, offsetting improvements in GHG emissions can be achieved by reducing technical losses in Transmission & Distribution (T&D) with greater benefits for the system as a whole.

The gas report assesses the potential for gas-fired power that might result from future hydrocarbon development in the Amu Darya and Afghan-Tajik basins located in Northern Afghanistan.

If discoveries are made at the oil-prone prospects of the Afghan-Tajik basin, they would produce associated rich gas that could be processed to strip out propane and butane. The Amu Darya basin has also deep gas deposits, possibly dry gas mostly, therefore increasing the potential for power generation capacity substantially.

Nonetheless, substantial additional work is needed to confirm the size of the reserves that could be used for gas-fired power generation to meet demands of not only Northern Afghanistan but also other parts of the country. Other uses also need to be considered, while larger reserves offer the potential for export.

The lack of infrastructure and absence of gas pricing mechanisms might reduce the incentives for the International Oil Companies to explore and produce.

## RAILWAYS

Many schemes for railway lines in Afghanistan have been conceived and proposed. It is unlikely that most of them could be constructed. Many, even if constructible, may not be financially viable. Their construction would create a drain on the Afghan national economy as the economic development generated would not be sufficient to cover the cost to the debt necessary to build, operate and maintain the lines.

A few railway lines are feasible along the northern border. These lines extend from Kunduz in the east to the Iranian border between Herat and Khaf and are extensions of other regional rail networks.

For any and all lines built or proposed, the most pressing rail need for Afghanistan's development of resource corridors is the commercialization of any railway and the provision of terminals and other facilities for local distribution of wagonloads to industries and for transshipment between roads and rail.

Another pressing need is for the development of rail expertise and a regulatory authority that can oversee safety and interoperability and ensure access to infrastructure.

A review of the proposal for the copper mines at Aynak strongly suggests that constructing a new major railway is not necessary for the operation of the mine. Copper products could be moved by road transport.

Analysis of the proposals for the iron ore mines and possible metallurgical works near Hajigak shows that the maximum projected output of the mines would exceed the current capacity of connecting Iranian or Pakistani networks without a major upgrading. Exploiting the mines and any steelworks at the scales described for full production requires the eventual construction of an entirely new medium-to-heavy duty railway through Afghanistan plus substantial upgrading of existing lines or, more likely, a new rail line to ports in Iran or Pakistan. Consideration of this railway must await geo-political developments.

It is possible that not all of Hajigak's output would need to move across a single route. It is more likely that it would start low and rise over time. The recently announced phasing of the Hajigak proposal, with initial output for a 1-2 million tpa steel mill, would likely require only a rail link to coking coal fields at Dar-i-Suf and then the mill, whose most likely markets would be the Central Asian economies to the north.

Because no subsidy mechanism has been identified to fund the inevitable major losses that light-density passenger services create, no investment or provision for this service should be contemplated at this time.

Instead investments in basic highways and roads appear to make more sense for local and regional corridor development. Indeed, transport investment should focus first on all-weather, high axle-load highways instead.

## ROADS

All weather, serviceable roads provide the greatest short- and medium-term potential for broader development among the Resource Corridor investments, given their easier access and connection to rural areas. They are essential in the operation of mining centers, servicing of electricity grids and transportation of mining products.

Since 2002 there have been substantial investments in the road network in Afghanistan. Several key segments of the Resource Corridor have newly built roads, and others have some new roads but missing links.

Maintenance though has lagged, and is critical. Investment in the development and rehabilitation of roads can be futile in the absence of effective maintenance mechanisms supported by appropriate institutional and legislative structures. A positive development has been the agreement of the ARTF Operation & Maintenance (O&M) funding window and another has been the approval by Government of a fuel levy to provide further maintenance funds. However institutional and procedural reforms should be put in place in order to build on the gains made hitherto.

The Resource Corridor initiative calls for a substantial and accelerated reform plan to enable maintenance of critical road links. A practical approach could begin by contracting out O&M, gradually reducing reliance on force account maintenance, while developing the domestic road construction industry.

The Salang Pass is one of the most crucial road assets and segments in the country. Its development, rehabilitation and serviceability are pivotal to maintaining connectivity between the north and the south. It currently faces challenges related to reparation works done as well as level of service and safety (ventilation-lighting and power generation) at the operation of the tunnel.

A feasibility study for new tunnel and road sections was completed during 2012, and a World Bank project to finance a bypass road from Doshi to Bamyan is about to start its preparation. Other development partners are also funding the short- and medium-term rehabilitation of the Salang tunnel.

The northern corridor will facilitate transportation of oil and gas products from Amu Darya as well as future connections to the Afghan-Tajik oil and gas basin and their respective oil and gas facilities. Maintenance of the newly-built A76 will be critical, particularly as oil trucks begin to travel down it in increasing numbers.

Copper deposits in Aynak, North Aynak and Zarkashan require the roads serving these areas are rehabilitated and a well maintained. The most critical need is to accelerate the rehabilitation and upgrade of the Jalalabad-Torkham road and to complete the construction of selected provincial and rural roads in the copper areas of the South.

**PRIVATE SECTOR DEVELOPMENT**

The Private Sector Development reports look at the Aynak and Amu Darya projects as opportunities to trigger the development of the Afghan private sector, especially the construction and civil works sectors.

With a focused and early program of capacity building, domestic Afghan firms could reach quality levels sufficient to supply around $800 million priority goods and services needed to construct the Aynak copper mine and the Amu Darya oil blocks. These local firms could also provide about $151 million worth of operational goods and services representing about 22 percent of the total expenditures.

Many local companies are keen to work in mining and oil and gas, but need better access to information and business connections so they can more strategically invest in the capabilities needed to reach sufficient quality levels.

Local procurement faces challenges of a) quality and availability of goods and services; b) insufficient information leading to uncertainty to assess revenues/ borrow at equity stakes; c) poor information flows to the private sector regarding available services; d) potential political and economic risks given the upcoming 2014 withdrawal of foreign forces and uncertainty about the timing of extractive industry investments.

The suggested support program would focus on local businesses that are already viable, established and have strong management. It would require active participation from multilateral and bilateral donors, the Aynak and Amu Darya investors, the Ministry of Mines, the Afghanistan Chamber of Commerce and Industries (ACCI) and other associations, investors and local businesses.

The proposal is to create enterprise centers that provide multiple services to local businesses in order to address some of these issues. The governing and coordination body would collect all procurement needs from private sector investors and distribute the information to suppliers through the development of a traditional and virtual marketplace.

These offices would also link local businesses and potential investors through conferences and communication campaigns as well as manage the capacity and skills development program provided by technical mentors from extractive industry investors, business mentors and independent bodies.

In addition, it would help integrate investment plans to upgrade local supply into work plans designed for companies meeting thresholds of capability to upgrade quality. The combination of mentorship and investment from funds, grants or private equity partners would result in an improvement of local production through increased capacity and better quality.

The program would be monitored and evaluated rigorously to assess effectiveness.

## SKILLS

The development of skills related to the mining, oil and gas sectors in Afghanistan is critical as the extractive industry is expected to be – along with agriculture- one of the two principal drivers of growth for the Afghan economy.

More than 16,000 jobs can be directly generated by the 10 biggest extractive projects currently envisioned by the Ministry of Mines. A wide range of skillsets will be needed, from top management to basic mining operations.

To ensure Afghans can seize these upcoming employment opportunities, actions are required to increase the quality and quantity of available professional qualifications.

Unskilled and semi-skilled positions will account for 70% of the employment estimates. High-end jobs, specialized in geology, resource management, and petroleum engineering represent only 10-15% of skills needed.

While most major donors have a program in place to address skills development through their education or workforce initiatives, no existing programs are specifically focus on skills related to the extractive industries.

In particular, it will be crucial to support domestic job seekers to access jobs in the extractive sector by improving the quality of relevant programs in educational facilities and encouraging engagement between job seekers and employers. To do this, a dedicated team in charge of the Skills Strategy Development (SSD) component of ARTF will serve as a liaison between donors/partners, the extractive companies, and recipients of assistance (Universities and Technical and Vocational Education and Training (TVET) institutions).

The biggest areas of intervention of the SSD are work placement and practical training. A key success factor in this respect is private sector participation especially information sharing with educational institutions as well as involvement in internship programs for prospective employees. As the Amu Darya project has already begun, immediate interventions are needed in order to ensure that locals can seize employment opportunities.

To cope with this requirement, the program design is divided into two phases: first, a pilot program focused on short-term interventions, leaving time for the project team to promote awareness of the skills strategy development program to Ministries and donors. Second, the launch of a broader skills development program will focus on a broader number of upcoming extractive investments.

## COMMUNITY BENEFITS

Mine development and other extractive projects create substantial economic, social and environmental changes that need to be carefully managed.

Involving affected communities in regions surrounding extractive sites and associated transportation corridors during the development process can help ensure that mining ventures are successful while also promoting sustainable benefits to communities.

The community benefits policy note prepared for the Afghanistan Resource Corridor Project (ARCP) offers the rationale for a benefits sharing framework, which aims to ameliorate negative impacts while capturing as many benefits as possible, especially at the local level.

If benefits are not captured at the local level they are lost or forfeited and many disadvantaged people are likely to be worse off.

The note also outlines a methodology for developing and implementing Community Development Agreements (CDAs), which is one way to promote community benefits sharing by anticipating and managing potential disparities that may emerge within affected communities such as inequalities in wealth, access to benefits, skills and education.

Community Development Agreements acknowledge the value of a community and its organizations as stakeholders in the communication and negotiation processes involved in extractive projects.

As such, CDAs support grievance and dispute resolution mechanisms, regular and transparent communication, strong relationships amongst all stakeholders and effective monitoring and governance of agreements.

Each of these key aspects is developed in detail in the policy note.

## STEEL MILL

The availability of low-cost iron ore and potential coking coal deposits, coupled with local and regional demand for steel and its by-products, may make Afghanistan an attractive location for an integrated steel mill. The current state of infrastructure, on the other hand, is a significant constraint.

The steel report examines the viability of the AFISCO consortium's initial commitment to build a steel mill with an annual capacity of 7 million tons in Afghanistan.

The consortium has been awarded three of the four blocks of the Hajigak iron ore deposit, and its steel mill proposal assumes that proximate coking coal deposits can be used.

The demand estimations for potential sales for an Afghan mill are projected at approximately 2 million tons by 2025, including sales into Central Asia. A mill with a capacity of 7 million ton is unlikely to be viable, except in the very long-term and with infrastructure available to export beyond Central Asia.

In regards of the immediate target markets the prime market for Afghan steel will be regional (Afghanistan, Uzbekistan, Tajikistan, Kyrgyzstan, Turkmenistan, and possibly Northern Pakistan).

China as a market is not suitable for Afghan steel. Although the country overwhelmingly dominates both production and consumption of steel in the region, it is expected to remain self-sufficient in steel.

India, on the other hand, is likely to remain a net steel importer over the medium term, but potential for self-sufficiency and current infrastructure constraints largely rule it out as a market for Afghan steel.

Since over-sized steel mills are highly liable to failure, and the most realistic market demand is for approximately 2 million tons, a phased investment is advisable.

Besides iron and steel, the mill would generate byproducts such as gas, tar, and slag, for which local markets are likely.

## LAND

ARAZI, the newly independent land authority, was created in 2009 by consolidating several government units to address the vast challenges of land administration and management.

ARAZI is responsible for land management in the fields of tenure clarification, resolving land disputes, leasing and transfer of land, recording and surveying of land, and other land issues.

Although reforms have been instituted to improve capacity, comprehensive dissemination, strengthening of, and delegation to regional offices, necessary and significant challenges remain for this to be successful.

One of the immediate challenges ARAZI faces is the need to increase its human and institutional capacity.

The recently developed land strategy document provides a series of recommendations for the political, legal, organizational, financial, operational, monitoring and evaluation, cadaster and dispute resolution issues.

The current governance framework will provide ARAZI with the organizational and operational means to provide its services in an open and transparent manner.

With respect to specific land services demands, the majority is expected to be generated by the major national infrastructure investments, which are being prepared (but not implemented) under the National and Regional Resource Corridors Program (NRRCP).

As part of the preparatory process, along with feasibility studies and Environmental and Social Impact Assessments, ARAZI will conduct cadaster surveys and land clearance as preconditions for sector ministry land acquisition as part of investment operations subsequent to the NRRCP.

ARAZI's functions regarding land management also includes the identification of state land to lease to private investors, which will also be a key activity under the NRRCP Secretariat.

## AFGHANISTAN AGRICULTURE SECTOR

Investing in agriculture in Afghanistan is critical as the sector accounts for a quarter of the national economy, and plays an important role in the livelihoods of the approximately 76% of the population and nearly 90% of the poor living in rural areas. The World Bank carried out an Agricultural Sector Review in 2014.

The Review proposes a strategy to serve as an initial phase in the national agricultural strategy, providing an early boost to productivity growth, employment, and poverty reduction.

The review takes into account the diversity of Afghan Agriculture and proposes a two-pillar strategy to achieve developmental goals in this context:

Pillar I: Prioritized Value Chains: Irrigated wheat and horticulture, and intensive livestock are the value chains that provide the most promising opportunities. Currently, these three sub-sectors account for 66% of agricultural GDP. With the right mix of policies and strategic investments, the three subsectors could double the value of agricultural production and add 1.3 million jobs in 10 years.

Pillar II: Addressing the Needs of the Rural Poor: The prospect for significant productivity gains in rain-fed and extensive farming systems is limited. Other complementary and non-farm interventions will also be required, especially for people with access to little land or livestock. These interventions include community development programs, relief programs, education and training, settlement programs, and social protection programs.

# TRAVEL TO AFGANISTAN

## US STATE DEPARTMENT SUGGESTIONS

**TRAVEL WARNING:** The Department of State warns U.S. citizens against travel to Afghanistan. We continue to receive threats from terrorists, including Usama Bin Laden, who is based in Afghanistan, that do not distinguish between American military and civilian targets. U.S. citizens who are in Afghanistan or considering traveling there should be aware that the U.S. Government reserves the right to retaliate against the facilities of those who harbor terrorists, as well as the terrorists themselves.

The Department of State urges Americans who decide to remain in Afghanistan in spite of this warning to exercise extreme caution, monitor their security situation closely and make plans for responding to a sudden deterioration in security conditions. All U.S. personnel at the U.S. Embassy in Kabul were evacuated in 1989, and no other diplomatic mission represents U.S. interests or provides consular services.

President Clinton signed an Executive Order effective July 6, 1999, imposing financial and commercial sanctions against the Taliban in Afghanistan, a faction that currently exercises de facto control over much of the country, for their support of Usama bin Ladin and his terrorist network.

In addition, frequent military operations continue in various regions of Afghanistan, sometimes involving intense fighting. Americans remain vulnerable to politically and criminally motivated attacks and violence, including robbery, kidnapping and hostage-taking. The estimated 5-7 million landmines scattered throughout the countryside pose a danger to all residents and visitors to Afghanistan.

U.S. citizens who decide to enter Afghanistan in spite of the Travel Warning are strongly urged to register and obtain updated security information at the American Embassy in Islamabad, Pakistan, or the U.S. Consulate in Peshawar, Pakistan, at the following addresses:

U.S. Embassy, Diplomatic Enclave, Ramna 5, Islamabad, telephone (92-51) 2080-0000, consular section (92-51) 2080-2700, fax (92-51) 822-632

U.S. Consulate Peshawar, 11 Hospital Road, Peshawar Cantonment, telephone (92-91) 279-801, fax (92-91) 276-712

## TRAVELLING TO AFGHANISTAN

Flight Operations UNOCHA/UNDP Islamabad
Tel: +92 (51) 211451-5
Fax: +92 (51) 211450
E-mail: unocha@undpafg.org.pk

Boy, if you hate crowded hiking trails and booked hotels, have we got a place for you. Although the U.S. State department says don't go, the Talibs say don't go and the north says don't go, Afghanistan is number one with a bullet for people who want to visit dangerous places. There is no U.S. embassy at the moment (hell, there's no anything at the moment), The NGOs keep their bags packed and no one quite knows who's in charge at any one time. The Talibs are here to stay, but that doesn't mean there is an long-term sense or logic regarding their entry policy for foreigners.

Journos and scribes are officially welcomed by the Taliban and then never given visas to enter. The Red Cross needs Talib approval for all journos before you can book a flight. Same goes for the UN. There are a number of restrictions, advance notice and permission requirements so contact:

Once inside journos have to comply with a two page list of do's and don'ts, which oddly enough includes having your picture taken in a place where taking pictures of living things is forbidden. Being beaten every time you whip out a camera does put a damper on bringing in a Betacam crew. If you are sponsored by an NGO you must only cover the activities of that group. If you somehow get it just to look around, you must stay at the Intercontinental, hire a guide and a driver who maintains his lonely vigil in the lobby. Figure on doubling the rate when you go to the front lines. Strangely, if you are not a journalist there are no laws to restrict your movement. And techncially, once outside Kabul you are free to do what you like (other than photograph people or, as a male, interview women). In the north, you must register in Mazar and stay at the UN guesthouse, whereas journos are forbidden from staying with the UN in Kabul. You will find the Taliban both pleasurable, exasperating and sometimes brutal, depending on circumstances.

DP called the embassy to get the latest travel stats. Apparently, Afghanistan is where all the journos were headed to earn their spurs. When asked who is going to Afghanistan, our contact replied, "Lots of journalists." The embassy needs $60, a couple of photos and a letter from your company saying why you want to be Afghanistan bound. If you enter from Peshawar, don't forget you need to arrange a double or multiple entry visa, a Khyber Pass permit and a gunman from the Khyber Tribal Agency office in Peshawar to get to Torkham. For some odd reason going back doesn't require this. You also need an exit visa (which can eat up half a day) if you leave from Kabul.

Pleasure tourists may find their visa request turned down unless they are truly persuasive. or bum a ride with an NGO car. The border crossings are as mercurial as they are dangerous. DP narrowly missed being caught up in a shootout at Torkham between slack-jawed Talib boy-guards and veddy British and veddy nervous Pakistani border guards. After the Talibs rocketed the top of the Pakistani post and shot through a demining vehicle, calm was restored and the Talibs went back to whipping urchins with their steel cables.

The Taliban-friendly U.S. embassy (locked in their usual time warp) told us that Massoud was getting support from "Russia and the Soviet Union" and when pressed for advice on how to stay safe, they came up with "Don't steal anything." Any other advice? "Well, you might have to grow a beard, or if you are a woman you might have to wear the chador, well no, now that I think of it, I guess Diane Sawyer didn't have to." We assume he meant the chador not the beard.

The London Afghan Embassy is run by Massoud's brother Wali. He can get you a journo visa for the north but can't do much about arranging a flight in. Tajikistan and Pakistan are your only safe bets for getting into the north. But just getting into and out of Tajikistan is its own nightmare (see the "Tajikistan" chapter).

All border crossings except Termez in Uzbekistan are technically open, but the embassy recommends that travelers use the crossings from Pakistan, Iran and Tajikistan only. The best way into the north and the south is from Pakistan. The intrepid can stroll into Afghanistan over the many mountain trails that connect the two countries in the north and along the Khyber Pass. Since these are usually drug smuggling routes, all travelers will be suspect. A few years ago the DEA (via the Pakistani antidrug agency) was actually offering tribesmen a bounty on any gringos caught buying drugs, so shop for souvenirs with caution.

Afghans are quite hospitable and will offer food and whatever lodging they have. You are expected to reciprocate with some type of gift or remembrance. Photos of your family are great icebreakers and gifts like flashlights, medicine or even clothes are received well. Make sure you pick the right guide, one on good terms with the tribes who control the regions you will be passing through. You will probably be the only tourist in Afghanistan. Camels can be rented to carry heavy gear for US$10 dollars a day, and guides go for about US$20 a day, plus baksheesh (a tip). Travelers would be ill-advised to go gem hunting or arms collecting in the hills at this time due to the prevalence of land mines-still the number-one killer and maimer of humans and other living things-and the propensity of Afghans to kidnap foreigners for a few quick dollars.

Most of the country is in the hands of the Taliban, who also control the entry and movement of all outsiders.The northwest is in the hands of the Tajiks and the Wahkan corridor is a no-man's-land under any condition due to the mountainous terrain and drug smuggling. Those who want to meet the Taliban can also contact them in Pakistan.

## DANGER OF KIDNEPPING FOR FOREIGNERS

Traditionally and historically the Afghans are among the most hospitable people in the world. Today their “hospitality” can go extreme. Foreigners can be just kidnapped. Kidnapping is actually a tribal tradition that goes back before recorded time. Recently, kidnapping has been a means to bring attention to tribal disputes or grievances. Locals, expats and tourists are routinely kidnapped in Afghanistan and near the border with Pakistan. Ransoms run from US$2,000 up to US$50,000 and more for foreign workers.

The positive side to this is that if you're traveling under the protection of one tribe and are kidnapped by another, your host tribe has an obligation to free you. The people in the greatest danger are foreign workers who travel in a predetermined route or stay in a fixed place.
http://travel.state.gov/afghanistan_warning.html
Any foreigner is going to be considered a suspect spy and enemy.

## LAND MINES

The Russians buried and dropped about 12 million mines in the ground. Some say at the current removal rate it will take 20,000 years to remove all the mines. HALO figures that 640,000 mines have been laid since 1979. In 1998 they cleared 100,000 individual items of unexploded ordnance, or UXO. HALO has 1,300 Afghan deminers working under the supervision of only two expats clearing the towns and countryside. They are working feverishly to demine the 95 percent of the country under peace so that more than 3 million Afghans can return to their formerly mined villages. There are currently 300,000 Afghans waiting to rebuild or move back into their homes in Kabul.

Most deminers will tell you privately that the UN estimate is a little over the top but makes them look good when they do it faster. There are more than 50 different kinds of mines, and not just Russian made. There are RAP-2s from Zimbabwe, and even NR-127s made in Belgium. There are neat battery-powered multicensored mines that blow up when they feel vibration. According to the UN, 162 of AfghanistanOs 356 districts are affected by mines. The most dangerous areas for mines are Helmand with 5 major fields, Kandahar with 47, Paktia with 118, Logar with 53 and Herat with 86. The areas affected are grazing land, irrigation systems, agricultural land and cities. Both the Taliban (who promised me they didnOt and wouldnOt use mines back in the bad old days) and the northern alliance is busy putting new ones in as you read this.

The UN estimates it needs $185 million to carry out all its programs, including demining. Afghanistan currently has the worldOs largest demining program and in seven years has destroyed over 200,000 devices, but has cleared only 80 square kilometers. The most heavily mined areas are security zones around the major cities along the Iranian and Pakistani borders (Herat, Kandahar, Jalalabad and Khost). Follow the basic rules and you will survive: Do not wander off hard surface (even when taking a leak). Learn to squat at the edge of the road to urinate like the locals do. Do not travel in snow. Land mines were laid in strength along mountain passes and can be more sensitive with ice and snow cover. Do not turn over or pick up any items, do not inspect abandoned military vehicles, do not run up a hill to get a better vantage point . . . and the list goes on.

http://www.un.org/Depts/Landmine/program/Afghan/partners.htm

What were people in Afghanistan doing when they were killed or injured by a land mine.
Fetching water 20 percent
Traveling 15 percent
Fighting 13 percent
Playing with a mine 8 percent
Demining 4 percent

## EVERYDAY LIFE INFORMATION

Electricity (when you can find it) is 220v/50Hz. The official languages are Pashtu (mostly in the south and east) and Dari Persian (in the north and west). Many people speak English and some Russian. The money is the Afghani and the black market is the only real place you can exchange notes. Figure on a U.S. dollar getting you 44,360 afghanis. Be forewarned that there are two afghanis. One, called Dostum money, is used in the north and is one-tenth of the value of the Talib afghani used in the south. They look identical except for the spacing between the type on the front. The way to remember is the type of the northern or Dostum money is "allied" or together and the south is apart.

The money changers are fair since this is how all people change money. Try not to use U.S. $100 bills printed before 1993 since many money changers won't take them. When shops are open they start at 8 a.m. and close between noon and 1 p.m. and then reopen until 4:30 p.m. Some shops are closed Wednesday and Friday. Traffic drives on the right and the normally paved roads are full of potholes from shells and disrepair. Jalalabad is the main smuggling area for cars, electronic goods and drugs into Pakistan, so be judicious when asking questions or taking photographs.

Web Sites: http://www.agora.stm.it/politic/afghanistan.htm

Even though things are settling down, medical care is not Afghanistan's strong point. Health care is available in the major cities through aid groups. Many prescription drugs and antibiotics (not opiates) can be bought over the counter. They will be old and dusty and we do not recommend self-medication. A traveler with a serious condition should seek help in Pakistan or Iran. Better yet, take the next flight home or to London. Expect that the most basic medical care is limited or nonexistent with war wounded and children getting priority treatment. Malaria (primarily the benign vivax form) is present below 2,000 meters (6,562 feet) between May and November in the southern area and falciparcium strain occurs in the warmer south. Chloroquine-resistant falciparcium has been reported. Rabies, tick-borne relapsing fever and cutaneous leishmaniasis are present.

## THE TALIBAN EVERYDAY LIFE RULES

Men must grow beards
No 24-hour All Mullah, All the Time, Talibvision
No Afghan space program
No book reading
No coed cheerleading
No drinking
No flying kites
No foreigners with Afghan women
No movies
No music
No paper bag jokes
No paper bags
No photography
No recycling the Koran
No schooling for females
No sneaking Colt 45s in a bag
No soccer
No theater
No TV
No videos
No Internet
No white socks for females

In Taliban areas, soccer, volleyball and even chess have been banned because they cause youths to miss some of their five daily prayers. Women must wear the burqa, a kind of shmoo-sack slash veil that covers the entire body, and men must have long beards, something that shocks naive journos but is quite normal outside of Kabul. Western pleasures like trashy novels, MTV, movies, beer and Nintendo are all forbidden. The idea is to not divert people's minds from God and family. Come to think of it, these guys might be on to something. To contact the Taliban stateside get ahold of:

Mulawi Abdul Hakeem Mujahid or Noorullah Zadran
55/16 Main Street
Flushing, NY
Tel.: (718) 359-0457
News Hotline: (718) 762-8095
Fax: (718) 661-2721
Web site: www.taleban.com
E-mail: AMujahid@aol.com
Nonofficial site:
http://www.ummah.net/Taliban/

## GETTING OUT

The bus system still operates, taxis are cheap (DP paid $25 to go the 200 miles from Torkham to Kabul) and depending on how many crashes Ariana has there are airliners flying in and out of the southern cities. Last time we checked the one-way fare from Kabul to Dubai was $175. Ariana, which was once run by Pan Am, now has three Boeing 727s, three Antonov 24s and is buying a wide-bodied Boeing 747 from Kuwait Airlines. The airport at Kabul is blown to bits but open. Ariana flies a lot of unknown cargo to Dubai, so it's hard for foreigners to buy tickets. Most journos drive in or fly on the Peshawar-based Red Cross and Islamabad-based UN flights.

Ariana Airlines
3rd Floor, Dudley House,
169 Piccadilly
London W1V9DD, UK
Tel.:+44-171-4931411
Fax:+44-171-6291611
Web site: http://fly.to/ariana
E-mail: arianaaf@brain.net.pk

# DANGEROUS PLACES IN AFGHANISTAN

## DRUGS

Despite the don't askDdon't tell antidrug stance of the Taliban, Afghanistan is the major poppy growing nation in the world (after Myanmar) and a major transporter. The latest word on the street is that bin Laden is buying up raw opium and using it to fight a second front in his war against the West. About $350 of opium gum can be refined into herioin worth a street price of $70,000 in New York. Farmers in Helmand and Nangarhar provinces grow poppies, which are cut to ooze gum. The gum is gathered and send to the 60 or so labs in the southeast and east of Afghanistan. Wrapped tightly in plastic or in glass jars it is shipped to Pakistan across Iran or through Turkmenistan to Turkey or north to Tajikistan, where the Russian military expedites its shipment to Moscow.

Afghanistan is the largest grower of poppies (4,600 tonnes in 1999 compared to 1,300 tonnes from Myanmar) and the largest exporter of hashish in the world. Up to 14 metric tons of hashish have been seized by the border states of Uzbekistan, Turkmenistan, Kyrgystan, Tajikistan and Kazakhstan. Badakhshan borders Tajikistan, where Russia has deployed 25,000 troops to help fight antigovernment Islamic guerrillas believed to have bases in Afghanistan. Strangely, Osama's efforts to corner the market has pushed the price down to $37 a kilo (2.2 lbs.) from $60.

http://www.afghan-politics.org/Reference/Drugs/drugs_main.htm

## MILITARY TRAINING CAMPS

Afghanistan has always had training camps for mujahedin. We know this because the United States paid for them to be built and expanded back in the '80s. So it wasn't that hard to crulse missile them on August 20, 1998, and it wasn't that hard to rebuild them in Khost and outside Jalalabad, Kabul and Kunduz by December, five months later. Osama, the son of a Saudi construction maven from Yemen, just can't stop building. He has about 3,000 people on the payroll in Afghanistan and is building everything from mosques to government buildings. Tomahawk missiles also hit Jamiatul Mujahideen and Harkatul Ansar camps, both run by Pakistanis, almost 21 kilometers away from Osama's exclusively Arab camp in Khost. The Salman Farsi camp and the Badar 1 and Badar 2 are for the training of Arabs, while the Pakistani-run camps of Pakistani-based Harkatul Mujahideen (former Harakatul Ansar or HUA) and Harkatul Jihad Al-Islami. Osama is one of the benefactors of the Harkatul Mujahideen who teach volunteers from as far away as North America, the Phillipines, Bosnia and Algeria to fight low-intensity terrorist wars.

Missiles also hit the ten-year-old Jamiatul Mujahideen camp commanded by the Kashmiri Mufti Bashir. This camp was for training up to 250 volunteers from Kashmir and Pakistan to fight in Kashmir, a war the Pakistani ISI funds and provides training for.

### TRIBAL AREAS

The Khyber Pass is still controlled by tribal chiefs who make a living by shipping drugs, taking money from truck drivers and kidnapping people that visit this historic route. Robbery, shootouts, murder, extortion and/or kidnapping are an everyday occurrence for the unwary, and it has only been the lack of foreigners that have kept this region out of the headlines.

http://www.javed.com.pk/Peshawar.html

### OUTFEET

Females have become the latest pawns in the war in Afghanistan. Reacting to a report by DP's co-resident at the UNICA guesthouse Zohra Rasekh, the Physicians for Human Rights and other junket journos have declared war on the Afghan people. By focusing on the burqa as a symbol of evil (something Zohra, a woman, forgets to mention she didn't have to wear in Kabul), she has demonized Afghan culture and blamed it on the Taliban. Any visitor to the north will tell you that the burqa is a part of Afghan life except in once-cosmopolitan Kabul.

The report goes on to clinically document the lack of health care for women as if the author has comparable statistics from Afghan women in Rochester, Minnesota. "PHR explored the reasons for decreased access to health care services. Of the 40 women interviewed, 87% (33 of 38) reported a decrease in their access to health services. The reasons given included: no chaperone available (27%), restrictions on women's mobility (36%), hospital refused to provide care (21%), no female doctor available (48%), do not own a burqa (6%), and economics (61%)." Taken the other way DP finds it amazing that 52% of afghan women had access to any doctor male or female. Women and their rights are being used as a pawn in this war but the endgame is they have lost either way. The lack of aid because of the way their unelected government treats them and another generation lost to poverty and hopelessness.

http://www.rawa.org/

http://www.phrusa.org/campaigns/af_exec1.html

## WEAPONS IN AFGHANISTANS

Taday, Afghanistan has more guns per capita than anywhere else on earth. England allowed the Pathans to manufacture their own guns 200 years ago, and the CIA delivered enough weapons to keep the region swimming in weaponry for years to come. But this was all dwarfed by the stockpiles of weapons the Russians abandoned or lost in the ten years of warfare.

The Affridi tribe of Afghanistan and Pakistan still produce about 900 to 1,200 copies of modern weapons a day in its gun factories in Darra Adam Khel.

The best place to buy guns is actually just outside Afghanistan in Pakistan. Anyone can hire a gunman for about $20 a day, but if you want to shop for that special hard-to-please someone, take along an Afghan guide and go visit the Smugglers Bazaar (20 minutes east of Peshawar) in Darra (about 40 minutes south of Peshawar). Although Darra has been officially closed for two years to outsiders you can still buy a worn but serviceable AK-47 for $200. Pros know to buy the short Chinese-made assault versions, since their barrels don't heat up as much and they can be concealed under your shwaler qamiz. These go for about $375D$1,000 Chinese- and Russian-made pistols are between $10D$100, with the Pakistani-made knockoffs at the low end of the price spectrum.

Anyone can buy Chinese and Russian rocket launchers for just under a grand and rockets by the case for 400 rupees (US$125) each. Grenades are a bargain at US$3 each. Perfect for that kidnap scenario when you threaten to pull the pin. Other items for sales at bargain basement prices include land mines, antiaircraft guns, bazookas, Stalin OrganDstyle rocket launchers (the self-propelled kind) and even lovely used Russian T-55 tanks.

Wanna-bes who don't want to be arrested in Darra can head north of Peshawar to Sakahot and see guns being made from cheap pig iron. Lookee loos who appreciate the smell of cordite and the sound of tinnitus can arrange to fire automatic weapons in the nearby gorge. One banana clip of 30 bullets will set you back about ten bucks. Cheap, even by Coney Island standards. The hottest selling items are still the pen guns that fire a single bullet and can be used to write ransom notes. They are a measly six dollars. Naturally, you will need a complete Soviet eraDuniform, bayonets, combat gear, watches, boxes of uncirculated rubles (wrapped and still in serial number order) and medals to complete your Cold War GI Joe play kit.

## GETTING AROUND

Afghanistan is sort of an Adventureland notch for journos-a place where you can take a cab to the front lines and be home in time to shop for carpets on Chicken street. The Talibs view most journos with a jaundiced eye since the rash of gender junkets trashed their ideas on women's fashion and law and order.

Although they told me that DP was the first North American the Taliban had talked to long ago, I am sure the thrill has long worn off as everyone from National Geographic to Dateline does their prerequisite Afghan Taliban adventure story. Areas under Talib control are safe but expect major league hassles from Talibs who want to know what your business is. Try taking pictures of them and you may end up walking like a chicken. The north is still wild and wooly and the last time I tried to get around on a fuel convoy I was told that I might be stopped by brigands and "teased" like one of their drivers was a while back. I learned later that this is a polite way of saying sodomized. Soooeii.

The favored modes of travel are by minibus (cheap and available in all small towns), private car (not as available) and pack animals, which are slow and a great way to see what land mines can do. There is no law inside Afghanistan other than the Taliban's industrial-strength version of sharia, usually mixed in with a little local tribal law and whatever the local commander feels like doing with you that night. If he wants you to watch a Ned Beatty movie with him decline, politely. (no more Deliverance jokes from here on in.)

It is helpful if Westerners understand Afghan culture and have a basic understanding of the Pakhtun (Pathan) language. Most important is knowledge of the customs of Islam. Despite what you read in the press most Afghans (and not just the Taliban) are devout Muslims and adopt traditional dress and customs. Currently, there is little animosity toward Westerners, but you will be lectured continuously on Islam and considered an oddity for not embracing what is essentially the only religion in Afghanistan. Any major affront to Islam could result in severe punishment or a sound beating. Travel only with the permission of each local commander and be prepared to drink a lot of tea.

Abdul Hakeem Mujahid is your man if you want to get into Talib-held areas. The Taliban's ambassador in Pakistan now works out of a small office in a third-floor walkup in Queens, New York.

### EMBASSY LOCATIONS

Because there is no U.S. embassy in Afghanistan and no country represents U.S. interests here, the U.S. government is unable to provide normal protective services to U.S. citizens in Afghanistan (as if they would even if they had an embassy). The nearest U.S. embassies and consulates are in Pakistan and Tajikistan. The telephone number for the (very helpful if you want reasons to stay out of Afghanistan) but under siege U.S. embassy in Islamabad, Pakistan, is: [92] (51) 826-161/179. There is little they can do for you once you are in Afghanistan.

U.S. Consulate in Peshawar, Pakistan
Tel: [92] (521) 279-801/2/3
U.S. Embassy in Tashkent, Uzbekistan
Tel: (3712) 771-407/771-081
U.S. Embassy in Dushanbe, Tajikistan
Tel: (3772) 21-0356/-0360/-0457
U.S. Embassy in New Delhi, India
Tel: [91] (11) 600-651

## BUSINESS TRAVEL

### BUSINESS CUSTOMS

Business meetings are usually conducted in Dari, Pashto or English in the principal's office. Green or black tea, nuts and raisins are served to greet guests. The form of greeting is “Asalam Aleikum” (Peace be with you), followed by a firm handshake and then, for courtesy and to pay homage to the host (you don’t necessarily have to), briefly place your right hand over your heart. It is best to take a few minutes initially to engage in pleasantries about each other's country, rather than going straight to business. Afghan interlocutors may appear vague and non-committal during meetings. In order to build trust and "get to yes," be patient, share meals and other social events and discuss matters other than business. Capture the essence of your business meetings and agreements in a follow up letter to your Afghan interlocutor. Be clear about what you have committed yourself or your U.S. firm to do, or in many cases, have not committed to do. A promise to "look into" or "research" an issue, quote, or pricing policy may be interpreted as a firm commitment.

**DO'S and DON’TS in Afghan Culture**
Don't show impatience if your interlocutor isn’t giving you direct answers. Afghans like to elaborate and want to be clear in communicating.

Don't panic. Afghanistan’s government can be bureaucratic. It may take you several days to get a simple authorization signed. Keep in mind that Afghanistan’s government is undergoing a reform process.

Don't call an Afghan "Afghani." Afghani is the currency, Afghans are the people of Afghanistan.

Don't drink alcohol in front of an Afghan.

Do greet everyone when entering a room. Shake hands with the men, but not with a woman unless she extends her hand first.

Do eat with your right hand as much as possible.

Do dress modestly.

Do accept a chair if someone brings you one to sit on, even if you would rather stand. This is a sign of respect.

Do read about the country's history, culture, and people before you come, as this will be treated as a sign of respect for Afghanistan.

## TRAVEL ADVISORY

While the U.S. Embassy in Kabul encourages U.S. companies to review business opportunities in Afghanistan, it is important to keep in mind the volatile security situation in the country. Travelers should consult the State Department Travel web site http://travel.state.gov prior to any travel and review both the Consular Information Sheet and Travel Warning for Afghanistan. These documents can be found at: http://travel.state.gov/travel/cis_pa_tw/cis/cis_1765.html

## VISA REQUIREMENTS

A passport and valid visa are required to enter and exit Afghanistan. Afghan entry visas are not available at Kabul International Airport. American citizens who arrive without a visa are subject to confiscation of their passport and face heavy fines and difficulties in retrieving their passport and obtaining a visa, as well as possible deportation from the country. Americans arriving in the country via military air usually have considerable difficulties if they choose to depart Afghanistan on commercial air because their passports do not receive stamps showing they entered the country legally. Those coming on military air should move quickly after arrival to legalize their status if there is any chance they will end up departing on anything other than military air.

For the most updated requirements to obtain an Afghan visa, please contact the Embassy of Afghanistan located at 2341 Wyoming Ave., NW, Washington, DC 20008, phone 202-483-6410, fax 202-483-6488), http://www.embassyofafghanistan.org

U.S. companies that require travel of foreign businesspersons to the United States should know that it could take weeks or months for an Afghan citizen to receive a visa to visit the United States. The U.S. Embassy in Afghanistan currently does not process visas for Afghan citizens. Please see the U.S. Embassy website for information on how Afghan citizens may apply in Islamabad, Pakistan.

State Department Visa Website: http://travel.state.gov/visa/index.html

United States Visas.gov: http://www.unitedstatesvisas.gov

U.S. Embassy in Afghanistan: http://kabul.usembassy.gov

## TELECOMMUNICATIONS

Local telephone networks do not operate reliably. Most people rely on satellite or cellular telephone communications even to make local calls. Cellular phone service is available in Kabul with coverage extending to 23 provinces . Teledensity is 3.5 percent of the population. There are currently two wireless service providers : (i) Afghan Wireless Communications Company (AWCC) (44% market share), a joint venture between U.S.-based Telephone Systems International and the Afghan Ministry of Communications and (ii) Telephone Development Company Afghanistan (TDCA) (56% market share), operating under the brand name Roshan. TDCA is an international consortium led by the Aga Khan Fund for Economic Development. A third provider, Investcom, is scheduled to begin operations in 2006. The country has multiple internet service providers.

## TRANSPORTATION

Several commercial airlines serve Afghanistan at Kabul International Airport. Pakistan International Airlines has three weekly flights to and from Islamabad. Azerbaijan Airways has twice weekly flights to and from Baku. Indian Airlines flights three times a week to and from Delhi. Kam Air has flights daily to Dubai . The U.S. Embassy does not recommend use of Ariana Afghan Airlines to any destination or Kam Air flights to and from destinations other than Dubai because existing civil aviation regulations in Afghanistan do not meet international aviation standards. Please see the State Department's Consular Information Sheet at http://travel.state.gov/travel/cis_pa_tw/cis/cis_1056.html for more information.

Taxis around Kabul should range between Afs 50 to 100 ($1 or $2 depending on where you are going) per trip, but a dedicated car and driver is recommended. For travel within Kabul, a car and driver (no English) will run up to US$30 to $100 per day. Public buses are not recommended.

## LANGUAGE

Dari and Pashto are the official languages of the country. Few native Afghans speak English, but many returning expatriate Afghans speak English or German. Rates vary widely; a reliable interpreter fluent in English, Dari and Pashto may earn anything between $150 - $3,000 per month.

## HEALTH

The weather in Afghanistan is very dry, with summer highs into the 100s F and winter lows into the 20s F with snow. Kabul is very dusty, and shoes and clothes are difficult to maintain.

Well-equipped medical facilities are few and far between throughout Afghanistan. European and American medicines are available in limited quantities and may be expensive or difficult to locate. There is a shortage of standard medical supplies. Basic medicines manufactured in Iran, Pakistan, and India are available, but their reliability can be questionable. Travelers should bring all necessary medications, both prescription and over-the-counter.

A couple of western-style private clinics have opened in Kabul in recent months: the DK-German Medical Diagnostic Center (http://www.medical-kabul.com), and CURE International Hospital (ph. 0799-883-830) offer a variety of basic and routine-type care; Americans seeking treatment should request American or Western health practitioners. American travelers may seek emergency medical services at the International Security Assistance Forces (ISAF) medical facilities in the Kabul area, but routine care is not available. The ISAF German Hospital, located about 10 kilometers from Kabul on Jalalabad Road (a road often off-limits to official Americans because of security concerns), and the combined forces ISAF clinic, adjacent to Kabul International Airport, may provide medical care to American citizens who can show a passport and request emergency care. Shino Zada Private Hospital located in Microrayon 4, opposite the central heating center, provides general surgery, maternity care, ambulance and pharmacy facilities 24 hours a day. Imran Clinic, across from the Ministry of Interior, has limited laboratory and x-ray facilities.

Afghan public hospitals should be avoided. Individuals without government licenses or even medical degrees often operate private clinics; there is no public agency that monitors their operations. Travelers will not be able to find Western-trained medical personnel in most parts of the country outside of Kabul, although there are some international aid groups temporarily providing basic medical assistance in various cities and villages. For any medical treatment, payment is required in advance. Commercial medical evacuation capability from Afghanistan is limited.

Information on vaccinations and other health precautions, such as safe food and water precautions and insect bite protection, may be obtained from the Centers for Disease Control and Prevention's hotline for international travelers at 1-877-FYI-TRIP (1-877-394-8747) or via the CDC's Internet site at http://www.cdc.gov/travel. For information about outbreaks of infectious diseases abroad consult the World Health Organization's website at http://www.who.int/en. Further health information for travelers is available at http://www.who.int/ith.

## LOCAL TIME, BUSINESS HOURS, AND HOLIDAYS

Local time is GMT +4.5.

Afghanistan observes a five and a half day workweek, with Thursday afternoon and Friday as the days off. Business hours are typically 8 AM to 4 PM. Commercial shops keep longer but varying hours, usually from 7am to 11pm.

Holidays vary year to year and are determined by the Islamic Calendar and the visibility of the lunar crescent. Holidays include three days for Eid-ul-Qurban in January, three days for Eid-Al-Fitr in December, one day for the Prophet's Birthday in May, February 9 (10 th of Maharam), March 21 (Nawrooz) and August 18 (Independence Day.)

## TEMPORARY ENTRY OF MATERIALS AND PERSONAL BELONGINGS

Afghan customs authorities may enforce strict regulations concerning temporary importation into or export from Afghanistan of items such as firearms, alcoholic beverages, religious materials, antiquities, medications, and printed materials. American travelers have faced fines and/or confiscation of items considered antiquities upon exiting Afghanistan. It is advisable to contact the Embassy of Afghanistan in Washington for specific information regarding customs requirements.

## WEB RESOURCES

U.S. Department of State Travel Website http://travel.state.gov
U.S. Department of State Consular Information Sheets and Travel Warnings http://travel.state.gov/travel/cis_pa_tw/cis/cis_1765.html
U.S. Department of State Visa Website http://travel.state.gov/visa/index.html
United States Visas http://www.unitedstatesvisas.gov
U.S. Embassy in Afghanistan http://kabul.usembassy.gov
Embassy of Afghanistan in the U.S. http://www.embassyofafghanistan.org
Center for Disease Control http://www.cdc.gov/travel
World Health Organization http://www.who.int/en and http://www.who.int/ith

# SUPPLEMENT

## IMPORTANT CONTACTS

### U.S. GOVERNMENT CONTACTS

**U.S. Department of Commerce**
Jana Nelhybel
Afghanistan Investment and Reconstruction Task Force
Washington D.C. 20230
Tel: (202) 482-1812
Fax: (202) 482-0980
Email: afghaninfo@ita.doc.gov
http://www.export.gov/afghanistan

**U.S. Embassy Kabul**
Great Masood Road
Tel: +93 (20) 230-0436, +93 (0) 70-108-001, +93 (0) 70-108-002
http://kabul.usembassy.gov

Ronald Neumann, Ambassador
Richard Norland, Deputy Chief of Mission
Douglas Climan, Economic/Commercial Counselor
Rian Harris, Commercial Officer, HarrisRH@state.gov , Ext. 8364
Economic/Commercial Assistant, Ext. 8395

**U.S. Agency for International Development**
Great Masood Road
Tel: +93 (0) 70-234-236
Alonzo Fulgham, Mission Director
Grace Agana, Assistant to the Director, gagana@usaid.gov , Ext. 4445
http:// www.usaid.gov/afghanistan

Note: Phone and fax communications in Afghanistan can be accessed. However, e-mail is the most reliable form of communication

**USAID Washington Office**
1300 Pennsylvania Avenue, NW
Ronald Reagan Building
Washington, D.C. 20523-1000
Sepideh Keyvanshad, Afghanistan Desk Officer
Tel: (202) 712-0324
Email: skeyvanshad@usaid.gov

**U.S. Embassy Islamabad**
Consular Section
Ramna 5, Diplomatic Enclave
Islamabad, Pakistan
Tel: +92 (51) 208-02700
Fax: +92 (51) 282-2632
http://usembassy.state.gov/pakistan/consular.htm

**U.S. Trade & Development Agency (USTDA)**
Dan Stein
Regional Director for Europe and Eurasia
Suite 1600
1000 Wilson Boulevard
Arlington, VA 22209
Tel: (703) 875-4357
Fax: (703) 875-4009
Email: dstein@ustda.gov
http:// www.ustda.gov

**Overseas Private Investment Corporation (OPIC)**
John Aldonas
1100 New York Avenue NW
Washington, DC 20527
Tel: (202) 336-8400
Fax: (202) 408-9859
Email: jaldo@opic.gov
http://www.opic.gov

**Export-Import Bank (ExIm)**
811 Vermont Avenue, N.W.
Washington, DC 20571
Tel: (202) 565-3946 (EXIM) or (800) 565-3946 (EXIM)
G rayson Wolfe
Tel: (202) 565-3450
Email: grayson.wolfe@exim.gov
http://www.exim.gov

### INTERNATIONAL FINANCIAL INSTITUTIONS

**World Bank**
Alastair J. Mckechnie, Country Director for Afghanistan
House 19, Street 15, Wazir Akbar Khan
Kabul, Afghanistan
Contact:: Abdul Raouf Zia
Tel: +93 (0) 70280800
Email: azia@worldbank.org

Mr. William Center, Senior Commercial Officer
U.S. Commercial Liaison to the World Bank in Washington
Tel: (202) 458-0120
Fax: (202) 477-2967
Email: WCenter@worldbank.org

http://www.worldbank.org/af

**Asian Development Bank**
Afghanistan Resident Mission
Bryan Fawcett, Country Director
126, Street 2, Haji Yaqoub Round About
Shahar-e-Now,
P. O. Box 3070
Kabul, Afghanistan
Tel: +93 (20) 210-3602
Email: afrm@adb.org
http://www.adb.org/afrm

## AFGHAN GOVERNMENT CONTACTS

**Afghan Investment Support Agency (AISA)**
Tel: +93 (20) 210 3404
Email: info@aisa.org.af, invest@aisa.gov.af
http://www.aisa.org.af/
Mr. Omar Zakhilwal
President & CEO
Cellular Phone: +93 (0) 799 322-735
Email: zakhilwal@aisa.org.af
Mr. Suleman Fatimie
Vice President
Cellular Phone: +93 (0) 799 336-616
Email: fatimies@aisa.org.af, invest@aisa.gov.af

Ms. Masouda Delawar
Secretary to the President
Cellular Phone: +93 (0) 70 293-173
Email: M.H.A@aisa.org.af

Mr. Mohammad Sharif
Investment Manager (Agriculture, Livestock, Water and Power, Banking and Environment)
Cellular Phone: +93 (0) 799 336-529
Email: sharif@aisa.org.af

Mr. Salam Zahid
Investment Manager (Manufacturing, Industry, Trade, Transport, and Industrial Parks)
Cellular Phone: +93 (0) 799 336-527
Email: ZahedA@aisa.org.af

Mr. Naseem Akbar
Investment Manager (Public Health, Education, Media and Services)
Cellular Phone: +93 (0) 799 336-529
Email: NaseemA@aisa.org.af

Mr. Abdul K. Safi
Investment Manager (Information Technology and Construction Projects)
Cellular Phone: +93 (0) 799 336-552
Email: Abdulksafi@aisa.org.af

**Embassy of Afghanistan**
Mariam Nawabi, Economic and Commercial Counselor
Economic, Trade and Investment Department
2341 Wyoming Avenue, N.W.
Washington D.C. 20006
Tel: (202) 483-6410
Fax: (202) 483-6487
Email: contact@afghanistanembassy.org, commerce@embassyofafghanistan.org
http://www.embassyofafghanistan.org/, http://www.afghanistan.business-gateways.com/

**Afghanistan Reconstruction and Development Service (ARDS)**
Email: procurement@afghanistangov.org
http://www.eafghanistan.gov.af/procurement/

**Ministry of Commerce**
Tel: +93 (20) 210-2365
Email: info@commerce.gov.af
http://www.commerce.gov.af/

**Ministry of Finance**
Tel: +93 (20) 210-3272
Email: info@mof.gov.af
http://www.mof.gov.af/

## OTHER USEFUL CONTACTS

**Afghanistan International Chamber Of Commerce (AICC)**
Azarakhsh Hafizi, Chairman
House #91, Street 2, Shash Darak
Kabul, Afghanistan
Tel: +93 (0) 70-033-799, 0799-014-493,
Email: chairmanaicc@yahoo.com & hafizi@yahoo.com
http://www.en.aicc-online.org

**Afghan-American Chamber of Commerce (AACC)**
Atiq Panjshiri, President
8201 Greensboro Drive, Suite #103
McLean, VA 22102
Tel: (U.S) (703) 658-2929
Fax: (U.S.) (703) 658-9103
Email: apanjshiri@a-acc.org
http://www.a-acc.org

**Afghanistan Builders Association (ABA)**
Abdullah Nadi, President
Tel: + 93 (0) 70-286-103
Email: AbdullahNadi@aol.com

# AFGHAN EMBASSIES

## Australia

Consulate of the Islamic State of Afghanistan
GPO Box 88
Canberra ACT 2601
Tel.: 612-62868445 Fax: 612-62868446
E-mail: admin@afghanconsulate.net
Website: www.afghanconsulate.net
Honorary Consul: Mr. Mahmoud SAIKAL

---

**Austria**

Embassy of the Islamic State of Afghanistan
Kaiserstrasse 84/1/3
A-1070 Wien
Tel.: 431-5247806 Fax: 431-5247807
E-mail: afg.emb.vie@chello.at
Charge d' Affaires: Mr. Farid AMIN
(non-Resident Ambassador to Hungary & Bosnia)

---

**Bangladesh (People's Republic of)**

Embassy of the Islamic State of Afghanistan
House No. CWN (C) - 2A
Road No. 24, Culshan
Dhaka
Tel.: 8802-9884767 Fax: 8802-9884767
Charge d'Affaires: Mr. Ghulam Mohammad SOKHAN-YAR

---

**Bulgaria (Republic of)**

Embassy of the Islamic State of Afghanistan
61 "Boryana" Street
Bl. 216-A App. 15, Ovcha Kupel
1618 Sofia
Tel.: 3592-8708394 Fax: 3592-9559986
Charge d' Affaires: Mr. Mohammad Fazel SAIFI

---

**China (People's Republic of)**

Embassy of the Islamic State of Afghanistan
8 Tung Chih Men Wia
Chao Yang District
Peking
Tel.: 8610-65321622 Fax: 8610-65322269
Charge d'Affaires: Mr. Abdul Bassir HOOTAK

---

**Czech Republic**

Embassy of the Islamic State of Afghanistan
Nakazance 634/7
17100 Praha 7 – Troja
Tel.: 4202-8544228 Fax: 4202-7650732
Charge d' Affaires: Mr. Mohammad Zahir SALJOOQI

---

**Egypt (Arab Republic of)**

Embassy of the Islamic State of Afghanistan
59 El-Orouba Street, Heliopolis
Cairo
Tel.: 202-4177236 Fax: 202-4177238
Ambassador: Mr. Sayed Fazlullah FAZIL

**France**

Ambassade de l'Etat Islamique d'Afghanistan
32 Avenue Raphael
75016
Tel.: 331-45250529 Fax: 331-45250529
E-mail: ambassade.afg@worldonline.fr Website: www.ambafghane.com
Charge d' Affaires: Mr. Mehrabuddin MASTAN

**Germany**

Die Botschaft des Islamischen Staates Afghanistan
Wilhemstrasse 65
10117 Berlin
Tel.: 4930-2292612 Fax: 4930-2291510
Charge d' Affaires: Mr. Amrullah JAYHOON

Generalkonsulate des Islamischen Staates Afghanistan
Uckesdorf, Liebfrauenweg 1A
53125 Bonn
Tel.: 4922-8251927 Fax: 4922-8255310
General Consul:

**India**

Embassy of the Islamic State of Afghanistan
Plat No. 5, Block 50F, Shantipath, Chanakyapuri
New Delhi 110021
Tel.: 9111-6882191 Fax: 9111-6875439
E-mail: Afghanspirit@yahoo.com
Ambassador: Mr. Masood KHALILI

**Indonesia (Republic of)**

Embassy of the Islamic State of Afghanistan
15 Jalan DR Kuskmas Atmaja
Jakarta
Tel.: 6221-335390 Fax: 6221-335390
Charge d'Affaires: Fat'h Mohammad SHERZAI

**Iran (Islamic Republic of)**

Embassy of the Islamic State of Afghanistan
Dr. Beheshti Avenue, 4$^{th}$ Street
Tehran
Tel.: 9821-625040, 625600 Fax: 9821-8735600
Consulate Section: 9821-8737531
Ambassador: Mr. Mohammad KHAIR-KHAWH

Consulate of the Islamic State of Afghanistan
Imam Khomeini Avenue, Doshahid Street

Sevom Isfand Sq.
Mashad
Tel.: 9851-827544 Fax: 9851-44404, 814797
Consul: Mr. Abdul RAHIM

**Iraq**

Embassy of the Islamic State of Afghanistan
Shareh Al-Maghreb
Aldifaeih Waziria 27/1/12
Baghdad
Tel.: 9641-5569508 Fax: 9641-5560331
Charge d'Affaires: Mr. Sayed Sharif YOUSEFI

**Italy**

Embassy of the Islamic State of Afghanistan
Via Nomentana 120
00161 Rome
Tel.: 3906-86216111 Fax: 3906-86322939
Charge d'Affaires: Mr. Hamidullah NASSER-ZIA

**Kazakhstan (Republic of)**

Embassy of the Islamic State of Afghanistan
Mir 12
Alma-Ata
Tel.: 73272-247660, 338711 Fax: 73272-323729
Charge d'Affaires: Mr. Abdul AZIZ

**Kuwait (State of)**

Surra, Block 6, Surra Street
Across Surra Co-op Society
House No. 16
P.O. Box 33186, Rawdah, 73452
Tel.: 965-5329461, 5328156 Fax: 965-5326274
E-mail: afg_emb_kuw@hotmail.com
Charge d'Affaires: Dr. Naseer Ahmad NOOR

**Kyrgyzstan (Republic of)**

Trading Representation in Bishkek
Tel.: 996332-284826 Fax: 996332-284826
Trade Attache: Habibullah MAHSHAR

**Malaysia**

Embassy of the Islamic State of Afghanistan
No. 1, Lorong Ru Kedua
Off Jalan Ampang,
55000 Kuala Lumpur Malaysia
Tel.: 603-4565199 Fax: 603-4564933
E-mail: murad1@tm.net.my Website: www.afghanembassy.homepage.com
Charge d'Affaires: Mr. Abdulsattar MURAD

**Poland**

Embassy of the Islamic State of Afghanistan
Ul. Staroscinska 1 lok. 25
02-516 Warszawa
Tel.: 4822-6460314 Fax: 4822-8480280
Ambassador: Mr. Abdul Hai HAIDAR

**Russian Federation**

Embassy of the Islamic State of Afghanistan
Sverchkov Per 3/2
Moscow
Tel.: 7095-9287278, 9217094 Fax: 7095-9240478, 9219563
Ambassador: Mr. Abdulwahab ASSEFI

**Sudan (Republic of)**

Embassy of the Islamic State of Afghanistan
Madinatol Riyadh
Shareol Moshtal,
Square 10, House No. 81
Khartoum
Tel.: 24911-221852, 221827 Fax: 24911-222059
Charge d'Affaires: Mr. Enatullah KHALIL

**Switzerland**

Permanent Mission of the Islamic State of Afghanistan to the UN
Consulate of the Islamic State of Afghanistan
63 Rue de Lausanne
1202 Geneva (CH)
Tel.: 4122-7311616 Fax: 4122-7314510
Charge d'Affaires: Mr. Homayoun TANDAR

**Syria (Arab Republic of)**

Embassy of the Islamic State of Afghanistan
Mozzo, West Villas
Juber Ben Hayan Bus Station
Damascus
Tel.: 96311-6667527, 6133783 Fax: 96311-6133595
Charge d'Affaires: Mr. Abdullah MOHSENI

**Tajikistan (Republic of)**

Embassy of the Islamic State of Afghanistan
Ul. Pushkina, House 34
Dushanbe
Tel.: 73772-062057 Fax: 73772-276061
Charge d'Affaires: Mr. Ibrahim HIKMAT

**Turkey**

Embassy of the Islamic State of Afghanistan
Cinnah Caddesi, No. 88 Cankaya
Ankara
Tel.: 90312-4381121 Fax: 90312-4387745
Charge d'Affaires: Mr. Ilmorad ARGHOON

**Turkmenistan**

Embassy of the Islamic State of Afghanistan
14 Gerogli Street
Ashgabat 744000
Tel.: 99312-395820 Fax: 99312-395821
Charge d'Affaires: Mr. Shah MARDANQOL

**Ukraine**

Embassy of the Islamic State of Afghanistan
Krasnozvyozdny Ave. 48
Kiev, 25037
Tel.: 738044-2448649 Fax: 738044-2448649
Charge d'Affaires: Mr. Sayed Mahmood FARANI

**United Kingdom**

Embassy of the Islamic State of Afghanistan
31 Prince Gate
London SW7 1QQ
Tel.: 44171-5898891, 5898892 Fax: 44171-5813452
Charge d'Affaires: Mr. Ahmad Wali MASUD

**United States of America**

Permanent Mission of the Islamic State of Afghanistan to the UN
360 Lexington Avenue, 11$^{th}$ Floor
New York, NY 10017
Tel. 212-9721212, 9721213, 9721221 Fax: 212-9721216
E-mail: AfgWatan@aol.com
Ambassador: Dr. Abdul Ghafoor Ravan FARHADI

**Consulate-General of the Islamic State of Afghanistan in New York**
360 Lexington Avenue, 11$^{th}$ Floor
New York, NY 10017
Tel.: 212-9722276, 9722277 Fax: 212-9729046
E-mail: Consulate@aol.com
General Consul: Mr. Abdul Habib SERAJ

**Representative Office in Washington**

1021 Arlington Blvd. Suite 1120
Arlington, VA 22209
Tel.: 703-469-3946, 362-9246 Fax: 703-469-3859
E-mail: mohammadseshaq@aol.com
Representative: Mohammad ES'HAQ

**Uzbekistan (Republic of)**

Embassy of the Islamic State of Afghanistan
Ul. Gogol, House 73
Tashkent 700047
Tel.: 99871-2354112 Fax: 99871-2342634
Charge d'Affaires: Mr. Hasham SA'AD

# BASIC TITLES ON AFGHANISTAN

***IMPORTANT!***
***All publications are updated annually!***
***Please contact IBP, Inc. at ibpusa3@gmail.com for the latest ISBNs and additional information***

| Title |
|---|
| Afghanistan A "Spy" Guide - Strategic Information and Developments |
| Afghanistan Business and Investment Opportunities Yearbook |
| Afghanistan Business and Investment Opportunities Yearbook Volume 1 Strategic Information and Opportunities |
| Afghanistan Business Intelligence Report - Practical Information, Opportunities, Contacts |
| Afghanistan Business Intelligence Report - Practical Information, Opportunities, Contacts |
| Afghanistan Business Law Handbook - Strategic Information and Basic Laws |
| Afghanistan Business Law Handbook - Strategic Information and Basic Laws |
| Afghanistan Business Law Handbook - Strategic Information and Basic Laws |
| Afghanistan Business Law Handbook - Strategic Information and Basic Laws |
| Afghanistan Constitution and Citizenship Laws Handbook - Strategic Information and Basic Laws |
| Afghanistan Country Study Guide - Strategic Information and Developments |
| Afghanistan Country Study Guide - Strategic Information and Developments |
| Afghanistan Customs, Trade Regulations and Procedures Handbook |
| Afghanistan Customs, Trade Regulations and Procedures Handbook |
| Afghanistan Diplomatic Handbook - Strategic Information and Developments |
| Afghanistan Diplomatic Handbook - Strategic Information and Developments |
| Afghanistan Ecology & Nature Protection Handbook |
| Afghanistan Ecology & Nature Protection Handbook |
| Afghanistan Ecology & Nature Protection Laws and Regulation Handbook |
| Afghanistan Energy Policy, Laws and Regulation Handbook |
| Afghanistan Foreign Policy and Government Guide |
| Afghanistan Foreign Policy and Government Guide |
| Afghanistan Healthcare Sector Organization, Management and Payment Systems Handbook - Strategic Information, Programs and Regulations |
| Afghanistan Immigration Laws and Regulations Handbook - Strategic Information and Basic Laws |
| Afghanistan Insolvency (Bankruptcy) Laws and Regulations Handbook - Strategic Information and Basic Laws |
| Afghanistan Investment and Business Guide - Strategic and Practical Information |
| Afghanistan Investment and Business Guide - Strategic and Practical Information |
| Afghanistan Labor Laws and Regulations Handbook - Strategic Information and Basic Laws |
| Afghanistan Land Ownership and Agriculture Laws Handbook |
| Afghanistan Mineral & Mining Sector Investment and Business Guide - Strategic and Practical Information |
| Afghanistan Mining Laws and Regulations Handbook |
| Afghanistan Recent Economic and Political Developments Yearbook |
| Afghanistan Reconstruction Handbook |
| Afghanistan Taxation Laws and Regulations Handbook |
| Afghanistan Transportation Policy and Regulations Handbook |
| Afghanistan: How to Invest, Start and Run Profitable Business in Afghanistan Guide - Practical Information, Opportunities, Contacts |

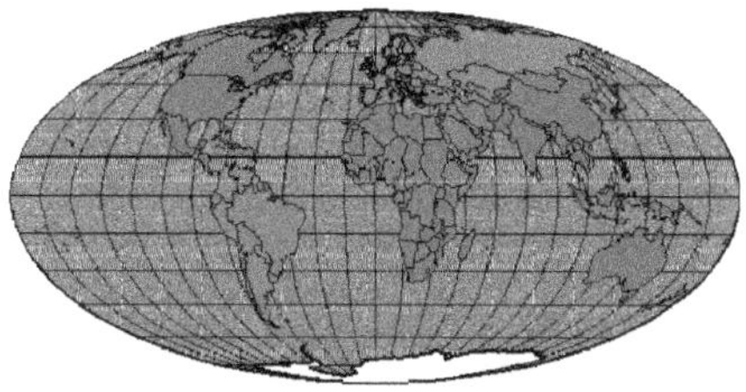

# WORLD INVESTMENT AND BUSINESS LIBRARY

| TITLE |
|---|
| Cape Verde Investment and Business Guide Volume 1 Strategic and Practical Information |
| Cayman Islands Investment and Business Guide Volume 1 Strategic and Practical Information |
| Central African Republic Investment and Business Guide Volume 1 Strategic and Practical Information |
| Chad Investment and Business Guide Volume 1 Strategic and Practical Information |
| Chile Investment and Business Guide Volume 1 Strategic and Practical Information |
| China Investment and Business Guide Volume 1 Strategic and Practical Information |
| Colombia Investment and Business Guide Volume 1 Strategic and Practical Information |
| Comoros Investment and Business Guide Volume 1 Strategic and Practical Information |
| Congo Investment and Business Guide Volume 1 Strategic and Practical Information |
| Congo, Democratic Republic Investment and Business Guide Volume 1 Strategic and Practical Information |
| Cook Islands Investment and Business Guide Volume 1 Strategic and Practical Information |
| Costa Rica Investment and Business Guide Volume 1 Strategic and Practical Information |
| Cote d'Ivoire Investment and Business Guide Volume 1 Strategic and Practical Information |
| Croatia Investment and Business Guide Volume 1 Strategic and Practical Information |
| Cuba Investment and Business Guide Volume 1 Strategic and Practical Information |
| Cyprus Investment and Business Guide Volume 1 Strategic and Practical Information |
| Czech Republic Investment and Business Guide Volume 1 Strategic and Practical Information |
| Denmark Investment and Business Guide Volume 1 Strategic and Practical Information |
| Djibouti Investment and Business Guide Volume 1 Strategic and Practical Information |
| Dominica Investment and Business Guide Volume 1 Strategic and Practical Information |
| Dominican Republic Investment and Business Guide Volume 1 Strategic and Practical Information |
| Ecuador Investment and Business Guide Volume 1 Strategic and Practical Information |
| Egypt Investment and Business Guide Volume 1 Strategic and Practical Information |
| El Salvador Investment and Business Guide Volume 1 Strategic and Practical Information |
| Equatorial Guinea Investment and Business Guide Volume 1 Strategic and Practical Information |
| Eritrea Investment and Business Guide Volume 1 Strategic and Practical Information |
| Estonia Investment and Business Guide Volume 1 Strategic and Practical Information |
| Ethiopia Investment and Business Guide Volume 1 Strategic and Practical Information |
| Falkland Islands Investment and Business Guide Volume 1 Strategic and Practical Information |
| Faroes Islands Investment and Business Guide Volume 1 Strategic and Practical Information |
| Fiji Investment and Business Guide Volume 1 Strategic and Practical Information |
| Finland Investment and Business Guide Volume 1 Strategic and Practical Information |
| France Investment and Business Guide Volume 1 Strategic and Practical Information |
| Gabon Investment and Business Guide Volume 1 Strategic and Practical Information |
| Gambia Investment and Business Guide Volume 1 Strategic and Practical Information |
| Georgia Investment and Business Guide Volume 1 Strategic and Practical Information |
| Germany Investment and Business Guide Volume 1 Strategic and Practical Information |
| Ghana Investment and Business Guide Volume 1 Strategic and Practical Information |
| Gibraltar Investment and Business Guide Volume 1 Strategic and Practical Information |
| Greece Investment and Business Guide Volume 1 Strategic and Practical Information |
| Greenland Investment and Business Guide Volume 1 Strategic and Practical Information |
| Grenada Investment and Business Guide Volume 1 Strategic and Practical Information |
| Guam Investment and Business Guide Volume 1 Strategic and Practical Information |
| Guatemala Investment and Business Guide Volume 1 Strategic and Practical Information |
| Guernsey Investment and Business Guide Volume 1 Strategic and Practical Information |
| Guinea Investment and Business Guide Volume 1 Strategic and Practical Information |

| TITLE |
|---|
| Guinea-Bissau Investment and Business Guide Volume 1 Strategic and Practical Information |
| Guyana Investment and Business Guide Volume 1 Strategic and Practical Information |
| Haiti Investment and Business Guide Volume 1 Strategic and Practical Information |
| Honduras Investment and Business Guide Volume 1 Strategic and Practical Information |
| Hungary Investment and Business Guide Volume 1 Strategic and Practical Information |
| Iceland Investment and Business Guide Volume 1 Strategic and Practical Information |
| India Investment and Business Guide Volume 1 Strategic and Practical Information |
| Indonesia Investment and Business Guide Volume 1 Strategic and Practical Information |
| Iran Investment and Business Guide Volume 1 Strategic and Practical Information |
| Iraq Investment and Business Guide Volume 1 Strategic and Practical Information |
| Ireland Investment and Business Guide Volume 1 Strategic and Practical Information |
| Israel Investment and Business Guide Volume 1 Strategic and Practical Information |
| Italy Investment and Business Guide Volume 1 Strategic and Practical Information |
| Jamaica Investment and Business Guide Volume 1 Strategic and Practical Information |
| Japan Investment and Business Guide Volume 1 Strategic and Practical Information |
| Jersey Investment and Business Guide Volume 1 Strategic and Practical Information |
| Jordan Investment and Business Guide Volume 1 Strategic and Practical Information |
| Kazakhstan Investment and Business Guide Volume 1 Strategic and Practical Information |
| Kenya Investment and Business Guide Volume 1 Strategic and Practical Information |
| Kiribati Investment and Business Guide Volume 1 Strategic and Practical Information |
| Korea, North Investment and Business Guide Volume 1 Strategic and Practical Information |
| Korea, South Investment and Business Guide Volume 1 Strategic and Practical Information |
| Kosovo Investment and Business Guide Volume 1 Strategic and Practical Information |
| Kurdistan Investment and Business Guide Volume 1 Strategic and Practical Information |
| Kuwait Investment and Business Guide Volume 1 Strategic and Practical Information |
| Kyrgyzstan Investment and Business Guide Volume 1 Strategic and Practical Information |
| Laos Investment and Business Guide Volume 1 Strategic and Practical Information |
| Latvia Investment and Business Guide Volume 1 Strategic and Practical Information |
| Lebanon Investment and Business Guide Volume 1 Strategic and Practical Information |
| Lesotho Investment and Business Guide Volume 1 Strategic and Practical Information |
| Liberia Investment and Business Guide Volume 1 Strategic and Practical Information |
| Libya Investment and Business Guide Volume 1 Strategic and Practical Information |
| Liechtenstein Investment and Business Guide Volume 1 Strategic and Practical Information |
| Lithuania Investment and Business Guide Volume 1 Strategic and Practical Information |
| Luxembourg Investment and Business Guide Volume 1 Strategic and Practical Information |
| Macao Investment and Business Guide Volume 1 Strategic and Practical Information |
| Macedonia Investment and Business Guide Volume 1 Strategic and Practical Information |
| Madagascar Investment and Business Guide Volume 1 Strategic and Practical Information |
| Madeira Investment and Business Guide Volume 1 Strategic and Practical Information |
| Malawi Investment and Business Guide Volume 1 Strategic and Practical Information |
| Malaysia Investment and Business Guide Volume 1 Strategic and Practical Information |
| Maldives Investment and Business Guide Volume 1 Strategic and Practical Information |
| Mali Investment and Business Guide Volume 1 Strategic and Practical Information |
| Malta Investment and Business Guide Volume 1 Strategic and Practical Information |
| Man Investment and Business Guide Volume 1 Strategic and Practical Information |
| Marshall Islands Investment and Business Guide Volume 1 Strategic and Practical Information |

| TITLE |
|---|
| Mauritania Investment and Business Guide Volume 1 Strategic and Practical Information |
| Mauritius Investment and Business Guide Volume 1 Strategic and Practical Information |
| Mayotte Investment and Business Guide Volume 1 Strategic and Practical Information |
| Mexico Investment and Business Guide Volume 1 Strategic and Practical Information |
| Micronesia Investment and Business Guide Volume 1 Strategic and Practical Information |
| Moldova Investment and Business Guide Volume 1 Strategic and Practical Information |
| Monaco Investment and Business Guide Volume 1 Strategic and Practical Information |
| Mongolia Investment and Business Guide Volume 1 Strategic and Practical Information |
| Montserrat Investment and Business Guide Volume 1 Strategic and Practical Information |
| Montenegro Investment and Business Guide Volume 1 Strategic and Practical Information |
| Morocco Investment and Business Guide Volume 1 Strategic and Practical Information |
| Mozambique Investment and Business Guide Volume 1 Strategic and Practical Information |
| Myanmar Investment and Business Guide Volume 1 Strategic and Practical Information |
| Nagorno-Karabakh Republic Investment and Business Guide Volume 1 Strategic and Practical Information |
| Namibia Investment and Business Guide Volume 1 Strategic and Practical Information |
| Nauru Investment and Business Guide Volume 1 Strategic and Practical Information |
| Nepal Investment and Business Guide Volume 1 Strategic and Practical Information |
| Netherlands Investment and Business Guide Volume 1 Strategic and Practical Information |
| New Caledonia Investment and Business Guide Volume 1 Strategic and Practical Information |
| New Zealand Investment and Business Guide Volume 1 Strategic and Practical Information |
| Nicaragua Investment and Business Guide Volume 1 Strategic and Practical Information |
| Niger Investment and Business Guide Volume 1 Strategic and Practical Information |
| Nigeria Investment and Business Guide Volume 1 Strategic and Practical Information |
| Niue Investment and Business Guide Volume 1 Strategic and Practical Information |
| Northern Cyprus (Turkish Republic of Northern Cyprus) Volume 1 Strategic Information and Developments |
| Northern Mariana Islands Investment and Business Guide Volume 1 Strategic and Practical Information |
| Norway Investment and Business Guide Volume 1 Strategic and Practical Information |
| Oman Investment and Business Guide Volume 1 Strategic and Practical Information |
| Pakistan Investment and Business Guide Volume 1 Strategic and Practical Information |
| Palau Investment and Business Guide Volume 1 Strategic and Practical Information |
| Palestine (West Bank & Gaza) Investment and Business Guide Volume 1 Strategic and Practical Information |
| Panama Investment and Business Guide Volume 1 Strategic and Practical Information |
| Papua New Guinea Investment and Business Guide Volume 1 Strategic and Practical Information |
| Paraguay Investment and Business Guide Volume 1 Strategic and Practical Information |
| Peru Investment and Business Guide Volume 1 Strategic and Practical Information |
| Philippines Investment and Business Guide Volume 1 Strategic and Practical Information |
| Pitcairn Islands Investment and Business Guide Volume 1 Strategic and Practical Information |
| Poland Investment and Business Guide Volume 1 Strategic and Practical Information |
| Polynesia French Investment and Business Guide Volume 1 Strategic and Practical Information |
| Portugal Investment and Business Guide Volume 1 Strategic and Practical Information |
| Qatar Investment and Business Guide Volume 1 Strategic and Practical Information |
| Romania Investment and Business Guide Volume 1 Strategic and Practical Information |
| Russia Investment and Business Guide Volume 1 Strategic and Practical Information |
| Rwanda Investment and Business Guide Volume 1 Strategic and Practical Information |
| Sahrawi Arab Democratic Republic Volume 1 Strategic Information and Developments |
| Saint Kitts and Nevis Investment and Business Guide Volume 1 Strategic and Practical Information |

| TITLE |
|---|
| Saint Lucia Investment and Business Guide Volume 1 Strategic and Practical Information |
| Saint Vincent and The Grenadines Investment and Business Guide Volume 1 Strategic and Practical Information |
| Samoa (American) A Investment and Business Guide Volume 1 Strategic and Practical Information |
| Samoa (Western) Investment and Business Guide Volume 1 Strategic and Practical Information |
| San Marino Investment and Business Guide Volume 1 Strategic and Practical Information |
| Sao Tome and Principe Investment and Business Guide Volume 1 Strategic and Practical Information |
| Saudi Arabia Investment and Business Guide Volume 1 Strategic and Practical Information |
| Scotland Investment and Business Guide Volume 1 Strategic and Practical Information |
| Senegal Investment and Business Guide Volume 1 Strategic and Practical Information |
| Serbia Investment and Business Guide Volume 1 Strategic and Practical Information |
| Seychelles Investment and Business Guide Volume 1 Strategic and Practical Information |
| Sierra Leone Investment and Business Guide Volume 1 Strategic and Practical Information |
| Singapore Investment and Business Guide Volume 1 Strategic and Practical Information |
| Slovakia Investment and Business Guide Volume 1 Strategic and Practical Information |
| Slovenia Investment and Business Guide Volume 1 Strategic and Practical Information |
| Solomon Islands Investment and Business Guide Volume 1 Strategic and Practical Information |
| Somalia Investment and Business Guide Volume 1 Strategic and Practical Information |
| South Africa Investment and Business Guide Volume 1 Strategic and Practical Information |
| Spain Investment and Business Guide Volume 1 Strategic and Practical Information |
| Sri Lanka Investment and Business Guide Volume 1 Strategic and Practical Information |
| St. Helena Investment and Business Guide Volume 1 Strategic and Practical Information |
| St. Pierre & Miquelon Investment and Business Guide Volume 1 Strategic and Practical Information |
| Sudan (Republic of the Sudan) Investment and Business Guide Volume 1 Strategic and Practical Information |
| Sudan South Investment and Business Guide Volume 1 Strategic and Practical Information |
| Suriname Investment and Business Guide Volume 1 Strategic and Practical Information |
| Swaziland Investment and Business Guide Volume 1 Strategic and Practical Information |
| Sweden Investment and Business Guide Volume 1 Strategic and Practical Information |
| Switzerland Investment and Business Guide Volume 1 Strategic and Practical Information |
| Syria Investment and Business Guide Volume 1 Strategic and Practical Information |
| Taiwan Investment and Business Guide Volume 1 Strategic and Practical Information |
| Tajikistan Investment and Business Guide Volume 1 Strategic and Practical Information |
| Tanzania Investment and Business Guide Volume 1 Strategic and Practical Information |
| Thailand Investment and Business Guide Volume 1 Strategic and Practical Information |
| Timor Leste (Democratic Republic of Timor-Leste) Investment and Business Guide Volume 1 Strategic and Practical Information |
| Togo Investment and Business Guide Volume 1 Strategic and Practical Information |
| Tonga Investment and Business Guide Volume 1 Strategic and Practical Information |
| Trinidad and Tobago Investment and Business Guide Volume 1 Strategic and Practical Information |
| Tunisia Investment and Business Guide Volume 1 Strategic and Practical Information |
| Turkey Investment and Business Guide Volume 1 Strategic and Practical Information |
| Turkmenistan Investment and Business Guide Volume 1 Strategic and Practical Information |
| Turks & Caicos Investment and Business Guide Volume 1 Strategic and Practical Information |
| Tuvalu Investment and Business Guide Volume 1 Strategic and Practical Information |
| Uganda Investment and Business Guide Volume 1 Strategic and Practical Information |
| Ukraine Investment and Business Guide Volume 1 Strategic and Practical Information |
| United Arab Emirates Investment and Business Guide Volume 1 Strategic and Practical Information |

| TITLE |
| --- |
| United Kingdom Investment and Business Guide Volume 1 Strategic and Practical Information |
| United States Investment and Business Guide Volume 1 Strategic and Practical Information |
| Uruguay Investment and Business Guide Volume 1 Strategic and Practical Information |
| Uzbekistan Investment and Business Guide Volume 1 Strategic and Practical Information |
| Vanuatu Investment and Business Guide Volume 1 Strategic and Practical Information |
| Vatican City (Holy See) Investment and Business Guide Volume 1 Strategic and Practical Information |
| Venezuela Investment and Business Guide Volume 1 Strategic and Practical Information |
| Vietnam Investment and Business Guide Volume 1 Strategic and Practical Information |
| Virgin Islands, British Investment and Business Guide Volume 1 Strategic and Practical Information |
| Wake Atoll Investment and Business Guide Volume 1 Strategic and Practical Information |
| Wallis & Futuna Investment and Business Guide Volume 1 Strategic and Practical Information |
| Western Sahara Investment and Business Guide Volume 1 Strategic and Practical Information |
| Yemen Investment and Business Guide Volume 1 Strategic and Practical Information |
| Zambia Investment and Business Guide Volume 1 Strategic and Practical Information |
| Zimbabwe Investment and Business Guide Volume 1 Strategic and Practical Information |

www.ingramcontent.com/pod-product-compliance
Lightning Source LLC
LaVergne TN
LVHW080026210926
848481LV00011B/3111
* 9 7 8 1 4 3 3 0 0 0 1 3 3 *